C0-DXC-681

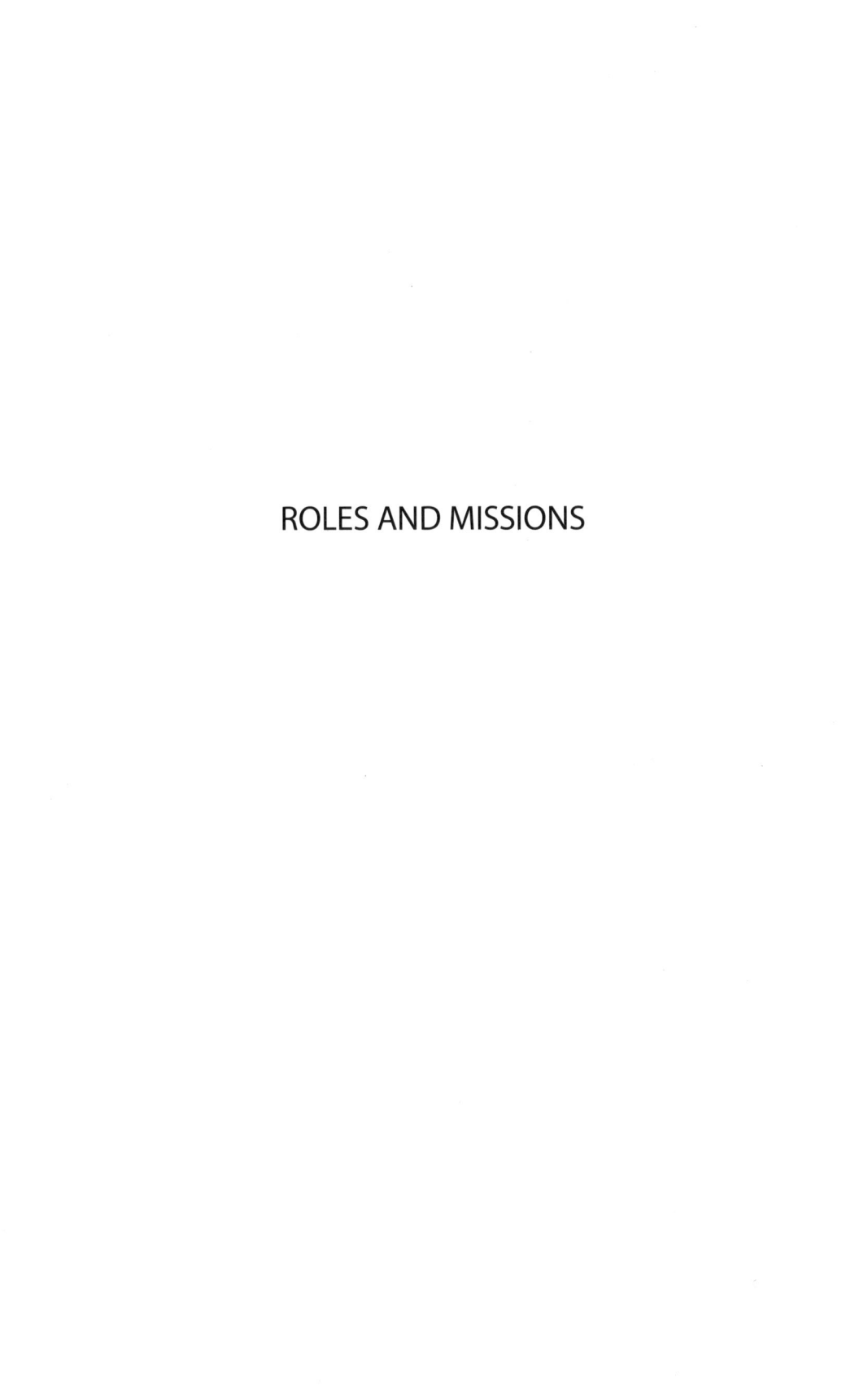

ROLES AND MISSIONS

Also by General Merrill A. McPeak

Hangar Flying
Below the Zone

Roles and Missions

GENERAL MERRILL A. MCPEAK
Former Chief of Staff, US Air Force

Lost Wingman Press
Lake Oswego, Oregon

LOST WINGMAN PRESS
123 Furnace Street, Lake Oswego, OR 97034
www.LostWingmanPress.com

Copyright © 2017 by Merrill A. McPeak
All rights reserved, including the right of reproduction
in whole or in part in any form. Published 2017.
Printed in China
22 21 20 19 18 17   1 2 3 4 5

Editor: Holly Franko
Illustrations: Keith Buckley
Cover and book design: Jennifer Omner
Set in Myriad Pro and Century Schoolbook

PUBLISHER'S CATALOGING-IN-PUBLICATION DATA

McPeak, Merrill A., 1936–
　Roles and missions / Merrill McPeak.
　　　pages cm
　Includes index.
　ISBN: 978-0-9833160-9-1 (hardcover)
　ISBN: 978-0-9916587-0-1 (pbk.)
　ISBN: 978-0-9916587-2-5 (leatherbound)
　ISBN: 978-0-9916587-1-8 (e-book)
　1. McPeak, Merrill A., 1936– 2. United States. Air Force—Generals—Biography. 3. United States—Military policy—Decision making. 4. National security—United States. 5. Persian Gulf War, 1991—Aerial operations, American.   I. Title.
UG626 . M4353 A3 2017
358.4`0092—dc23

2014904864

For Brian

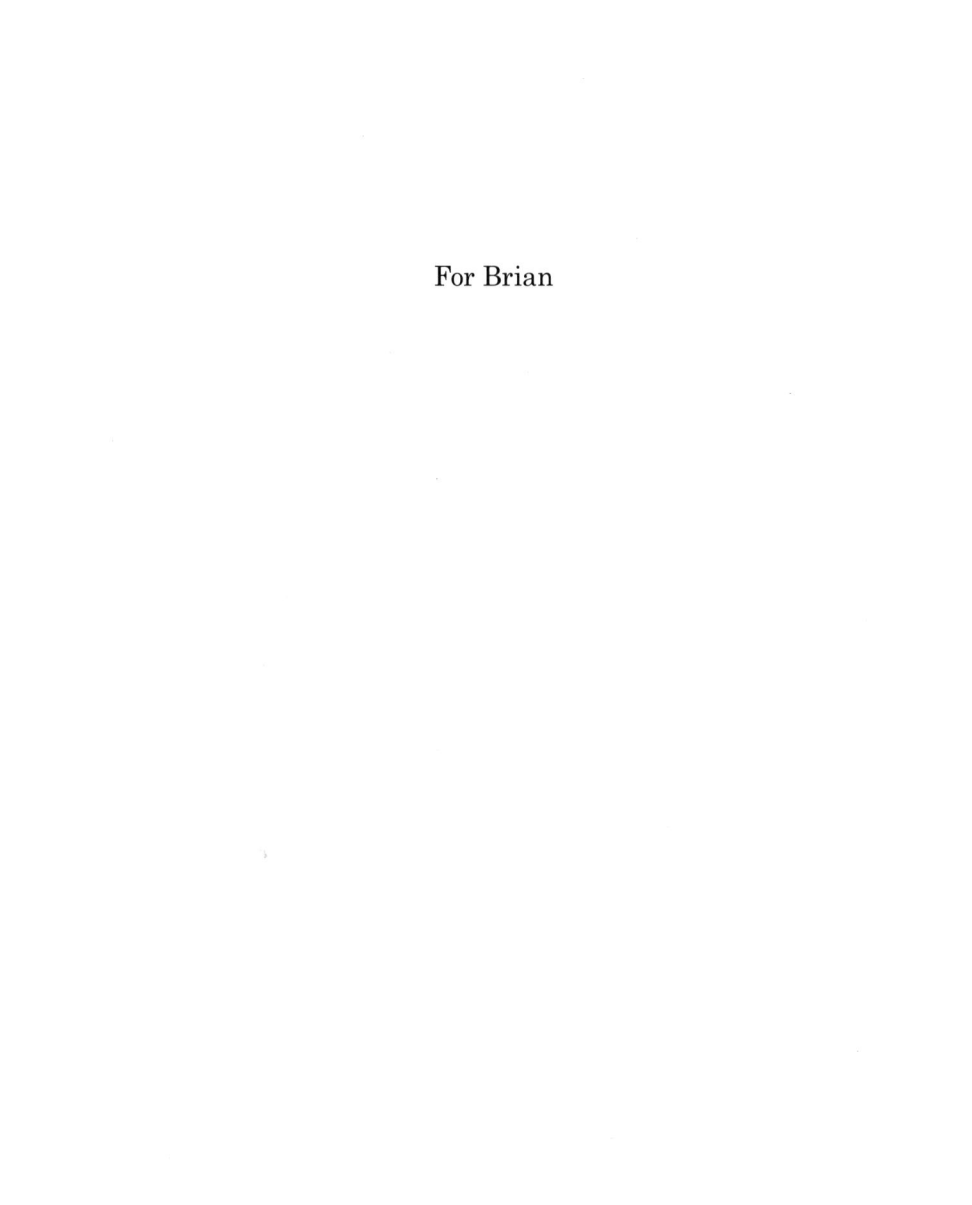

Contents

Preface		1
Chapter 1	Desert Storm	5
Chapter 2	Lessons of the Gulf War	34
Chapter 3	1991: Organize	63
Chapter 4	1992: Train	122
Chapter 5	1993: Equip	172
Chapter 6	Bosnia	228
Chapter 7	The War on Biology Part I: Women in Combat	247
Chapter 8	The War on Biology Part II: Gays in the Military	271
Chapter 9	Somalia	297
Chapter 10	Roles and Missions	306
Chapter 11	Followed by More	357
Appendix: Battlefield Control Measures		367
Index		381

Preface

As I returned to Washington to become the Air Force's 14th chief of staff, I'd accumulated much experience dealing with security problems in some of the world's most interesting spots. I'd spent 11 years in various NATO and national assignments in Europe, flown combat missions in Southeast Asia, worked the Arab-Israeli problem for three years as a Pentagon staffer, led the Air Force component responsible for operations in Central and South America, and commanded Air Force units serving in Japan, Korea, Alaska, Hawaii, Guam, the Philippines, and elsewhere throughout the Pacific. This would seem ideal preparation for a job sometimes described as being a principal military adviser to the secretary of defense and the president. As it turned out, military aspects of international security were the domain of the chairman of the Joint Chiefs of Staff, the service chiefs playing only a cameo role. I watched from the sidelines and did not always have the strength to stay quiet, as will be seen. But the problems were someone else's. Here, I report observations, for what they are worth.

Happily, there was much to do inside the Air Force. There is a sort of second law of bureaudynamics at work in large organizations, arising from an urge to elaborate that approaches the status of a physical constant. Left unchecked, social structures become complex, opaque, messy. Recurring failure is the result we should expect and is, in fact, what we get—and what we make worse, as each new disappointment calls for a customized solution, new prohibitions, an office of its own, some furniture and carpeting. It's hard to understand why we let this happen, since the more complex a mechanism, the less likely it will work under any but the best conditions, with armed conflict being a sort of limiting case for social disorder. Simplifying, tidying up the Air Force, making it more suited for use in combat, was a problem I could and did take on.

But rationalizing how the services *collectively* provide integrated combat forces at reasonable cost is a job for the secretary of defense, or even the president. In my experience, the topic of who will do it is of only theoretical interest, since nobody with authority actually tried. An imaginary effort would start with a review of who should be doing what on the battlefield. This is the *Roles and Missions* question, an important one, and one not yet answered as this is written.

Have you looked at a modern airplane? Have you followed from year to year the evolution of its lines? Have you ever thought, not only about the airplane but about whatever man builds, that all man's industrial efforts, all his computations and calculations, all the nights spent over working draughts and blueprints, invariably culminate in the production of a thing whose sole and guiding principle is the ultimate principle of simplicity?
—Antoine de Saint-Exupéry, *Wind, Sand and Stars*

Chapter 1

Desert Storm

Never send a man where you can send a bullet first.
—Samuel Colt

Washington can be a miserable place in the best of times, but being trapped in the Pentagon during a shooting war is surely one of the city's more exquisite agonies. That I'd taken up duties as the Air Force's chief of staff following Mike Dugan's dismissal did nothing to lighten the load. Dugan's predictions about the war were in line with the views of most airmen, mine included. He'd committed the capital city's gravest sin: being right too soon. So here I was, with nothing much in the way of fresh ideas to offer, manifestly a second-stringer, the substitute whose unanticipated insertion into the game can only disappoint the crowd.

More to the point, the Gulf War was coming on fast. One could argue it made little sense to switch service chiefs in the midst of a buildup for war. Frankly, it didn't matter much, the chiefs having been marginalized in an era of "jointness." But if I had any illusions about my importance in upcoming events, they quickly dissolved. In Washington, uniformed leadership was firmly in the hands of General Colin Powell, who dominated military discussions and decision making and who embodied the sole connection to higher civil authority. Powell was smart and gutsy, so worse things can happen to the country.

Powell had played a role in bringing me to Washington. He wanted a quick replacement in view of the situation in the Gulf, and I was an obvious choice, having come second to Dugan only a few months earlier. Powell had met me in Honolulu during one of his visits to outposts. He checked with Vice Chairman David Jeremiah, who said we'd worked well together as component commanders in the Pacific. Jeremiah described me as a "team player"—unlike Dugan, evidently.

By way of professional background, Powell was an infantryman and Jeremiah a surface sailor. As for the other service chiefs, Carl Vuono was an artilleryman, Al Gray a Marine infantryman, and Frank Kelso a submariner. None of these gentlemen had a reputation for passionate airpower advocacy. I'd be the outlier, convinced airpower would prove decisive in the coming combat. (Of course, Dugan had already been removed for saying this, though maybe not in just the right way.) In JCS deliberations, I'd also be the new guy, someone who should perhaps observe a period of respectful freshman silence. As a consequence, I worried a little about the lack of an authoritative Washington voice able to address the problems and prospects of the impending air campaign.

Happily, the situation was different where it mattered most, in the theater of operations. There, for the first time, an officer who had never worn an Army uniform, who had spent his entire career practicing and preparing for aerial warfare, would lead the air campaign.

Chuck Horner

According to the way the Pentagon subdivided the world for military operations, the Middle East was part of Central Command, which had its peacetime headquarters at MacDill AFB, in Tampa, Florida. Army General Norman Schwarzkopf was in charge there. Lt. Gen. Chuck Horner, commander of Tactical Air Command's

Ninth Air Force, located at Shaw AFB, South Carolina, headed up Central Command's Air Force component, known as Central Command Air Forces (CENTAF). At the start of Desert Shield, Horner had been running Ninth Air Force and CENTAF for more than three years. Having visited the Gulf many times, he knew and worked well with local political and military figures. In command at Riyadh for phase one of Desert Shield, Horner did an impressive job coordinating initial defense preparations and the early stages of reinforcement by all the services.

I'd known Chuck Horner for a long time. An F-100 pilot at Lakenheath, he had later transitioned to the F-105 and flown a noteworthy combat tour in Southeast Asia as a "Wild Weasel," stimulating, then attacking surface-to-air missile defenses—fun work but not calculated to enhance longevity. As a three-star, he stayed current in the F-16, earning the respect of aircrews and keeping him trained, *practiced* in modern air combat. A cutup as a youngster, he'd matured a bit but was still cheeky, something of a jester with friends. Scruffy, a little disheveled, having lost the battle of the waistline, he might not be what one thought of as the picture-perfect military officer, but he was comfortable inside his skin and sneaky smart. When it came to the mission and the people entrusted to him for its accomplishment, he was engaged, deeply serious, the opposite of frivolous.

Planning the Air Campaign

By the time I arrived in Washington, Horner had already put together an overall concept for air operations and was assembling a team to draw up tasking orders for its first few days. To help with detailed planning, Horner tapped Brig. Gen. Buster Glosson, who had arrived to be deputy commander of the Joint Task Force Middle East just as Iraq invaded Kuwait. In Riyadh, Glosson ran a compartmented planning cell eventually nicknamed the "Black Hole"—information went in, nothing came out—that did much of the work. Its members got help from the Air Staff's "Checkmate" office, a group of savvy young officers headed by Col. John Warden.

Early in the buildup phase, Checkmate drafted the outline of an air campaign notable for its rejection of the gradualism that had hobbled our effort in Vietnam. Warden briefed this plan, called Instant Thunder, to Schwarzkopf, at CENTCOM's Tampa headquarters. Schwarzkopf liked it. Warden took it to the Gulf, accompanied by Lt. Col. Dave Deptula, a very bright officer assigned to Secretary of the Air Force Donald Rice's personal staff. Warden returned to the Pentagon, but Deptula stayed in-country, taking on a continuing planning role.

As originally structured, the air campaign would unfold in four phases. To open phase one, "D-day" featured an overwhelming night attack on Iraqi air defenses, command and control facilities, and high-priority sites known to support Scud short-range ballistic missiles and Iraq's nuclear, biological, and chemical weapons programs. Follow-up attack on phase-one targets would continue as necessary throughout the campaign, but we thought we could inflict adequate levels of damage in about seven days.

Phase two called for attacking the logistics infrastructure—roads, bridges, the rail network, en route supplies—supporting Iraq's army deployed in and near Kuwait. We aimed to isolate that army and run it out of food, ammunition, and POL.

Phase three would be the direct aerial attack on the deployed Iraqi Army—a "softening up" phase, during which we hoped to destroy or immobilize something like 50 percent of their heavy equipment, especially tanks, artillery, and armored personnel carriers. Together, phases two and three should require another three weeks, but we saw them as open ended in the sense that our own ground attack, called G-day, would start only when Schwarzkopf judged we had inflicted appropriate damage levels.

Phase four was the post-G-day direct air support of our ground attack.

An Embarrassment of Air

Horner had overwhelming force available for the air campaign. Already by 1 November 1990 the US Air Force alone had brought in 700 aircraft, more than half of them combat types or "shooters," and more than 31,000 people. At this point, CENTAF by itself easily outclassed the entire Iraqi Air Force. But on 8 November, the day after I swore in as chief, President Bush announced we would enter a second phase of Desert Shield. Thereafter, US forces in the Gulf nearly doubled in size. By D-day, 17 January 1991, CENTAF alone possessed more than 1,100 aircraft of all types and 47,000 people. We continued to augment during the active combat phase so that by 1 February the US Air Force had 693 combat and 487 support aircraft, and more than 55,000 people in-theater.

But CENTAF constituted only a little more than half the total friendly air order of battle. To complete the picture, on 1 February the US Navy had 318 combat and 117 support aircraft, and the Marine Corps 182 combat and 293 support aircraft in-theater. All of these figures included helicopters. The Army also brought in a very large number of helicopters—more than 1,500—and a few support aircraft. Coalition partners added even more airpower. Saudi Arabia, the United Kingdom, France, Canada, and Italy all made sizable contributions. Bahrain, Kuwait (the Free Kuwait Air Force in exile), Qatar, and the United Arab Emirates (UAE) were important participants. Symbolic but much appreciated assistance came from the air forces of Australia, New Zealand, South Korea, and Argentina.

There was simply no way the Iraqis could expect to make a fight of it. Iraq's air force had about 550 fighter, bomber, attack, and reconnaissance aircraft in frontline service. These numbers made it the world's sixth-largest air force, about three-quarters the size of Britain's Royal Air Force. But many Iraqi aircraft were of marginal quality, training levels were suspect, and they were badly organized.

Iraq's air combat force was split between two organizations: Air Defense Command and Air Support Command. Defense Command was responsible for protecting strategic targets and airfields. It controlled all fighter-interceptor units, air-surveillance radars, the control and reporting system, and those army units equipped with SAMs and antiaircraft artillery assigned to defend strategic targets. Support Command was responsible for reinforcing the operations of the Iraqi Army and Navy. Into this command went all fighter-bomber, bomber, and reconnaissance units. The Scud missiles belonged to the Iraqi Army, as did mobile AAA, SAMs, and all battlefield helicopters. Thus, command of Iraqi air was disjointed, some units controlled by the air force but structurally compartmented, and some belonging to the army.

As a consequence—and in common with the armed forces of many countries—Iraq had given little thought to the difficult problem of conducting integrated air operations, including how to sort friendly from hostile aircraft in a confused tactical situation. During the Iraq-Iran War of the 1980s, the Iraqi Army put a SAM and AAA umbrella over its ground forces; gunners and missile crews considered all approaching aircraft hostile. Reportedly, more than three-quarters of Iraqi aircraft lost during that war were downed by "friendly" fire. In the Desert Storm engagements about to occur, Iraqi pilots had every reason to believe both sides would harass them continuously until they got back on the ground.

Considering the weakness of the threat, coalition air forces enjoyed an embarrassment of riches. Such an airpower glut is the reverse of the normal battlefield situation: usually, commanders manage shortages. How is it that Horner was so blessed? First, nearly all US military officers occupying leadership positions were Vietnam veterans, united by a firm resolve not to repeat what we saw as the mistakes that led to defeat there. People at the top, epitomized by Colin Powell, believed we must be "decisive."

But service parochialism reinforced the obsession with decisiveness. We competed to send the most and best. Schwarzkopf asked for three carrier battle groups, the Navy sent six. The Marines showered air on their two deployed divisions, providing a level of support unknown in normal operations. I joined in the bidding, calling Horner often to make it clear he could have more of anything he wanted. He finally told me he'd run out ramp space to park airplanes.

It's hard to imagine an argument against decisiveness, but I considered the race to get service-branded assets into action a little unseemly. I finally went to Powell, telling him we were making this look too hard, throwing in everything we had and taking six months to get ready to fight over real estate not much bigger than New Jersey, against an enemy with a GDP about a third the Air Force's budget. Obviously, we were going to win, but we wouldn't earn any style points.

Powell thanked me for my interest in national security.

Camp David Meeting

On 1 December Powell arranged for the chiefs to meet with President Bush at Camp David, a "speak now or forever hold your peace" session that would give each of us a chance to express reservations about the operations soon to begin in the Gulf. All the president's senior civilian advisers were present, most notably Jim Baker, Dick Cheney, and Brent Scowcroft. A wooden model of the torpedo bomber Bush had flown in World War II sat in the middle of the conference table.

Having been chief of staff a grand total of three weeks, I was expected to assess preparations for the upcoming air campaign, regarded by all as crucial to success. When my turn came, I talked about the planning Horner was doing, the various phases of the air campaign. I made a number of predictions, the most important of which was that the air campaign would be "over"—meaning we'd have destroyed enough Iraqi military equipment to be confident about ground operations—in 37 days (pretty close, as it turned out). I tried to prepare the president for bad news. Although we'd do everything possible to avoid it, some collateral damage would inevitably occur. I estimated we'd kill perhaps as many as 2,000 Iraqi civilians (also fairly accurate), drawing widespread, punishing press coverage. I predicted we'd lose 150 aircraft (wildly wrong, thank goodness, but I aimed to underpromise and overdeliver). These predictions and a few others I made lacked the skillful equivocation one gets used to at high-level Washington powwows. In the years since, President Bush has told the story: as the meeting broke up, he drew Scowcroft aside and asked, "Who is this guy McPeak? Does he know what he's talking about?"

Trip to the Gulf

Early in January 1991, I flew to the Gulf for a quick readiness assessment. We'd tentatively scheduled D-day for the middle of the month. With a view to Dugan's experience, I took no newspaper reporters with me. I touched down first in Riyadh for meetings with Schwarzkopf and Horner. I didn't know Schwarzkopf, a bear of a man with a reputation for volatility.

At a high level, leadership often involves a show of openness and the simultaneous contrivance of a little mystery, something Colin Powell clearly understood. But there was nothing enigmatic about Schwarzkopf. I guessed he'd get along well with Horner. In many ways they were of a type: what you saw was what you got. My meeting with him was pleasant enough, though clearly he was not anxious for Horner to get more "help" than necessary from me or other Pentagon functionaries.

In-theater, I hopped around, visiting as many bases as I could, nearly always flying the F-15. This gave me the best possible look at operations, including aircrew training levels and mental preparation for the coming campaign. Many of our people had been in the desert for a while, waiting for the president to build a coalition and prepare the nation for war, and for the other services to catch up. After six months of running in place, I worried our guys might be getting a little stale.

The visit had a personal angle. My sister, Norma, had two children in the Air Force, both deployed to the Gulf. My niece, SSgt Shannon McGinnis, was a communications specialist stationed with the air support operations center for the XVIII Airborne Corps. SSgt Kevin McGinnis, my nephew, was a security policeman at Al Dhafra Air Base in the UAE, where we'd stationed F-16s.

I talked their commanders into giving the kids a couple of days off so they could accompany me. They were both doing a great job, like many others. Shannon, living with the Army, had it tougher than all but a few Air Force people in-theater.

In all, I visited a dozen bases. The Saudis had recently completed airfield pavements for a new base at Al Kharj (eventually, this would become Prince Sultan Air Base) and invited us to use it. It wasn't a real base yet, more like a runway, taxiways, and some airfield lighting, but we pitched in to put up the vertical infrastructure supporting a wing of aircraft. I was on the ground there when an Air National Guard squadron from South Carolina landed and taxied in. Civil engineers handed the squadron commander carpentry tools and showed him where he could build his flight-line facilities.

My visit to the excellent base at Khamis Mushait, near the bottom of the Arabian Peninsula, was a highlight of the trip. Our stealth fighter, the F-117, was stationed here, well away from attack (unless staged from Yemen). But as a consequence the crews would fly long missions: six hours to the target and back. I learned we'd told stealth pilots to take "go pills," amphetamines that would help keep them awake on those long, straight-and-level legs up to Baghdad and back. This didn't make sense to me and, though I did not intervene, I left unhappy.

My most interesting and enjoyable flight was a rehearsal of D-day operations out of Al Dhafra. I flew number four in an F-15 combat air patrol sweeping ahead of a 40-ship F-16 package. The F-16s carried live 2,000-pound bombs targeted on an abandoned desert airstrip. (I asked why we were dropping live, rather than practice or inert, ordnance. We were certainly going to chew up the desert. I should have known the answer: we hadn't brought practice munitions to the theater.) We had Airborne Warning and Control System (AWACS) aircraft and a gaggle of KC-135 tankers supporting us. Tornado fighter aircraft from the Italian Air Force played opposition air, trying to break up the package. We conducted all operations "comm out"—that is, in radio silence. A captain, Fighter Weapons School graduate, briefed and led the mission. In 30-plus years of flying fighters, I'd never been more impressed with a training exercise.

White House Lunch

Back in Washington, someone (probably Powell) mentioned to the White House I'd been off in the Sandbox playing fighter pilot, and the president invited me to lunch. We met upstairs in the family quarters. We had scheduled mid-January, only a few days away, as the kickoff for Desert Storm, but the Army was having trouble getting ready and, in any case, Powell thought we'd not yet exhausted diplomatic options or given economic sanctions "a chance to work." So once again we were hearing talk of delay.

At lunch, the president asked my impressions. I told him we'd been training hard in-theater since mid-September and were more than ready to go. Our guys had their game face painted on; further delay would be a mistake, in my judgment. He nodded and told me not to worry. I think he'd already decided to launch on schedule. Scowcroft and Cheney lunched with us. I came away feeling good about our political leadership, though Cheney preserved his careful, even slightly ominous silence, a personality trait I was getting used to.

After lunch the president took me to meet the first lady. Barbara Bush had fallen at Camp David and hurt her leg, which was now in a cast. The president led me to their bedroom. She was in pajamas, the leg sticking out from under covers. The dogs, Ranger and Millie, assisted. Mrs. Bush gave me a hearty welcome, as though strangers often paraded by to see her in bed. I was completely charmed, but figured nobody in Grants Pass, Oregon, was ever going to believe this.

A Deputy for Schwarzkopf

During the run-up to actual operations, the JCS had to deal with the matter of Schwarzkopf's deputy. In accordance with the power-sharing arrangements customary at joint commands, someone from a service other than the Army should hold the post of deputy commander. My old friend Air Force Lt. Gen. Buck Rogers was the incumbent, but Schwarzkopf wanted to leave him in Florida, in charge of the residual staff at the peace headquarters. Schwarzkopf would need an in-theater deputy, especially inasmuch as he was repeating an old Army mistake: dual-hatting himself as commander of land forces.[1] Powell asked the services for nominations.

For several reasons, I thought the deputy should be an airman, and not just because the post was by custom ours under the job-apportionment scheme. There was much more at stake than mere cosmetics. It was obvious airpower would play a key role in the coming fight, making it especially important that an airman's point of view have weight in decisionmaking.

Moreover, true jointness would become a reality only if we insisted on it when it mattered. Pretend jointness had a long history, showing itself whenever the chips were down. In recent memory, only Eisenhower got it right, taking an airman, RAF Air Chief Marshal Arthur Tedder, as his deputy. (Eisenhower did dual-hat himself as Army component commander, though here the issue was how to avoid putting Bradley's Army group under Montgomery.) In Korea, MacArthur ran the war out of Far East Command headquarters, an Army organization dressed up as a joint command. He, too, refused to establish a land component, reserving the role for himself. The commanders of the Navy and Air Force components therefore had no ground counterpart; any negotiation with the Army commander was also a discussion with the boss. The story was the same in Vietnam. Starting with General Paul Harkins, commanders of Military Assistance Command, Vietnam, weighted the staff heavily in favor of Army officers and refused to

---

1 Lt. Gen. John Yeosock served as Army component commander and Lt. Gen. Walt Boomer commanded the Marine component. Schwarzkopf retained for himself overall command of the two together, the joint ground forces.

take an airman as deputy. Each time the Air Force recommended doing so, it heard a claim that the ground battle was the important task and therefore the deputy had to be a soldier. Once again, in Vietnam the overall commander dual-hatted himself as land component commander.

I said nothing of this history in making my case at the JCS meeting called to deal with the issue of Schwarzkopf's in-theater deputy, but I did argue that we expect joint commands to act with a minimum of parochialism, service bias tempered by the common mission and by associations formed in the course of normal business. This would happen only if there was balanced representation in the headquarters, with each service having a voice in decisions.

Although I thought Schwarzkopf's deputy should be an airman, I agreed we should not stick him with cheap goods. I therefore nominated Chuck Horner for the job. Like any red-blooded American, Chuck wouldn't relish leaving his command, but air campaign planning was well advanced and many others could execute the plan. In my view, considering the airpower arrayed on our side, defeating Iraq's air force was not much of a test and, as Schwarzkopf's deputy, Horner would in any case be nearby and in position to help if there were any hiccups. Certainly no one doubted Horner's quality. He'd done a first-rate job commanding the whole show in-theater during the initial reinforcement phase, before Schwarzkopf showed up. Plus, Schwarzkopf liked and respected him.

Powell turned away this nomination, citing the importance of keeping Horner at the head of the air component. The argument made sense and I bowed to it, but was not ready to concede the issue. I nominated Butch Viccellio—a world-class officer, a dead certainty to become a four-star and already regarded as a runner to replace me as Air Force chief. Powell would shortly select Viccellio for the key position of director of the Joint Staff, so I believed Powell knew and liked him. Though primarily an operator, Butch had a very strong background in logistics, something that was giving the Army fits. In short, he'd be the perfect deputy.

Instead, the JCS approved and sent in the Army nominee, Lt. Gen. Cal Waller. Powell argued the Army was having the most trouble getting ready; Schwarzkopf needed green suit help. I agreed the Army was tangled up, but couldn't figure out why it should be rewarded for that, or why Waller was the needed antidote.

When Powell took the chiefs into executive session, I made clear my views about form versus substance in jointness. Powell cut me off, visibly agitated, the only time I ever saw him show anger toward any of the service chiefs. Bellyaching at this point was counterproductive. Time to get on the team.

I'd hit a nerve in questioning Powell's sincerity about jointness. His image was an interest-bearing, offshore account into which he made carefully measured, regular deposits. He was not interested in seeing the balance looted, or even submitted to independent audit. True, Powell was in and of the Army, green oozing from the bone marrow, but the likeness was of someone grown above this, somehow larger than the Army, like Marshall or Eisenhower, an iconic image that would oxidize if anyone thought he was just playing the old Army game.

He concluded the executive session with the standard stump speech about "our" commitment to jointness, but I'd seen the thing itself, in grainy detail. On this issue, at least, Powell's sincerity was virtual, something invented and seemingly genuine in all dimensions, but not real.

The Storm Begins

As the buildup continued, the president did what I considered a masterly job of preparing the US public for the coming combat. On 29 November, UN Resolution 678 authorized force to eject Iraq from Kuwait. In early January, the president sought congressional approval for "offensive use" of US troops. In the Gulf when Bush made this decision, I winced, wondering what we'd do if Congress said no. The president took a considerable political risk. Senator Sam Nunn of Georgia and others did speak out against the proposal, but on 12 January, Congress approved using military force to implement the UN resolution, affirming the president's political instincts—though it was a cliffhanger in the Senate, 52–47. Maybe we hadn't declared war, but now no one could argue this was unilateral action by the president. On 15 January, only three days after the congressional resolution, the UN deadline for Iraqi withdrawal from Kuwait passed.

On 17 January 1991, at 0238 hours local time, Operation Desert Storm began. Coalition aircraft opened the action with a massive blow against numerous Iraqi targets. On the first night, we hit virtually every entry on the master attack list, more targets than the entire Eighth Air Force struck in all of 1942 and 1943. We hit 50 of the initial targets in the first 90 minutes. This was a new kind of aerial warfare—not serial but parallel attack—simultaneous wreckage of key targets to create maximum shock effect, followed by continuous pressure everywhere to prevent recovery.

The first objective was to take down Iraqi air defenses through a combination of active attack and electronic warfare. As one indication of success, at the outset, we monitored radar emissions from nearly 100 Iraqi air defense sites. By four hours into the operation, this number had dropped to 15, with radar coverage becoming sporadic soon thereafter. We could now operate with relative safety at medium altitude, mostly unmolested by radar-guided SAMs.

Only eight hours into the action, we'd realized our goal of overwhelming Iraq's command and control system, fitting Saddam with both a blindfold and a gag. From this point forward, he could neither understand the tactical situation nor order an appropriate response.

Capt. Jon Kelk, an F-15 pilot from Eglin AFB, claimed the first aerial victory, downing an Iraqi MiG-29 in the opening minutes of the war. Thereafter, air-to-air kills piled up rapidly. The final USAF score was 31 to zero. All our kills came from Sparrow and advanced medium-range air-to-air missile (AMRAAM) shots, underscoring the transition to a new sort of aerial combat, waged head-on, from beyond visual range.

The Iraqi Air Force put up almost 250 sorties the first day but quickly throttled back, flying only 40 on 23 January, a week into the war. As the Iraqis thought it safer to keep their aircraft locked in hardened shelters, we switched to attacking bases and airfield pavements, with only five of 24 main operating bases still functional by the 23rd. We then began a big push against nearly 600 aircraft shelters, using 2,000-pound laser-guided bombs with spectacular success. This triggered a mad dash of Iraqi jets to Iran, where eventually more than 130 Iraqi aircraft would sit out the war. We scored a few more aerial kills by putting up an F-15 patrol along the Iranian border, catching some of them on the way out. Perhaps half of Iraq's air force emerged from the war, much of it parked in Iran, the sanctuary from which it would not soon return.

The Great Scud Chase

On 18 January, the war's second day, Iraq attacked Israel and Saudi Arabia with Scud missiles. As military weaponry, the Scud didn't amount to much. A development of the German V-2, it packaged a relatively small warhead in a short-range, inaccurate missile, a weapon for attacking cities rather than military targets. But the psychological and strategic consequences were serious. Certainly, if Iraq could goad Tel Aviv into a reaction, Israel's involvement in the war would undermine, and perhaps destroy the coalition.

Iraq had three versions of the Scud: the Soviet-supplied 160-mile-range SS-1, and two indigenous variants, the 325-mile Al-Husayn and the 400-mile Al-Hijarah. Although we don't know the exact number of Scuds held by Iraq, we thought the Soviets had delivered at least 600, some of them cannibalized to build the extended-range versions.

Scud accuracy improved a bit when it was launched from fixed sites. In the western desert near the Jordanian border, Iraq had constructed five such sites, with a total of 28 launch positions from which the Al-Husayn version could reach all large Israeli cities. Crews required about an hour to set up and launch from a pre-surveyed site. Alternatively, Scuds could launch from anywhere, even off the back of trucks that served as transporter-erector-launchers (TELs), but with degraded accuracy. Estimates of the number of Scud TELs in service at the start of the war ranged from a low of 12 to a high of 22.

We were deeply concerned that Saddam might configure the Scuds with chemical or biological warheads, which would put them (along with nuclear munitions) in the category of weapons of mass destruction. So configured, the missile posed a genuine military threat and, of course, raised even graver psychological and strategic questions. We had already made it clear we would not use chemical or biological weapons in the Gulf, but if attacked would respond "appropriately," a tacit threat to go nuclear. Of course, the Israelis also had nuclear weapons, though they'd always been cagey about it, believing a certain ambiguity served their purposes.

Having anticipated the Scud problem, we attacked fixed launch sites and suspected missile-storage facilities from the beginning. Since we also wanted to destroy Scuds en route from the warehouse to launch sites, we had to find the TELs. The chase started immediately, absorbing much of our attention and many of our highest-quality attack and surveillance assets. We used every reconnaissance trick we knew, keeping the roads from Baghdad to the launch sites under continuous watch, day and night. We put a very substantial fraction of all sorties flown by the F-15E—our best and most advanced ground-attack aircraft—into orbit over launch sites, ready to pounce. During 43 days of battle, the Great Scud Chase cost us something like 2,500 sorties—no less than 25 percent of the F-15E's total number, removing these valuable aircraft from alternative, high-priority tasking.

In addition, the Army tried to shoot down Scuds with the Patriot air defense missile. Designed to knock down incoming aircraft, not ballistic missiles, the Patriot was nevertheless the best thing available. We'd already positioned them in Saudi Arabia and quickly delivered two batteries to Israel, where their presence provided some comfort for the urban population. However, the Scuds kept coming, and the Patriots kept missing. Since it was not their hardware, the Israelis were objective in their assessment of the Patriot's performance, which they regarded as a joke.

I suppose a case can be made that we were at least partly successful in dealing with the Scud. Sixty percent of all Scud shots occurred in the first 10 days of the war, when launches averaged five a day. Over the next 33 days, the firings dropped to one a day. Moreover, by the end, the Iraqis were launching from inside Baghdad, putting Israeli targets out of range, so we can assume they could no longer move from surviving storage facilities to the pre-surveyed firing sites. In the end, only a single Israeli citizen died as a direct result of the Scud attacks, a fact that helped keep Israel out of the war.

Still, the Scud launch rate was rising again as the war wound down and, in any case, it sure felt like we were unsuccessful. In all, Iraq fired 88 Scuds at us and Israel, and our defenses stopped few, if any. We have no hard evidence we ever destroyed a single mobile Scud launcher by air attack. We know at least 19 launchers survived the war. Accordingly, we seem to have joined our Army colleagues, matching the dismal results chalked up by the Patriot missile.

On 25 February, the day after G-day, a Scud missile hit a barracks housing Army reservists in Dhahran, killing 29 and wounding 99 others, a heavy blow accounting for a sizable fraction of our total combat losses.

Meanwhile, we had effectively merged the first three phases of the air campaign. Predictably, Schwarzkopf wanted us to begin working on the Iraqi field army at once, especially regular army formations facing our initial jump-off positions and the elite Republican Guard divisions being held back to reinforce their lines or exploit any breakthrough. Had it been in short supply, we certainly would have argued against diverting airpower from higher priority targets, but with so much capacity in-theater, we started the flow of sorties into the Kuwaiti theater of operations (KTO), including B-52 attacks, immediately.

On 22 January, Iraq declared war on the environment, setting two Kuwaiti oil fields afire, then opening manifolds at offshore terminals to pump crude into the Gulf. Precision bombing attacks soon damaged and shut down the pumps, but before it was over, at least 517 Kuwaiti oil wells were burning, one of the great ecological disasters in history.

The Battle of Al Khafji

During the run-up to Desert Storm, Schwarzkopf asked that we deploy Joint Surveillance Target Attack Radar System (JSTARS) aircraft to the theater. Still in technical development, JSTARS carried a large radar optimized to detect and track moving ground targets. We had two prototypes flying and we sent them, with contractor-provided civilians manning the back end of the aircraft, where the ground target tracking work was done. On the night of 29 January, the crew of one of these aircraft, searching for Scuds in western Iraq, took a radar look into southern Kuwait and saw signs of an attack in the making. Twelve days into Desert Storm, Iraq was about to abandon the strategy of just sitting there and getting pounded. Forces from two Iraqi divisions, the 5th Mechanized and 3rd Armored, were moving south toward the border, apparently aiming at the unprotected town of Al Khafji, on the northeast Saudi coast. Almost four weeks before our G-day, Iraq was trying to start a ground war.

So far, nothing had worked for the Iraqis. Scud attacks were painful but had not succeeded in bringing Israel into the war. Our destruction of aircraft shelters caused the Iraqi Air Force to run and hide, slamming the door on any air option they might have. Setting Kuwaiti oil fields afire and pumping oil into the Gulf had created an environmental catastrophe without any strategic payoff. The last real chance to take the initiative might be this southward attack aimed at drawing us into ground combat before we were ready. They could not hope for outright victory, but during the long war with Iran, Iraq had launched probes that sometimes drew opposing forces into carefully prepared defensive positions, traps in which the Iraqis inflicted heavy casualties. Perhaps this was what they had in mind with this foray toward Al Khafji.

The Al Khafji attack came at an awkward moment for the coalition. The Army was midway through a three-week deployment from the coast to jump-off positions hundreds of kilometers inland. Any disruption of this movement would upset Schwarzkopf's timetable. Schwarzkopf therefore decided neither to reinforce Al Khafji nor launch a ground counterattack, as perhaps the Iraqis had hoped. Instead, he pulled back on the ground to give coalition air more working room and told Horner to stop the Iraqis.

Horner responded quickly, diverting hundreds of sorties for use near Al Khafji. Coalition air attacks were pretty effective, and by the morning of 30 January only a few hundred Iraqi troops had made it into the town. Bringing up reinforcements was now the Iraqis' only chance to regain the initiative. They pressed these forward under cover of darkness. Again, JSTARS saw this movement and we stopped it, exacting a heavy toll. By next morning, the entire Iraqi offensive had unraveled: we had destroyed 350 tanks, 150 armored personnel carriers (APCs), and nearly 100 mobile artillery pieces, forcing a ragged retreat. A captured Iraqi soldier reported his brigade had been cut to pieces, hurt more by 30 minutes of air attack than in eight years of war with Iran. For the next three days, coalition aircraft continued to pick over stranded Iraqi forces. Much of what was left of the Iraqi 5th Mech ended up trapped between two of its own minefields for the rest of the war.

The main phase of the Battle of Al Khafji lasted less than 48 hours, but word got around. Subsequently, Iraqi ground forces looked for the surrender queue.

AC-130 Loss

In the early daylight of 31 January, a heat-seeking missile shot down Spirit 03, an AC-130 gunship participating in the Battle of Al Khafji. All aboard were killed.

Gunships had been taken away from the Air Force component and put in the Special Operations Force upon its formation in 1987.

These formidable aircraft provided the most powerful fire-support element the SOF had. But there was nothing "special" about the action around Al Khafji, a military operation we would describe as entirely conventional. Nevertheless, the gunship operated under control of the theater SOF commander, not Horner, who was surprised to learn it was still in the vicinity of Al Khafji at sunup, when the Iraqis would be able to see the aircraft and bring it down. Horner hastily called for its withdrawal, an action that came too late.

In the end, the Air Force would lose 20 people in Desert Storm, 14 of them in this AC-130.

Tank Plinking

Not long after the Battle of Al Khafji, we concentrated attention on Iraqi armor, hunkered down, awaiting our ground attack, already beaten in spirit but not yet wrecked. On the night of 5 February, Horner put up a few F-111s equipped with Pave Tack, an external pod combining an infrared sensor with a laser designator, and 500-pound laser-guided bombs. We had not anticipated this novel use of the F-111, but we were having trouble verifying the destruction of Iraqi equipment fast enough to meet Schwarzkopf's schedule for the ground assault. We thought Pave Tack's infrared avionics might be able to see armored vehicles in the evening hours because uneven heat dissipation would create a temperature gradient between metal hulls and the surrounding desert. It turned out we could see armor well enough from safe, medium altitudes to shine the Pave Tack laser on tanks, armored personnel carriers, and artillery. We scheduled 44 more F-111 sorties the following night with results so good we thereafter used three-quarters of the F-111F sorties in this way. Over the course of the war, F-111s got credit for destroying nearly 1,000 of some 6,000 armored vehicles the Iraqis had brought to the fight. It was a little like taking potshots at tin cans, so the aircrews promptly named it "tank plinking," a usage some officers in our own Army found disagreeable.

If anything, the psychological impact of tank plinking was more important than the sheer physical destruction. Previously, tank crews assumed that if they came under air attack, they could dig in and make it expensive in airplanes—maybe work their way out of the hole. It was now obvious this approach led nowhere. The combination of spread-eagled Iraqi air defenses and guided air munitions made one-way attrition unavoidable and also unmistakable. Now, Iraqi soldiers simply abandoned armored vehicles, distancing themselves from their equipment.

The 'Air Campaign'

Another term the Army didn't like, at least back in Washington, was "air campaign." What with the Battle of Al Khafji and tank plinking, it was beginning to look like airpower might be capable of decisive, independent operations against ground forces, a notion that using the term "air campaign" seemed to legitimize. Of course, the Army knew stand-alone air operations could never be decisive because its doctrine told it so, granting the matter immunity from questioning. It therefore objected to the term "air campaign," which it regarded as an advanced marketing concept. The Army suggested we call what we were doing an "air operation" in support of a combined-arms campaign, the centerpiece of which was the ground action still to come.

Once imprinted, doctrine is something like a mother tongue. It hardwires the cortex and shuts down further science, especially the objective observation and recording of new information.

The Al Firdos Bunker

In the early darkness of 13 February, two F-117s attacked the large underground bunker at Al Firdos, dropping one bomb each. Intelligence reports indicated the Iraqis were using Al Firdos as a command post. What we did not know was they were also sheltering civilians on its top floor.

If home in bed, Iraqis were pretty safe at night in Baghdad, so putting civilians in a military bunker was a fairly dumb thing to do. Iraq subsequently claimed 200–300 civilians were killed. Television coverage showed rescue workers removing children's bodies.

The international reaction soon had Powell running for cover.

He talked it over with Schwarzkopf, who decided we could attack downtown Baghdad only with his express permission, effectively ending bombing in the city. Though Horner subsequently made a number of requests to hit bridges and leadership targets in the Iraqi capital, approval never came. For all intents and purposes, the air campaign "downtown" was over.

When one thinks about it, our "strategic" bombing of Iraq (that is, the bombing in and around Baghdad) reached maximum intensity on the opening night of the war and declined thereafter, coming to a virtual stop after Al Firdos. This is an interesting reversal of precedent. Always before, in World War II, Korea, even Vietnam, strategic bombing increased as the war progressed and political constraints fell away. In Iraq, part of the explanation was that we'd planned all along to switch at a certain point from the capital to Iraq's army in the field as our principal target. Still, the bombing restrictions in downtown Baghdad had much to do with television reporting. Powell showed great sensitivity to any press coverage that included pictures. Straight print or radio journalism didn't seem to faze him, but look out if it's shown in living color.

Ford's Theatre

On the evening of 21 February, President Bush invited Justice David Souter, newly named to the Supreme Court, and me to dine with him at the White House and afterward go to a performance of the play *Black Eagles*. The play is based on the experience of our Tuskegee Airmen. Of course, the Air Force is very proud of these fliers, and I was honored, if a little uneasy, to sit next to the president at Ford's Theatre. Thinking about how Lincoln met his fate kept me checking the balcony seats.

By this point in mid-February, it was clear the air campaign was going well, so the president and I did not talk about it much. The real decision concerned the timing of the ground attack. Our planning assumption was that G-day would fall on 24 February, but President Gorbachev had made a grandstanding peace proposal aimed at giving Saddam an opportunity to withdraw from Kuwait before we began the ground campaign. At the same time, Schwarzkopf had developed a case of the jitters. He was concerned about the weather and, as always, the Army wanted more prep time. As he dropped me off after the play, the president disappeared into the White House to meet with Cheney, Powell, and others to decide how to handle these pressures.

For my part, I didn't think it mattered much when we started the ground war. We were demolishing the Iraqi Army and could continue the air campaign indefinitely. Time was on our side.

G-day

The story of Desert Storm's ground operations is well known. Happily, air preparation of the battlefield and a strong performance by the Army and Marines made things go as quickly and as well as anyone could hope. Still, I wince a bit when I hear the Army's formulation: the "100-Hour War." My guess is the Iraqis will always think of the preceding 39 days as war. Although it would seem fairly hard to do, 973 Iraqi soldiers had already found a way to surrender before the ground attack began. Perhaps as many as 100,000 more had deserted, a figure that seems even more remarkable when compared with the perhaps 10,000–12,000 who died of injuries sustained under air attack.

In the end, psychological attrition beat Saddam's army. At first ground contact, Iraqi units began surrendering en masse, and on 25 February, Baghdad broadcast an order for its forces to withdraw from Kuwait. But withdrawal was under way already and was anything but orderly, turning into the "mother of all retreats." Thousands of military and civilian vehicles clogging the four-lane highway running north out of Kuwait City got blown to pieces by repeated air attack.

In JCS meetings, Colin Powell seemed uncomfortable at this point. He'd done all he could to manage the press, metering it in and limiting access, so that positive coverage would emerge from the action. We were on a worldwide public opinion high, the figure of Powell himself at the center of this feeling. Now, here were these pictures of the "Highway of Death," Iraqi teenagers with whom we had no real quarrel, barbecued and bloody. Our standing in the world started to turn brown at the edges.

Well known for his views about decisiveness, Powell had indulged in some bellicose posturing. (Regarding Iraq's army: "First we're going to cut it off, and then we're going to kill it.") But now that it was time to paint the fence, he looked for an exit.

On 27 February, coalition forces led by our Marines liberated Kuwait City, encountering little resistance. To the north, Republican Guard divisions being encircled by our armor showed some fight, igniting a one-sided tank engagement in which two Iraqi divisions were decimated. The outcome was absolutely sure, ordained.

Managing the Ground War

In the end, we paid a high price for Schwarzkopf's decision to keep for himself a double role—the joint commander's job of integrating ground, sea, and air forces and the land component commander's job of directing ground operations. One might argue, though I would dissent, that combining the jobs was essential in the planning phase. But when the ground war started, there was too much work and too little time. Our mistakes kept us from destroying the Republican Guard and gave Saddam a reasonable shot at retaining power.

The first problem was getting Freddie Franks going. Army Lt. Gen. Frederick Franks, at the head of the powerful VII Armored Corps, moved slowly by day and stopped altogether at night. He wanted to synchronize his units, an agonizing process made more tedious by questions of air integration. This sluggishness much reduced his effectiveness in rolling up Iraqi forces, but wasn't a total disaster because we could attack retreating Iraqis by air. In the finale, it was the placement of the fire support coordination line that created a larger problem.

For the Air Force, the fire support coordination line (FSCL) is perhaps the most important battlefield control measure. Inside its limits, no air attack takes place unless requested by and under the tactical control of the ground commander.

It's the ground commander who decides where to draw the FSCL, though he should coordinate its placement with the air commander. Beyond the FSCL, we presumably have no worry about the safety of our own troops, so the air commander is free to attack targets under the supervision of the joint commander, without the ground commander's having an overriding, controlling voice. Crossing the FSCL outbound, we arm-up weaponry, and the fight's on.

Much is at stake in the placement of the FSCL, in terms of the infighting for roles and missions. From the Army point of view, the farther out the FSCL, the more likely lots of air action will take place inside it and therefore the more airpower the ground commander controls. The airman's view is that, first, the FSCL should be located to provide an adequate safety buffer for friendly troops; but otherwise, placement should maximize risk for the enemy. It often does, especially when the Army is under pressure. In late stages of the Korean War, we drew the FSCL as close as 300 meters in front of our own troops.

On 27 February (G+3), the envelopment of Republican Guard formations approached a critical phase. Without coordinating with Horner, the FSCLs for both the VII Armored Corps (Franks) and the XVIII Airborne Corps (Lt. Gen. Gary Luck) were set far ahead of their ground advance. Even though his movement was at best deliberate, Franks put the VII Corps' FSCL 50 miles beyond his forward positions. The XVIII Airborne Corps' FSCL was placed north of the Euphrates River, which had the effect of protecting retreating Iraqi forces from unfettered air attack. Horner finally called the situation to Schwarzkopf's attention and got it straightened out, but only hours before the fighting stopped.

'Every War Must End'[2]

Colin Powell telephoned from the White House on 27 February, following a meeting with the president. At the Pentagon, Vice

---

2 "Every War Must End" is a chapter title from Powell's book, *My American Journey*.

Chairman Dave Jeremiah was meeting with the Joint Chiefs. Powell asked Jeremiah to tell us the president had decided to suspend hostilities shortly. Surprised by this, I looked round the table at the others. Maybe they knew something I did not. From what I could see, we'd slipped the noose around Saddam's neck but hadn't pulled it tight. A lot of equipment was getting back into Iraq—much of it because of the misplaced fire support coordination line—and plenty more would escape unless we continued fighting for a while. We needed another 24 hours, maybe 48 at the outside. Why the preoccupation with wrapping it up? Like the other chiefs, I wasn't interested in wheeling around and hiking to Baghdad, but we should at least finish the work in Kuwait.

I suspected Powell stage-managed the decision to quit early. He'd wanted to avoid a fight in the first place, much preferring great-power diplomacy and economic sanctions as remedies to Saddam's behavior. Then, too, in our last couple of JCS sessions, Powell had made clear his concern about the press coverage turning negative. The most recent polls had shown the American public rating the military the most respected profession, ahead of education and medicine. Morale inside our ranks was at a post-World War II high. Powell's worry, I think, was that one-sided fighting in the endgame would tarnish this newly brightened image. Moreover, he argued that if we didn't watch out, we'd weaken Iraq too much, creating a power vacuum at the north end of the Gulf, which Iran, no friend of ours, would gladly fill.

Powell was certainly right about our image and the need for balance vis-à-vis Iran. But there was something more at work here. Blessed with the talent to elevate himself above the routine and see big issues, Powell was a man with a point of view—sometimes wrong, maybe, but always honest and thought out. His public face was that of a hedgehog, clamped down on a few simple truths: be slow to anger; use military action only as a last resort; if, finally, action is unavoidable, go big. But he was a fox in hedgehog clothing, understanding the complexities and paradoxes of national security policy as well as anyone in Washington. That said, like Freddie Franks, he was a supreme gradualist, dedicated to slow motion, low-risk action. With Desert Storm, unwillingly and seemingly as a last resort, he had rolled the dice. It was as if he'd bought stock and watched it make a spectacular rise. There may be more upside, but let's not get greedy. Bank the gain. It was not so much that he was afraid to win as that he hadn't prepared himself for such a big, easy win. Having survived more than 30 years in the Army and two tours in Vietnam, he knew we were not this good.

Though I didn't know it at the time, out in the theater, Schwarzkopf's new deputy, Cal Waller, came close to redeeming himself: "Why are we stopping at this point?" he asked. "Why not go ahead and complete what we were going to do?" Why not, indeed. Back at the Pentagon, I didn't have the courage even to ask the question. I was the junior guy at the table, I'd already been given the lecture on jointness and, in any case, the decision had been made. What was I supposed to do? Call the president?

So I joined in the round of backslapping. Too eager for peace, we wouldn't give war a chance. Active operations ended at midnight Washington time (8:00 a.m. Riyadh time), on 28 February. After inspired huddling, determined blocking, sharp passing, and solid running, we fumbled on the one-yard line.

Briefing the Press

DOD Public Affairs asked each of the chiefs to brief the Pentagon press corps on his service's role in the fighting. I was up first, on 15 March, briefing on aspects of the air war. In preliminary remarks, I was careful to share credit:

> Before I begin, it is largely a story about airpower, a success story for US and coalition air forces. But I need to remind myself and everybody here that we were only part of a larger air, land, and sea campaign—what we call a combined-arms operation, in which all the services made a very important contribution, and, of course, all our allies did as well.

I then went on to describe the contribution made by the air operation. In 39 days of continuous aerial assault and four days of joint air-ground operations, coalition air forces put up 110,000 sorties and delivered 70,000 tons of munitions. The US Air Force was the makeweight, flying 60 percent of the combat sorties and dropping 75 percent of the ordnance—and 90 percent of what really mattered, the precision-guided munitions. We employed nearly 1,000 combat aircraft—800 fighters and 80 bombers—and lost 14. Only 20 Air Force people died in 43 days of intense fighting. If we set aside the 14 airmen in the AC-130 operated by the Special Operations Force—and, of course, we cannot—we lost just six people in combat: one a week, an astonishing result. We demolished Iraq's air force and air defense force. Of 35 credited air-to-air kills, we scored 31; of six helicopter kills, we got five. And, of course, we more or less comprehensively defanged Iraq's army, paving the way for the walkover that followed.

Like the press everywhere, the corps of Pentagon reporters gets paid to provoke quotable one-liners. I was a reliable supplier, often to my regret. Following my briefing on our performance in Desert Storm there was a question-and-answer session, during which I spoke my mind:

> Q: Is it conceivable that by continuing the air war alone for another period, the Iraqis would have been totally defeated without a ground war?
>
> A: My private conviction is that this is the first time in history a field army has been defeated by airpower. It's a remarkable performance by the coalition air forces. But there are some things airpower can do, and does very well, and some things it can't do, and we should never expect it to do—that is to move in on the terrain and dictate terms to the enemy. Our ground forces did that. I think, by the way, again, they did a remarkable job.

It was that first sentence that got Powell's attention. He rang me up. He didn't want to second-guess me. He conceded the point.

He, too, thought airpower had been decisive. But the first defeat of a field army from the air? That was a really unfortunate formulation, didn't I think? Mightn't I tone it down a bit? Though he didn't say so, he must be wondering whether in replacing Dugan he'd traded one hair-on-fire airpower zealot for a worse one.

But he did not raise with me another exchange he might have viewed as pointed at him:

> Q: At the end of the ground war, the Army was saying that going after the Iraqi soldiers was sort of like clubbing baby seals. At that point, the Air Force swooped in on one of the convoys going from Kuwait to Iraq. Was that an excessive use of violence?
>
> A: As far as attacking retreating troops, I think you have to understand a little bit about military history. When enemy armies are defeated, they retreat, often in disorder, and we have what is known in the business as the "exploitation" phase. It's during this phase that the true fruits of victory are achieved—when the enemy is disorganized. The alternative is we should never attack a disorganized enemy. We should wait until he is stopped, dug in, and prepared to receive the attack.
>
> You may recall how disappointed Lincoln was with General Meade when he failed to pursue Lee after Gettysburg. It certainly prolonged the Civil War a year or so, and many more young Northern and Southern men were killed as a consequence.
>
> All American generals should remember that lesson. If we do not exploit victory, the president should get himself some new generals.

Chapter 2

LESSONS OF THE GULF WAR

The United States relies on the Air Force, and the Air Force has never been the decisive factor in the history of war.
—Saddam Hussein

One can argue that Desert Storm was at best a strategic standoff. Saddam endured long after the departure of George Bush the Elder, there was no better state of peace, no significant shift of power in the region. We spent three Iraqi GDPs on a 43-day war with them that did not settle the underlying issues. The UN economic sanctions continued and, if we are to believe the critics, were responsible for a good deal more suffering than was ever induced by the bombing.

Maybe we won at the operational level, though even this would be a close call. We did not entirely incapacitate the Republican Guards, used ruthlessly, and almost immediately, to bring the Kurds and the "Marsh Arabs" back in line. We signed up to a lengthy, expensive air policing commitment. And, if we did win, it was at unnecessarily high cost. Though this is said of nearly every war, the gross extravagance was pretty clear in this case.

But at the tactical level, we scored a victory as lopsided as any since Pizarro took a handful of Spaniards up into the Andes and wiped out the large, professional armies of the Incas. Our 149 combat deaths (out of the 511,000 troops deployed) represented a loss rate about a tenth of that suffered by Israel in the Six-Day War of 1967, rightly regarded as a dazzling Israeli victory.[3] We lost fewer military personnel to hostile fire during five weeks of actual shooting than we did in routine accidents during the five months of preparation. Young American males were safer in the war zone than in large cities of the United States.

On the other hand, our initial estimate of 200,000 Iraqi casualties was wildly inaccurate. It turned out to be more on the order of a fifth of that number, perhaps as low as 8,000 killed.

What we did achieve was the reality of a well-nigh bloodless battlefield victory and the illusion of a conclusive military triumph. Much credit for both substance and shadow should go to Colin Powell.

It was a remarkable performance, especially on the part of the Air Force, and conclusions drawn from it should have helped shape the nation's defense establishment in the years since. But it is very hard for large organizations to learn through success. Even failure has to be catastrophic before the evidence will be admitted. In any case, victory in the Gulf has not, to date, made much difference and, for the Air Force, it didn't need to. The principal technical lessons, stealth and precision, were initiatives of long standing. The main outlines of reorganization, a primary thrust of my tenure as chief, had already been agreed between Secretary Rice and me by early January, before the curtain rose on the air campaign in the Gulf. In other words, for the Air Force, the impact of Desert Storm was to confirm we were on the right track in courting large-scale technical and structural change.

---

3 Sadly, of US killed in action, 35 died as a consequence of that terrible oxymoron "friendly fire," 14 in the SOF AC-130, 29 in the Scud barracks attack, and 21 from handling unexploded ordnance. Arguably, at least 99 of our 149 combat deaths were preventable.

Aside from the Air Force, in our approach to overall defense reorganization and reform, and especially to defense budgeting in the decade of the 1990s, we acted as though Desert Storm hadn't happened. So, it might be a good idea to review a short list of Lessons Ignored.

The Role of Air Forces

Warfare has a history that predates the appearance of humankind, but the question of what to make of the airplane has arisen only in the last 100 years or so. What we should do with a new military technology depends on how we answer a more important question: what is our purpose in offering battle? If defeat of enemy ground forces is the only definition of success, then the work is not well started until we close with, engage, and either destroy them or move them off contested territory. These are the *decisive* acts, the stuff of victory. Airpower can be an important adjunct to a successful ground campaign, but it makes no sense to employ it alone or in pursuit of some more remote objective. Here we see deep into the wellsprings of Army thought: only sustained military operations on land will settle the issue.[4]

World War I saw the first large-scale combat use of the airplane. Following it, airpower evangelists predicted a future in which ground forces would lose pride of place. They would engage one another, to be sure, but they could be overflown, ignored, waved at in passing. Deep attack—on the enemy's industrial base, capital, population, communications—would determine the outcome.

Accordingly, the first doctrinal issue separating the Air Force and the Army is whether, independently, airpower can be decisive in this way. Soldiers show a skepticism that is first of all intuitive

---

4 See for instance *Certain Victory: The United States Army in the Gulf War:* "Desert Storm confirmed that the nature of war has not changed ... the strategic core of joint warfare is ultimately decisive land combat." Such a claim stands in interesting contrast with, for instance, Sun Tzu's view of the army as an instrument for delivering the *coup de grace* to an enemy previously made vulnerable.

but also springs from their view that claims about airpower's effectiveness have so far been inflated. Both the Navy and Marine Corps hold a watching brief in favor of the Army but are not anxious to join the argument, since these services each have large air arms, quite capable of independent battle operations.

As is standard procedure in doctrine debates, the Army starts by pushing forward question-begging definitions: engaging and defeating the enemy army on the ground falls within the established meaning of the term "decisive." Absent this, it can't be decisiveness we're talking about.

On this semantic foundation, the Army builds a concept of how airpower should be employed. It sees the Air Force as a powerful auxiliary, a deliverer of critical support. It relies on air transport to get to the fight, and likes air reconnaissance to increase its understanding of the situation, but it's close air support (CAS) the Army has in mind. CAS is regarded as much-improved fire support: artillery on steroids. Airplanes deliver munitions that do not need to be as ruggedly packaged as artillery shells and therefore can be mostly explosive charge, rather than mostly steel jacket. In addition, airplanes get to the target quickly, overcome terrain obstacles, maneuver to align their attack axis with the most vulnerable aspect of the target. All this is excellent, but hardly revolutionary. It can be thought of as the linear extension of earlier combat experience—say in the US Civil War or World War I—when artillery became the first line of offense, the infantry following up after each barrage. The Army's excellent (though hardly objective) official account, *Certain Victory: The US Army in the Gulf War*, states the view succinctly: airpower is "the means to weaken the enemy and shape the battlefield."[5]

As for the enlargement of airpower beyond close air support,

---

5 The claim is presented without convincing evidence. Our ground forces certainly did fall, at last, on a weakened enemy. But one could as easily assert the reverse: that ground forces shaped a battlefield on which air forces did most of the actual killing.

the Army agrees that air superiority is needed. But, push come to shove, they have their own means to achieve it—guns and missiles that can create local air superiority where they regard it as meaningful, in the air just overhead. They view deep attack as important mainly because it will have delayed effects on the close battle. Therefore, deep attack must be "synchronized," by which is meant planned and executed against targets selected by the ground commander.

The Army's argument is a fair one, if we allow the distinctive definition of terms. We should not. Airmen rightly regard "decisive" as meaning something quite different: that we cause the desired change in enemy behavior, however this is done.

But scholarship is tiresome so we often skip the matter of definitions, bringing the debate around to various interpretations of airpower's actual performance. Unhappily, airpower's track record has been mixed, at best. One could certainly argue that air campaigns before Desert Storm took too long, to do too little, at too high a cost. As a consequence, it was difficult to counter the Army proposition that independent air attack is not worth the diversion of sorties that might otherwise go to close air support.

However, with less than a century or so of aerial combat behind us, we shouldn't be quite so ready to close the books. We learned a lot about this new instrument of war, in Europe and the Pacific, in Korea and Vietnam. Over the years we'd mastered the technology, techniques, and procedures making for purposeful employment. A changed organizational culture was even more important: our senior leadership now came from officers who had spent their entire professional lives thinking about and practicing the uses of airpower.

Hence, our performance in the Gulf War was entirely different. As one study observed, ". . . when one can conduct a 4 corps offensive operation against a 42 division opponent with less than 200 casualties, something significant has happened." Given any spark of curiosity, we might have asked the obvious questions:

"Why were results so unlike our earlier combat experience? What adjustments should we make?" The essence of scientific method is not to rely on the writings of Aristotle to answer questions like these, but to observe the phenomena and decide for ourselves. Objectivity would be a great liberator, here.

The Battle of Al Khafji is a turning point in the debate about airpower—and, for that matter, in the history of armed conflict. This is the engagement that should be studied at the war colleges, especially Carlisle Barracks, the Army school. Aside from Scud attacks, Khafji was Iraq's only offensive action of any consequence, and it was simply smashed by airpower, and airpower alone. An incontestable specific finding is that airpower will stop moving armor—at night, on short notice, and without a coordinated ground counterattack.

But can we make a more expansive claim regarding the question of decisiveness? Well, it sure looked like the combination of precise attack and 24-hour pressure shocked the Iraqi Army into submission. The body continued to twitch. What resembled ground fighting, but might more accurately be described as vigorous decomposition, dragged on after G-day until we invited surrender. The ground offensive was important and deserves our respect, but it is nonsense to depict it as the deciding factor. On the face of it, it was airpower that was decisive, that determined the outcome for the Iraqi Army, just as in the Pacific during World War II it had settled the fate of navies.

But in the late spring of 1993, long after the Army had time to digest the Desert Storm result, their chief of staff, Gordy Sullivan, gave me a bound, autographed copy of *Field Manual 100-5, Operations*, the Army's cornerstone doctrine publication. Among its assertions: "It is the Army's ability to react promptly and to conduct sustained land operations that make it *decisive*" (emphasis in the original).

To believe that airpower, on its own, can coerce an opponent to change his behavior is not to hold that airpower should always be used alone, which would be silly. Airpower is not the answer to every security challenge or in every combat scenario. Maybe our next engagement will be mostly a ground party, like the 1989 Operation Just Cause in Panama, or the 1993 "invasion" of Haiti. In any event, we all understand that the normal war-fighting mode employs all our forces, fighting in harness. But we may now confidently assert that airpower occupies the central role in high-end combat operations.[6] It is clearer than ever that the outcome of armed conflict between great powers will be decided in the contest for control of the air. It's the winner of this high battle whose forces will survive and prevail at the Earth's surface.

The Question of Command

The Air Force exists as a separate service because the airplane is not simply a technical achievement. A century of experience with manned flight has shown that the most important rationale for independence is cultural.

The day after I swore in as of chief of staff, the president announced the decision to send another 200,000 troops to the Gulf. Though it seemed to me we were already in pretty good shape to do whatever we wanted, it was claimed that this additional measure would position us for "offensive" option. Schwarzkopf himself explained the rationale:

> Any student of military strategy would tell you that in order to attack a position, you should have a ratio of approximately 3 to 1 in favor of the attacker. And, in order to attack a position that is heavily dug in and barricaded, such as the one we had here, you should have a ratio of 5 to 1 in the way of troops in the favor of the attacker.

In the military art, what we regard as ancient history depends on point of view. Descriptions of the battlefield and how it works—theories and mathematical models—that do not incorporate ideas about airpower might be called "classical" theories. Thus, Schwarzkopf's

---

6 What I elsewhere call Type A war.

1990 official photo.

Secretary Dick Cheney and Pentagon General Council Terry O'Donnell swear me in as the Air Force's 14th chief of staff.

Retiring Grace and Mike Dugan from active service.

The Joint Chiefs meet with the president in the Oval Office.

In the desert, at the corner of Jones Alley and McPeak Blvd.

Breakfast in the desert.

After action, briefing the Pentagon press corps.

*The Desert Storm JCS: CSAF Merrill McPeak,
CNO Frank Kelso, CMC Al Gray, CSA Carl Vuono,
CJCS Colin Powell, VCJCS David Jeremiah.*

description of the problem he faced conformed exactly with the classical view, and judged by this criterion, he was a classical general, every bit as much as Napoléon or Ulysses S. Grant.

I mean no criticism of Schwarzkopf, who led brilliantly. But, as might be expected, Schwarzkopf started with the foot soldier's foxhole perspective (as did Colin Powell). Military forces operating at the Earth's surface must be concerned with developments immediately in front of them, so this mindset is entirely understandable.

But the military art changed in a radical way in 1903—the year the Wright brothers flew—at exactly the same time and in much the same way the twin theories of special relativity and quantum mechanics began correcting our picture of the physical world. There is an aerial view. By instinct and training, even the most junior pilot sees it. The battlefield looks different from 40,000 feet, and it is a difference of kind, not simply degree.

In Desert Storm, the air campaign was certainly the centerpiece of the Allied effort. Under the circumstances, it's hard to see why overall command could not have gone to an airman. Why must we assume that only an officer with surface-based qualifications is suited to lead such an enterprise?

Leaving aside the Desert Storm result, America has not performed exceptionally well in armed conflict since the end of World War II. One reason may be that airmen were for decades systematically excluded from command of a theater of operations. During my time as chief, I tried hard and repeatedly to get an airman assigned to lead a joint, geographic command. I was unsuccessful.

We do not need airmen in command everywhere and at all times. The most competent officer of whatever service should be selected, a policy that would both ensure substantial Air Force representation and be a big step toward true jointness.

Organization

Though both are important, effectiveness in battle is connected more to ideas than hardware. For years airmen have argued that air operations, both offensive and defensive, are an entity and therefore the strength and flexibility of air forces can be fully exploited only through central direction and control. The idea that more than one person should have his hands on the controls of an air campaign reminds us of the French saying about divided command: "One dumb general is better than two geniuses."

The air operation designed by Horner involved sophisticated targeting, complex electronic warfare support, and intricate patterns of air refueling. The air arms of all our services and of many foreign countries, most using unique national or service-specific techniques and procedures, flew together in confined air space. All sorts and varieties of equipment were employed, including some aircraft, like the French Mirage, used by both sides. As one indicator of how important integration was, we put 2,000 sorties a day into a relatively small combat arena, and there was not even one instance of air-to-air fratricide, an eye-catching achievement and one that could not have been possible without top-down direction and control.

This conviction that the air operation is a system and has to be managed as a system is bitterly opposed by the other services, who see it as an undisguised Air Force grab for control of their air arms. The prospect of an Air Force officer having tasking authority over Army, Navy, and Marine Corps aviation is, to say the least, unpalatable to these services.[7]

Control is a manhood issue. Even inside the Air Force—here, despite our own doctrine—we have been reluctant to integrate air capabilities. Over the years, Strategic Air Command went to great lengths to retain control of bombers and tankers, wherever or for whatever purpose they were employed. Military Airlift Command

---

7 Ironically, there is tacit agreement in all services about the need for centralized control of air. At some level, in each service, aviation assets are collected and managed centrally. Every infantryman does not get his own helicopter or his own Patriot missile to use as he sees fit. So, the real issue is not whether air assets should be controlled centrally, but at what level such authority should reside, which is another way of saying who will do the controlling.

did much the same thing with transports. This approach prevented the senior airman in a theater of operations from organizing truly integrated Air Force operations, let alone integrated joint air operations involving the participation of the other service components. We've paid a high price for this foolishness, and not just in dollars. Air operations in Korea and Vietnam were never properly integrated, and it cost lives.

Had responsibility for the nation's military aviation been assigned to the Air Force in 1947, or if being right were sufficient to prevail on an issue, the matter would have been settled long ago. Our failure to make the hard decisions in the post-World War II reorganization means that just about everybody in Washington has his own air force and wants to keep control of it.

However, today's joint command structures are considerably stronger than they were at the time of Korea or Vietnam. If they wish, joint commanders can now create something like a single air arm. This is what Schwarzkopf did. Ignoring the misgivings of his other service components, Schwarzkopf gave Horner the job of integrating the air campaign and backed him when attempts were made to assert independence. This was a courageous and excellent decision but, in my view, it is the choice almost certain to be made by any joint commander with brains and backbone.

Horner's control was by no means absolute; the process required endless negotiation. The Navy established a "fleet defense" allocation that withheld sorties not only for air defense but also for "related naval missions." When, as in Desert Storm, the Navy operates so close to shore they are in essence part of one integrated air defense system, retaining sorties for separate tasking is very inefficient. By the end of Desert Storm, 38 percent of all Navy "shooter" sorties were tasked for fleet air defense, while at the same time, only 12 percent of Air Force sorties were defensive, and it was the Air Force sorties that got all the kills. In other words, the Air Force protected the fleet in the process of protecting everything else.

As for the "related naval missions," in practice this meant the

Navy also retained sorties to attack on-shore targets they regarded as important. The Navy's tacit assertion: we should conduct two or more air wars in a theater of operations, one against targets of interest to the joint commander and another one (or more) against targets of interest to individual service component commanders. The question of how to coordinate these separate air wars, or how to prioritize in case of conflict, was finessed.

The Marines agreed to provide Horner sorties "in excess of their direct support requirements." This meant they withheld all the aircraft they regarded as strictly for close air support—helicopters and Harrier jump jets—as well as all C-130 air refueling tankers and a hefty portion of their F/A-18s, capable of participation in the deeper battle. They offered up all A-6 and EA-6B sorties and half the F/A-18 sorties, at least at the outset. As G-day approached, the percentage of F/A-18 sorties tasked by Horner gradually dwindled, these being withheld on the claim they were switching to close air support. But the Marines encountered little opposition on the ground, and therefore did not require much actual close air support during their dash to Kuwait City. The bulk of the sorties the Marines flew and *classified* as CAS went after targets well forward of the line of ground contact, in the part of the battlefield where we do interdiction, which needs, and should have had, central tasking and control.[8]

The Army never agreed that Horner could task its helicopters. (The Army Apaches that fired the first shot at Iraqi air defense radars were from the Special Operations Forces, not the Army.)

Thus, the cooperation of the other services was grudging and reluctant. Horner made many lasting contributions, but among

---

8 In the US Naval Institute's November 1991 issue of *Proceedings*, Maj Gen. Royal N. Moore Jr., who commanded Marine Corps air in the Gulf, published an article titled, *Marine Air: There When Needed.* He was frank: "This way, I didn't have to play around with the (joint air planning) process while I was waiting to hit a target. I kind of gamed the ... process."

his most important was keeping peace in the airpower family. He knew when to insist on integration and when he could compromise in order to make integration as nonthreatening as possible. He also had the personal qualities to make this go down with his fellow component commanders. But in the final analysis, Horner held the high cards. He had much more air capability than needed, even if the other services stayed on the sidelines. Cooperation was the price of admission. They could either get in the game or be left out. (They anyway complained of being left out.) For the most part, and especially for operations outside Kuwait and its immediate confines, the other services accepted Horner's control.

The much-increased authority conferred by the Goldwater-Nichols reforms means that a joint commander will have the loudest voice in deciding how airpower is organized for combat. Joint commanders are very likely to decide that at least the assigned air assets with any reach—that is, all the aircraft not tied absolutely to the close air support role—will be centrally tasked at the theater level. To do the tasking, joint commanders will likely appoint an overall air commander.[9] In theory, the joint commander might choose an overall air commander from any service. There will be qualified aviators in the Air Force component, in the aviation branches of each of the other service components, and in the air element of assigned Special Operations Forces. However, the combat aviation resources of the other services report to the commanders of these components, while the Air Force component is unambiguously the joint commander's own air arm. Accordingly, we can expect the Air Force component to lead the integrated air effort. This is the iron logic of joint air warfare, and it is an unwelcome development for the other services, who will quite likely see

---

9 As this is written, the overall air commander is called the "joint force air component commander," or JFACC. Of course, there isn't any "air component," so it is a lawyerly question just what the joint force air component commander commands.

control of "their" aviation assets taken away just as the prospect of action looms large.

The practices established by Schwarzkopf in the Gulf War—designating an air commander, adopting an overall concept for the air campaign, centralizing air planning and tasking—resulted in history's most effective use of airpower—far from perfect, but good enough for the league we played in.

Intelligence

We spend a lot of money on intelligence. Much of our experience to date has been thoroughly unsatisfactory, our failure in the Gulf War to track down Scud missiles being just one case in point. In general, targeting is the intelligence problem that has to be solved, and it should be given even higher priority, as against the other sorts of intelligence work we do.

Before the advent of precision bombing, targeting was rather like measuring with a micrometer, marking with caulk and cutting with an ax. Since you were likely to miss anyway, selecting exactly the right aim point and assigning it exactly the right priority did not count for much. But now we can hit dead center what we're aiming at, and the entire success or failure of air combat operations rides on our ability to identify, locate, and prioritize targets. From now on we are likely to judge commanders by how well they target.

As a rule, the sensors that identify and locate targets should be wired into the closest possible loop with the operator.[10] Sensors onboard the shooter aircraft—eyeballs, infrared, cockpit radar—provide the best intelligence because they present target information that can evaluated by the operator and acted on immediately. Off-board sensors that are in close and continuous contact with the shooter—AWACs, JSTARS, the ground radar environment—are

---

10 As an example, note the recent apparent success, in Type B war, of Predator drones, the result of attaching missiles to what was in essence a surveillance platform.

second best because they, too, give timely advice that can be acted on quickly. Overhead and other strategic sensors are least best because their information often must be downloaded and analyzed at some remove. Even if information from these sources could be routed directly to the cockpit (and some of it can and should be), well intentioned, rear-echelon civilians will likely choose what information to display and what to withhold. We would be wrong to assume otherwise, as such evil springs from the reality that knowledge is power.

BDA

Battle damage assessment (BDA) is a specialized form of target intelligence. To understand its importance, it is useful to make an analogy with living systems. Any living system is certainly more capable than the sum of its parts. The body is made up of trillions of cells but can do things no pile of similar cells can do. The key reason a living body does more interesting things than an equivalent pile of cells can is that it accepts and acts on feedback, the various inputs from the environment that convey information. Even the most primitive human activity, like shaping flint for a knife, involves feedback in which the brain uses information to modify subsequent actions of the body.

BDA is the feedback mechanism for air operations, separating effective employment from random results. To date, our air operations, including those for Desert Storm, have been characterized by bad feedback, or worse. This is a problem to be solved and probably will be incrementally, as all the various battlefield sensors improve in performance. The same principles for fixing the larger intelligence system should be used here.

Fratricide

Incidents of fratricide, in which US aircraft killed our own or allied ground troops, accounted for 24 percent of all coalition casualties. In the future, there may be good technical solutions to the IFF (identify friend or foe) problem. Despite a considerable effort, we haven't yet found one. For now, we should think about social or organizational solutions. The Marines have one: they do their own close air support (CAS). This is not a perfect answer, but when capabilities that must routinely be combined in the heat and pressure of combat are collected in the same service, the associated problems can be dealt with using the strongest management tool available: command.

Stealth

Surprise is the difference between expectation and reality. An idea that shouldn't need much discussion is that, when you can pull it off, surprise conveys overwhelming advantage at every level—strategic, operational, and tactical.

Owing to its relatively high speed, the airplane has always had the potential to surprise—to appear suddenly, before defenses can be prepared—witness the Japanese success at Pearl Harbor or the Israeli attack that opened the Six-Day War. Various sensors have been mobilized against the aircraft to prevent surprise, starting with the human eye and ear. During World War II, we set up listening and observation posts on our coastlines, employing these biosensors. The Navy still stands watch, constantly scanning the horizon with binoculars. Once we suppressed their radars, the Iraqis did the same thing, establishing looking and listening posts in the desert. But, more often than not, approaching aircraft are seen or heard pretty late in terms of organizing an effective defense.

Of all our sensors, radar's range is the greatest, and so, over the years, it is principally radar that has eroded the aircraft's ability to surprise. By the time of our attacks into North Vietnam, surveillance radars were so effective that we made no attempt to surprise, relying instead on mass and electronic confusion to overwhelm ground defenses. We ran between tackles, using muscle rather than finesse—we knew it and they knew it—and our resulting losses were high. Happily, the Air Force did not give up entirely on trying to achieve surprise. In fact, a lot of "black" money and much scientific and technical effort went into "stealth," a catchall description for various initiatives to reduce every sort of observable feature, most notably radar reflectivity. The F-117 was an early and interesting result.

Restoring tactical surprise to the air engagement has benefits so obvious that, in testimony before a congressional committee following the Gulf War, I said the Air Force would "never again develop and procure a nonstealthy combat aircraft." Regarding other categories of equipment, this would be good advice for all services.

Surprise has the status of a principle of war, so it is worth mentioning here only because we continue cranking out military equipment thought to be "modern," even though, in use, it has little or no hope of being able to achieve surprise— like, say, the helicopter. Why? The only good answer is we can think of no practical alternative (and there almost always is an alternative). But advocates for nonstealthy systems often go further, attacking the value of stealth: it isn't that important ("tactics contributed to the F-117's excellent combat record") or it doesn't work that well ("the F-117 was tracked by Iraqi radar").

The motives for resisting progress are often obvious. Change has real political, budgetary, and bureaucratic consequences. But in the defense business the tendency to remain committed to obsolete systems is unfathomable because so much is at stake. Sometimes the resistance can be understood only as an aspect of man's fall from grace.

In 1645, Cromwell dyed the uniforms of his New Model Army with a compound derived from insects the Spanish had found during their conquest of Central America. Brushed off Mexican cacti, these little critters could be dried and ground up to produce an amazing scarlet dye. The result was the highly visible British soldier; indeed, they quickly became known as redcoats, a message they somehow did not immediately grasp. As firearms lethal at some remove were perfected, the tactical consequences of wearing these outfits should have been obvious, but in the late 1700s and early 1800s, when Crown troops were sent to fight in America, they still dressed in scarlet, by then a proud tradition. Our side wore buckskin or other apparel more suitable for fighting in the wilderness—or anywhere else, for that matter.

It is sometimes said that armies prepare to fight the last war. The implied criticism is mistaken, as such a condition would improve the actual state of affairs. Most armies do not study war at all in any systematic way. Certainly the British Army of the nineteenth century missed some of the lessons of their various engagements in North America. In February 1881, at the Battle of Majuba, British troops suffered a humiliating defeat that effectively ended the First Boar War. The British dead included their field commander, the scarlet-clad Sir George Colley, who caught a bullet in the forehead.[11]

It is an undeniable fact that the F-117 fighter flew 1,297 sorties in Desert Storm, many of them into downtown Baghdad against the most heavily defended targets. No F-117s were lost, or even scratched, notwithstanding heavy ground fire encountered along the way. Anyway, the argument about the value of stealth simply does not pass the Farmer Jones Logic Test. Tanks and tents are not given a coat of fluorescent paint. If it were free and quickly available, we would all have all the stealth we could get, in all the equipment we bought.

Precision

Desert Storm highlighted some remaining issues with guided air-to-ground munitions. First, we didn't have enough of them. Fewer than 10 percent of the bombs dropped in the Gulf War were guided, but it was obvious that these munitions made the biggest difference. They dominated the conflict in two ways: they were

---

11 We should not think Colley was a Blimpish dimwit. Indeed, he had a well-earned reputation for competence. And he'd served in India, where British soldiers had earlier (1845) learned to soak their white uniforms in a concoction of mud, curry, and coffee to produce khaki, a color that blended with the landscape. That someone as smart as Colley didn't get it shows how debilitating cultural influences can be.

used to attack the most important targets, and by and large, they hit what they were aimed at.

The usual problem with precision is it costs a lot. At more than a million dollars a round, the Navy had a hard time building a substantial inventory of Tomahawk missiles. They fired 288 in Desert Storm, nearly all the attacks coming in the first two weeks, and ran out completely after 28 days.

The "smart" bomb grew out of an earlier effort to get precision at low cost. We hung a laser designator on the airplane, giving the aircrew a way to shine light on a target. We took conventional dumb bombs, of which we had plenty, strapped a cheap laser seeker on the front and movable fins on the back, and produced the laser-guided bomb (LGB). It turned out to be very accurate, going right to the spot illuminated by the aircrew. The cost, nominally $10,000 a round, was also right. But you can't "laze" through cloud; both the aircrew and the bomb have to see the target. In fact, in the Gulf, bad weather was the most serious obstacle we faced using these munitions.

In the aftermath of Desert Storm, Air Force Secretary Don Rice and I resolved to turn up the temperature of a program to give us a relatively cheap smart bomb that could be used in any weather. We called it the Joint Direct Attack Munition (JDAM).[12] In our concept, JDAM started as a regular dumb bomb, but the strap-on kit consisted of an autopilot and a cheap receiver that was updated by the GPS satellite navigation system. Rice and I hoped to get accuracy on the order of 10 meters at a full up cost of about $20,000 per round. The key points: JDAM could be used in any weather and could be acquired in quantity—an inventory could be built.

Only a small distance separates a home run from a long fly ball, but the result is binary. In much the same way, hitting what you

---

12 In Pentagonese, calling something "joint" confers on it automatic, uncritical support. But the Navy soon attached itself to the program, making it truly joint.

aim at, instead of missing close, is an inflection point in aerial warfare, a small percentage difference that changes everything.

Ethical Considerations

In combination, stealth and precision raise interesting ethical issues. Reduced aircrew exposure means we take much less risk. Moreover, if we wish, we can cause a lot less indiscriminate death and damage. Of course, anything that reduces the cost of war or makes it seem more attractive can be counted on to spark high-minded hand-wringing. In the decade since Desert Storm, some otherwise sensible people have argued with a straight face that any combat involving us is now so one-sided as to have become immoral. Somehow it would be more ethical were we to take a few casualties.

In a way the critics are right. The Air Force is not looking for a fair fight. We've thought and worked hard since 1947 to make sure any fighting we do is as unfair as possible. But, here, Protestant dread lies heavy over martial impulse. No use arguing; this is the same crowd that found mutual assured destruction such a handsome article.

Mass

Like surprise, "mass" is a principle of war, this one calling for concentration of force. Voltaire said God is on the side of heavy battalions, this because "bigness" was needed to create mass effects; that is, to insure the opposition was outmanned and outgunned at the point of contact. And until quite recently it was still possible to maneuver relatively large formations in some safety because reconnaissance was hit or miss. Stonewall Jackson's night march at Chancellorsville allowed him to fall on an unprepared Union flank. In August 1914, the British Expeditionary Force arrived in France with something like 80,000 troops, the Channel crossing unobserved, their presence a nasty surprise to the Germans. The introduction of an entire Chinese Army in Korea came as a shock to MacArthur. Unseen by the Iraqis, our own VII Armored Corps moved northwest to G-day jump-off points in a bumper-to-bumper convoy that stretched for miles across open desert under clear skies.

Modern reconnaissance methods herald the end of this sort of maneuver. Sensors like JSTARS give us good 24-hour situation awareness across an entire theater. Opposing surface forces now face a difficult choice. It must be assumed that any movement will be quickly detected. In this situation, no surface maneuver force—on land or at sea—stands any chance of reaching its destination, unless it can somehow wrest air superiority from us—showing again that airpower is the key enabling capability making all other sorts of combat power usable.[13] Bigness now translates as a one-to-one increase in visibility and attractiveness as a target, with little if any corresponding payoff in performance. We had better be careful, here, because the technology trend that is weakening the link between size and effectiveness is accelerating.

Of course, precision attack is a much more economical means to concentrate energy and create mass effects.

The availability of precision mandates a radical redesign of forces to make them "small"—by which I mean to reduce their observability—a fact having noteworthy implications for large formations like divisions and corps, for large installations like bases and port facilities, and for classes of equipment like main battle tanks and surface ships.

In considering how they might survive in the age of information warfare, all our forces must improve their stealthiness. To do this, they'll have to get small. Our Army needs to look more like the Special Operations Force (assuming we can keep the SOF small). For the Navy, the model is the submarine, a stealthy boat. A modern diesel submarine can be purchased for a large sum of money and has some stealthy features. But to achieve multidimensional stealth, a submarine must be "quieted," and that costs a lot more,

---

13 Here I refer to modern, Type A war.

starting with the nuclear power plant that enables long-range submerged cruise. Just as with aircraft, we have found that true stealth is worth the premium price.

Submarine warfare is a role and core competency of the Navy and should be funded appropriately. But, since the Navy has an effective monopoly, they feel no pressure to invest in the activity and, as this is written, the submarine force is being allowed to atrophy so that money can be diverted into tactical air, a capability already oversubscribed. This is a serious mistake that should be corrected quickly. The submarine has been around a while, but it is still a sunrise system, as opposed to large surface vessels, which are simply semi-immobile, high-visibility targets.

We should expect a last ditch stand by those who have a stake in bigness. In particular, armored vehicles and ships have been a dominating presence for a century or more. Why should anyone suppose it might be different in the future? To sum up the answer in one idea: it is now possible to hit any target that can be located, to hit it with uncanny accuracy, and to hit it from a safe distance. This is a hard problem, with no single, cheap solution. But survival in combat will require us all to create uncertainty about our location.

Logistics

Desert Storm required an extensive, even bloated logistic support. In part, this was a product of a "decisiveness syndrome" that demanded much more combat force than was needed to do the job; in part, it was a characteristic inherent in armed forces of the industrial age. For whatever reason, it took us six months to deploy, and we required 25 bases in the region to defeat a small country with a third-rate military.

Support economies are important in any deployment scenario. We simply must reduce the volume of logistic support required for deploying forces. When we do this, we will cut down the time needed to prepare for combat and diminish our attractiveness as a target—not to mention earning a wholesale reduction in the cost of maintaining forces in peacetime.

Missile Defense

We now have some actual experience on the receiving end of ballistic missile attack. It wasn't pretty. In this regard, we are our own worst enemy, since we continue to work on missile defense in a political and financial straitjacket. There has been a technical and conceptual bright spot here: the Air Force's Airborne Laser Program. The issue is whether it will survive the bureaucratic and political infighting.[14]

Defending the country against incoming missiles (both ballistic and cruise) is a good idea because protecting the people, property, and institutions of the United States is a good idea. If for political or financial reasons we cannot yet construct comprehensive missile defenses, we should put in place a thinner shield aimed at preventing accidental or terrorist attack, then gradually bolt on enhancements to build a more complete system.

The argument against defending ourselves from missile attack goes back to the notion of mutual assured destruction (MAD), according to which nuclear-armed opponents must stand utterly exposed to retaliation in order to create stability in the relationship. It was asserted that the side fielding missile defenses might be tempted to attack on the expectation they could defeat a prospectively weaker retaliatory response. This argument wasn't valid, even for the Cold War condition that gave rise to it. Defenses are inherently stabilizing, as any schoolyard bully knows. It's offense that destabilizes. (Imagine a world in which the number of nuclear missiles is zero. Would missile defenses be destabilizing?) And the anti-missile defense view is even less sound for the post-Cold War world, in which threats to us transmute and proliferate into the hands of nondeferrable, nonstate actors.

---

14 It didn't.

It's only a matter of time until ballistic or cruise missiles are used against us. The loss of a single city to missile attack would be orders of magnitude more expensive in lives and material than the most extravagant missile defense program we could devise. And who is to say it would be only a single city?

While we certainly need to defend ourselves, antimissile defenses should, in principle, be deployed globally, so the threat of missile-delivered weapons of mass destruction can be eliminated, like smallpox.

It also makes a lot of sense to defend against missile attack in a theater of operations, and for many of the same reasons. Here, our excuse for failure has less to do with ideology than with politics and bureaucratic strength. The Army now plays a lead role in theater missile defense (TMD), and that is a good choice if you think defeating incoming ballistic missiles is close combat and needs to be integrated with the rest of the combined arms battle. But there is little doubt that the best way—maybe the only way—to deal with theater ballistic missiles is to attack them en route to the launch pad, or on it, or early in their ascent phase, or outside the atmosphere. We also should play goalie, attempting the extremely difficult—indeed, nearly impossible—endgame defense. But all logic tells us TMD must be integrated with what is otherwise happening deep, high, and in space, and the job should go to the Air Force.

Readiness

Our squadrons deployed quickly and were ready on arrival. We did not need a lengthy transition from our normal, in-garrison mode to a deployed, combat-ready posture. Admittedly, this is a somewhat easier problem for the Air Force than for the other services. We are by nature a force-in-readiness, doing more or less the same thing in peacetime we do in combat, so the transition is transparent and, while not effortless, relatively straightforward. Nevertheless, we can be bad at it, as well as good. It turned out we were good. We always will be, as long as we are willing to pay the price—and this means dollars, equipment, and people—to maintain high readiness standards in peacetime. When Marshal of the Imperial Russian Army Alexander Suvorov said, "Train hard, fight easy," he was talking about today's readiness, and he was right.[15] Our aircrews found the Desert Storm fighting less of a challenge in many ways than routine training exercises.

However, we should also be concerned about tomorrow's readiness. In 1939, the Polish Cavalry may well have been in wonderful condition—horses fit, harness oiled, sabers sharpened. Ready or not, they were irrelevant when confronted with modern military capabilities. Equipment modernization is future readiness.

People

The postgame analysis always seems to focus on budgets and programs but, at the end of the day, Desert Storm was a human victory, from President Bush down to the lowest ranking grunt. We were better organized, better trained, and better led than the competition. I wouldn't like to do this, but we could have traded Saddam our hardware for his and still have won going away. This is worth mentioning only because we so often ignore the human dimension in deciding how to organize, train, equip, and use our armed forces, treating combat formations and individual soldiers as though they were so many colored pins to be pushed around on a map.

---

15 Suvorov, Alexander (ca. 1729-1800): Born a commoner, he enlisted, some say at age 13, and earned a commission in 1754, a significant achievement in an age when aristocracy provided the officer class. Rising through the ranks, he introduced simplified tactics and a training program that emphasized the physical stamina needed for rapid maneuver. He delegated to subordinate commanders authority to think and act independently, making a virtue of necessity, since he usually led from the front. This habit of sharing the dangers of battle—so unlike the typical gentleman officer—endeared him to his soldiers. Though often faced by forces of greater size, he never lost a battle.

Wrong Lesson

Some have claimed the Gulf War was a setup for airpower. Their suggested bumper sticker: "We do deserts—not jungles or mountains." (Under the heading Consistency 101, this assertion was often made in tandem with the contention that airpower was, anyway, ineffective.)

Open desert is indeed congenial for air employment, though it is important to note that it works reasonably well for everybody, including the opposition. Even on our side, soldiers I know do not welcome bad weather, or fighting in a mountain, jungle, or urban setting.

On the other hand, the Gulf War happened halfway round the world. After getting there, our aircraft were typically based some considerable distance from the target. At best, the weather was not good and had an enormous negative impact on the effectiveness of offensive air operations. The important factors in our success—organization, readiness, stealth, precision—apply with equal effect to any combat environment.

Being easy should not be confused with making it look easy.

Chapter 3

1991: Organize

Generally, management of the many is the same as management of the few. It is a matter of organization.
—Sun Tzu, *The Art of War*

At the end of calendar 1990, the Air Force was by any measure a giant organization. Our active-duty strength was 535,000; the Air National Guard and the Air Force Reserve added another 200,000 or so uniformed personnel; there were nearly 250,000 full-time civilians on the payroll; altogether, say a million people in the Air Force. We operated 139 large installations in the United States and overseas. Applying the customary force-structure metric, we possessed 36 fighter wings—24 in the active component and 12 in the Guard and Reserve. Additionally, we had 300 bombers and 365 strategic transport aircraft—in all, more than 6,000 airplanes of various types, as well as 1,000 ICBMs, many space systems, and so forth.

So the Air Force was a big outfit but, from a resource perspective, in decline. The high-water mark of the Reagan defense buildup had been reached in 1985. In doing the programming for 1986, I had told our chief of staff, Larry Welch, I thought we could have a great

Air Force for $100 billion, down maybe 10 percent from where we then were. Now, as I became chief, we were at the front end of executing the FY 91 budget, which in then-year dollars stood at $91.2 billion, off 25 percent in real terms from the spending peak. The fat had been squeezed out. But I was quite sure we'd slide further, making this point forcibly in public statements and, more important, acting on this assumption in our internal planning and budget execution. In retrospect, we know this is exactly what happened. The Air Force experienced a further four straight years of real budget decline so that by the end of my tenure we had an additional 30 percent less—more than $20 billion a year—to spend.

The Cold War was over for sure and, for sure, we were going to be poorer and smaller. But if I had one nonnegotiable condition of employment, it was this: I'd leave behind an Air Force better than the one I had inherited. The challenge would be to do this while spending a lot less money. Business as usual wouldn't be good enough. We'd have to reorganize.

The reorganization of the Air Force was a complex undertaking, the details not perhaps of universal interest. In what follows, I'll discuss only some of the main ideas that went into the redesign and only the most important structural changes.

Put the Mission Front and Center

In setting out to redo organizational structures, I had several prejudices, the first being an attachment to the mission. Technically, the Department of the Air Force—I mean the department itself, in contrast with its operating arms—has no mission. Instead, by law (Title 10, US Code) the *functions* of the Department of the Air Force are to organize, train, and equip air combat forces, then provide them to the various joint commanders for operational use.

I would not like to overwork the distinction between a mission and a set of functions, but there is a link from these concepts to the menu of choices available in selecting organizational style. Much depends on whether we're inclined to organize by mission or by function. If by mission, it's first necessary to ask: *What is to be done?* (what's the desired *output?*), then select someone to head the effort and give him the resources (people, equipment, dollars) needed to do the job. Most important, the person charged with the mission makes the resource allocation decisions. It's his budget, his people, his equipment, his facilities.

If, on the other hand, we organize by function, we turn the question around: *What inputs will lead to a desired result?* To use commercial analogues, we might think that good engineering, or excellent financial controls, or world-class marketing will guarantee a successful project. Since getting these functions right is the key, we decide real professionals must supervise them. All the engineers will report to a chief engineer, the accountants to a chief financial officer, the salesmen to a vice president for sales, with these department heads retaining resource control. There will also be somebody "in charge" of the overall project, but he will reach into the functional departments for support. He's a project coordinator, in charge of blending someone else's resources.

No large organization I know of is pure regarding organizational style; all are some mix of these two approaches. Moreover, the factors affecting the decision about how to organize are quite dynamic: objectives change, new threats arise, external factors adjust the resource mix. Given constant flux, an organization's structure is seldom perfect and must be fine-tuned as circumstances vary. The question for those charged with oversight is, what bias do I want to run through the organization? What mistake am I willing to live with?

In thinking about this issue, definitions are important, the terminology more likely to confuse than clarify. People who man functions can and usually do state their purposes in mission-like terms. For instance, at the beginning of 1991, the Air Force had an Air Weather Service (AWS), an organization with a long and honorable history. It was what we might call a functional "stovepipe." That is, everybody in the weather business, no matter at what level or where assigned, was inside this vertical construction.

Air Weather Service certainly had a purpose: to provide weather observation and forecasting to the operating Air Force (and, as it happened, also to the Army, though not the Navy). This sounds like a mission, and AWS was good at it. Weather forecasters and observers seemed happy—comfortable is perhaps a better term—with the arrangement. They enjoyed a well-established career track, with increasingly senior weather professionals in charge at each level, and sitting atop the whole structure was the Air Weather Service commander, a brigadier general.

Except, nobody believed the business of the Air Force was to furnish itself weather forecasts. This was clearly a kind of functional support for the real mission. So how should it be organized? Suppose I gave you an air combat task and you failed, in part because of bad weather forecasting. Who do I fire? You, or the Air Weather Service commander?

In January 1991, many essential parts of the Air Force were built on this stovepiped model.[16] In reorganizing, I wanted to connect everyone as closely as possible with the mission, which I saw broadly as "operations," rather than with any particular job specialty. The mistake I was willing to live with was having too much focus on the real job.

Simplify, Streamline, Flatten, Decentralize

At all levels of the organization, a unifying theme would be to simplify, to prune optional detail, to identify and chop off elaboration, to pare down to essentials. I knew there were limits on how far we could go in this regard. Einstein put it best: "Everything should be made as simple as possible, but not simpler." Given our

---

16 Oddly, this was not true of the traditional professions. At base level, the heads of the medical, legal, and chaplain functions all worked directly for a local operating commander. We were in the awkward position of believing operational commanders could directly supervise doctors and lawyers, but not weather forecasters.

size and responsibilities, the Air Force would always be a complicated organization. And I reckoned we would not get it precisely right. My mistake of choice was to make it too simple.

If possible, I wanted to de-layer the Air Force, make its structure flatter. A flat structure would force us to unify responsibility for task accomplishment at the lowest level possible, to decentralize authority and move it closer to the problem. There are said to be only two rungs in the ladder from village priest to pope. While I was skeptical about this claim, the church had been remarkably successful for many centuries, and the horizontal design of its organization was one reason why.

Consolidate, Where Possible

Our reduced circumstances made consolidation unavoidable, but I did not want to consolidate based merely on assumptions about presumed economies of scale. In my view, the claims made for efficiency through consolidation were nearly always extravagant and at the same time ignored far more important factors, like the impact on human spirit and motivation. Too often, the practical consequence of consolidation was centralization, the movement of authority to the center and up in an organization. Any action to consolidate had to meet the Farmer Jones Logic Test: did it unify resources and responsibility without undermining the even more important organizational goal of decentralization?

Strengthen the Chain of Command

The nation's armed forces are granted a monopoly on violence only because it is assumed they respond to and carry out the public will. The basic mechanism for ensuring they do so is called the chain of command, which accordingly ought to be treated with some reverence. The chain of command has too many links for comfort—something like eight or 10 between the president and the pilot who pulls the trigger. There is a lot of noise in any circuit with this many soldered connections and the whole lash up will no doubt come under the greatest stress just when its integrity is most important. Even so, the realities of size, mission, and geography impose span-of-control limits on how much we can reduce the number of links.

In reorganizing, I wanted to pay attention to what we were doing with the chain of command, to keep it as clean as possible, make it a point to strengthen the links every way we could.

Promote Human Values

People, not org charts, win wars. What we were after was a structure in which desired human qualities could take root and grow. For example, I thought we could increase the ratio of good to bad jobs. Looking back on my own career, I'd not intended to stay in the Air Force, doing so only because I kept being given interesting work to do. I wanted to underscore this sort of human value, to the extent this could be done through improved organizational design.

It was then necessary to apply these principles to each level of organization. In implementation, I described an "objective" organization, not necessarily the existing structure, and maybe not even one we would ever get to, but a Platonic ideal, the desired target of organizational evolution.

The Objective Squadron

The squadron was the basic unit the Air Force provided to joint commanders for employment. It corresponded roughly to the Army battalion and, as with the battalion, a lieutenant colonel commanded. The squadron was also the first level at which we represented the spirit of comradeship with official emblems or symbols—the patches and plaques, the badges of heraldry we accord recognized military units.

In law, the corporation is said to be a natural person. In fact, the squadron has a better claim to such status. The battle ebbs and flows, people go and are replaced, the building fills with ghosts, but the thing itself—the squadron—remains alive, its standard a faithful arbiter of the relative wind. It's the squadron that goes to beer call and holds reunions.

Put in simplest terms, the commander of an operational squadron takes his unit to a theater of operations, makes contact with and fights the enemy.[17] What resources should we put at his disposal to carry out these tasks? At a minimum, he needs people and airplanes, and we might think he should have command of both the people who fly and the people charged with primary care of the aircraft. Aircrews are necessarily part of the operations squadron; indeed, it wouldn't be an ops squadron without them. And, at the atomic level, an individual pilot and his crew chief form the electron and proton, the elemental fighting team of the Air Force. It was never clear why we would want to break up this team.

But at home station, at least, it was possible to do so, assigning flight-line maintenance personnel and even the airplanes to somebody outside the operating squadron. That's because, at base level, there were two echelons of aircraft maintenance. The first echelon was the flight line, where a crew chief met, parked, refueled, and prepared the aircraft for launch. If he was any good, he'd be more than just a gatekeeper, discovering and referring problems to a specialist. Like the family physician, he'd do much minor repair himself.

The second maintenance echelon was located in specialist shops—electrical, hydraulic, engine, and so forth—where experts performed off-aircraft diagnostics and repair. Air bases typically had more than one ops squadron and since we couldn't afford to buy every squadron its own set of specialist shops, we centralized second-echelon maintenance and provided consolidated support to all squadrons.

Thus, there were two ways to organize first-echelon aircraft maintenance: flight-line crew chiefs could be part of the operational squadron, along with the pilots they supported, or they could be part of an aircraft-maintenance organization that included the

---

17 Examples cited in this chapter are mostly from fighter unit operations. Close parallels exist in other kinds of units, flying and nonflying.

second-echelon specialist shops. In November 1990, they were part of the maintenance establishment. In essence, we had decided that flying airplanes was pretty easy but preparing them for flight was hard. Since the critical path to mission success ran through aircraft maintenance, we mustn't give this problem to a flying squadron commander, who probably wouldn't know much about it. Accordingly, we'd removed the crew chiefs—indeed, the aircraft themselves, in many cases—from operational squadrons and consolidated them into a central maintenance organization.[18] In a classic case of managing inputs, the team I thought responsible for combat results—a pilot and his crew chief—had been broken up and put in separate stovepipes.

Meanwhile, we'd accumulated plenty of evidence showing that flying squadron commanders do just fine when put in charge of flight-line maintenance. In the early 1960s, my F-104 wing had kept a squadron in Moron, Spain. When deployed, we took our crew chiefs with us. It made no sense to reorganize for every deployment, so we stayed in this configuration when back home at George. At RAF Woodbridge, in my second operational posting, the 79th Squadron was separated from its wing and the headquarters at RAF Wethersfield. The 79th therefore owned and operated its own flight-line maintenance—again, doing very nicely. Of course the Thunderbird Squadron, in which I served in the late 1960s, stayed on the road all the time, had always been responsible for its own flight-line maintenance, and was pretty good at it. So I'd seen squadron maintenance in action and knew it worked well. But in addition, if we looked outside, at the Navy or Marines, or at overseas air forces we respected, like the Brits or Israelis, it seemed everybody who understood the flying business put first-echelon aircraft maintenance in the operational squadron.

---

18 This treats the airplane as a tool, a piece of technology, rather than a weapon. The airplane is more rightly seen as an extension of the pilot. Together, they form a *system for combat*, like the samurai and his sword.

The argument that should have been determining was that when provided to joint commanders for use, many combat squadrons move from home base to a theater of operations and take flight-line maintenance with them. They had to. It's a bit of an exaggeration—but only a bit—to say that without crew chiefs, we are a one-sortie Air Force. As a consequence, when we didn't put the airplanes and crew chiefs in the ops squadron in peacetime, we were obliged to *reorganize* for war. The first day of combat is the wrong time to begin teaching the squadron commander a whole new set of skills.

I also sought to stimulate leadership growth at every level. For example, many general officers were selected from the pool of former flying squadron commanders. If we exclude flight-line maintenance from what he has to do, a flying squadron commander is in charge of 50 people or so, nearly all of them officers, highly motivated college graduates. This should not be regarded as a world-class leadership challenge. But, put flight-line maintenance in the squadron and it swells to maybe 200 people, all still good folks, but now the squadron is enlisted-heavy, with a whole new set of problems to solve.

Accordingly, we decided to return to operational squadron commanders the ownership and control of their aircraft and crew chiefs. This important change for the better met every one of our reorganization objectives, especially mission focus, decentralization, and emphasis on human values.

The Objective Group

In the chain of command, several squadrons form a group, several groups, a wing. But here the story gets a little complicated. In the Second World War, the group was a real organization, serving as the basic administrative echelon for combat elements of the Army Air Forces. Many of these World War II groups had particularly illustrious histories. Former members of RAF Eagle Squadrons formed the nucleus of the 4th Fighter Group, which began operations in October 1942, flying Spitfires. The 23rd Fighter

Group absorbed Claire Chennault's American Volunteer Group, the magnificent "Flying Tigers." In those days and in the immediate postwar period, a rough measure of the size and strength of the Air Force was often expressed in terms of the number of combat groups it could field.

After the establishment of the independent Air Force in 1947, the group went into decline. Instead of putting ops squadrons in an operations group, they reported to somebody called a deputy commander for operations, or DO, who inhabited a sort of twilight zone between being a commander and being part of the wing staff. Ops squadron commanders were in no doubt they worked for the DO, so the palimpsest of a command level existed, but the DO had neither the title nor the formal authorities of a real commander.

We decided to revitalize the group. At a typical base, squadrons would be part of a group, each group with a commander and almost no staff. The *operations* group would contain the flying squadrons, now to include flight-line maintenance. This group would remain officer-heavy and the other groups in the wing enlisted-heavy, but putting flight-line crew chiefs into ops squadrons moved a lot of enlisted end strength into the operations group, producing a much healthier officer/enlisted ratio across the wing. A new *logistics* group would include second-echelon maintenance as well as the supply and transportation squadrons previously belonging to someone called the deputy commander for resources, or RM, an office that disappeared. The old combat support group became simply the *support* group, with most of its functions intact, but the title "base commander" going by the wayside.

We adopted a scheme called skip-echelon staffing that declared every other echelon purely tactical and sought to eliminate all forms of administrative activity. The group was stripped of functional staffing, getting the group commander out from behind a desk. We pulled together such staff functions as the DO had formerly performed, like command post manning, weapons officer, standardization/evaluation, and so forth, and put them into a squadron called an "operations support squadron." Each group would have such a squadron—a way of turning staff jobs into line service. In addition, we specified that deputy group commanders would be lieutenant colonels. No more ADO (Assistant Director of Operations) colonels, as I had been at MacDill. This eliminated many colonel slots, but the real impact was to convert the deputy group commander position from a bad job for colonels to a good job for lieutenant colonels.

Reorganizing at group level strengthened the chain of command and considerably reduced overhead. By itself, getting rid of the RM saved nearly 300 colonel slots across the Air Force.

The Objective Wing

Groups combine to form a wing. Although the Air Corps of World War II and earlier included a few formations described as wings, they bore little resemblance to the contemporary version. Where they existed, they might control several combat groups or service organizations spread out at widely separated locations. The 1st Bombardment Wing, one of our leading formations between the wars, exemplified this sort of thing. Commanded in the mid-'30s by Hap Arnold, it conducted much of the Army's pursuit, bombardment, attack, and observation activities in the western part of the United States, reporting to the so-called General Headquarters Air Force, the early version of an independent air arm. It was inactivated in 1945, and nothing of its heritage survives into any currently active wing.

A new kind of wing emerged when the Air Force became a separate service and began to organize on its own. Wings took charge at a single airfield, conducting operations through a combat group and that group's operational squadrons, and controlling all the elements needed to support the mission activity. Air Force headquarters "authorized" the wings expected to be permanent, giving them one-, two-, or three-digit numerical designations. The idea was to number permanent wings in a single series, beginning with the Arabic "1st." As this is written, surviving examples include the 1st Fighter Wing, at Langley Field, Virginia, and the 2nd Bomb Wing, at Barksdale Field, Louisiana.[19]

Since they formed starting in 1947, these new postwar wings had no real heritage at the outset, but in most cases a wing's number came from the combat group incorporated into it. Then, in 1954, Air Force headquarters began issuing orders that "bestowed" on wings the history and honors of its associated group. For instance, the leading fighter ace of World War II, Richard I. Bong, served with the 49th Fighter Group in the Pacific. This group evolved into and gave its number to the 49th Fighter Wing, later equipped with the F-117 stealth fighter and stationed at Holloman Field, New Mexico. In this way, wings that began with little or no actual history were able to trace their lineage all the way back to Army Signal Corps days, and, as a consequence, the wing, like the squadron, is a vessel containing our traditions.

The postwar wing was a fundamental level of organization because the Air Force does so much important business at bases and the wing was roughly congruent with the air base itself—but not quite. As we began working on reorganization, some important support functions were not part of a local wing. I earlier cited the example of weather support. In 1990, weather squadrons were tenants on air bases, belonging to a weather wing located at some remove. In the same way, the people responsible for controlling local air traffic—the operation of the control tower and approach navigation aids—were part of Air Force Communications Command.

---

19   Here I use the archaic "Field" instead of "Air Force Base" because it is so much more authentic a descriptor, akin to the Army "Fort" or Navy "Station." I thought about pushing to restore this older, more redolent usage, but we would have had many signs to repaint and much stationery to reorder. Nevertheless, I used the term as often as possible, hoping to delay its extinction.

For a flying wing, few matters were more important than weather forecasting or air traffic control. As part of the reorganization, we decided to close down the weather and communications wings and incorporate their functions into the objective wing.

In addition, every base had inside its fences a grab bag of small organizations—"detachments," "operating locations," "branches," "offices," and so forth—that were not part of the local wing. Too often these little appendages were free-floating, with absentee supervision or none at all. Some of these small offices perforce had to stay outside the wing. For example, the Air Force Audit Agency had compartmented reporting responsibilities that might be compromised if we placed it under local authority. But we found no convincing rationale for the independence of many support functions stationed at a base but held outside the wing. Where it made sense and could be done at small or no cost, we rounded up the strays and made them part of the objective wing. An abundance of alternative, virtual, pseudostructures disappeared.

What about bases with two or more wings? Often, there was a senior formation, called an "air division," to which wings reported at such bases. Sometimes, the combat support group belonged to the division, so neither operating wing controlled base support functions. Usually, different types of mission equipment were involved. At George, when I was there as a lieutenant, we had an F-100 wing and an F-104 wing. Had we wished, we could have put all the squadrons in one wing. The argument against doing so would be we couldn't find a wing commander with talent enough to supervise an organization containing two types of aircraft. Of course, the point that complexity can be dealt with only by increasing specialization makes sense. You just have to judge how far it should be pushed, or you end up with left eardrum surgeons.

I thought the air division redundant because a wing commander should be able to supervise the operation of two or more types of airplanes. Real system expertise was needed at squadron level, where the boss had to be hands-on the equipment. In other words, we wanted an F-16 pilot in charge of an F-16 squadron, a chopper pilot at the head of a helicopter squadron, a missileer commanding an ICBM squadron. Above squadron level, we should be able to rely on less explicit supervision. By the way, this approach encourages decentralization, making the squadron commander the expert who must be trusted by commanders above him.

In sum, I aimed to consolidate into the objective wing everyone assigned to a base and everything that happened there. Any other arrangement had to be argued for and approved as an exception to policy. Our motto for the new setup: "One Base, One Wing, One Boss."

Accordingly, we abolished the air division as a level of organization.

The 100-Wing Air Force

At the beginning of 1990, there were 205 things called "wings" in the active Air Force. During my time, this number came down to 100. A third of the reduction was on account of actual force structure given up in the post-Cold War drawdown. But most of the loss was the result of deactivating weather wings, communications wings, and the like, and consolidating operational wings at bases that previously had two or more. Cutting the number of wings in half led to large savings of senior personnel and overhead, as we turned in the manpower, office space, and fittings of redundant wing headquarters. More important, the surviving 100 organizations were "real" wings, embodying real combat power, located one each on our (by that time) roughly 100 major installations. By the end of calendar year 1992, all 100 of the wings that survived the drawdown were in something approaching the objective configuration.

I wanted general officers in command of our restructured wings. Our manning documents already called for generals at the most important wings, but the policy had been to fill these slots with promising colonels targeted for promotion after proving themselves.

This approach had two bad consequences. First, wing commanders were sometimes junior by date of rank to other colonels in the wing. (We published special orders to put the junior man in command.) This neither helped the wing's performance nor fostered a healthy command relationship. Older colonels felt slighted; indeed, this was a not very subtle message to them that they should stop working at their Air Force jobs and start looking for postretirement employment. Moreover, the military culture is such that we cannot ignore the fact of seniority. It affects—indeed, it should affect—daily relationships. Putting general officers at the head of objective wings would remove any ambiguity about seniority.

Second, colonels that we tested as wing commanders often failed. Commanding a wing was a big, complicated job (and would be more so in the new, reorganized wings) and often we misjudged either the capacity or luck of theoretically talented colonels. In any case, this was exactly the wrong place to experience failure. As an institution, the Air Force could accommodate a certain amount of rear-echelon incompetence, but excellent performance at wing level, where the service transacts so much of its actual business, was essential to our success. Some general officers would surely fail as wing commanders, but to put a general in charge was to take our best shot at providing solid leadership at wing level.

At the start of our reorganization, we had one-star generals in command at only three wings. I established a goal to put flag officers at 60 wings. But where was I to get 57 generals? Congress controlled of the number of flag officers in each service and had already decreed the Air Force must cut its total, leaving us in 1991 with a planning figure of 229 general officers of the line. Half of these, 115, would be one-star, brigadier generals. To meet my goal, I'd have to put most of them to work in the new objective wings.

Abolishing the air divisions freed up 19 brigadier generals. A second source was the Air Staff and other senior headquarters. I cleared generals out of staff slots and sent them back to the field, with the good result of opening some rather more important staff postings for colonels being watched for promotion. In addition, we learned something about our one-star force. Good generals relished returning to command, but some retired in lieu of reassignment, a not altogether bad thing.[20]

I made steady progress toward the goal of 60 general officer wing commanders. Already by the end of 1992, 44 wings had generals in charge and, as I left office, we were actually a little above 60, and still climbing.

The new career-development path we established tested colonels with command at group level—a tactical, flight-suit, fatigues-wearing echelon that demanded a deep understanding of professional specialties, but where they would camp out under the watchful eye of a general-officer wing commander. If they navigated this assignment successfully, they would be candidates for senior service school—the various war colleges—and broadening staff assignments, the best of them in major command, Air Staff, or joint billets. If they continued to grow, they would be competitive for (1) promotion to one-star, and (2) return to a wing as commander, providing perhaps the best example of unmixed pleasure since childhood.

The Objective Numbered Air Force

Usually, wings reported to a numbered air force (NAF), for which the naming convention differed somewhat. The numbers were not Arabic numerals; they were spelled out, as with my old command, Twelfth Air Force.

The first numbered air forces came along near the beginning of World War II, when the expansion of the Air Corps required some delegation of headquarters authority to allow closer supervision of training and operations. The United States was subdivided into four districts, designated for First, Second, Third, and Fourth Air Forces. These four remained in the United States, but other

---

20 When Lincoln came to town, Gen. Winfield Scott, hero of the Mexican War, weighed 300 pounds and couldn't get on a horse without help. It took Lincoln a while to find someone to run the Army.

NAFs were established for duty overseas, and these are the ones we remember: the Mighty Eighth, carrying the load into Germany through heavy flak, Ira Eaker in command; the Ninth, clearing a way into Normandy and saving the bacon at the Battle of the Bulge, Lewis Brereton and Hoyt Vandenberg among its leaders; the Fifteenth, at Anzio and the Siegfried Line, Jimmy Doolittle there, back from his raid, and followed by Nate Twining when Doolittle went to relieve Eaker; the Fifth and Seventh, making possible the brilliant island-hopping strategy in the Southwest Pacific, a competent George Kenney lashing things together with duct tape and bailing wire; the Twentieth, firebombing Tokyo, Curt LeMay at the controls.

At a time when the Air Force was bound to shrink, I wanted to keep these formations. There always seemed to be pressure from Pentagon bean counters to reduce or abolish the numbered air forces, but these were line outfits with long and storied service. I even hoped to reactivate some that had been on the shelf for a while. But they couldn't cost much—and wouldn't—since, according to our concept, in a normal, peacetime configuration, the objective numbered air force would be a tactical echelon with little or no functional staff support. This approach made it possible to cut the head count of the objective NAF headquarters from an average of about 300 to fewer than 50 people.

However, we also envisioned the numbered air force forming the nucleus of the Air Force component in a theater of operations, and when so employed, we'd have to beef it up. Ninth Air Force had provided the template, morphing into a much-enlarged CENTAF for Desert Storm. The same thing would happen to Seventh Air Force, in case of renewed conflict on the Korean Peninsula, or Twelfth Air Force, for active operations in Latin America, and so forth. Thus, the objective numbered air force was a slimmed down, purely tactical headquarters in peacetime, augmented as needed when provided to joint commanders as the echelon in charge of active air operations in a combat theater.

We viewed the numbered air force commander as having a leadership, as opposed to management role, though at this level the qualities demanded were not simply military but also diplomatic and political. At the head of the objective numbered air force, we envisioned a field commander, a competent operator, someone still comfortable in a flight suit and high-speed, high-*g* office, but also someone with the character and temperament to deal with the daunting problems of joint and alliance warfare—someone like the virtuoso leader of Desert Storm, Ninth Air Force commander Chuck Horner. At any time, there were only 20 or so numbered air forces and I wanted them led by our most promising generals.

Secretary Don Rice

The idea of bottom-to-top organizational reform would eventually bring me into conflict with sizable portions of the Air Force. Some of the resistance came from smart, thoughtful people—mostly functional specialists—who disagreed in principle. But the greater part of the opposition was reflexive. Change is hard for people to accept, and this was going to be wholesale change. Happily, the secretary of the Air Force wanted more or less the same things I did.

Don Rice had been the long-term head of RAND Corporation, which had gotten an early line of business as the Air Force's think tank, but which had expanded and diversified under his leadership. He had a strong background in the physical sciences and engineering as well as a good understanding of economics and management. He was active and aggressive, had a first-rate mind, an intense interest in the Air Force, and he worked hard. (In fact, too hard. This was another case of an early riser—me—being paired with a boss who'd rather work late into the night.)

In November of 1990, after my confirmation by the Senate, the ongoing Desert Shield and the upcoming Desert Storm occupied most of our attention. Nevertheless, Rice and I began talking privately (and often well past dinner time!), sketching our thoughts on reorganization. We saw eye to eye on most items, Rice perhaps a little surprised he'd been issued a chief of staff with such progressive ideas. He wanted detail, which I provided. By Christmas we'd agreed in principle on nearly all the moves to be made at lower echelons: putting flight-line maintenance into operational squadrons, restoring the group as a command level, consolidating authority at our bases in a single wing commander, revitalizing and streamlining the numbered air forces.

We continued to discuss only two issues. I wanted to reduce the number of major commands and cut their size and cost. Though he was inclined to agree, Rice worried about how best to do it. The major air commands were vastly different from one another. There could be no "objective" major air command; each would need a custom redesign. And these were, after all, large, important enterprises. We could do a lot of damage if not careful.

The Major Air Commands

Each of the major air commands (MAJCOMs) was a large headquarters with the full range of functional staff and often a four-star commander. These were named (not numbered) units: Strategic Air Command, Pacific Air Forces, and so forth. Aside from SAC, not much in the way of Air Force heritage was at stake in the perpetuation of any major air command.

The major air commands fell into two categories: operational and departmental. Major operational commands, such as SAC, TAC, MAC, PACAF, and USAFE, had under them the subordinate numbered air forces and wings that provided air combat units to joint commanders. The seams between these MAJCOMs were fairly clean, except we were organized as though bombers and tankers (in SAC) and fighters (in TAC and the overseas major commands) participated in different wars. Neither our doctrine nor our actual experience supported this view. We were supposed to hold the firm belief that air combat was a system, an integrated, unified whole, and all our actual experience showed this was true. Always, when shooting for score, we blended bombers and fighters—reorganizing on the fly, as it were. Often, we'd not managed the mix well. The secretary and

I reasoned we could and should consolidate the fighting elements for air warfare into a single command, organizing in peacetime in accordance with combat practice. Our concept called for disestablishing SAC and TAC and combining their assets in a new command, tentatively identified as Air Combat Command (ACC).

On the other hand, the departmental commands—Training Command, Systems Command, Logistics Command—were responsible for aspects of preparing forces for frontline use, the "train" and "equip" functions. Various problems were cooking with this arrangement. For instance, we had two large, four-star commands in the "equip" business. Air Force Systems Command did research, development, and acquisition of new equipment; Air Force Logistics Command and its large depot network did heavy maintenance of fielded equipment. We did not do a good job of managing the seam between these two organizations. Because Systems Command was in the technology-push business, it tended to field equipment that, when it worked, performed beautifully, but was difficult and expensive to maintain, something we didn't find out until Logistics Command began trying to keep it flying. I thought merging the two commands and eliminating the seam might prove very helpful in applying advanced technology to the problem of equipment reliability, maintainability, and supportability. Moreover, much responsibility for system acquisition had shifted to the secretary's office under Goldwater-Nichols reforms, sharply reducing the scope and authority of Systems Command. It was increasingly hard for me to see the advantage of having two big headquarters, instead of one, in the "equip" business.

Secretary Rice was prepared to accept my expertise regarding the operational commands, but I believe he thought (accurately, as it turned out) that I didn't know a great deal about equipment acquisition and support. Moreover, the two organizations, Systems and Logistics Commands, were together responsible for spending most of the Air Force budget. He suggested we go slow, first getting the views of the two commanders, Ron Yates and Chuck McDonald.

If they did not oppose a merger, we could have them study the idea and give us a definitive proposal. That's what we did.

The "train" function was also quite disjointed. Air Training Command did not include, for instance, Air University (AU) at Maxwell Field, so officer and NCO professional military education lay outside its scope. Training Command controlled two of the three officer sources—ROTC and Officer Candidate School—but the Air Force Academy was a stand-alone organization, reporting to the chief and secretary. Moreover, Training Command did not do combat crew training. Rather, it passed along brand-new flight crews to the using commands, which put them through additional, often quite extensive, formal training before they could go to operational squadrons. The secretary and I wanted using commands to focus on combat employment, an objective undercut by the time and attention they had to give their formal schoolhouses. In any case, in principle, I regarded it a departmental responsibility—part of the "train" function—to issue combat-ready aircrews to the operational commands.

As the secretary and I thought our way through the problem, we saw that failure to separate responsibility for the "organize, train, and equip" functions from responsibility for active use or "employment"—the one, a set of issues belonging to the Department of the Air Force, the other, a responsibility of joint commands—lay at the heart of much organizational distress. We needed to look at everything we did and judge whether it was "departmental" or "operational," then decide where and by whom it would be done. In the end, we established an objective Air Combat Command to combine the war-fighting elements of the old SAC and TAC, an objective Air Force Materiel Command to hold the merged Systems and Logistics Commands, and an objective Air Education and Training Command, into which we put Training Command, Air University, and as much of the combat crew training function as we could.

Thus, through rationalization and consolidation, we were able to reduce the number of major commands in the Air Force from

13 to eight, with most of the important actions taken before the end of 1992.

Air Force Headquarters

The headquarters structure was duplex: the Secretariat reported to Rice; the Air Staff reported to me. The matter that took Rice and me a while to resolve was the relative size and division of labor between these two structures. In approaching this issue, I had two objectives. First, I aimed to reduce the headcount in both. Second, the two staffs often worked the same issue, sometimes at cross-purposes, and always increasing the difficulty of coordination. Rice and I thought matters should be considered once, with unified advice provided to both the chief and secretary. Regarding how staff work might be divided, if the matter under review was clearly "military," I wanted responsibility for it in the Air Staff. If, on the other hand, it could be thought of as a "business" issue, I was willing to have the Secretariat deal with it. In concept, the secretary agreed, so we went to work on realignment.

The simplest case involved the Air Force's senior security policeman. Our head cop was a brigadier general, who had a small staff and reported to the inspector general, a three-star officer in the Secretariat. The sort of investigations the inspector general might be tasked to do would be of great interest to the secretary, but airbase security and law enforcement were local, military concerns, and I wanted policy oversight for this function in the Air Staff.

How to supervise operational requirements was a harder problem because it involved more headcount. For years, the major commands had been the key players in establishing operational requirements. (What sort of equipment do we need, and why?) Air Force headquarters had played a largely administrative role—recordkeeping, validating program elements, Washington advocacy. In headquarters, staff responsibility for handling requirements had moved around from office to office. (It should always have been part of the deputy chief of staff for operations (DCS/Ops); these were, after all, "operational" requirements.) As luck would have it, requirements were being tracked by the DCS for research and development (DCS/R&D) when the Goldwater-Nichols Act took responsibility for equipment acquisition away from military staffs and gave it to the service secretariats. So requirements had disappeared into the Secretariat, along with the rest of DCS/R&D. I knew establishing operational requirements was a military rather than business issue, and therefore wanted to move responsibility for it back to the Air Staff.

Secretary Rice agreed in principle with the Air Staff's reassuming responsibility for things like security police and operational requirements. And as for the Air Staff, Rice was content to let me reduce its numbers. But he thought the Secretariat, if anything, needed to be bigger, or at least better balanced with the Air Staff. As things stood, the Air Staff was five times the size of the Secretariat and in addition carried the authority and prestige of hands-on military experience. When the two staffs disagreed, Big Blue tended to steamroll the Secretariat. Of course, moving the manpower spaces associated with "military" issues to the Air Staff would make the imbalance worse, so it was not going to happen unless I could more than offset the headcount the Secretariat would lose in such a transfer.

Looking around for a bargaining chip, I selected the staff supervising foreign military sales (FMS). It was mainly a business-type activity and probably should have been in the Secretariat all along. Although the FMS function had a sizable presence in the Air Staff—more than enough to offset the requirements and security-police spaces I wanted back from the Secretariat—most of the actual work was done at Wright Field, in Logistics Command. I offered it to the secretary in trade and he agreed. Done deal.[21]

---

21 In the end, we reduced the size of Air Force headquarters—the Secretariat and Air Staff combined—by about 15 percent, from more than 3,000 spaces to fewer than 2,600. In the process, the Secretariat gained spaces, growing to about 40 percent the size of the Air Staff.

I set down in these pages only highlights of the most far-reaching, fundamental reorganization of the Air Force in its history, then reaching back 45 years. Yet, in the late evening of 15 January, two days before the kickoff of Desert Storm and after less than three months as chief, I walked out of Don Rice's office with complete agreement, subject to Yates and McDonald reporting they could merge Systems and Logistics Commands, which they did, 60 days later. I can't imagine this would have been possible with any other secretary. It required both brains and courage. Luckily, Don Rice had both.

'Go' Pills

As soon as I returned from my quick trip to the Gulf just before Desert Storm, I asked the surgeon general to tell me why it was a good idea to force feed "go" pills—amphetamines—to aircrew members. Of course for many years these had been issued to pilots facing flights of unusual length, it being thought safer to take the drug than risk the consequences of accumulated fatigue. My first experience with "uppers," or "speed," had been during transatlantic deployments in the early 1960s. "Go" pills were issued at the mass briefings before such deployments, together with sedatives meant to reestablish the sleep cycle after crossing multiple time zones. But the use of all such drugs was elective and, because of a personal hang-up, I never took any, just giving them back or throwing them away after the briefing. I didn't have any scientific or ethical reason for rejecting drugs. I certainly used alcohol, though not owing to any conviction it made me a better or safer pilot. But I thought if you weren't physically up to the demands of the job, you should either get in shape or find other work. Altering the body's chemistry seemed to me a form of cheating. Real toughness, not the chemically induced kind, is or ought to be the building block for combat success.

The surgeon general couldn't defend the practice, so I ordered that aircrews not be required to take amphetamines. Moreover, I let it be known that I did not and would not take them, which was enough to sharply reduce their consumption.

Physical Fitness and Weight Control

During all of my Air Force years, we'd had some sort of physical fitness program, weakly administered and usually focused on weight control. To the extent we enforced the program at all, it was to establish maximum weights for various combinations of height, age, and gender. A medic could waive even this modest requirement if on examination he found a person "big boned," or some permutation of this condition. Such programs seemed to me yet another example of management by input. As I told the *Air Force Times*, "I place a high premium on physical fitness, and I put the weight-control program in that context. I'm not as interested in how much people weigh as in how physically fit they are."

But my feelings went well beyond this. In my view, part of the heritage of the Air Force, and a big reason I took to it as a career, was the idea of readiness for combat. To a considerable degree, fighting is a physical act that everyone wearing a uniform must be ready at a moment's notice to undertake. I wanted this message understood, even at a time when we were all preoccupied with Desert Storm. The February 1991 issue of *Airman* magazine quoted me:

> I feel being a warrior is a special job. It has special benefits, privileges and rewards. But it also makes special demands on people who decide to take up the profession of arms. I do not understand how people who are not physically fit can be ready for combat. So, I try to maintain a certain standard of physical fitness. I urge everyone to do the same. We are not civilians in uniform. We are warriors. We need to act like, feel like and be warriors.

US Strategic Command

Among the Air Force's reorganization moves, the most eye-catching would be disestablishing Strategic Air Command and redistributing most of its assets to the new Air Combat Command.

But SAC had special responsibilities for central nuclear warfare that ran outside Air Force lines. So Secretary Rice and I could not do this on our own; we needed support from the secretary of defense and the chairman of the Joint Chiefs of Staff. Secretary Dick Cheney was no problem. He seemed to appreciate what we were up to, perhaps because Rice had privately kept him in the picture about our plans. Characteristically, Colin Powell was more cautious, but on the principal issue that affected him, he certainly agreed that nuclear warfare was not a monopoly mission of the Air Force. The Navy also had a big role with its ballistic-missile submarine force. A new, joint Strategic Command that unified responsibilities across the services made a lot of sense. SAC's commander had always been an airman, of course, but I proposed to Powell that we rotate the top job at the new Strategic Command between Air Force and Navy, which added to the idea's attractiveness.

Lee Butler

Powell and I knew it was essential to get the right guy in position at SAC to make the transition happen. The best candidate was Lee Butler. He was very bright (the first Rhodes Scholar from the Air Force Academy), had a good background in strategic operations and was working for Powell at the time, in the Joint Staff. I made sure he bought into the idea of shutting down SAC before nominating him to replace Jack Chain as commander. Chain was a talented officer who often succeeded where others failed. The Air Force would miss him when he left its ranks. But Lee Butler was the man for this new challenge. He turned out to be a real innovator, tickled with the opportunity to help bring about change. We could not have reorganized the Air Force without him. To his eternal credit, the usual question that arises when people are asked to do hard things—what's in it for me?—never figured in the conversation.

Lee Butler was the last commander of Strategic Air Command and the first head of the new Strategic Command. As was the case with the other joint commands, the Air Force would provide combat units to him for use in executing war plans, these forces coming to him from reconfigured numbered air forces.

State of the Union

On 29 January 1991 I attended my first State of the Union address. I got a kick out of it. The chairman and chiefs (plus the Coast Guard commandant) sat up front, to the president's right as he faces the chamber. The justices of the Supreme Court sat near the center, with the president's cabinet arrayed between the JCS and the court. Most of the remaining floor space was given over to the diplomatic corps. Of course, congressmen and senators occupied the elevated rows of seats.

There was a nice protocol for applauding what the president had to say. On many issues, the president was sure to be given a receptive hearing by his own party. But the Supreme Court and the Joint Chiefs were supposed to be nonpolitical. We all watched the chairman and clapped when he did. The chairman watched the chief justice.

End of the Warsaw Pact

On 25 February 1991 the Warsaw Pact military alliance dissolved. The full Pact, including its political elements, would disappear by 1 July.

Force-Structure Metrics

One hundred real wings on roughly one hundred actual bases was a measure of Air Force size and strength that made sense to me, but in making decisions regarding our force structure, both Congress and the executive branch used a term of art: the Tactical Fighter Wing Equivalent, shortened to TFWE by insiders. This was a horrible way to describe our force structure, conveying little understanding and putting us at a sizable disadvantage when compared with the other services. The public dialogue sized the Army and Marine Corps in divisions, the Navy, in ships. A division, or a ship, is a real thing you can see and count, even touch, if you like. But the TFWE was an abstraction, a notional force of three fighter squadrons, each containing 24 aircraft. To be sure, some fighter wings were in this exact configuration, but many were not. Moreover, the TFWE described only a fraction the Air Force, giving no weight to bombers, tankers, transports, missiles, space capabilities, and so forth. For instance, at the start of FY 91, the active Air Force operated 251 flying squadrons, of which only 70 were fighter units. If these 70 squadrons all possessed 24 aircraft (which they did not), they constituted 23 and a third TFWEs, an important piece, but hardly a comprehensive picture of our force structure.

For us, a much better, simpler and clearer description of force structure would be total wings, just as we had measured ourselves in groups during and immediately after World War II.[22] In a way, the handicap was of our own making; we'd allowed the number of things called wings to proliferate out of hand.

I tried to change the vernacular, describing the Air Force according to its number of operating wings, without modifier, using this terminology in internal discussion and congressional testimony. But my "100-Wing Air Force" never caught on as the standard descriptor of our actual size. The TFWE metric had too much momentum. In the debate that followed, it brought a tear to the eye when we sounded taps for an honored division, or scuttled an excellent ship. It was much easier to let the air out of that vague generalization called a "tactical fighter wing equivalent."

The Base Force

Colin Powell came to the chairmanship in October 1989 understanding we could no longer rely on the Soviet threat to legitimize defense budgets. Moreover, he saw that if DOD could not agree on

---

[22] In late-1944, Hap Arnold set up a planning committee to recommend the size of the postwar Air Force. The planners, led by Ira Eaker, concluded that a minimum of 75 groups would be required, manned by some 550,000 personnel. This would have been a huge cut from the 218 groups and 2.5 million military and civilian personnel on duty with the Army Air Forces at war's end. Even so, it was a dream. By December 1946, only 52 groups remained in the AAF, of which two were judged combat ready.

an approach to reduced spending, Congress would impose cuts to below prudent levels and at a rate that might wreck the residual force. Even so, his subsequent action was remarkable. Although it takes no great genius to understand a severe resource climate, senior military leaders are by instinct loath to adjust, hoping some miracle will make the problem go away. This attitude has the ugly consequence of perpetuating inefficient resource allocation, in the long run further weakening the nation's defenses. Rather than let this happen, Powell spent much of his first year working on and getting consensus for reductions of about one-third, producing what he called the Base Force.

The rationale for the Base Force was that America needed to retain the capacity to act in an uncertain world. Granted, the Soviets were much diminished as a threat, rolled back from Central Europe in both space and time, and no longer so serviceable as a yardstick for judging how big our forces should be. But we could predict instability, uncertainty, a reordering of alliances, and the very high likelihood of regional conflict. The design intent of the Base Force was to take a large but acceptable and carefully calibrated reduction, while holding on to force structure and capabilities needed to exercise the authority of a superpower.

Powell outlined a strategy: we needed the capacity to fight and win two simultaneous major regional contingencies (MRCs). Thirty years earlier, the Kennedy administration had put forward the ambitious "two-and-a-half-wars strategy." A large war against a Communist government could break out in each of Europe and Asia, while Castro might threaten a "half war" close to home. We could never have afforded the force structure consistent with this strategy and, anyway, the Vietnam War got in the way. By 1969, Nixon had revised the goal downward to "one and a half wars." The "half war" is another name for a major regional contingency, a rather large, but contained (as opposed to global) conflict—Korea, say, or Vietnam. When we did stage what amounted to a half war in Desert Storm, the MRC gained credibility as a scaling device.

Powell had hard work selling the two MRC strategy inside the Pentagon. Defense Secretary Dick Cheney and his undersecretary for policy, Paul Wolfowitz, were anything but convinced the Russians had gone away. Marine Corps commandant Al Gray was an ardent and effective opponent to any drawdown of the Marines. The other service chiefs were at best lukewarm supporters. In the ensuing fight, Powell maneuvered well and had won by the time I showed up. On 29 November, at one of my first meetings with OSD executive staff, Cheney directed the services to implement the Base Force. However, the Gulf War quickly consumed the administration, and we did not formally present the proposal to Congress until six months later.

Had I been present for duty, I would have tried to help Powell because he was right for all the right reasons. But I did agree with my brother service chiefs in one respect: the Base Force was more likely a ceiling than a floor. Powell had shown our hand regarding the drawdown we'd accept without a fight. Advocates for deeper cuts would pocket the concession and scrub for additional surgery.

However, there was another, much more important problem: inside the Pentagon, the Base Force concept left the services with dollar and force-structure targets, but no blueprint for remodeling the force. In the staff work running up to sizing the Base Force, we'd initially discussed structural cuts as if they would be taken in combination with changes in the character of the force, so as to make it more suitable for post-Cold War security challenges.[23] But concerns about force characteristics and capabilities got lost in the fight about size, and the services ended up cutting combat capability in increments and in a way that preserved the essential features of the Cold War force. We gave no attention at all to overlap

---

23 Bill Clinton, in his first presidential campaign, ridiculed the Base Force, calling it "Cold War Minus," saying its design was entirely inadequate for addressing our new security circumstances. The criticism was right on the money.

and duplication of capabilities across service lines and not much to the infrastructure-reduction issue. Our so-called tooth-to-tail ratio, already shameful at 50-50, eroded further to something like 30-70.

To meet the Base Force we had to peel off nine active tactical fighter wing equivalents (TFWEs), going from 24 to 15. The target date by which the services were to achieve mandated cuts jumped around a bit, so the pace at which we were supposed to draw down was never clear. But for the Air Force, speed wasn't an issue since, to my way of thinking, keeping force structure on life support was a waste of money. If we were going to end up at 15 active fighter wings, with matching cuts in other force elements, I wanted to close redundant units as fast as I could and put our dollars on the care and feeding of the residual force. By and large, the other services did not share this view, preferring to fold flags only after the last, sad bugle note had faded.

Desert Island Discs

In mid-March 1991, Washington's public FM radio station, WETA, asked me to be the guest on Desert Island Discs. The rules of the game, based on the familiar BBC program: if cast away on a desert island, what five pieces of music would you want with you? Pretty simple. No one can argue about it—it's personal, a matter of taste—and the selections do not have to fit together as a program. My list: *Goldberg Variations*, J.S. Bach (Glenn Gould's 1955 studio recording); Symphony no. 25 (*Little G Minor*), W.A. Mozart; Ninth Symphony (*Choral*), L. v. Beethoven (Bernstein, massed orchestras in Berlin, with "Freiheit" substituted for "Freude"); String Quartet in F (*American*), A. Dvorak (Air Force String Quartet); "Georgia on My Mind," (Ray Charles).

Air Force String Quartet

As can be seen, by the time of my Desert Island Discs appearance, the Air Force had a string quartet. I had something to do with putting it together. I knew we would do a lot of entertaining in our quarters at Fort Myer. The Air Force Band was justly famous for its quality, including especially two groups, the Singing Sergeants and the Strolling Strings, who made frequent appearances around Washington, including in the White House. But I judged them a little large for our quarters and thought we should try chamber music. I went to work on this early, asking the band commander to form a quartet from his string sections. My idea was to start with Haydn and work through as much of the standard repertoire as we could in four years. I auditioned the players, who turned out to be both accomplished and enthusiastic about the concept. We had to replace the second violin midway through my tenure but otherwise managed to hold the group together for the whole four years.[24]

Mike Carns

By March 1991 we had moved Mike Loh from vice chief of staff to Langley, where he replaced Bob Russ as TAC's commander, and waited to become the first commander of the new Air Combat Command.

To replace Loh as vice chief, we nominated Michael P. C. Carns. I'd known and admired Carns going back to my days as an action officer on the Air Staff. I worked with him again in the Pacific, where he was deputy to Admiral Ron Hays at PACOM. He'd moved from that job back to Washington to serve Colin Powell in the important position of director of the Joint Staff. As always, he turned in an impressive performance, and Powell was more than happy when I suggested his return to the Air Force, with promotion to four-star.

Carns was smart, selfless, and absolutely reliable, a simply great wingman. I was very comfortable having him in charge when I was outside the Building. As our relationship matured, I'm not sure he was entirely happy with me. On matters I considered of greatest importance, I worked without a lot of collaboration. Often, I kept

---

[24] By midpoint in my term, an informal competition sprang up so that during my overseas travel there was sometimes reciprocal entertainment by *their* string quartet. I can report that only the Israeli Air Force ensemble matched ours, and they were reservists.

my own council, spending no time explaining things, leaving it to him to catch up. This is an admittedly defective leadership style, even counterproductive, but I am who I am. Anyway, Mike did a lot better without supervision than most people do with it, and I made good use of the time he freed up.

No-Fly Zones

Almost immediately following the Gulf Storm ceasefire, Saddam Hussein started whacking the Kurds in the north and the Marsh Arabs, Shiites living downstream from Baghdad in the delta of the Tigris and Euphrates Rivers. The United Nations passed mandates demanding protection for these people, and on 10 April 1991 we established a no-fly zone in the airspace above 36 degrees north latitude. By the following August, we'd instituted a similar regime south of 32 degrees. These two no-fly zones evolved into Operation Northern Watch and Operation Southern Watch, and for the next decade we exercised air sovereignty over these parts of Iraq, establishing rules for who could enter the airspace, doing daily reconnaissance and shooting back when shot at, which was often.

State Dinner

On the evening of 18 June 1991, my wife and I were invited to the White House for a state dinner in honor of President Collor of Brazil. As we worked our way into the dining room, we were handed slips of paper giving us table assignments, me at Table 1, Ellie at Table 13. She said, "Here we go again, you with the biggies, me next to the kitchen." It turned out she was seated on the president's left, and I was quite close to the swinging door into the service area, as in, "Don't let the door hit you on your way out!"

Gloria Estefan entertained.

Preserving Air Force Heritage

From the beginning of my tenure as chief, it was obvious we would draw force structure down from our Cold War high, the only question being how much and how quickly. But as I came into office, there was little anxiety about the impact this might have on Air Force heritage. The attitude seemed to be that we had evolved quickly in a short period of time, our dimensions had waxed and waned considerably, and we'd never worried much about the effect of change on our heritage and history. We were a hardware outfit, a technology outfit. We'd be OK.

I had a different idea. In my view, heritage lies at the core of fighting spirit. In World War II, the Army Air Forces lost 52,173 people killed in battle, a number I lamented because so much of it was unnecessary or plain stupid, but one I also celebrated because of the human values it illuminates. Excellent personal conduct in battle is the artifact of both values and training. We must train hard—and train hard, and train hard—and if we do, we can build solid, load-bearing structures that will carry the weight of combat. But we should never rely on training alone because close contests will come down to a question of values. Heritage is all about values, hopefully embedded in the genetic makeup of an organization and, if we are not careless about it, usable as the sturdy underpinning, the foundation of combat readiness.

As I came on board, it looked like we would end up with three fighter wings in Europe—one each in England, Germany, and Italy. Many fine, long-serving NATO-committed wings, like the 20th (Upper Heyford), 36th (Bitburg), 50th (Hahn), and 81st (Bentwaters) were programmed to inactivate, their numbers already headed for the deep freeze. All the same, we were planning to retain some wings with much less distinguished histories simply because they populated domestic bases that would survive the downturn. The accident of location was about to play a key role in determining our future order of battle.

Instead of letting this happen, we set up a system for grading wings and squadrons from a heritage standpoint. Organizations scored points for each year of active service and each campaign ribbon, for combat kills, or Medal of Honor winners, and so forth. We awarded special points for specific outstanding achievement or connection to historic events. For instance, the 509th Bomb Wing was activated near the end of World War II for the sole purpose of dropping atomic bombs on Japan. Its performance otherwise had been unremarkable, but we thought it important to keep the only wing in anybody's air force that had ever used nuclear munitions in anger. We settled the 509th at Whiteman Field, Missouri, where we intended to bed down our new stealth bomber, the B-2. The 89th Wing, at Andrews, with no combat record, also earned special consideration after many years of supporting high-ranking dignitaries. Among its other responsibilities, the 89th operated Air Force One, the president's airplane. Through the whole grading process, we paid close attention to our oldest units, usually having single- or two-digit designations. Because of their tenure, these were the outfits in which the most Americans had served, where roots run deepest into American communities.

Naturally, there were winners and losers in this process. My old wing, the 20th, resettled at Shaw, South Carolina, gaining some protection against future disturbance. Ed Eberhart, a friend and future four-star, had recently commanded the wing displaced at Shaw, the 363rd, a unit with a good but not remarkable heritage. Similarly, the much-decorated 35th Wing, made available when we closed operations in Iceland, dislodged the 432nd Wing at Misawa. The 432nd was Charlie Gabriel's old wing (also formerly commanded by Mike Ryan, a future chief of staff), and I regretted standing down this organization.

We saved some distinguished wings by relocating them at places where we formerly had off-brand organizations. For many years Training Command operated "technical training centers," large schools that taught nonflying specialties. For example, officers and airmen went to Keesler Technical Training Center, Biloxi, Mississippi, to learn how to do air traffic control. We converted all of these "centers" to wings, allowing us to save the numbers and heritage of, for instance, the 81st Wing, formerly at Bentwaters and resettled at Keesler. Among others, Robin Olds and Rock Brett had commanded the 81st, and I was glad to save it, even as a training wing.

The scoring and reshuffling of squadrons was, if anything, even more important. Going forward, the way we organize for combat is likely to be much more ad hoc, or oriented on specific tasking; squadrons rather than wings will probably incorporate much of our future heritage. It was crucial that we keep historic squadrons alive. So, for instance, we saved the 555th Fighter Squadron ("Triple Nickel"), bedding it down at Aviano, Italy, as a unit of the 31st Fighter Wing. This squadron had included some famous MiG killers in Southeast Asia, like Steve Ritchie, our leading pilot ace from that war. We kept our most storied squadrons and, where we could do it, kept consecutively numbered squadrons in the same wing. At Holloman, for instance, we made sure the 49th Fighter Wing incorporated the 7th, 8th, and 9th Fighter Squadrons.

As part of the evolution that retained the older, more revered wings and squadrons, we were able to breathe new life into inactive numbered air forces. We put the ICBM force into a rejuvenated Twentieth Air Force. Twentieth formed in 1944 exclusively as a heavy-bombardment organization, with command retained in Washington by Hap Arnold, making it a precursor of Strategic Air Command. The B-29s used in the war-ending atomic attacks on Japan belonged to Twentieth Air Force. Going forward, the ICBM wings would report to Twentieth, stood up at Warren AFB, Wyoming, where we put a three-star in charge. In Space Command, launch and on-orbit operations were consolidated under a reactivated Fourteenth Air Force, headquartered at Vandenberg. Fourteenth had played a big role in World War II's China-Burma-India theater as headquarters for the groups forming the Flying Tigers. In the remodeled Training and Education Command, we reactivated Nineteenth Air Force to supervise wings doing flying training, including the combat crew training removed from the major operational commands. On the occupational-training side, we brought wings that had displaced the old technical training centers under the command of a reactivated Second Air Force. I was delighted to bring these historic numbered air forces back to active duty.

In some ways, First Air Force was unique. By the early 1990s, squadrons of the Air National Guard handled almost all the air defense mission. The Air Guard was a perfect fit for this role, operating in a decentralized style and committed to NORAD for employment. First Air Force, located at Langley as a unit of TAC, served as the administrative headquarters for the operation. I saw no reason why a Guard officer should not lead continental air defense, so we moved First Air Force to Tyndall Field, in Florida, and assigned Phil Killey, previously director of the Air National Guard, to command it. As far as I knew, this was the first time a general officer of the National Guard commanded an active numbered air force.

Numbering

Regarding Air Force wings, the original idea was to number them in consecutive order, with no number duplication. But following World War II, the history and heritage of combat groups was incorporated into wings. This made for some confusion. For instance, *Air Force Combat Units of World War II*, the official guide, lists 14 "1st" groups of various kinds. One of these organizations, the 1st Fighter Group (earlier, the 1st Pursuit Group), is the World War I outfit of Eddie Rickenbacker and Frank Luke and the forerunner of today's 1st Fighter Wing at Langley Field. But from time to time, we'd also had the 1st Air Commando Group, the 1st Combat Cargo Group, the 1st Photographic Group, the 1st Sea Search Attack Group (Medium), and so on, all of which might have evolved into postwar wings.

In 1991 we had on active service three "1st" wings: the 1st Tactical Fighter Wing (Langley), the 1st Air Commando Wing (Hurlburt Field, Florida), and the 1st Space Wing (Peterson Field, Colorado). We also had two "2nd" wings. We decided to follow the original intent and give each surviving wing its own unique number. We would do this by replacing duplicate numbers with honorable designations that would otherwise retire during the post-Cold War contraction. We folded the 1st Space Wing designation and moved the

21st Wing from Alaska to Peterson to become the 21st Space Wing. We backfilled Alaska with the 3rd Wing, made available when it came out of Clark Field, in the Philippines. As a result, we eliminated a duplicate "1st" wing while preserving in Alaska a fine old single-digit wing with a great combat heritage.

In the case of the 1st Space Wing, there was no controversy, as the organization had stood up recently and had little history. By contrast, I got some hate mail from alumni of the 1st Air Commando Wing. The Air Commandos rightly regard themselves as special. Moreover, the wing's lineage ran back to World War II's 1st Air Commando Group, which had been commanded by Phil Cochran and made legendary by the cartoonist Milton Caniff, of "Terry and the Pirates" fame. When I asked the Air Commandos to become the 16th Wing, they did, but it went down hard.

Naming

What we call something is important. So in addition to deciding which unit numbers to keep on the rolls, we paid some attention to the matter of names.

That over time we give objects more complex names ought to be regarded as a physical law, linked to entropy. Too often, the modifiers do not pay their freight. Going forward, we decided to opt for the simplest designation. As part of the reorganization, we were able to strip "Strategic" and "Tactical" from squadron and wing titles, so something like the 90th Strategic Missile Wing became simply the 90th Missile Wing, and the 4th Tactical Fighter Wing, the 4th Fighter Wing. We shortened "Bombardment" to "Bomb," as in the 5th Bomb Wing, at Minot Field, North Dakota. We took "military" out of the transport business; "military airlift squadrons" became "airlift squadrons." At Kadena, where, following reorganization, the wing incorporated fighters, tankers, AWACS, and helicopters, the host unit, formerly the "18th Tactical Fighter Wing," became simply the "18th Wing," with many future keystrokes saved and nothing valuable lost in the process.

If one judged only by the names we had given them, I started with 43 different types of wings, 58 different kinds of groups, and 181 different sorts of squadrons. By early 1994, those numbers were down to 18, 31, and 84, respectively. So much for fancy packaging.

As for the major commands, "Air Combat Command" was the logical term for the replaced SAC and TAC. Putting most of the former SAC's tankers into MAC evolved it to Air Mobility Command. As for changing ATC to Air Education and Training Command, left alone, I would have kept the old name. But Ike Skelton, the powerful Missouri congressman (and friend), had made a big deal of reforming professional military education in all the services. When we merged Air University into ATC, he wanted the name changed to highlight the importance of "education," and the secretary and I accommodated him—in my case, reluctantly.

Heraldry

We reviewed in detail all the symbols and emblems associated with organizations remaining in our thinning lineup. Typically, the earliest squadron and group patches were simple and elegant. Even during the rapid expansion of World War II, much grand symbology was invented, especially the Walt Disney-inspired squadron patches. But the early years of the Cold War produced some appalling designs, reflecting much committee work and local option. The representations got more and more elaborate and ugly. In 1952 somebody let the 7th Bomb Wing change its patch from a splendid design—a plain blue crest with 3 Maltese crosses on it—to one featuring a spread-winged eagle clutching a refueling boom. Worse yet, the old crest was a retained feature, sort of hanging in the space below the extended refueling probe. Not wanting to leave anything out was the characteristic design impulse of many modern patches, with the result that most of them resembled nothing so much as an odd-shaped pizza, with everything.

With respect to the colors and emblems of older units, we decided to look at each and, where possible, return to the original design. We did run into limits on our flexibility. Some of the early patches featured a skull and crossbones or Grim Reaper-style figures, no longer attractive in an era of kinder, gentler combat. With more women in the force, cheesecake had perhaps lost its universal appeal. So in a few cases, we settled for less meritorious, more politically correct revisions of pioneer designs.

Regarding the newer, Cold War-era patches, many died quietly as units were retired or replaced in the drawdown. But we retained a few line organizations with unattractive modern patches, and I asked the units concerned to do a redesign. This led to some interesting submissions, followed by much give-and-take, the upshot of which was we all agreed that simple is good—simpler, better.

But this was a problem like shaving: it had to be done every day. As late as 12 November 1992, I sent the following message, personal for all senior commanders:

> Once again I have been surprised by a unit patch, this time of the 366th Wing, being changed while we were all looking the other way. We must act more effectively to protect Air Force heritage. Well-meaning, well-intentioned people, doing what they believe is right, need to understand this matter better. AFR [Air Force Regulation] 900-30 specifies the procedures to be used when requesting a change to unit emblems. This regulation is now undergoing a rewrite. As an interim measure, all changes to unit patches will be approved by me. Warm regards.

I was a big-time supporter of decentralized decision making, but there are some issues that only the whole organization can address. One of these is the symbols people will fight for. No one at any level should be allowed to change Air Force heraldry on a whim.

Three-Sentence Limit

I'm not superstitious, preferring natural explanations. And though I want and seek advice, I don't like it force-fed to me. I found the invocations given by Air Force chaplains often at odds with these two organizing principles—and they went on at tiresome length, as well. I asked the chief of chaplains to limit invocations to three sentences at events I attended as senior officer. He passed the word and the result was dramatic. Our public prayers became little wonders of form as each chaplain sought an ingenious syntactical solution. Better yet, the thought expressed lost its flabbiness in the boiling down. Best of all, much time was saved for everyone, always excepting the chaplains, who had to put a lot more work into the blessings they offered.

NATO Air Chiefs

Our Air Force chief of staff sits at the center of a web of relationships with airmen of other countries. Eleven years of service in Europe gave me some understanding of the importance of NATO Air Chiefs, an organization meeting alternately in Washington and the various alliance capital cities. My Twelfth Air Force responsibilities south of the border had introduced me to CONJEFAMER, the association of Latin American Air Chiefs. Of course, I'd founded Pacific Air Chiefs when I was at PACAF.

The air forces of the North Atlantic alliance had worked in harness for many years, though this fact had not dissolved entirely the tensions that spring up, even in the closest families. One thinks, for instance, of the uneasy relationship between Greece and Turkey. I was lucky to have friends on each side, Stathas Athanasios of the Royal Hellenic Air Force, and Siyami Tastan and, later, Halis Burhan of the Turkish Air Force. These airmen genuinely liked each other on a personal level, and the business and social contact made possible by gatherings of the NATO Air Chiefs helped dampen tensions.

CONJEFAMER

General Tommy White started CONJEFAMER in 1961. White had been air attaché in Buenos Aires, where he developed a strong affection for the air forces of South America. When he became chief of staff, he proposed establishing what he called a Conference of Jefes of American Air Forces, shortened to CONJEFAMER. A small standing organization was set up to promote the interests of military aviation in the hemisphere—better mapping, postal support, weather forecasting, etc.—and the chiefs agreed to meet annually. The venue was on rotation, usually in the United States every other year. On alternate years, one of the other member air forces sponsored the meeting in its country.[25] These gatherings were lots of work and lots of fun. As with NATO, some of the countries had an unhappy relationship, so these meetings were a rare opportunity for senior military people to get to know one another in a relaxed setting. I formed many close friendships with the other jefes. Cultural barriers never disappear entirely, but English is the more-or-less universal language of aviation, and airmen share a storehouse of common experience.

Airmen of the Americas have often provided progressive leadership as their countries moved toward greater democracy. Maybe the best example was Fernando Matthei, chief of Chile's air force for 13 years and by the early 1990s the senior serving air chief in the world. During much of Matthei's tenure, General Pinochet ruled Chile. Matthei did a lot, often at considerable personal risk, to bring Chile gradually back to civilian rule. When he retired to civilian life, I flew to Santiago to be present for the ceremony.

Manual Salvatierra was the brand new Nicaraguan air chief when he showed up at the first of my four CONJEFAMER gatherings. He was out of place because not a pilot, and a little embarrassed about this. A student activist in law school, he'd gotten on the wrong side of Samosa and fled the university to join the Sandinista movement in the jungle. I suppose when the Sandinistas came to power, they had no better candidate to lead their diminutive air force. A large man with a disarming sense of humor, I liked Salvatierra immediately. Back home, he was taking flight

---

25 Because others wanted the honor, I agreed to meet in Bogotá, then Tegucigalpa, then Santiago, hosting in Washington only the 1994 CONJEFAMER XXXIV.

instruction in helicopters with results that were spotty at best, to hear him tell it.

Mount Pinatubo

In June 1991, Mount Pinatubo, quite close to Clark Field, in the Philippines, blew its top—the largest volcanic eruption of the twentieth century. Seismic monitoring had given warning and early evacuation saved many lives, but an immense outpouring of ash combined with heavy rains to create deadly mudslides that cascaded down into the valleys, destroying life and property over a wide area. Clark was directly in the path of this mudflow. Once truly a jewel of the Western Pacific, the base was a write-off.

We were involved at the time in negotiations with the Philippine government to extend our tenure at Clark, Richard Armitage supervising the talks. I liked Armitage, an action-oriented, classy guy, though he came across as overly respectful of my rank and position, a quality that always made me uneasy. Then, too, his top shirt buttons were under a lot of stress. I'd done some light weightlifting as part of an exercise program for many years, but Armitage was a power lifter whose specialty must have been bench presses.

In any case, the talks with Manila didn't go well, the Philippine government radicalized and seeming to want us out. Eventually, we decided to throw in our hand, walking away from Clark Field.

START I

After a decade of difficult, fitful negotiations, President Bush and Soviet president Mikhail Gorbachev signed the first Strategic Arms Reduction Treaty (START I) accords on 31 July 1991. Under its terms, the United States and Russia (plus three other post-Soviet nuclear states) would each reduce "accountable" nuclear warheads to 6,000 and bring their "launchers"—ICBMs, SLBMs, and bombers—below a ceiling of 1,600. There were many important technical provisions; there would be a fight on both sides to get the treaty ratified; but as a rough approximation, nuclear capabilities were cut by about a third. Moreover, the stage was set for further reductions in START II.

I believe the JCS could have halted START in its tracks and perhaps an earlier JCS might have done so. Under Powell's leadership, we were unanimous in support. Nothing I helped do as a member of the JCS was more important or made me prouder.

The reason to possess nuclear weapons was to deter others from attacking us. But our superiority in conventional warfare was so pronounced we had no need for an additional deterrent. As a consequence, the fact that nuclear weaponry existed anywhere in the world constituted for us more a threat than a protection. During my short tenure as chief, the number of strategic weapons in our inventory was cut about in half. I can't claim any credit for this, but I did nothing to stop it.

Coup Attempt in Moscow

On 19 August 1991, one day before the scheduled signing of a new treaty that would make official the dismantlement of the USSR, hardline opponents staged a coup against Gorbachev, who was placed under house arrest at his vacation home in the Crimea. The outcome was in doubt only briefly. Boris Yeltsin led resistance to the coup, making a memorable speech from atop a tank that persuaded many uniformed troops to defect. By 21 August most of the coup leaders had fled Moscow. Though Gorbachev was rescued from the Crimea and restored as a figurehead, Yeltsin became the effective leader of Russia.

Russia Visit

I had already resolved to meet the air chiefs of Eastern Europe as soon as I could work it into the schedule. My Russian counterpart, Yevgeny Shaposhnikov, extended an early invitation, and when the Warsaw Pact formally disbanded, I had a good reason to ask for permission to go. As this would be the first post-Cold War contact at service-chief level, the trip had to be cleared not only by the JCS, DOD, and the State Department, but also by the NSC staff at the White House. It was approved, then postponed because of the August coup attempt. Defense Minister Dmitri Yazov had been among the coup plotters. Shaposhnikov's refusal to join in the coup attempt earned him promotion to replace Yazov as the USSR's minister of defense. My new counterpart was Shaposhnikov's successor as Air Force commander, Col. Gen. Pyotr Stepanovich Deynekin. After the dust settled, my trip was reapproved.

The fall of 1991 was a period of rapid transition in Russia. The old Soviet Union was dead, but the body was not scheduled for official burial until December. There would be no bona fide replacement for the USSR, though a toothless umbrella organization of former Soviet republics, the Commonwealth of Independent States (CIS), would last for some years.

In Moscow, I met with Shaposhnikov, in transition to his new role as defense chief of the CIS. But I spent nearly all my time with Deynekin, the new commander of the Russian Federation Air Force (VVS). We quickly formed a warm relationship, notwithstanding the fact that he was a bomber pilot by background, with English only marginally better than my Russian, which was limited to "yes," "thank you," "goodbye," and "wadka." I addressed faculty and students at the Gagarin Air Forces Academy, briefing on air operations in Desert Storm. As often happened in such presentations, I had to pause after each sentence for consecutive translation. Spontaneity suffered somewhat, but the audience was rapt. Here was an airman describing operational concepts and results they could only dream about. I went to the VVS Museum at Monino, a nice collection of historic aircraft, deteriorating rapidly in an outdoor setting. I toured the flight research center at Zhukovsky and the Ramenskoye flight test center, their version of Edwards. The facilities were impressive, but little was happening at these locations, unless you counted résumé writing. I visited the aviation garrison at Kubinka, part of Moscow's integrated air defenses. Here, the Russian Knights, their version of the Thunderbirds, put on a flying display, in SU-27 Flankers. They managed a pretty impressive show in this large fighter aircraft.

Deynekin's air force was in the middle of a painful transition to much-reduced status, an evolution that contained some danger for the rest of the world. Deynekin had responsibility for the tactical fighter (Frontal Aviation), long-range bomber (LRA) and air transport forces (VTA) of Russia. He did not command the Air Defense Force (PVO) or the Strategic Rocket Force (SRF), which, in the Soviet model, were organized as separate branches of the armed forces. I met with the officers heading these branches, as they also were my counterparts.

The Rocket Force commander was an older officer, very senior, the appropriately named Field Marshall Maximoff. Powerfully built, used to being listened to, Maximoff was a man who had trouble not poking you in the chest as he made his point. He took me to Russia's ICBM training site and showplace, Balabanovo. There, he was at pains to emphasize that Russia's nuclear command and control systems were, as we Westerners said, "failsafe." There was no possibility of inadvertent or accidental launch.

This had been an issue as recently as mid-August, when Gorbachev had been arrested while on vacation. The officer assigned to carry the nuclear launch codes—the so-called football—had taken them and returned to Moscow, without Gorbachev. Of course, we regarded this as a period of grave risk for the West and the world. At any rate, Maximoff apparently expected me to take back a message that we ought not be concerned about command and control of "his" missile force. He took me through an elaborate prelaunch training exercise with an actual missile crew seated at a launch control panel, demonstrating all the checks and procedures supposed to insure positive control. We then went down into a missile silo. He paused on the catwalk about halfway down. Through an interpreter, Maximoff continued to stress the absolute security of his launch control mechanisms. Not once, but several times, he compared his procedures favorably with those he supposed to be employed by us. I took it all in stride until, finally, his voice rising a bit, he thumped a fist on the catwalk railing, saying something like, "Our failsafe procedures are as good as yours. Perhaps even better. Yes, our procedures are even better, in fact, much better than yours!"

I turned to the translator, affecting the nonchalance fighter pilots trot out for use in the darkest emergencies, and asked, "How do you say 'bullshit' in Russian?"

The translator laughed a little nervously and relayed the question to Maximoff, who forced a thin smile that released the tension.

Deynekin and I got along exceptionally well, another case of airmen being on the same wavelength. Our stay in Moscow found us there on a Sunday, which the Russians had scheduled as a down day. Ellie asked whether instead we could have dinner with a typical air force family, in their quarters. The Russians liked the idea. Sunday morning, Deynekin, his wife, Nina, and their son showed up to take us in tow, stopping first at a high-rise apartment building into which they were slated to move soon. His new quarters were nearing completion and he was awfully proud of the place, two bedrooms, maybe 1,200 square feet. He ushered me into the small single bathroom to point out a mixing faucet he'd somehow acquired from the States. Then we went on to the apartment of a Russian Air Force colonel who was an old friend of the Denynekins. The flat was barely large enough for the seven of us. We dined around a coffee table in the tiny front room. A "typical" Russian meal was helped down with several bottles of vodka, everybody's English improving as the afternoon wore on.

Deynekin's deputy was a fighter pilot by trade, a veteran of multiple Warsaw Pact assignments. When he and I compared assignments, we satisfied ourselves he had been stationed at Peenemünde during the early 1960s, when I had pulled fighter nuclear alert with that airfield as a target.

Before going to Moscow I was asked by Colin Powell to check on the status of his former counterpart, Marshall Mikhail Moiseyev. In the aftermath of the Moscow coup, he'd been elevated from chief of the defense staff to defense minister, then dismissed after only one day on the job, and now had vanished. Powell considered him a buddy after they and their families had spent time together. I put the question to Deynekin during an evening event at the state guesthouse where the Russians put us up. He gestured we should go outside. As we strolled into the nearby woods, Deynekin explained with body language that the guesthouse was rigged for electronic eavesdropping. He told me Moiseyev was under house arrest, but otherwise OK. Or at least I thought that's what he said and that's what I reported to Powell.[26]

At one point during my visit, Deynekin disappeared entirely. It turned out he flew overnight to Chechnya to see Dzhokhar Dudayev, the first Soviet Air Force general of Chechen ethnicity, who had resigned from the service, been elected president of Chechnya, and was leading a breakaway effort. Apparently, Russian authorities hoped that Deynekin could appeal to Dudayev's old air force loyalties to bring him back in line. It didn't work. Dudayev was later killed, and the Chechnya problem spiraled out of control.

In Moscow I managed a visit to the Pushkin Museum to see one of the world's great collections of French Impressionists. Later, in St. Petersburg, I did the same thing at the Hermitage. Other cultural highlights included the Moscow State Circus (trained cats!) and a performance of *Swan Lake* at the Kirov Ballet.

The Russian Air Force has its own flag, flown alongside national colors on their bases. As I departed Moscow for Washington, Deynekin took one of these flags and tied it around my neck as a kind of scarf. It was a touching gesture, not of surrender, though Deynekin understood who'd won the Cold War, but of reconciliation.

---

26 As of the turn of a new century, Moiseyev seemed alive and doing well in post-Communist Russia.

Plaques Program

Unit symbols figure prominently in our heritage and become part of the inner life of a military professional. Visit any active or retired military person at home, and you're likely to see the "I Love Me" wall, with its array of plaques representing a succession of assignments. For the Air Force of my time, these plaques appeared in an ample variety of shapes and sizes. In my too few days at the helm of the 20th Wing, I had not been able to gather standardized plaques of my own squadrons for display in the command post, eventually having a set made in the civil engineer's carpentry shop. Typically, squadrons, wings or other organizations contracted individually with plaque manufacturers, ordering and producing models of varying quality and design. This state of affairs was in marked contrast with that of, say, the RAF. In any RAF facility, worldwide, you'll see unit plaques produced according to a standardized format.

Setting out to correct the situation, I chose a standard design format for unit plaques and asked the Air Staff's Morale, Welfare and Recreation (MWR) office to solicit bids centrally and procure plaques in large lots, driving down the cost. MWR then resold the plaques to units, a typical end-use being the going-away gift for members leaving on reassignment. We fixed the problem and saved money at the same time.

Eliminating Club Debt

Over the years, many officer and NCO clubs had gotten into financial straits. A well-run club might keep its nose above water, but there was certainly no way for it to accumulate the funds required to recapitalize facilities. This became an awkward problem when Congress began refusing to appropriate funding for club modernization. At the Pentagon, the Air Force had a central account into which we deposited a percentage of membership dues, or "nonappropriated" funds, and from which we made loans for large construction projects. These loans had to be repaid, with the result that many bases had been saddled with debt they couldn't retire unless they cut service, which further reduced membership participation, creating a typical death spiral.

The indebtedness was money we owed ourselves. I simply forgave the debt and it disappeared, instantly restoring the financial health of many clubs in distress. During my term, we continued to aggregate nonappropriated funds and finance local club construction, but we did it with grants, rather than loans.

Creating Consensus

Although the organizational redesign was top-down directed, I understood we needed to get buy-in from the internal Air Force audience. Already by December 1990, in an interview with *Airman* magazine, I spoke of the reorganization to come in terms of building a "leaner, tougher, more reliable force." This was the beginning of an internal-education effort that climaxed in November 1991, with release of a training video meant for screening during all-hands calls at our bases, in which I talked about "Tomorrow's Air Force."[27]

The Brown Papers

A series of "Brown Papers," unsigned pieces satirizing the reorganization, presented the opposing view. (Famously, buildings on bases of the old Tactical Air Command had been painted in earth tones, so the color brown had become identified with fighter pilots. The paper's title may have had even earthier overtones.) The first Brown Paper emerged in August 1991, carrying the title, "TAC-umsizing the Air Force: The Emerging Vision of the Future." The paper asserted that the restructuring aimed only to glorify "the manly man"—that is, the fighter pilot—"the single-seat combat warrior who must command at all levels and within all functional forms." Another Brown Paper appeared a year later, "Back to the Future: The Second Coming of the Manly Man," and in

---

27 The 75-minute video was admittedly a demand on attention span. Still, I think the *Washington Post's* description—"excruciating"—was harsh.

October 1994, just as I retired, came "A Manly Man for All Seasons: The Final Chapter."

I got a kick out of these documents—relished them, really, made no attempt to suppress or find out who wrote them. But the criticism had a hidden, not-so-noble agenda. Whereas I didn't see why we couldn't all be winners, the authors of the Brown Papers obviously thought somebody had to lose in the reorganization and that it would be them and others like them. They saw their futures shrinking. I did not share or even understand this careerist concern, but I did ask that people watch what I was doing and, over time, what I did. I promoted Paul Stein to become superintendent of the Air Force Academy and in the years ahead would promote Billy Boles to run the reorganized Air Education and Training Command, the first nonflyers ever put into these key positions. When time came for Mike Carns to step down as vice chief, I elevated Tom Moorman, only the second officer not a pilot to hold this position. I pulled the ICBMs together into a numbered air force, put a three-star missileer in charge of it, and made the two large airlift numbered air forces three-star billets. These moves and many others provided enhanced career opportunity for nonfighter pilots.

The Air Force doesn't need to be led by fighter pilots or, for that matter, any kind of pilot. But it had better be led by warriors, a category that would include people like Paul Stein and Billy Boles.

Reorganization Mistakes

Most reorganization gets (un)done in the following way: (1) the new boss spends six months to a year getting his feet on the ground and assessing what needs to change; (2) he forms a committee, with representation from everybody who can lose in the change process; (3) the members study the matter thoroughly and shuffle much paper; (4) they pad a list of diminutive proposals, puffing it up to disguise the emptiness; (5) even so, the proposals run into major-league opposition and are quietly shelved; (6) steps one through five take years off the calendar; and (7) the boss has his going-away party.

I avoided the trap described above. We truly imposed this restructuring from the top down, but because I rushed to get it done, I made mistakes, a couple of them unforgivable.

In establishing the new Air Combat Command, I assumed that all of the war-fighting elements of SAC would be combined with those of TAC to create ACC. That is, I thought about the problem in terms of air-breathing fighters and bombers and couldn't see much difference between them. (Targets can't either.) It seemed to me that air refueling and precision munitions had removed the systemic distinctions, turning short-range fighters into long-range bombers and much reducing the payload requirement. But I should have thought more about the ICBMs and tankers. We included SAC's ICBMs in the new Air Combat Command but left out nearly all of the tanker aircraft. Putting the ICBMs in was a bad mistake; leaving the tankers out, a tragedy.

The argument for combining the commands rested on the need to fight integrated air warfare, but I saw the business of ACC as fighting modern, conventional war. Of course, nuclear-tipped ICBMs do not integrate in conventional war, in any meaningful sense. I'd simply stuck the ICBMs into ACC without thinking about it. On reflection, it seemed to me the ICBMs fit best in Space Command, which already was launching rockets to put satellites in orbit. Of course, ICBMs were also rockets and, if ever actually employed, would travel out of the atmosphere and through space, so there were physical similarities in the mission. Moreover, putting the ICBMs in Space Command would give it a combat mission with a sharper edge, allowing its people to move back and forth between silo and launch pad. We finally did move the ICBMs to Space Command, but only after yanking a lot of people around and causing many to wonder whether I was brain dead.

On the other hand, with tankers, no one could contest the case for integration. Absent aerial refueling, it's pretty hard to plan and conduct modern air combat operations. But I'd let most of the tankers go from SAC into the new Air Mobility Command (AMC),

Roles and Missions 115

the replacement for Military Airlift Command. (AMC would also replace MAC as the Air Force component of US Transportation Command.)

One of my objectives in setting up Air Mobility Command was to remove "theater" airlift, mostly C-130s, from the stranglehold of the old MAC. Again, the Air Force had over time gone back and forth on this issue. The question was whether to think of theater airlift as a combat asset or as part of the transportation function. In my view, the answer was pretty clear. Typically, C-130s go to a theater of operations and stay there for the duration. We had C-130s permanently assigned overseas for just this reason. In this regard, theater airlift differs significantly from the "strategic" lift that gives us worldwide reach, flying across oceans to connect with any theater, as needed.

In debating how to organize airlift, professional transporters highlighted the strategic-to-theater "interface" as an overriding issue. Cargo arrives in-theater and changes hands. If our people don't handle this transfer well, essential equipment and supplies will sit on the ground—won't get to the user. So management of this interface is certainly an important problem. If you think it's the *most* important problem needing a solution—a variation on the theme of input manipulation—then you might put the transportation organization in charge, as we had done with Military Airlift Command. If you think (as I did) that in-theater transportation is only one of a number of combined-arms elements the war fighter must integrate, then C-130 transports belonged under local command. Some kind of mechanized transportation (and various "interfaces") is a characteristic of nearly all combat assets—wheeled vehicles, tracked vehicles, winged vehicles, bicycles. This is not a good reason to put them all in Transportation Command.

The secretary agreed to let me move US-based C-130s into Air Combat Command but worried about ACC becoming too large and powerful. I shared his concern, to a degree. Moving all SAC's assets—the bombers, tankers, and (at first) ICBMs—plus all of

MAC's nonstrategic airlift into ACC would produce among our major commands a condition not unlike that of the planets as seen by an outside observer—Jupiter and some miscellaneous orbital debris. So in the name of balance, Rice and I compensated the old MAC for removal of its C-130s by giving it most of SAC's tanker force, then renamed it Air Mobility Command.

At first glance, this seemed like a good idea. After all, mobility involves more than just airlift. In addition, tanking is essential in extending the reach of airlifters, as we learned in spades during the Yom Kippur War and again during Desert Shield, when we practically built an aluminum bridge across the North Atlantic. But, like C-130s, tankers are essential, in-theater, combat assets. At the end of the day, we should have put everything needed for modern, integrated air combat in Air Combat Command—and its overseas counterparts, PACAF and USAFE. We should have been proud that the command designed to hold our CONUS-based combat assets would dwarf all others in size. We should have left MAC's name the same but retained in it only those strategic lift assets that perforce support all theaters. This sort of MAC would provide functional (not combat) support and be unambiguously part of the (functional) Transportation Command. It would rely for air-refueling support on the combat commands, principally ACC but also the overseas Air Force components, instead of vice versa.

We did put a handful of tankers into ACC and all the tankers assigned overseas into PACAF and USAFE, but most of the tanker force went to AMC, my mistake and one not yet corrected, as this is written.

One big thing we did to descope ACC was to remove from it as much as practical of combat crew training. This job was given to Air Training Command (ATC), along with the bases at Luke and Tyndall and important tenant relationships at Kirtland, where ATC would do training for the Special Operations Force, and Altus, where it would train airlift crews. This big increase in ATC's responsibilities and assets helped restore internal balance. It also meant people would rotate back and forth between using commands and the formal schoolhouses, giving them a shot at being instructors and a look at a major air command of another style. And it infused frontline equipment into ATC, something badly needed, especially in connection with training enlisted maintenance specialties.

We went further and consolidated Air University into ATC and renamed it the Air Education and Training Command. AETC would be a departmental command, reporting to the chief and secretary. Like the new Air Force Materiel Command that would spring from the merger of Systems and Logistics Commands, it worked for the Air Force, not a joint commander.

I realized that the new, much strengthened AETC needed more clout and a first-rate commander. Closing Systems Command freed up a four-star billet. Then, in 1992, I got Colin Powell's support to promote his Joint Staff director, Butch Viccellio, and move him to take over our remodeled training business. One of our very best, Butch was a big-picture guy with great instincts. Nobody would do a better job of tooling up the new command.

But a significant error was to leave the Air Force Academy out of the new AETC. Though not heading a major air command, the academy superintendent reported directly to the chief of staff. Influential alumni thought this gave the academy prestige it would not have if subordinated to a major command. Butch Viccellio had been a standout athlete at the academy and I thought putting him at AETC would help bring the alumni around. It did help some, but not enough. In the end I yielded to internal pressure, thinking that other aspects of the reorganization were more important and needing to pick my fights. It was clear then (and events since have only underscored this reality) that the academy would be much better served by closer supervision than it's ever likely to get from a chief of staff.

Returning to Israel

In early December 1991 I made a swing through Portugal, Turkey, and Israel. It was a productive trip, the highlight Israel. I met with Moshe Arens, the defense minister; Lt. Gen. Ehud Barak, chief of the general staff; and Maj. Gen. Avihu Ben-Nun, IDF/AF commander, an old friend. I visited Tel-Nov Air Base and got a hop in their version of the F-15, unhappily in the back of a two-seater, as they wanted to demonstrate a helmet-mounted aiming system of their design, which required that I become a passenger.

A very special dinner was held, attended by every former Israeli Air Force commander except David Ivry, then serving as director general in the Defense Ministry and therefore pretty busy. My old buddy Moti Hod was there, as was Amos Lapidot, the then newly appointed head of the Technion, their marvelous engineering school at Haifa. Today, it would no longer be possible to duplicate this feat, as some of these founding aviators are gone. Even in 1991, it was remarkable that all of any country's former air chiefs would still be alive.

We raised a glass to Joe Alon and Avi Lanir.

Jack Anderson

On 6 December the *Washington Post* published a Jack Anderson column, headlined "Air Force's Stealthy Renovation Project." In it, Anderson alleged that, while in command in the Pacific, I had "ducked the spending rules" in authorizing a "$5 million, first-class renovation" of PACAF's headquarters building. A job this size would ordinarily require congressional approval as part of the Military Construction budget but, according to Anderson, I reclassified the headquarters as 14 separate buildings so the remodeling would look like a series of smaller jobs that could be done with Operations and Maintenance (O&M) funds that I controlled. This was "fancy footwork" that showed my "preference for form over substance," a trait I continued to display as chief of staff by ordering "the design of new uniforms" and personally modeling "the $1.5 million prototype." Air Force auditors had "landed at Hickam" and:

> ... discovered the secret renovation scheme ... A simple, 50-year-old building was being turned into digs the likes of which the average soldier never sees: carpets, wallpaper, wooden baseboards and oak chair railings around the walls.

Anderson's column said I was "not available for comment."

The facts were as follows: The PACAF headquarters building had been built and was still shown on civil engineer drawings as 14 separate structures. Over many years, these buildings had been connected incrementally by passageways and corridors to form a single facility. The entire edifice was badly in need of renovation. In Hawaii, my civil engineers had argued we could do the renovation legally by taking advantage of the technicality. I gave the go-ahead but was increasingly uncomfortable with the decision, "project pyramiding" being a well-explored path to trouble. While the various renovation projects were still under way, I asked the auditor to take a look to make sure everything was legal and aboveboard. (This was, by the way, my own auditor, stationed at Hickam, not someone flown in and "landed" there.) When the auditor made an adverse ruling, I ordered the projects stopped.

Jim Lynch, Anderson's staffer, had rung up my Public Affairs folks on 21 November, outlining the story and asking for a statement. Far from being "not available for comment," we had subsequently been in contact with Anderson's office on a daily basis and provided written answers on 2 December, four days before the story appeared in the *Post*. Among other points, we noted that Air Force office workers were by now pretty used to carpet and wallpaper. Our suggested revisions went unacknowledged.

As part of an "openness" campaign, Jack Anderson was among the many media personalities I had invited to lunch with me in the Pentagon. He had not accepted the invitation so, after his "exposé" appeared, I asked to see him. His staff said OK, and I dutifully turned up at his Georgetown office. I wanted to talk about the large baloney content in his article. He would have none of it. It wasn't that he bristled or took offense. He just wouldn't talk about it. He seemed heavy, slow moving, old, disconnected. (He soon retired with Parkinson's disease.) The subject he wanted to talk about was flying saucers, and space aliens the Air Force would not admit had landed at Roswell, New Mexico.

Most newspapers printed his column in the comics section.

Summing Up Reorganization

It is said that publishing the best dictionary is simple: copy the one that is currently best and correct one error. Thus, by tiny tweaking of the status quo, we can claim famous victories. This was not my approach. Separately, the changes outlined in these pages would have been important. Separately, they (and many others not mentioned here) were, after all, only a question of trimming, combining, improving, simplifying. All together and all at the same time, the changes added up to headfirst, deep-end, radical reform unparalleled in Air Force history. I think Secretary Rice and I can make a fair claim to having "reinvented" the Air Force. So we risked reaching too far, of doing damage to the Air Force, though I knew the outfit was strong enough to take it and emerge stronger still.

But why do this? Compared with the competition, the Air Force was already well organized. Certainly we had shown quality results in Desert Storm. Many said, "If it ain't broke, why is the chief fixing it?"

It is a fact that we did not reorganize because we were getting poor results. But everyone recognizes the need for change after failure. The real test of an organization is how it handles success. The secretary and I felt we should not wait until it was "broke," as Detroit had done when faced with auto competition from Japan. And we had whatever it took—good sense, dumb luck, whatever— to insist on improvement in an already outstanding organization. Not having to be right all the time on every issue freed me to take risk and to take the heat when something went wrong, as inevitably it does in dealing with complex, highly dynamic situations.

Near the end of my time as chief, *Air Force Magazine* did a sort of retrospective. Commenting on the reorganization, Senior Editor James Canan wrote:

> . . . the main purpose of the top-to-bottom restructuring was to strengthen Air Force management and operations in order to make the post-Cold War Air Force, despite its downsizing and its diminishing financial resources, even more potent than it proved to be in the Gulf War.

Bull's-eye.

Regarding reorganization, unlike some of the issues thrust on me from the outside—"roles and missions," "gays in the military," and the like—I never got bored, or sour, or felt undermined by a sense of futility. But already in my first days, I felt the pressure to move quickly. It's never a good idea to put the roof on before the foundation is dry, but I had only four years to get this done. Let those who came after me argue the supposed benefits of slower, more deliberate change.

Chapter 4

1992: Train

No, it's just a machine. I'm the weapon.
—Tom Cruise, as Commander Jack Harper, in *Oblivion*

It was, of course, impossible to pack all concerns about organization into 1991, but in that first full calendar year, I could and did highlight the topic, give it special attention. In much the same way, I planned to tackle the other two departmental functions—train and equip—in 1992 and 1993, respectively.

From the beginning, Secretary Rice and I knew the Air Force would be smaller. In the event, Air Force end strength peaked in 1986, after which we cut nearly 300,000 people, a decline of about a third in total headcount. Most of the cutting occurred on my watch, well after the budget had started to shrink. Some of the delay was due to natural lags in the system, but the truth is I pushed hard to cut payroll quickly. I was not worried that end-strength loss would translate automatically into diminished combat effectiveness, if we could free funds to train people properly and buy them better equipment.

Thinking about the Air Force as a business, we'd been able to achieve disproportionate gains in labor productivity. In World

War II, the B-17 had a crew of 10, got shot down a lot, and achieved bombing results that were nothing to brag about. By contrast, the B-2 had two people in it, penetrated the fiercest defenses and attacked multiple targets with precision so it didn't need to go back again. I couldn't quantify the productivity improvement, a version of infinity, like the difference between surviving and being killed, or hitting instead of missing. No matter how you measure it, the gain had been massive, making our much smaller force a much more formidable one.

In any case, within reasonable limits, size is no longer the most important factor in preparing forces for success in combat, if it ever was. Indeed, the "soft" assets of an organization—its morale and culture, its training and tactics—pile up more value. Even for tangible assets, within wide limits the way they're combined (the recipe) is more important, in my view, than gross size.[28] I therefore had no problem with reducing payroll, and did so with speed, where I could influence the matter.

But, while being smaller wouldn't stop us from being better, realizing that ambition, actually getting stronger and tougher, would require improved training.

Personnel Classification

As with reorganization, the details of how we reformed Air Force training are unlikely to be of interest to everyone. In broad outline, we began with an overhaul of our 40-year-old personnel classification system to reduce the number of occupational specialties. We wanted to train people more broadly and employ them more flexibly. In our early years, enlistments were short and the idea was to push lots of people through job training quickly so we could send them to units in time to get some use out of them before their

---

28 Lenin said that, for armies, quantity is a kind of quality, an observation that is at the same time astute and obtuse, the insight of a professional civilian. More often, especially in modern war, bigger is simply bigger.

hitch was up. To reduce schoolhouse time, we narrowed and specialized career fields. By the early 1990s, we had for many years been working on a different problem. We recruited many fewer people, trained them better, and tried hard to keep the good ones for prolonged service. Our classification system needed to be remodeled to reflect this changed approach.

In parallel with increasing flexibility in classification, we imposed a requirement for more formal, or classroom, as opposed to on-the-job training. And we tightened the rules governing how people progressed from apprentice to journeyman to craftsman, aligning these career milestones better with promotion phase points and enlisted professional military education, like the NCO Academy.

The old system spread officer skills over 20 career groupings and did not use these same groupings to classify enlisted personnel. The new system concentrated officer and enlisted specialties together into just nine career groups, then renamed and numbered the groups to align them better with the new objective organization. Overall, we cut the number of officer specialties by 40 percent and reduced enlisted skill categories by about 10 percent. We had no less work to do and no magic scheme for changing the kinds of work we did, but changing our classification system in the way we did meant we would train people more broadly and assign them to a wider range of jobs, tendencies mirroring an Air Force in which we employed people more flexibly.

Enlisted Technical Training

On the enlisted side, our system for describing skill level was quite traditional:

1-level	Trainee
3-level	Apprentice
5-level	Journeyman
7-level	Craftsman

The way the system was supposed to work, enlisted inductees began a career by going to basic military training at Lackland

Ellie, with Golda and me on the steps to Air House.

With Secretary Don Rice.

The Air Force honors Bob Hope.

In the Rose Garden, President Bush gives Don Rice and me the Commander in Chief's Trophy, part of my string of four in a row.

Air Force headquarters staff, 1991. Seated, from left: Tom Hickey, Mike Loh, me, Charlie May, Brad Hosmer. Standing: Bob Ludwig, Skip Rutherford, Butch Viccellio, Monte Miller, Leo Smith, John Jaquish, Mike Nelson.

At his Moscow headquarters, Piotr Deynekin wraps me in the flag of the Russian Air Force.

With the Deynekins, in St. Petersberg.

Golda prepares to receive dinner guests.

*Air Force chiefs have dinner at Air House: Larry Welch,
Dave Jones, Lew Allen, me, Mike Dugan, Charlie Gabriel.*

*Air Force first ladies: Dottie Gabriel, Skip Brown, Grace Dugan,
Ellie McPeak, Lois Jones, Barbara Allen, Eunice Welch.*

In Calcutta, Ellie and I meet Mother Teresa.

The Air Force String Quartet, at Air House.

Ellie meets first lady Barbara Bush.

Next-door neighbors Colin and Alma Powell have us to dinner.

AFB, Texas, for a short introduction to military life, then moved on to a technical training school, where they learned the fundamentals of an occupation. During this initial schooling, we classified trainees as 1-levels. We awarded a 3-level qualification to those who successfully completed technical training, sending them on to bases to begin an apprenticeship. With time and on-the-job training (OJT), apprentices became 5-level journeymen, the core of our enlisted workforce. With additional seasoning and service, journeymen grew into the senior NCO force, 7-level craftsmen who provided much in-office, in-shop, and flight-line supervision.

This broad description held true for many people, but there were also numerous exceptions. For instance, some occupational specialties had no technical school. People in these jobs simply went directly from basic training at Lackland to their first duty assignment. There, they learned primary job skills, either through OJT, or by correspondence course, or through some combination of these two. This progression was the case for some rather sizable career fields, like supply warehouseman and vehicle operator. Some career fields had technical schools, but funding limitations prevented everyone from attending. For instance, some of the carpenters who worked in our civil engineer squadrons went to the technical school at Sheppard AFB, Texas, and some did not. Still others—most importantly, many in the aircraft-maintenance career field—went to technical training but did not receive a 3-level qualification on graduation. Instead, after arrival at their first operational base, they attended courses taught by a field detachment of Training Command, only afterward becoming 3-levels. For a variety of reasons, some, like security police, were awarded the 3-level before they completed technical training.

The inconsistencies did not stop with initial technical schooling. When it came time to advance to journeyman and later to craftsman, some—weather forecasters, for example—went back to tech school for more formal training. Most did not, relying instead on yet another correspondence course and still more on-the-job training.

In fact, we leaned very heavily on OJT. For many enlisted occupations, the initial trip through tech school was their last skill training having the hallmarks of formal schooling: an indoor classroom setting; professional, full-time instructors; well-designed training aids; and so forth. Almost none of these advantages applied to OJT. Make no mistake, OJT was valuable, even irreplaceable. We just needed to keep it in perspective, to do it properly and in balance with more formal training.

So our enlisted training *system* was not systematic enough—and not rigorous enough. At an air base, 3-levels worked in a controlled environment, whereas we regarded 5-levels as fully qualified, their performance not supposed to require close supervision. But across the Air Force, the average time to upgrade from 3-level to 5-level was 13 months, not a very long apprenticeship to qualify somebody to troubleshoot the F-15 flight-control system or control air traffic at a large aerodrome. Moreover, the rules allowed these same 5-levels to conduct and certify completion of training done under the OJT system. Thus, in many cases, we authorized journeymen who had only a year or so experience in the field to train newly assigned apprentice airmen. Likewise, the day a buck sergeant (E-4) was notified of promotion to staff sergeant (E-5), he could immediately enroll in upgrade training for the 7-level. If the training—usually another correspondence course—was completed before the promotion became effective, the individual could become a 7-level the same day he sewed on staff sergeant stripes. This phenomenon was commonly referred to as the "one-day 7-level." We had aimed at high performance, but in the press of business, we'd not carefully applied strict standards to skill-level progression. We should have reserved the craftsman rating for midcareer NCOs—usually technical sergeants or master sergeants with 10 or more years of service. But as it actually operated, the system allowed—even encouraged—enlisted members to get a craftsmen rating as soon as they became junior NCOs, typically at the five- to seven-year point, and typically without any return to school for additional formal training.

Technical Training Reforms

As our first initiative in the Year of Training, we directed that everybody go to a technical school after completing basic military training. We did not have a job so straightforward that it required no formal skill training, and even if we did, we shouldn't want to acknowledge it, to send this message to someone starting an Air Force career. Second, we decided to send everyone back to Training Command for additional *formal* training before he or she could become a 7-level craftsman. Obviously, this sharply reduced our dependence on OJT and correspondence courses, though these would continue to be important in the upgrade from 3-level apprentice to 5-level journeyman. We also mandated that our enlisted people could not go back to tech school for advanced training until they had become stripe-wearing staff sergeants, thereby eliminating the one-day 7-level. In fact, we slowed down the skill-level upgrade process across the board, with the intent of producing journeymen and craftsmen who were more mature, more experienced, and better qualified.

Enlisted Professional Military Education

There was another sort of training called "professional military education," or PME, meant to prepare NCOs for increased rank and responsibility, as opposed to advancing technical proficiency. Enlisted PME started with Airman Leadership School, continued at midcareer with the NCO Academy, and culminated with the Senior NCO Academy. At the NCO Academy, for example, technical sergeants refined the leadership skills they would need when joining the "top three" ranks of master sergeant on up. Thus, the NCO Academy was (or should have been) a school for making master sergeants. At the Senior NCO Academy, senior master sergeants prepared to become chief master sergeants, the highest enlisted grade.

However, our review of enlisted PME showed uneven attendance patterns. Students at the NCO Academy, for instance, ranged anywhere from staff sergeants with eight years of total service to master sergeants with more than 16. Some NCOs attended in residence, some by correspondence, some not at all. Without going into detail, the inconsistencies that characterized occupational training extended as well to leadership training.

On the PME side, we decided to put much greater emphasis on training in residence rather than by correspondence. We also regularized rank requirements, directing that only technical sergeants could attend the NCO Academy and that they must do so in residence and before promotion to master sergeant. We followed suit for senior master sergeants in line to attend the Senior NCO Academy.

Training Costs

Our cost projections showed the reforms to enlisted training would produce big savings in the out-years, in the shape of more efficient and safer operations. We also had under way a number of initiatives that would cut training overhead. Already we were reducing the number of large technical training centers from six to four, closing Chanute AFB in 1993 and Lowry AFB in 1994, harvesting economies of scale at the four remaining centers (now converted to wings). Shrinking the number of occupational specialties meant we could scrap many of the old, narrower technical courses we had offered.

Even so, we needed a little seed money to initiate the changes, an up-front investment the secretary and I offset by moving funds from lower-priority programs. Predictably, the bean counters in SECDEF's staff deemed this step offensive and, first chance they got, took the funding away from us—simply snatched it out of our budget. Mind you, we'd found the dollars to enhance enlisted training from inside the total Air Force allocation, taking money from elsewhere. It was not as though we'd increased the burden of national defense.

The deputy secretary of defense oversaw the Pentagon's annual budget exercise, and I almost never intervened with him in person. But I made an exception in this case, writing Don Atwood a note:

> Sir,
>
> This is an important issue for us. Small dollars (~$20 million in 94) to improve training programs, all found inside the AF top line. The Comptroller takes this money because he thinks our training standards are high enough already!
>
> Please help.
>
> VR
>
> Tony

DEPSECDEF did help, but the comptroller always finds a way to get even.

Enlisted Rank and Insignia

At the same time we instituted training and education reforms, we retooled the enlisted rank structure. Previously, we'd partitioned the enlisted pay grade of E-4 (three-striper), calling the upper tier "sergeant" (or "buck sergeant"), specifying a different style of stripes to wear, and claiming this was the entry level for noncommissioned officer status. But if this was so, NCOs made up 77 percent of our enlisted force. And in fact, fewer than half of the E-4 sergeants actually could be placed in positions of increased responsibility. So, we told them they were NCOs, but it was largely atmospherics—and they knew it.

We eliminated E-4 tiering, designated all E-4s "senior airman," and made E-5 "staff sergeant" the first NCO grade. We still had an NCO-heavy enlisted force—52 percent—but this was more realistic, more fulfilling, and more in keeping with our drive toward professionalism.

In connection with the effort to redesign the uniform (see below), we made all enlisted stripes brighter and more conspicuous. Previously, a master sergeant wore six chevrons, all of them "rockers," a sort of U-shaped stripe. Going forward, master sergeants, because of our other initiatives now typically 7-level craftsmen and NCO Academy graduates, had a stripe above five rockers to make clear their status as part of the NCO stratosphere—the top three of master, senior master, and chief master sergeants.

The reforms introduced in enlisted training and education made for a more logical career progression, a building-block approach that was cleaner, clearer, and more consistent. Officers had long followed a kind of road map as they progressed through the grades. For the enlisted force, we'd found it difficult to define a good career path, in large part owing to variability in training programs that we had now fixed. Each member of our enlisted force, which, after all, added up to more than 80 percent of our uniformed population, could now plan a rational career progression.

Enlisted Retention

The increased training costs we incurred would not have made sense without high retention rates. Typically, airmen choosing to stay in the Air Force until retirement reenlisted twice. At each stage, we identified the people we wanted to keep and set a goal of retaining 65 percent of these reenlisting the first time and 90 percent for those signing up for a full 20-year career. We were not meeting these goals in 1990, the rates of 51 and 84 percent, respectively, but we improved steadily and by 1994 the rates stood at 62 and 89—nearly there and headed in the right direction. At least from the standpoint of enlisted retention, we were doing something right.

Quality Air Force

Our training initiatives took place against the backdrop of a movement sweeping through government and business: Total Quality Management (TQM). The product excellence and low cost achieved by Japanese industry, notably in automobiles and consumer electronics, had been a shocker. Much credit was claimed for methods like statistical quality control introduced in Japan by American management gurus, most notably W. E. Deming.

I was a little skeptical about TQM. The Air Force had been a quality outfit from the beginning, and I didn't think we had much to learn from the Japanese experience. But Secretary Rice was marginally more enthusiastic, and I came around to thinking there might be a few prizes in that grab bag (like a later variation called "lean" manufacturing). But I insisted on calling our effort "Quality Air Force" (QAF), not TQM, and used the QAF motif to reinforce attributes we wanted to see in the organization anyway. We dressed up ideas like decentralization, for instance, in QAF clothing. The pitch went something like this: pre-QAF, we centralized everything possible. Accountability was diffuse and ambiguous. Cost controlled quality, under the rubric "Quality Is Expensive." We worked at getting inputs right. Rules and strictures governed behavior and creativity. The climate: "Tight Supervision." Fair treatment—equity—was a prime motivator. We made employee commitment a slogan. The human spirit mattered little. By contrast, a Quality Air Force decentralized everything possible, tied accountability to authority, and distributed authority widely. We wanted a focus on outputs, with quality a way of life: "Unquality Is Unaffordable." Superiors gave wide latitude for action, fostering initiative, innovation, and ingenuity in a climate of trust and mutual respect. Motivation would flow from ownership and reward, with real and pervasive involvement. The human spirit would shape all else. Thus, rather than changing the Air Force on a TQM model, I tried to pick and choose aspects of the quality movement and give them an Air Force flavor, turn it into an Air Force thing. As a consequence, we stiff-armed the more bureaucratic aspects of TQM and may actually have gotten some good out of it.

The Tank

On 10 February the JCS gathered at the old Department of the Interior Building to commemorate 50 years of regular meetings. There had been no such meetings prior to February 1942, but the demands of Alliance coordination led Roosevelt and Churchill to establish the Combined Chiefs of Staff, a move that led quickly to the realization we should follow the example set by the British, whose service chiefs had by then been meeting as a body for nearly 20 years. The first JCS meeting was held at the Interior Department in a sort of bomb shelter that gave the feeling of being stuck inside a tank. Thereafter, the Joint Chiefs continued to meet in the "tank," even though it was an otherwise unremarkable conference room on the Pentagon's second floor.

Mary McGrory

In March, Mary McGrory joined me for lunch in my E-Ring office. More than just a *Washington Post* columnist, she was an institution, a large figure in American journalism. Among her distinctions: a Pulitzer Prize and membership on Nixon's "enemies list."

I invited McGrory over because I'd always admired the clarity of her prose. At lunch, we spoke of the power of language, and she mentioned in passing a poem by W. B. Yeats, *An Irish Airman Foresees His Death*. I admitted I didn't know it. When she got back to the *Post*, she faxed a copy.

Gongs for JSTARS

On 13 April I flew an F-15 to Melbourne, Florida, to visit the Grumman plant then producing the JSTARS aircraft. We had requisitioned developmental versions for service in Desert Storm, with the back end or "mission" part of the airplane manned by Grumman civilians. They'd done an outstanding job, so I lined up 17 of them and decorated each with the Air Medal, the only nonmilitary people involved in Desert Storm to be so honored.

Meeting with Canada's Military Chiefs

The US and Canadian armed forces chiefs met every year, at a site nominated in turns by the sides. Canada's chief of defense staff (equivalent of our JCS chairman), General John de Chastelain, hosted the 1992 meeting in Quebec City. Very bright and possessing great personal charm, De Chastelain served twice as chief of defense staff, the terms interrupted by a posting as Canada's ambassador to the United States. Still later, he was deeply involved in disarming Northern Ireland's Provisional IRA. De Chastelain was an unusually able man of notable accomplishment, in and out of uniform.

Should the Chief Fly Single-Seat Fighters?

In Washington, I flew a variety of aircraft when traveling on business. For shorter trips, I piloted a Learjet or Gulfstream. For overseas travel, I used a modified KC-135, nicknamed Speckled Trout, which had for decades supported the transportation requirements of the secretary and chief.

At PACAF, I'd kept my F-15 qualifications current by flying with the Hawaii Air National Guard. It was pretty rare for a four-star to fly single-seat jets, but I found it useful both with aircrews in our squadrons and with senior allied officers, who couldn't help noticing. After coming to Washington, I decided to continue the practice. It certainly was an advantage when I went to Saudi Arabia to inspect readiness just prior to Desert Storm. But when I got back from the desert, someone showed me an Air Force regulation having the effect of prohibiting me from flying single-seat fighters. I rescinded the directive on the spot and made a note to review the whole matter of Air Force regulations, which anyway needed adjustment.

About this time, my flying got connected to reports of improper use of aircraft stationed at Andrews Field, Maryland. Our transport aircraft stationed there supported political figures, the travel supposedly limited to official use only. But it's pretty hard for the Air Force to police travel requests that emanate from the White House or from the offices of powerful congressmen, so the potential for abuse was obvious. In early 1992, Fred Francis of *NBC Nightly News* was at the center of a ruckus that reached a high point when John H. Sununu, a former governor of New Hampshire then serving as President Bush's chief of staff, took one of our planes to Boston and subsequently attended an auction of rare postage stamps.

About the same time, Francis discovered I was still flying the F-15, reporting this fact on 23 April:

TOM BROKAW: Government perks have gotten a lot of attention recently: limousines, official planes. But NBC News has learned that the Air Force chief of staff is top gun when it comes to expensive perks. NBC's Pentagon correspondent Fred Francis has exclusive details for us tonight. Fred?

FRED FRANCIS: Tom, the Air Force's top four-star general, according to his own officers, is abusing his position by using $40 million combat jets as personal taxis and escorts . . . To the dismay of many of his own officers, he has flown combat F-15 fighters more than 38 hours in 18 months, unprecedented for a desk general, an indulgence that has cost the taxpayers more than half a million dollars . . .

And during all of his flights, McPeak is accompanied by at least one and often three other F-15s, which doubles or quadruples the cost of each trip.

McPeak also flew the F-15 on patrol near Iraq six times during Desert Shield. One critic said that took precious flying time from younger combat pilots . . .

General McPeak insists his flying gives him hands-on control of the Air Force, an institution he is radically reorganizing in a style that has earned him a lot of praise and a lot of enemies in the ranks.

Francis repeated the gist of the piece the next morning, a Friday, on NBC's *Today* show, for Katie Couric and anybody who had missed it the night before. I'd gotten to know Couric when she was on the Pentagon beat, before she took over the *Today* show anchor seat. She was an Army brat, and I liked her. When she clucked her tongue in reaction to the Francis broadside, I knew I was in hot water.

I spent most of Friday at Carlisle Barracks, Pennsylvania, giving a lecture at the Army War College. The rest of the time I spent in the office, busy with normal routine but waiting for the phone to ring. I heard nothing from either Secretary Cheney or Chairman Powell. I guessed that Cheney would be his poker-faced self, throwing words around like manhole covers, so I didn't expect expressions of support from him. But Powell and I had gotten over the rancor about who should be Schwarzkopf's deputy, and he'd become a friend. We were next-door neighbors at Fort Myer, though our schedules meant we saw little of each other across the fence. The chiefs were on a first-name basis with the chairman, so he occasionally called me "homey," the gangsta-rap term for guys from the neighborhood, the ones you not only like, but also trust. I sometimes gave his first name its British, short "o" treatment. Since others (and he himself) used the long "o" (KOH-lin), I asked him if my occasional mispronunciation gave offense. He said he couldn't care less, and meant it. A man's man, Powell's easy charm made him impossible to dislike and at the same time kept the inner steel out of sight.

Powell didn't ring me up either, but the Associated Press's Sue Shaffer came by my office for an interview, giving me the chance to start a backfire.

The story continued to build over the weekend. Under the headline, "Air Force Chief Hits Heavy Weather," the *Washington Post* calculated I could fly in a nice, roomy C-135 for $1,585 less an hour than the official F-15 rate. The article did point out I was pressing to restore the service's "warrior orientation" and that I'd never made a secret of my regular flights in single-seat aircraft.

Shaffer's AP story also appeared on Saturday, in smaller outlets across the country. The treatment given by the *Sentinel* of Carlisle, Pennsylvania, was typical. It quoted me as saying,

> I can't just sit here in this office and look out the window and maintain contact with the Air Force . . . Do I fly F-15s? Guilty . . . I've been concerned maybe we're getting a little too soft . . . We don't need chair-borne leadership in the Air Force.

The article also pointed out that some people in the Air Force were unhappy about the radical organizational changes I was making and the pressure I was bringing to force senior officers out of staff jobs and "onto the tarmac."

Monday and Tuesday came and went, the story continued to play. I started getting cards and letters from all over the country, mostly very positive. Secretary Rice was mildly supportive, or at least not yelling at me, but still no reaction from the two big bosses, Cheney and Powell.

On Wednesday, my outer office got a call from the White House saying to expect a package. About noon, a Secret Service guy walked in with a large envelope. Inside it, nested like Russian dolls, a smaller envelope, then another and another. The tension mounted. At last, a greeting-card-sized note in the president's hand: "I saw the cheap shot fired your way on flying a fighter. Free advice! Don't let the bastards get to you or get you down." George Bush had affixed his runic scrawl.

Word of the presidential dispensation raced around the Pentagon—the outer office network in action—and my direct line soon buzzed, first from Secretary Cheney, then from Chairman Powell. They assured me they'd been in my corner all along. At the Pentagon press conference, Cheney's spokesman Pete Williams said his boss wished others would follow my example: "It's the kind of hands-on experience the secretary would like to see in all the Joint Chiefs."

Deynekin in the US

In May, when Piotr Deynekin and his family returned my visit to Russia by coming to the United States, Ellie and I met them in San Francisco, then drove north through Santa Rosa and down the Russian River to the Pacific Coast. He was touched, I think, when locals danced in native costume at Fort Ross, site of the deepest penetration Russian fur trappers made into North America. Then we went to Nellis to get Deynekin a hop in the B-1. We'd found a Russian-speaking lieutenant colonel who was a B-1 instructor pilot. He and Deynekin got airborne; I hurried after them in an F-15. The aerial intercept I accomplished must be the only instance of mock combat by the chiefs of our two air forces.

Breakfast with Strom

Civic groups from communities where the Air Force is a big player came to town often. They usually had enough clout with their congressional delegations to get some sort of séance scheduled, often a breakfast on Capitol Hill. Naturally, their own senators and congressmen showed up, but what amazed me was how many times I ran into Strom Thurmond, then approaching 90 years old, at these events. I recall one memorable breakfast, sponsored by friends from Clovis, New Mexico. I knew most of the group, having formed friendships during my time at Twelfth Air Force. But what was Senator Thurmond doing there? No telling what the connection was, except he sure liked breakfast and, for an older man, could put it away. After asking, "Do you want those eggs?" he helped himself to mine. He'd say a few words, witticisms repackaged for each state delegation, wrap some biscuits in a napkin, and be out the door.

Flying Training

Naturally, I took a special interest in flying training. It had always been pretty good, but, again, I wanted it to be as exacting and combat oriented as possible, within commonsense limits imposed by safety considerations and cost.

In thinking about flying training, I found it useful to divide it into two main types: formal training and continuation training. Formal training was done in some sort of "schoolhouse," purpose-built for the training mission. Instructors, specially trained and certified for the job, did the training in a controlled, indoor setting—a classroom or platform environment. Students followed a course syllabus, with established standards for progression and graduation. Primary and basic flying training was formal training, as was the combat crew training given prior to assignment to operational squadrons. During my time with the Luftwaffe's F-104G program at Luke, I'd been an instructor in the formal training system.

By contrast, continuation training was the routine, day-to-day work of operating squadrons, where the mission was readiness, and training was a function supporting that purpose. Improving combat readiness was important—we judged commanders according to their ability to do this—but in operational squadrons, training was much less structured, done mostly under the supervision of IPs selected by the squadron commander from among the most experienced and capable line pilots.

So the natural break between types of training involved thinking of formal training as a departmental responsibility and continuation training as an operational responsibility. Making combat crew training the business of Air Education and Training Command improved it because that command was responsible for the bulk of the department's formal-training business. On the other hand, taking combat crew training away from the operating commands relieved them of a large supervisory burden and meant they could give more time and attention to the continuation training that supported and improved readiness—their principal product.

T-3 Firefly

By the early 1990s, the Air Force had for some years given pilot candidates a few hours in powered aircraft before entry into flying school. We did this as a cost measure, hoping to eliminate quickly those with chronic airsickness or fear-of-flying problems. Officers produced by ROTC programs reported to a contractor-operated school; the Air Force Academy had its own program, run in-house. Both places used the T-41 aircraft, a military version of the Cessna 172. The venerable 172 had given many decades of honorable service as a family-style cross-country aircraft, but it simply was not a good match for our requirement to produce adventure-oriented warrior-pilots.

A program to replace the T-41 was already under way when I became chief. The prototype, a variant of the Slingsby T-67, began flying in the summer of 1991. I tried out the airplane in 1992 and didn't much care for the side-by-side seating but thought it otherwise a great little trainer, fully capable of military-style traffic patterns, aerobatics and spins, none of which the T-41 could do. The Air Force put the airplane through a thorough test program, redesignated it the T-3 "Firefly," and took delivery of an operational version in February 1994. (Others, notably the Royal Air Force and the Canadian Air Force, also adopted the aircraft as a preflight screener and primary trainer.) The training was so worthwhile we eventually increased the T-3 flying syllabus to 18 sorties and 25 flying hours.

The T-3 got in trouble after I retired. Although the civilian contract school never had a problem, a series of accidents at the Air Force Academy killed three cadets and their instructor pilots. I caught a little postretirement flak for this, it being claimed that I'd put lives at risk in an overzealous quest for more rigorous training.[29]

Following the accidents at the academy, the Air Force took the T-3 back to Edwards and again subjected it to several hundred hours of flight testing, reported in *Aviation Week* as bordering on "abuse of the aircraft." According to a pilot assigned to the test project, "We did everything we could to create a worst-case scenario . . . everything 'dumb' we could think of." The test pilots determined there was nothing wrong with the airplane and recommended returning it to service. Even so, in the spring of 1997, the Air Force grounded the T-3 and eventually disposed of the aircraft. This had the effect of causing flying school attrition to jump and eventually the screening program was reinstituted using another aircraft, with all the training done under civilian contract.

No doubt the academy made mistakes in administering the T-3 program, but a deeper, cultural problem was to believe that any

---

29 For example, in January 1998, *Time* magazine ran an article titled "The Deadly Trainer," saying, in part:
> . . . the T-3's introduction to Air Force training was a particular passion of General Merrill McPeak, the service's chief of staff in the early 1990s. McPeak, a fighter pilot who had flown with the Thunderbirds, the Air Force's precision-flying team, is now retired but still flies his own homemade, acrobatic RV-4 aircraft.

rated pilot on the academy's faculty or staff was well suited and safe to teach spins and aerobatics. Instructors for this type of training need themselves to be screened. As an institution, the Air Force had a hard time acknowledging this problem, let alone fixing it.

Having tougher, more combat-oriented training is just the ticket for the Air Force. But you better know what you're doing, as we should have.

JPATS

In 1956 the Air Force began replacing the primary flight trainer I'd first soloed in, the T-34, with the T-37 "Tweety Bird," so that by 1990 we'd been using this aircraft for 30plus years. Pairing the Tweet with our basic trainer, the T-38, allowed us to claim a virtue of our own invention, that we provided "all jet" training.

The T-37's performance deficiencies meant it was never more than adequate as a primary trainer. The side-by-side crew seating arrangement was another problem. At a certain point, we perforce transition many pilots into this configuration, the traditional arrangement for big airplanes, but early in a fledgling flyer's career, we should cultivate self-reliance, a quality not in harmony with this cockpit layout. We also experienced problems manning the T-37 instructor force. Nobody wanted to be a Tweet IP. We had to dragoon people into the duty, after which they exited the Air Force at the first opportunity and in large numbers. The attitude of the pilot force should have told us all we needed to know: we had to do better than this.

In the 1980s, we began a T-37 replacement program called the Next Generation Trainer, or NGT. Fairchild won the NGT competition with the T-46—like the T-37, a small twinjet with side-by-side seating. We soon abandoned the ill-managed T-46 program for budget reasons, with few tears shed.

Meanwhile, the Navy also needed a new primary trainer, so in the late 1980s, they joined us in a program called the Joint Primary Aircraft Training System. Proposed JPATS candidates were already flying before I became chief. In fact, I'd flown some of them.

One, the Swiss Pilatus P-9, was a single-engine turboprop that I rated very highly. A tandem two-seater, it far outperformed the T-37, had good handling qualities, and was a fine aerobatics and spin trainer. The jet-powered trainers in the candidate pool did not seem to have an important edge in performance and, over the life cycle, ownership cost would be a good deal lower with a prop-driven aircraft.

Some in the Air Force felt we should not "go backwards" on the matter of pure jet training. On the other hand, I thought a combination of prop and jet-engine training was, if anything, a plus. Airmanship accumulates in layers, the more kinds of experience the better. Even if we left aside cost considerations (and we shouldn't), a mix of prop and jet training would be a good thing, so I worried that entrenched attitudes would keep a propeller-driven aircraft like the P-9 from getting a square deal in the evaluation process.

About a year into my tour as chief, I scheduled a JPATS "summit," a meeting of all the senior people who had a vote in the matter. I wasn't going to dictate selection of a propeller-driven airplane, but I wanted to make sure we addressed all the objections to doing so. We met at Randolph, Training Command headquarters, putting the using command on its home turf, face to face with the acquisition community. It became clear that the users had no objection to selecting a propeller-driven design if it met performance requirements. Because JPATS was a joint program, we invited the Navy to the meeting. They also were OK with selecting a prop job, if that was the evaluation outcome. Back in Washington, I called the chief of naval operations, Frank Kelso, and made sure he was on board.

As it turned out, the Pilatus did win the subsequent competition. An upgraded version, the T-6 "Texan 2," has since provided years of superior, lower-cost pilot instruction.

Assignment Selection

When I graduated from pilot training, we lined up according to class standing and picked from the list of available advanced-training choices. Usually, fighter assignments went to the top graduates. The big airplane commands, SAC and MAC, objected to this procedure, arguing they got leftovers. Eventually they prevailed, and we switched to an administered system that allowed for more "equitable" distribution of the talent.

I believed in competition, in rewarding winners, in reinforcing success, and I thought our strongest people felt the same way. We were assigning new pilots out of flying school as if talent, hard work and luck counted for nothing. I directed an immediate return to the old system.

Pilot Production Rate

The drawdown in force structure meant we were closing squadrons right and left, releasing both experienced and inexperienced pilots for reassignment. Older, experienced pilots could be moved to staff jobs, but I wanted to keep younger pilots flying, which meant we had to reassign them to still-active squadrons, soaking up openings usually filled by new pilots coming out of flying school.

I began by diverting more than half of all new pilot graduates into nonflying jobs. We trained them in a support specialty—security police, intelligence, civil engineer, and so forth—and planned to keep them in these career fields for three or four years. They could return to the flying mainstream after some slack developed in the system. This was not what they (or we) wanted. It was a draconian measure thrust on us by the collapse of our force structure. But it would have the advantage of giving us a more broadly trained officer force in the years to come if, in fact, we got them back to flying and kept them in the Air Force.

But it wasn't enough simply to divert graduating pilots. I saw no alternative but to reduce the output from our flying schools, and to do so rapidly. Entering the early 1990s, pilot production was running about 1,500 a year. I drew this down in stages to 500. A lot of newly commissioned officers were denied entry into flying training. We cut way back on ROTC graduates ticketed for flying school and even reduced the number of entrants we took from the academy. In every case, we put these new lieutenants into a support career field and promised we'd circle back later and get them into flight training before they got too old. But it was bad news all around for many young men and women, and I heard about it, especially from parents.

Chopping pilot production so drastically also built in a world-class management challenge downstream as the affected year-groups aged. But we didn't go far enough for some sharp pencils in the Pentagon bureaucracy. During the program objective memorandum cycle for the 1993 budget year, OSD analysts proposed the Air Force cut pilot production even further. Once again I took the unusual step of sending Donald Atwood, deputy secretary of defense, a handwritten note:

Sir,

PBD (Program Budget Decision) 029 reduces AF pilot production to about 250 per year. Secretary Rice and I have already driven down pilot training to 500 per year, a very low rate by historical standards, with lots of problems attendant on our decision to go this low. To go to 250 is really going to be a showstopper. Please help us keep this problem manageable.

VR

Tony

He did help, and pilot production bottomed at 500 a year.

Pilot Retention

I worked hard on pilot retention because, once we produced a pilot and got him through combat crew training, we'd made—in some systems, literally—a million-dollar investment. For years we'd had up and down retention results. At the time, something like two-thirds of all airline pilots came out of the military, so our retention rates were often the complement of airline hiring rates, our good retention years matching those in which the airlines struggled.

We'd dealt with the problem mostly by imposing a service obligation on graduating pilots. When my class got wings, we all agreed to stay in the Air Force four more years. As training costs escalated, the commitment notched up so that by the time I took over as chief, it was eight years. One of the first staff briefings I took urged a further increase to 10 years, since the airlines were in one of their periodic hiring phases.

I didn't like the idea of a service obligation and didn't approve the proposed lengthening of the contract period. It went against the grain. We were an all-volunteer force, and I didn't want to keep anyone in the Air Force who didn't want to stay. In fact I wished we could walk back the service commitment to some lower number. But training costs in modern systems like the F-15 were very high, so I left it at eight years.[30]

A year of pilot training followed by the eight-year obligation brought pilots to the nine-year-service point, by which time they provided experienced, valued air leadership. We could count on keeping most pilots from the 15-year service point until they were retirement-eligible at 20 years. So the problem was to find a way to bridge the gap, to retain pilots in the important nine- to 15-year category.

We used something called the cumulative continuation rate to judge our success at this. For various technical reasons, it tracked the percentage of pilots entering their sixth year of service who would still be with us at the completion of their 11th year of service, based on existing retention rates. Our goal was 65 percent, and as I came to office, we weren't close to meeting it.

If I didn't like the idea of a longer service obligation, I'd have to find another way to retain pilots. We already had a proposal on the table to increase pilot compensation, asking Congress to approve bonuses for pilots who stayed on after the nine-year point. It wasn't an easy sell. I was in the embarrassing position of asking for stay bonuses at the same time we were closing squadrons wholesale and

---

30 In 1998, then chief of staff Mike Ryan increased the active duty commitment to 10 years.

therefore had too many pilots. Luckily, key congressmen and senators understood, and Congress funded the bonus program, which helped a great deal. But we weren't going to beat the airlines if pay was the only consideration.

My view was that, whereas we recruited men and women, we retained families. More and more Air Force families featured two income earners, with a spouse working outside the home. In the old days, we could just pick up families and plop them down somewhere else, willy-nilly. But with working spouses, reassignment could be a financial disaster and a cause of deep unhappiness in the family. If we could figure out how to do it, we needed an assignment system that sent people where they wanted to go and left people where they wanted to stay. I asked the personnel folks to tell me how to implement such a system for everybody, starting with pilots.

The Volunteer Assignment System

Our Military Personnel Center was located at Randolph Field, in San Antonio. Officers assigned there had to work out how we might implement my notion of an all-volunteer assignment system for pilots. After some staff work, a team flew to Washington to brief me on findings. The upshot was it couldn't be done. Nobody (or, anyway, not enough people) would ever volunteer for certain jobs—for example, Kunsan Air Base in Korea, home of the 8th Fighter Wing. We did not allow families at Kunsan because we had no housing for them, so we manned this wing by sending people there unaccompanied, on one-year assignment. Personnel detailers coped by spreading the pain, using "equity" as a mantra. Nobody went to Kunsan twice before everybody went once.

Equity was an idea I didn't much like because so many bad things were done in its name. If there was a problem at Kunsan, why not attack the problem rather than use our arbitrary assignment power to paper it over? If we thought about it, we could make Kunsan more attractive—budget more flying hours there, put junior people in leadership positions, authorize more choice coming out of Kunsan into follow-on assignments—anyway, use our imagination.

So I asked the team from the personnel center to stay over in Washington. Don't tell me it can't be done; come back and tell me how to do it—this on a Tuesday, they having flown up from Texas without a change of underwear because they were going to give me the bad news and go home. By Thursday they were back in my office with another briefing, the opening line of which was, "Chief, we can get you to a 90 percent all-volunteer assignment system for pilots." I heard them out, pocketed the 90 percent, and told them to go get the other 10. On Friday, needing to get back to Texas, they told me how to do it—and that I was making a big mistake. I said, OK, let's do it anyway.

The voluntary assignment system for pilots worked fine for the rest of my tenure. None of the predicted dire consequences materialized (though we did have to pretty-up Kunsan and some other places, and should have kicked ourselves for not having done so already). We got the needed movement in the pilot force, in part because younger pilots realized they couldn't simply homestead at a nice base and expect to get ahead in the career sweepstakes and in part because we did arbitrarily reassign older pilots who were locked in for 20-year retirement. Most important, we tackled the real issue: bridging the gap from the end of the eight-year flight-training commitment to the 15-year service point. The pilot cohorts in this category were married, had working spouses and young children in school, and didn't want to move. They were also precisely the midlevel, experienced people we counted on heavily for leadership in operating squadrons.

The Cumulative Continuation Rate

The volunteer-assignment policy improved retention until it got too good. The health of the pilot force requires a little turnover—the reason we set the retention goal at 65 instead of 100 percent. It got much better than the target goal, topping out at 87 percent in FY 95.[31]

Care and Feeding of Pilots

Including the reserve components, the Air Force logged over 3 million flying hours every year from 1976 through 1991. The number peaked at nearly 3.5 million hours in 1985. By 1991 we were down to just over 3 million hours. From then to the end of my tenure, the flying-hour program dropped sharply, down to 2.3 million hours in 1995. But in parallel with the dramatic dive in total hours, we reduced the number of airplanes and crews, so average flying hours per pilot held steady at 19 to 20 a month for fighter pilots. We were therefore able to maintain high training standards and keep our accident rate down.

Time spent in the air is important, both to keep skills sharp and to motivate. It has much to do with career retention, especially of the best people, who won't stay if they think we're not serious about flying. So even in a declining resource environment, I wasn't about to let the flying-hour program go pear-shaped. In fact, I thought we should fly more.

The feeling was reinforced annually, when the Navy's budget documents asserted a claim that its pilots were averaging 24 to 25 hours per month. I never trusted this figure, not knowing how the Navy derived it. Whenever I compared logbooks with a Navy or Marine contemporary, I was ahead on flying time. No matter, I wanted the Air Force, not the Navy, or anybody else, to set the standard for flying training. So I kept trying to bump up our flying-hour program, taking money from other activities I regarded

---

31 The volunteer assignment policy was revoked shortly after I left office. Even though it worked well and saved a lot of money, it didn't conform with our view of ourselves as part of a monastic brotherhood, with a "calling" that not only prepared us for sacrifice, but also required it. Of course, pilot retention in the key nine- to 15-year category plummeted.

I believe in a culture of warriors, not monks.

as less important, only to have the additional funding removed by OSD in annual budget drills. OSD civilian analysts were convinced we were already good enough, that we met *their* standards.

At length, I gave up, but the experience was disheartening.

Eliminating Regulations

Dealing with the system of Air Force regulations turned out to be a large undertaking. For one thing, when I took over we had 55,000 pages of regulations, all supplemented by many thousands of additional pages published by the major commands, numbered air forces, and so on down the line. Naturally, nobody ever read all this stuff. Even if you limited yourself to documents covering your occupational specialty, there was way too much painful, boring elaboration. What happened was, if you were well trained and if you had some specific problem or question, you could figure out which was the right regulation and look it up—often getting an unsatisfactory, user unfriendly answer because there was so much mindlessness that had been made mandatory somewhere, in some regulation. It was a system for lawyers, not operators.

I started out thinking we could rewrite regulations and change them from "how to do it" to a "what we want done" approach. In connection with round one of the attempted rewrite, I mandated, (1) a reduction of 35 percent in the number of regulations and, (2) that the page count of surviving regulations be cut 50 percent. (I knew these targets were precisely wrong, but you have to start somewhere.) When I took a look at the product at the end of this phase, it was still awful, so I ordered that all regulations simply be thrown out.

I even did away with the term "regulation," because it was clear we needed a changed mindset. I asked the chiefs of every Air Force function to produce new, readable documents called policy directives, no longer than two or three pages each. Each directive should answer the questions, "What do we think is important?" and, "What is our policy with respect to this important matter?" What's important and has company policy connected to it should be committed to memory and understood by everybody in the business, so functional chiefs who thought there were scores or even hundreds of things that were important were sent back to the drawing board. I didn't want to predicate policy direction on the assumption that people can remember 100 things. I had the new policy directives run by me for signoff before they became official.

In the end, Air Force headquarters produced 165 policy directives that replaced 1,800 regulations. These were supplemented by about 750 sets of instructions, crafted by field agencies and using commands, dealing with the "how-to" questions. The new approach resulted in virtually no paper publications. All policy directives and instructions for the entire Air Force were put on a single compact disk, with copies sent to each squadron. Anybody could pop the CD into a computer and call up any directive or instruction they wanted.

Training Video

I put together another video called "Two Kinds of Change" for use at commander's calls throughout the Air Force. In it, I spoke of the changes being forced on us—lower budgets, reduced force structure, shrinking end strength—and contrasted them with self-induced change, the reorganization and training reforms producing a better, higher-performing organization. Nineteen ninety-two was the Year of Training because the Air Force was shrinking rapidly, people who wanted out were leaving the service early, and we were becoming more professional day by day. In such circumstances, one might say the time was right for raising training standards, as, in fact, we were doing. But, we would have raised training standards anyway, whatever the circumstances, and if ever the time came to reconstitute a larger Air Force, we should raise standards again.

Ron Fogleman

A big part of getting an organization to change is convincing people that change is needed. I could not get this done across the board. I never did manage to generate much enthusiasm from H. T. Johnson, then heading the new Air Mobility Command and dual-hatted as commander of the Unified Transportation Command. We finally agreed on his retirement, and Secretary Rice and I nominated Ron Fogleman to replace him. Fogleman had been in Misty with me and had worked for me in the Pentagon during my tour as the Air Force's programmer. He was a superstar performer, and when I took over PACAF, I'd helped get him promoted and sent to run Seventh Air Force, in Korea. A career fighter pilot, Fogleman would have something to learn about the airlift business, but I was confident he'd bring the right combination of skill and enthusiasm to the transportation business.

Giving Up Single-Seat Flying

I eventually gave up flying single-seat fighters, not quite halfway through my term as chief. Staying current required me to visit F-15 units, which was a good thing but took lots of time. And while I was safe enough in the bird—the airplane was very forgiving—I sure was getting beat up in mock air-to-air combat. Averaging one sortie a month will not keep anybody sharp, especially at the play of fingers, the touch-typing of fire control buttons and switches decorating stick and throttles. We sometimes called this "playing the piccolo," and it must be done with dexterity if you want to stay in the fight.

I flew my last F-15 flights on 26 September 1992, a cross-country from Eglin to NAS New Orleans and return. At New Orleans, I flew 1 v. 1 against an Air National Guard pilot, a Weapons School graduate who spent most of his time camped out at my six o'clock, inside firing range. During debrief, he said he was having an off day.

When a great batter goes 4 for 4 and tells you something's not quite right, believe him. The good ones always know when they're having a bad day. As for me, if I couldn't do better than this, it was time to hang it up. I resigned myself to a life in family-model aircraft—not happy about it, and doing it without fanfare.

Trent Lott

Don Rice and I had brought Buster Glosson back from Desert Storm to take over the secretary's legislative liaison post. All services regarded this as a sensitive assignment, and I knew Buster's personality was just right for the job. It didn't hurt that he'd emerged from Gulf with a reputation as a smart planner and combat leader.

One day Glosson came by to say I'd have to go see Trent Lott. The then-junior senator from Mississippi was unhappy, thought I didn't respect him. This mystified me. I had no feelings one way or another about Trent Lott. I'd certainly accorded him the normal deference owed any senator, which is to say, plenty. Anyway, I agreed to meet him, was ushered into his office, and got tap danced on. Respect is what makes this town work. It's a measurable commodity. If you don't have it, you're finished here. And so on. I assured the senator I liked and admired him, after which he seemed happier. But I left wondering what the heck I'd done to deserve the lecture. (I never found out.)

In the armed forces, you get a little automatic respect based on rank and position. And otherwise all you can earn.

Air House

In the summer of 1960, the Army agreed to set aside Quarters Seven at Fort Myer, Virginia, as an official residence for the Air Force chief of staff, on the understanding we would eventually construct appropriate quarters elsewhere, presumably at one of the nearby air bases, either Bolling or Andrews. Located next to Arlington Cemetery, Fort Myer is a five-minute drive from the Pentagon, a big advantage over any possible alternative location. Moreover, Quarters Seven is a large house, suitable for entertaining, with a nice view down the district's monumental corridor. Every chief since Tommy White has been grateful to the Army for being allowed to live there.

The arrangement had also caused a certain amount of vexation in the Army. For the services, few matters are more sensitive than senior officer housing. This particular set of quarters was one of the grandest in the inventory, and a very senior Army officer had been displaced. Indeed, over the years, the choicest houses along

General's Row at Fort Myer had become "joint." The JCS chairman had occupied Quarters Eight for many years. More recently Quarters Six had been requisitioned for use by the vice chairman, following the creation of that position in the Goldwater-Nichols Act. Quarters Seven, sitting between these other two, was, after all, only on loan to the Air Force. So, the Army raised the question of its status from time to time.

In response to one of these periodic forays, Larry Welch tried to get money appropriated to enlarge and redecorate one of the houses at Bolling Field. The cost estimate came in at over half a million dollars, and the plan was eventually shelved by congressional committee. Some in the Army suspected the Air Force had made only a half-hearted effort. When our reorganization of the Air Force led to closure of Systems Command, a fine set of four-star quarters became available at Andrews, on the edge of the Beltway. I certainly was in no mood to trade living at Fort Myer for the brutal commute from Andrews to the Pentagon.[32]

To put us on firmer footing at Quarters Seven, I started to call the place "Air House." Invitations to social functions changed to reflect the new name. I also called attention to the honored place Fort Myer occupies in the history of military aviation.

In December 1907, the Army Signal Corps released Specification No. 486, calling for bids to deliver an air machine that could carry a crew of two, fly faster than 40 miles per hour, remain aloft for at least an hour and—probably the most onerous requirement—be transportable by four-wheel mule-drawn wagon. (The specification was tailored for the Wright brothers, the only feasible provider. Incredibly, responses came from 40 bidders.) The Wrights signed

---

32 While the issue was still in doubt, I began a checkout in the UH-1, preferring even a helicopter to sitting in traffic. I ended up with about 10 hours left seat UH-1 time, in the process much increasing my respect for chopper pilots. Thankfully, I never had to finish the checkout.

a contract in February 1908. In September, flight tests began, at Fort Myer. Orville managed to stay aloft for one minute and 11 seconds. Two weeks later, he crashed from a height of 150 feet, hurting himself badly and fatally wounding Lt. Tom Selfridge, the first serviceman killed in powered flight. Orville spent six months in Fort Myer's hospital. One of the gates to Arlington Cemetery is named after Selfridge. Next year, the Wrights returned to Fort Myer with an improved military flyer. On 20 July 1909, Orville flew with Lt. Frank Lahm for one hour, 12 minutes and 40 seconds, meeting one of the specifications. Three days later, Orville averaged 42.583 miles an hour over a two-way course. The airplane also passed the mule-driven transport test, and the Army accepted its first flying machine on 2 August 1909.

I had a scale model of the military flyer made up as a weather vane and put it on Air House's roof.

I also hit on the idea of producing a book about the house. Ellie wrote the families of previous chiefs and drew together a collection of photographs and stories that became the nucleus of the book. I made sure a photocopy of the document allocating Quarters Seven to the Air Force, signed by President Eisenhower's chief of staff, Andy Goodpaster, was an exhibit in the publication. Then I walked downstairs in the Pentagon and gave Gordy Sullivan, the Army's chief of staff, a personal copy of *Air House, A History.*

The Grey Eagle

For many years, the Navy had a program called the Grey Eagle that recognized the naval aviator with longest rated service. I felt this was a wonderful tradition and wanted to emulate it, but I couldn't think of a better name. Grey Falcon, Bald Eagle, Ancient Aviator—no title was as good. So, I wrote the CNO, Frank Kelso, and asked if we could use the same name. He was kind enough to interpose no objection (but then, he was a submariner!). At my urging, the Air Force Association commissioned the statue of an eagle, made using metal recycled from old airplanes. We placed this figure outside the chief's office, in the Pentagon hallway, attaching name tags to identify the officers who, in turn, and according to the date of their initial pilot rating, survived to become our most senior aviator on active duty. As each Gray Eagle retired, a new one would be identified.

For many years, the secretary, the chief of staff, and senior officers of the Air Staff had met twice a year with the leadership of the major air commands. These so-called CORONA gatherings aimed at across-the-board harmonization, especially on high-profile, Washington-centered issues. I instituted a third annual meeting, where four-star commanders were joined by numbered air force commanders, these together comprising the top two echelons of operational leadership. I saw this as a gathering of warriors, a knights of the Round Table, the sole topic for discussion being how to improve our fighting effectiveness. Each commander brought a representation of his organization's heraldry to the dinner held at these meetings. I presented the Grey Eagle at the first of these "heraldic dinners."

I knew if I served a full term as chief, I would be accorded this recognition and, indeed, I was the Air Force's third Grey Eagle.

The New Uniform

By the early 1990s, after more than 40 years of independence, the Air Force service dress uniform—our equivalent of the business suit—was still in essence a blue version of the Army uniform. Ours was a little toned down, without quite so much chrome and detailing, but nevertheless the two uniforms tracked quite closely in the years following World War II. Consequently, we also displayed lots of gadgets and doodads—something I thought not in keeping with the ideas of the founders of the Air Force, who were said to have wanted a "plain, blue suit." Somehow—maybe because the Korean War came along or owing to the press of other business—we never got around to designing our own uniform.

I felt we needed to revisit the issue. In a newspaper interview, I said,

> We've just proven in Desert Storm that we are an independent force in combat. It's time we had a uniform that expressed our coming of age as a service—a distinctively Air Force uniform.

A new uniform might also serve as a symbol of our reorganization, which in many ways also reflected a restoration of earlier, more streamlined structures.

I set up and chaired a uniform-design committee, becoming the "acquisition authority" for the new uniform, the only time I involved myself at this level in a procurement action. I put my deputy for personnel, Lt. Gen. (later General) Billy Boles; Chief Master Sergeant of the Air Force Gary Pfingston; and some others I trusted on the committee. I also asked half a dozen women to serve, including the head of Materiel Command's clothing branch, Capt. Cathy McGinn, and my assistant executive officer, Lt. Col. (later Brig. Gen.) Denny Eakle.

Our working concept called for designing and producing a distinctive airman's uniform and keeping it as simple as possible while at the same time making it smart enough in appearance that we could toss out an assortment of high-cost regalia kept in the closet for use on special occasions or by special units, like honor guards. We had so-called dress whites and dress blues for these purposes, trappings that were expensive and seldom worn. Anyway, it always seemed odd to me that we should discard our service dress uniform in favor of something else when we wanted to "look good."

Our existing uniform, like the Army's, was made of polyester material—a fashion highlight of the 1970s. The uniform committee immediately abandoned this material in favor of a wool blend we knew would be more expensive. We were quite confident of finding savings to more than offset the increased cost. The current uniform color, a deep blue, was excellent and the committee quickly decided to keep it. We stripped the uniform down to bare essentials: a blue jacket and matching trousers. Anything added had to fight its way onto the property. Pockets? For years the jacket had featured outside, cargo-style pockets whose only purpose was to add complexity and cost in the manufacturing process. Anything put in them caused an obnoxious bulge; by common practice the pockets went unused. We discarded them. The contemporary jacket's buttons featured the official Air Force seal, an indecipherable amalgam of heraldic elements having no practical connection to our aviation heritage. We took as a new button design Hap Arnold's simple winged star, a symbol I'd already brought back to life as the unofficial badge of the Air Staff.

Another of our design objectives was to make the uniform standard for both the officer and enlisted force. On initial entry into the Air Force, our practice was to issue enlisted men a dress uniform of lower quality than that worn by officers. At their own expense, airmen could go to the BX and purchase the better, "optional" version—and nearly everyone did so. In designing a replacement, I wanted to reflect a shift in attitude about the officer-enlisted relationship. In a modern Air Force, the separation of officer and enlisted was (or should be) increasingly blurred. Officers have strong technical competence and NCOs assume broad leadership responsibilities. Where do we draw the line between management and labor? If this question was not hard to answer, we should change the organization, the people, or the job to make it so.

This view led me to believe that the rank for both officers and NCOs should be worn on the sleeve. This required no big change for enlisted ranks, though we made their chevrons brighter and bolder and put three stripes on top instead of a previous maximum of two, changes popular with the NCO force. For officers, we removed the shoulder epaulets and adopted the ring scheme used

1993 official photograph, in the new uniform.

*Chuck Horner, Ron Yates, and I have a laugh
at one of our heraldic dinners.*

With Defense Secretary Cheney and the Rev. Billy Graham.

Piotr Deynekin lands at Andrews to return my visit. Maybe we're happy we didn't have to fight each other.

On the Pentagon's E-Ring, I show Deynekin the Gray Eagle Award, given in succession to the Air Force's senior pilot by length of rated service.

Nellis AFB: Deynekin and I debrief after the first mock combat between Cold War air chiefs.

From USAF's art collection: "The Chief."

by the RAF and many other air forces (as well as the Navy and most airlines).³³

I also wanted to streamline the uniform by removing ornamentation. We changed instructions on wearing the uniform to permit display of only one aviation or occupational badge. We required grades through colonel to wear all decorations earned, but allowed general officers to wear all, some, or none, according to their wish. When I stopped wearing decorations, nearly all general officers noticed and followed suit. Epaulets, medals, colored ribbons, and flourishes of all kinds seemed to me more appropriate for the armed forces of lesser, more tranquil states.

One of my controversial decisions was to remove the "U.S." devices worn, again following the Army's lead, on the jacket lapel. Pinned on, these metal insignia did a little fabric damage each time and were difficult to get straight. Moreover, nobody confused us with anybody else's air force, so the identification function added no value. But my removal of the "U.S." collar devices prompted a strongly negative reaction within the Air Force. I persisted because we wanted design elegance that can be found only in simplicity. As I told the *Washington Times*, "We have de-glitzed the uniform, we like the look, and we plan to keep it that way. Let the next chief of staff worry about it." As was often the case, the question for me

---

33 This decision sparked great controversy, and Ron Fogleman, my successor as chief, immediately reversed it—too bad, since sleeve-style rank insignia for officers was linked, in a way, to our history. Specifically, in the run-up to forming an independent Air Force, Hap Arnold authorized a design effort for a distinctive airman's uniform. Four prototypes were developed, all with officer sleeve insignia like the RAF used. This was the design approach preferred by our first chief of staff, Carl Spaatz, and, incidentally, by Jimmy Doolittle. However, to speed production of the new uniform, we adopted Army rank as an interim expedient—and got stuck there until I took on the problem.

was, what sort of mistake do I want to make? I opted for too simple a uniform.[34]

In the end, we fielded a much higher quality, more comfortable, better looking service dress uniform that we issued as part of a lower-cost clothing inventory.[35] The new uniform was meant for all the troops, from basic airman to general officer, the only difference being insignia of rank. We set a five-year transition period in which airmen could wear either the old uniform or new one. Nevertheless, when it went on sale, the new uniform was an immediate hit, with many sales outlets running out of stock.

Some of our uniform design decisions have been reversed (as I fully expected), especially the lapel "U.S." devices and the matter of displaying officer rank. But the returning gadgetry is in some respects only trimming for the new uniform we created and, as this is written, continues to be worn.

The Air Force should be cautious when adding back the sartorial splendor. There are several versions of a famous list called "What Every Officer Needs to Know about Combat." It consists of

---

34 Too simple, indeed, for Jack Murtha, powerful chairman of the Defense Subcommittee of the House Committee on Appropriations. When I needed money to produce and begin testing a batch of the new uniforms, I went to see him, wearing a prototype of the design. He asked, "Where are your decorations?" I told him I didn't want to wear any. He said, "You better wear some if you want the money." Thereafter, I took to wearing a single row of ribbons. Again, most Air Force generals followed suit.

35 We projected total savings of about $3.5 million a year across the Air Force, but it was pretty hard to capture and verify this figure. For sure, the elimination of "optional" white and blue ceremonial uniforms saved individual service members $360 each. Also, the Air Force paid an annual cash clothing allowance to enlisted personnel to help defray the cost of replacing worn-out uniform items. The new design allowed us to lower the basic allowance (for members with three years' service or less) about 15 percent, to $187.20 for men and $212.40 for women.

one-liners, the last inventory I saw having 35 of them. Each piece of advice has been earned the hard way: "If it's stupid but works, it ain't stupid." "If your attack is going really well, it's probably an ambush." Piece of advice Number 35 is, "The side with the simplest uniforms wins."

Chapter 5

1993: Equip

The English Navy, since its inception by Alfred, has arguably been the most successful and efficient military construct ever made. It went on longer than the Roman legions, achieved more than Alexander's hoplites, Tamerlane and the Khan's cavalry, and it did so almost entirely by threats and blockades, and being too expensive to risk using.

—A. A. Gill, *The Angry Island*

Nineteen ninety-three was the Year of Equipping the Air Force. Why put it third? Why single out organization, then training, before turning a spotlight on the many vexing problems of equipment acquisition? I suppose Title 10 of the US Code establishes an order, making "organize, train, and equip" the accredited functions of a service department. But it is also true I put organization and training ahead of equipage as having more to do with combat success. Figuring out how to organize is the most important management decision affecting operational results. As for the importance of training, it can take a decade to develop a new weapon system but, if my case was typical, 20 years or more goes into producing a reliable wing commander.

Moreover, organization and training were subjects I thought I understood, whereas I was anything but an expert on hardware procurement, a process that was by then administratively complex in the extreme, every previous misstep having inspired extended, line-item remediation. Moreover, inside the Pentagon it seemed we were trusted to fix matters of organization and training. Though the equipment acquisition system was badly broken, and everybody knew it, we enjoyed no such autonomy regarding its repair.

But, in truth, I did not, could not ignore acquisition issues until year three. Big procurement programs are minefields that must be cleared and crossed in real time. More often than I like to say, a troubled hardware program slid under my office door, all covered with hair, wriggled across the room on its own excreted lubrication, hopped up on the desk, and tried to smile.

JDAM

JDAM was the exception. Something like 90 percent of all the munitions used in Desert Storm were dumb bombs, with which we achieved roughly the same results we had in Vietnam. Secretary Rice and I talked about the problem and agreed to push the design of an inexpensive, all-weather smart bomb. The idea was to take a general-purpose bomb and strap on a guidance kit consisting of movable fins and a cheap autopilot. Before drop, the aircrew provided target coordinates and the bomb received periodic GPS updates during fall. We stated an absolute minimum of requirements: 10-meter accuracy and a cost of $20,000 for the guidance package.

Acquisition experts quickly came back to argue for relaxed requirements: initially, a 13-meter CEP and $40,000 price tag. In order to get the program moving, I agreed, but never stopped pushing the original accuracy and cost goals. As it turned out, the program met the $20,000 cost objective and demonstrated a CEP of less than 5 meters. With this sort of miss distance, the main accuracy consideration is target location error—in other words, intelligence, rather than weapon guidance.

JDAM was not a miracle weapon; it did not solve every combat problem. For instance, iron bombs don't glide well, so you can't stand off as far as you'd like when attacking ground defenses. In its early format, it was not so good against moving targets. But it was cheap, and it didn't care about the weather. In addition, because it didn't need laser designation or electro-optical guidance, it could be dropped from internal bomb bays, suiting it for use by stealth aircraft. The performance of JDAM in subsequent engagements—Kosovo, Afghanistan, Iraq II—shortened the duration of intense combat and reduced casualties in exactly the way envisioned by the early airpower advocates.

I suppose Rice and I can claim to be the fathers of JDAM. If so, we can be proud of it.

START II

On 3 January, President Bush and Russian President Boris Yeltsin signed the START II Treaty. The treaty obliged each side to reduce total deployed strategic nuclear warheads to the range of 3,000–3,500 by the end of its final phase. All the land-based missiles would be single warhead, eliminating the most destabilizing and dangerous Russian weapon, the multiwarhead SS-18. START II continued the remarkable progress in diminishing both the number and threat of nuclear munitions already made in the Intermediate-Range Nuclear Forces (INF) and START I Treaties. Along with the chairman and the other service chiefs, I was delighted to support it.

Camp David Farewell

The president asked the Joint Chiefs and the justices of the Supreme Court, with spouses, up to Camp David on 16 January. Former prime minister and Mrs. Brian Mulroney of Canada were there also, along with Warren Christopher, Vernon Jordan, and

Boyden Gray. Country and western singer George Strait entertained with a nice version of "All My Ex's Live In Texas." This was only a few days before a new president would be inaugurated and George Bush, too, was about to be an Ex who lived in Texas, at least part time. Barbara Bush was her usual, upbeat self.

Clinton Inaugural

Three nights later Ellie and I were at the Capital Centre for Bill Clinton's inaugural gala, sitting next to Donna Shalala, about to become secretary of Health and Human Services. The entertainment was luminous, Fleetwood Mac, Thelonious Monk, and Michael Jackson among the performers.

Defense Budget Dynamics

Like the economy as a whole, we can think of defense spending as having components of investment and consumption. The investment accounts fund major construction and procurement—research, development, test, and purchase of new equipment. Consumption takes the rest of the money for training, equipment repair, consumables, and payroll.

It's not easy to keep defense investment and consumption accounts in equilibrium. The emphasis nearly everywhere is on consumption, a tendency reaching extremes in the developing world, where nearly all the money goes for pay, the army being a kind of jobs program in disguise. Even in countries fielding advanced military capabilities, it's the consumption part of the budget that enjoys strong public backing. These accounts pay, feed, and support people; if spent wisely, they create current readiness, an outcome seen as laudable even by political factions not ordinarily considered pro defense. At best, investment accounts may produce future readiness, though more likely evidence of incompetence or scandal, as every important defense-procurement program comes under continuous, withering political attack. Thus, defense investment is savaged during periods when security concerns are less stressful, a perverse outcome because the time to invest is when the threat wanes, when readiness can be relaxed somewhat, freeing resources to cultivate future capacity.

Among the services, the Air Force invests most and therefore as I came to office the Cold War's end had already had outsized impact on us. As a fraction of recent budgets, our investment accounts peaked in the late 1980s at about 48 percent, the crest of the procurement wave started by the Reagan administration. By 1991, Air Force investment had dipped to 40 percent of its budget, a number bringing us perilously close to the edge of causing much damage, in my view. I therefore tried hard to protect investment during the budget cuts associated with the Base Force, finding savings through reorganization and consolidation, quickly cutting wings and squadrons I knew we could not sustain, and diverting freed-up funding into equipment modernization—mostly to finish the B-2, continue the C-17, and start up F-22 production.

B-2

I was a big fan of the B-2, our stealthy long-range bomber then in development. Its imaginative design put us in a league by ourselves, gave us the unique capacity to project power quickly to any spot on the globe, against any defenses. The airplane was also very expensive, and the cost kept climbing, putting pressure on the size of the total buy. We aimed to procure 75 airplanes, already down from the original requirement for 132, and even before we got the first one fielded at an operational base, we were having big problems getting approval to go beyond the initial 20. (The House of Representatives had already voted to kill the program.) Northrop, the builder, rallied its considerable political muscle behind continued production, but the math was entirely too simple. Everybody saw we were getting the first 20 B-2s for an all-in cost of $40 billion. I had to face the reality of a resource environment in which the Air Force could not afford to buy airplanes at 2 billion dollars each.

So in the run-up to the FY 93 budget, we sent down to OSD a

proposal that stopped B-2 production at 20.[36] I got a call from Secretary Cheney. Might I come see him? We met privately. He wanted to hear it from me personally. The Air Force really didn't want more B-2s? I said we'd be delighted with twice as many, or more, but at the cost projections coming across my desk, I couldn't find room for it in the budget.

It was always hard to read Cheney, but I got the feeling my answer disappointed him. At any rate, he never raised the matter again.

F-22

In 1990 the Air Force selected a winner in the advanced tactical fighter competition. We required an air superiority aircraft to replace the F-15, moving us into the era of fifth-generation jet fighters. We wanted stealth, with no compromise in aircraft performance to achieve it. In addition we were looking for supercruise (the ability to cruise at supersonic speeds while in normal or "military" power, as opposed to afterburner),[37] very good maneuverability, and a high degree of avionics integration. Lockheed's F-22 won in a fly-off against Northrop's F-23—the right choice, as the F-22 was a better design in every respect.

After coming to office, I helped make a couple of decisions as the program moved into its development phase. For instance, there was much agitation about whether to use a side stick controller or the more conventional control-stick-between-the-knees configuration. The fight was between members of the F-15 community, who liked the center stick and who were, after all, the air superiority experts, and F-16 drivers, who by then had lots of experience with the side

---

36 Eventually, we ran the development test vehicle back through the line and brought it up to production standards, giving us 21 B-2s.
37 As one would expect, using afterburner increases the heat signature, but the much bigger jet wake also significantly boosts the aircraft's radar return.

stick controller. The argument got loud. I favored the side stick controller. It established a symmetrical condition—your other hand on the throttle—and seemed to set you up well for a high-g fight, making you feel tougher, if not actually become tougher. It also cleared out a lot of cockpit real estate between your legs. I rang up Mike Loh, who was by this time running TAC, and said I'd done it both ways and voted for the side stick. Why not just issue it to the F-15 guys? He agreed.

'Multiroling' the F-22

Many air superiority advocates wanted F-22 "purity," to make air-to-air combat the airplane's only possible use. Preserving stealth characteristics meant the aircraft would carry its weaponry internally, and when the production design was briefed to me, the weapons bay would accept only air-to-air missiles. There was some logic to this approach. For example, aircrews flying the multirole F-16 fighter were by design all-rounders, pretty good at a lot of things but usually not best at any one thing. On the other hand, F-15 pilots were really good at air-to-air because that's all they did.

Secretary Rice and I were convinced too much specialization would be a mistake. Naturally, we wanted to field the indisputably best air superiority aircraft, but we also knew that controlling airspace involved more than shooting down airplanes. We also had to clear out surface-to-air defenses. In fact, if we fielded the F-22 and if its capabilities came anywhere near meeting the requirements we'd set, it seemed unlikely we'd find anybody who wanted to fight us, air-to-air. Our control of battle airspace would more likely be contested by SAM defenses, and we had only the F-117 and B-2 for stealthy attack of this target set. Because of their aerodynamic shortcomings, these airplanes were usable only at night. (That's why we painted them black.) So if we wanted to maintain round-the-clock pressure on surface-based defenses, we'd need to make sure the F-22 carried air-to-ground munitions. The secretary and I therefore directed redesign of the weapons bay so we could download some of the F-22's air-to-air missiles and put in two 1,000-pound-class bombs. This made the F-22 a true dual-role aircraft—and, in my opinion, saved the program from cancellation at a later stage.

We were a little discouraged that not everyone in the Air Force welcomed, or even understood, this decision. Apparently some of the air superiority purists thought only about killing enemy fighter aircraft. But the real aim of air superiority is being able to operate anywhere, in any airspace you want.

Nunn's F-22 Input

The most painful F-22 issue concerned the various assaults on program size. We started with a requirement for 750 aircraft, which I'd helped establish when I was on the TAC staff at Langley and had programmed as Larry Welch's deputy for resources. With the price going up, we were down to 648 jets by 1992, and it seemed to me we'd not get even this number if we didn't figure out a way to hold down cost. So I went to see Sam Nunn.

In addition to the power he wielded as chairman of the Senate Armed Services Committee, Nunn was one of the few military veterans in Congress. He worked hard on military issues; his colleagues respected his expertise and listened to him. Lockheed was set to build the F-22 at its Marietta, Georgia, plant, which had a rich cargo aircraft heritage but no recent fighter experience. Our early observations confirmed Marietta's reputation as a high-cost producer. I simply didn't trust the factory to bring in the airplane at anywhere near our projected cost numbers. By contrast, another big Lockheed plant—the F-16 factory in Fort Worth—operated the most efficient, lowest-cost fighter production line in the world. I explained all this to Sam Nunn, asking that he support me in moving the program to Texas. He said, "Sure, go ahead and move it—if you want to lose it."

The program was much too important to risk losing Nunn's support. I'd been naive even to ask for this concession. I took a deep breath, crossed my fingers and hoped Marietta would get better at the job. As I expected, though, the price kept going up, and we were under constant pressure to resize the buy to keep total program cost in line. By the time I retired, we were down to 442 aircraft, not quite enough for four-and-a-half wings instead of the seven-and-a-half we'd first programmed.[38]

Nobody to Fight?

Defending the F-22 program proved difficult in the face of many who claimed it had been designed against a potent Soviet threat, but in the post-Cold War conflict environment outclassed any possible opponent. In other words, it was too good. If so, that was fine with me, and I thought it ought to be fine with the American people. We need to distinguish between forces we put in place to bound and manage future military competition and those we actually use in their primary role. We never used nuclear weapons during the Cold War, but it is highly unlikely we could have won it without fielding them and keeping them modern. The F-22 was an analogous capability whose existence meant we could operate over any part of the globe we wished, and no one in their right mind would come up to fight us.

Ron Yates

Following the demise of Air Force Systems Command (AFSC), the management workload for equipage was centralized in the new Materiel Command. AFSC had been badly needed in the early years of the Cold War when the Air Force was at the vanguard in such matters as computer and missile design. But now the commercial sector provided technical leadership where it mattered most, in the information technologies and, in addition, most responsibility for system acquisition had transferred to the secretary's staff under the Goldwater-Nichols reforms. So we now had one major

---

38 At this writing, the total F-22 program has been stopped at 187 aircraft, fewer than enough to outfit two standard wings, with associated training and maintenance bases.

command in charge of hardware development, acquisition, and support, a single organization providing life-cycle management for all our equipment. A giant, the new Air Force Materiel Command had 100,000 people and was responsible for spending most of the Air Force budget.

We put Ron Yates in charge, a selection that helped work many social issues. The "loggies" seemed to be winners in the merger because the new Materiel Command was located at Wright-Patterson, home of the old Logistics Command, whereas Systems Command, at Andrews, was shuttered. But selecting Yates to lead the new combination meant the first boss at Wright-Patterson would be the old boss at Andrews.

This wasn't the only, or even the most important reason to pick Yates. An accomplished research test pilot, Ron had much to do with building and fielding our two outstanding fighters—the F-15 and F-16—giving him world-class credentials with the research and development community. But he was much more than just a hard-core techie. An outsized character, brilliant and tough, Yates immediately won the affection and respect of the logistics community. He brought just the right set of qualities to clear away the underbrush and blend the two previously competing cultures into an integrated acquisition command—no easy job.

Option C

Congressman Les Aspin, chairman of the House Armed Services Committee, had taken a serious run at the Base Force in early spring 1992. Bringing good credentials and a good argument to the debate, he said the "top down" approach to reductions adopted by the Pentagon would simply produce "a smaller version of the force we built for the Cold War,"—he called it "Cold War Minus"[39]— not one reengineered for twenty-first-century security challenges.

---

39 The phrase was picked up and used by Bill Clinton during the 1992 presidential campaign.

In this, he was right. Instead of what we'd done at the Pentagon, he proposed a bottom-up or building-block approach, based on an "Iraq equivalent" threat we knew we could defeat with a "Desert Storm equivalent" of force structure. According to Aspin, a Desert Storm equivalent consisted of seven Army divisions, eight Air Force fighter wings, four aircraft carriers, and one and one-third Marine divisions. This was the baseline, Option A, for a series of force-structure alternatives developed by Aspin and his staff. His clear favorite, Option C, had more force structure in it than Option A because it was supposed to handle not only a Desert Storm, but also a Korea-sized contingency, a Panama-sized contingency, and various humanitarian missions—as well as provide a rotation base for forces stationed overseas. Option C could do all this, according to Aspin, and still cut the Base Force by a further three Army divisions, five active Air Force wings, and 100 or so Navy ships. Having bracketed Option C with the more draconian Options A, B, and D, Aspin showed he occupied the reasonable, middle ground.

I had a lot of heartburn with Aspin's proposal. For starters, Option C played favorites in the matter of who should supply the nation's airpower. Every service came equipped with its own large, highly capable tactical air force. As a consequence, the country had, to be sure, bought and paid for too much tactical airpower, in the process shorting other essential elements of military strength. There was no good reason for this; it was all part of a game—more like a long war of attrition, really—that started when we failed to consolidate airpower in the defense reorganization that followed World War II. Tactical airpower (TACAIR) was the arena in which the services competed for market share.

By the early 1990s, the Air Force was in pretty good shape to hold our own in this competition, since our fighter squadrons were by any objective standard both of better quality and less expensive to acquire and operate than the other flavors, an advantage I was fully prepared to leverage in the Pentagon in-fighting leading up to approved budgets and force levels. But Aspin's Option C, if accepted, would virtually decide the matter. Option C protected Navy carrier-based TACAIR. Moreover, though a cut was proposed for the Marines, their political clout would keep this from happening, as Aspin knew very well. So without saying so or providing any analysis to support the proposition, Option C made a pro forma determination that the Navy Department provided the sort of TACAIR the country should keep—a big mistake, in my view. Of course, my acquiescence wasn't required, but I had no intention of rolling over. I prepared to fight the issue both inside the executive department and in congressional testimony.

Desert Drizzle

I also did not like Aspin's arithmetic. His Option A, the "Desert Storm equivalent," was the product of creative accounting. The Air Force had sent 33 full fighter squadrons to the Gulf. I knew, because I pushed hard to get them into the theater. We'd fought Desert Storm not with the eight wings Aspin loaded into Option A, but with 11. Moreover, our wings were joined in the Gulf by fighter squadrons from the air forces of Britain, France, Saudi Arabia, and other alliance members. Thus, the land-based TACAIR that defeated Iraq was at least twice the size of the eight-wing force specified by Aspin as a "Desert Storm equivalent."

In March 1992 I appeared before the Defense Subcommittee of the House Appropriations Committee and was asked to comment on Aspin's force structure options. Under leading questioning from ranking Republican congressman Joe McDade, I described the analytical approach as "wrong in detail." Far from the equivalent of Desert Storm, Option A was more a Desert Drizzle, a picturesque usage invented on the spot, and one I regretted almost immediately. It caught the headlines and certainly resonated with Chairman Aspin. He hit back, releasing a statement that excoriated my testimony.

Returned from the Gulf War and serving as director of our

liaison office with Congress, Buster Glosson came by to say Aspin was irate. If the Air Force ever wanted anything out of House Armed Services—and we surely did—I'd better go make peace. I got an appointment and had a private chat with Aspin. I'd meant no offense. I was participating, as one would expect a service chief to do, in the debate about national security. Like the congressman, I wanted to do the right thing for the country. (I did not add that, regarding Desert Drizzle, I should be acquitted on the grounds that truth is no libel.) A thoroughly nice man, Aspin was gracious. We put the matter behind us, forgiven if not forgotten.

Aspin hired on as an adviser to Bill Clinton during his successful run for the White House, and the president-elect quickly chose him to succeed Cheney as secretary of defense.

That sinking feeling on the Pentagon's E Ring might just have been mine.

Bottom-Up Review

The Bottom-Up Review (BUR) was the opening salvo of Aspin's brief tenure as secretary of defense.[40] The secretary said he wanted a thorough reexamination of budget projections that would do two things: (1) further cut defense spending below reductions already made, and (2) produce forces better suited to address post–Cold War security concerns. Of course, these very parameters were stipulated (and, regarding point two, ignored) for the budget drill that had produced the Base Force. But Aspin was explicit: the BUR would provide written, analytical justification showing precisely how each proposal put forward achieved both objectives.

Major Regional Contingency (MRC)

In sizing the Base Force, Colin Powell had argued we must be big enough to conduct two simultaneous MRCs. The Clinton administration did not want to be seen as backing off this requirement, so

---

40 The study's name was a little unfortunate. The uniformed military started calling it the "Bottoms Up Review." Annoyed, Aspin and his staff were always careful about pronunciation.

the threat scenario for the Bottom-Up Review set the same objective. It then identified force levels needed for each MRC: four to five Army divisions, 10 Air Force fighter wings, three to five aircraft carriers, and something under two Marine divisions. Sized to do two MRCs, the result was a sensible 10 Army divisions, 20 fighter wings, 10 aircraft carriers, and three Marine divisions.

These totals established *active duty* force-structure targets, except for the Air Force. For the Air Force, and *only* for the Air Force, the goal of 20 fighter wings was for combined active and reserve force structure. Thirteen of the 20 proposed wings were to be active, the other seven coming from the Reserve or Air National Guard. I objected to the practice of separating us from the rest in this way, of measuring, marking, and cutting the Air Force differently from the other services, and lost this argument.

And then, force-on-force analysis done by the services and the Joint Staff during the Bottom-Up Review showed a painful shortfall of certain Air Force assets, like AWACS and reconnaissance aircraft, which are especially important in the early phases of any engagement. Since it seemed we couldn't afford to buy more, Aspin simply relaxed the timing requirement, which became two "near simultaneous" MRCs. Our critical assets would "swing," that is, put out the fire in the first MRC, then sequence to a second and, hence, near-simultaneous MRC.

Once told the answer, we could do the math.

Presence

The Bottom-Up Review validated the Navy's assertion that they must have four or five large-deck aircraft carriers in order to be sure of having at least one available for a major regional contingency. During staff deliberations, some had questioned the four or five multiple, but I thought the Navy was right. Counting time in the shipyard undergoing refit, an aircraft carrier spends by far the majority of its operational life tied up to a dock. Then there is steaming time spent in training and work to prepare for deployment, then cruising time to and from the area of employment. It was therefore quite reasonable to calculate, as the Navy did, that if you want to keep one carrier forward-deployed and available for use in a MRC, you must have three to five for Atlantic and Pacific stations, and perhaps even more for operations in the Indian Ocean or Persian Gulf. (The requirement is somewhat reduced for the Western Pacific when Japan-basing is assumed). Overall, the four to five guestimate is probably about right for planning purposes. The Navy can surge for the occasion, as it did with the six carriers sent to Desert Storm, but in normal times, one aircraft carrier buys us the capability to fight one-fourth or one-fifth of an MRC. To handle two MRCs, we therefore needed 10 large-deck aircraft carriers.

But 10 was not a large-enough number to justify the Navy's then existing and programmed carrier fleet. In another embarrassing adjustment, Secretary Aspin scrambled for a rationale: "If we base our carrier needs solely on the regional threats, we could end up with fewer than we need to maintain a strong carrier battle group presence around the world." He decreed that 12 large deck-aircraft carriers were needed for "peacetime presence."

Certainly, I did not object to sizing forces based on the requirement to deter, as well as to defend. And I agreed it was often productive to move naval forces so as to influence a situation, especially when it was impractical or would take too long to bring forces ashore. But just then the Navy was selling "presence" as a role belonging to them. In a crisis (they said) they had shown repeatedly that nothing can stop them steaming in international waters, or close ashore or just over the horizon, on station, present for duty. On the other hand, (they said) we could never be *sure* of getting access to bases needed to establish an on-shore presence.[41]

---

41 Our post-World War II experience should convince us of at least this: if we do not have international support that gives us access to bases in an area of operations, we should take another look at what we're about to do.

In response, my argument went something like this: "presence" is neither a role nor a mission. It is, rather, a force characteristic, like speed or mass or maneuverability, and all armed forces possess it to a greater or lesser degree. Ground forces have presence in that it is they who actually take and hold real estate. The Army (and the Air Force) had been physically present in Europe, Japan, and Korea, protecting our most vital interests for longer than half a century. After Desert Storm we'd imposed an air-policing regime over North and South Iraq. As we sat in Washington debating "presence," Air Force fighter aircraft occupied half of Iraq's airspace, night and day.

Of course, this sort of presence is all about geography or location, but we could also think of it as a function of time. The Red Army was less present in Europe, not only because of its removal from NATO's former Eastern frontier but also because it would need to mobilize to return, giving us time to react. In the same way, any foreign power contemplating action against us had to reckon with the speed at which we might deploy forces. F-15s had launched from Langley, Virginia, and landed in the Gulf only 15 hours later to begin forming Desert Shield. A B2 parked on the ramp in Missouri could be present at any spot on Earth in 24 hours or less, certainly faster than surface combatants could get there unless they started pretty close to the scene. So it was a mistake to think anybody had a monopoly on the business called "presence." It was a quality, an attribute of the combat forces of all services.

Moreover, using their own four to five multiple, one aircraft carrier buys us about three months of presence per year. Even if the Navy was granted an exclusive franchise on presence, they should find a less expensive way to fill the requirement. In Pentagon debates, the Navy preferred that only large-deck supercarriers be counted as providing presence. By far the largest combat vessels ever built, these ships were running to roughly 100,000 tons displacement, carried up to 85 aircraft and cost about $5 billion to build. (The embarked air wing added maybe another $5 billion investment and, to be sure, there was the added cost of the escort ships and submarines that comprised the carrier battle group.) No other country could afford even one such warship. We had 12, plus another dozen amphibious carriers used by the Marine Corps. Though these also were impressively large ships, they cost about a third as much to build and operate as the large-deck variety. While there was a clear difference in combat capability between the two types of ships, I saw no convincing evidence amphibious carriers were not every bit as "present" when they showed up somewhere—maybe more so, since they embodied the capability to come ashore with infantry.

I also argued we should rethink the whole issue of forward presence. In the new security circumstances of the post-Cold War era we were likely to have far fewer forces based overseas, at least in legacy occupation countries like Germany, Japan, and South Korea. Where we could build new bases relevant to new threats, we were likely to have smaller permanent parties—more of a rotational presence, at least for a decade or so. The presence that engenders confidence—trust and influence that will stand up in crisis times—is gained by sustained *engagement* with our allies through periodic deployments, military exchanges, and a well-designed military sales program. It was this continued engagement, the reality and perception that we were committed and involved, that we needed to protect, not necessarily the permanent (or even transient) deployment of forces.

This vision of a different kind of future presence would be much enhanced by a larger fleet, that is, not bigger ships, but a larger number of ships. I wasn't trying to tell the Navy how to spend its money, but our inventory of surface combatants and submarines was shrinking rapidly, an opportunity cost resulting from the commitment to build and operate more supercarriers than needed to execute the country's war-fighting strategy.

Cost

In Pentagon budget exercises, bare-knuckle prizefights refereed by political appointees, the senior civilian leadership is often bright enough to see what needs doing but is understandably reluctant to jump between uniformed officers who have spent a lifetime training for and practicing real combat, especially as the ability to compare capabilities and make tradeoffs is undermined by the absence of objective, agreed data on value and cost.

Value determination is always going to be at least somewhat subjective. It will never be easy to say whether an attack helicopter was worth two tanks or a carrier air wing was worth three cruise missile ships. Exchange value will be guessed at based on witness testimony or fashioned artificially in simulations that yield results the question-begging assumptions predict. It's real combat that determines real value, and that's too high a price to pay for the information.

But accounting for cost can be fairly scientific. During my time in the Pentagon, it was not. It was against the law and you could go to jail if you spent money Congress appropriated for one thing on something else. Pentagon accounting systems were therefore very good at telling you if you were about to do this. Appropriations had to be spent before they expired. As fiscal year-end approached, you could track with great confidence how much you still needed to spend. The Planning, Programming and Budgeting System (PPBS), set up by Robert McNamara, was pretty good for roughing in budget proposals and out-year funding. But a big part of the problem in doing something like the Bottom-Up Review was we could not agree on what anything actually cost.

At his first meeting with the Joint Chiefs, Aspin went around the table, asking each of us to recommend an important thing he should try to accomplish during his time as secretary. When my turn came I told him the Pentagon sorely needed an accounting system that would allow us to compare costs. He should hire an outside accounting firm to design and install such a system, and mandate its use in the Building and by all services. He would not see it done, I said, because it would take a decade, maybe more. But he should get it started. He said nothing, maybe surprised I didn't follow the lead of the other chiefs, all of whom supported a favorite weapon system.

The Blind Budget Cut

As will be seen from the table below, I was not effective in defending the Air Force position in the Bottom-Up Review, the upshot of which was to cut our active fighter force to about half the size it had been when I became chief. Worse, as with the Base Force, the BUR called for significant dollar and manpower cuts while refusing to consider roles-and-missions or tooth-to-tail reforms that might have made the smaller, less costly force a better servant of national security. No matter. Two months after coming to office, the Clinton administration chopped the already sharply reduced five-year defense budget by an additional $131.7 billion, based on little more than wishful thinking. All defense spending categories took hard hits. Investment accounts came under the most pressure as we went on something of a procurement holiday, with consequences we would fully understand only years later.

Force-Structure Iterations				
	FY 90	Base Force	Aspin's Option C	Bottom-Up Review
Army: Active Divisions	18	12	9	10
Marines: Active Divisions	3	3	2	3
Navy: Ships	545	451	340	346
Large Deck Carriers	13	12	12	12
AF: Active Fighter Wings	24	15	10	13

Aspin told the Air Force to meet the BUR force-structure objective of 13 active fighter wings by FY 99. Again, in order to plow money back into investment, I laid plans to get there faster. As a consequence, during the first half of the 1990s, the Air Force underwent something akin to demobilization, lopping off about 40 percent of the active force structure that had been present for duty during Desert Storm.

Visiting the Council on Foreign Relations

In April 1993 Army Chief Gordy Sullivan, Marine Commandant Carl Mundy, and I went to New York City for a Council on

Foreign Relations Roundtable Dinner. The subject was "Redefining the Roles and Missions of the Armed Forces." Admiral Stan Turner presided. It was nice to be back for a dinner at the council, where I still had friends on the staff, but my after-dinner remarks offended Gordy Sullivan. The council wants a frank give-and-take and encourages it by a policy of nonattribution. I was therefore candid in my assessment of the mess we'd so far made of service roles and missions. This seemed to catch Sullivan by surprise. He may have anticipated we would dish up the pabulum senior officers usually serve on this topic, which would have been an insult to the council. Never all that quick to adjust, he came off badly and may have felt ambushed because he had not prepared for lively debate.

Carl Mundy disagreed with me without being disagreeable. Like the Marine Corps he headed, Mundy did not feel threatened.

The Defense Planning Guidance

In an era of US military dominance (which may be short lived), it's pretty hard to create scenarios that can justify forces of the size we need or want—witness Aspen's drift from concurrent to "near simultaneous" MRCs, or his argument for aircraft carrier presence. Never mind. I couldn't imagine a force-sizing approach that was better or more realistic.

However, I was often at odds with OSD's Defense Planning Guidance (DPG), a slender, classified document used to set out rules for developing force structure plans. Often, the DPG went beyond policy to deal with employment concepts, which of course had force-sizing consequences. For instance, the document usually specified that, in some future trouble spot, we would first rely on allies to stop an invasion, then the United States would send in and build up combat power in preparation for a decisive counterattack. Finally, when everybody was ready, air, land, and sea forces would carry out a well-orchestrated, simultaneous attack. This format tracked best with Army doctrine and provided work for everybody, especially ground forces. The frustrating part: during the buildup, airpower would perform the limited roles of air defense and reconnaissance, in essence flying holding patterns until everybody else was ready to go.

Eighth Air Force did not sit in England waiting for D-day before starting to bomb Germany. The results were not so good, our technical capabilities pretty thin in the 1940s and our organizational and cultural fitness to employ airpower still shaky. But Albert Speer, an acute observer, understood. "The real importance of the air war," he said, "consisted in the fact that it opened a second front long before the invasion of Europe. That front was in the skies over Germany."

C-17

For many years, the Air Force relied on jet-powered C-141s and C-5s to carry time-critical cargo to overseas operating bases. Shipments were downloaded and transferred to the ground transportation system or put on the C-130, a turboprop that could fly into less-developed forward operating bases. The combination worked pretty well, but cargo handling and transfer took time, and equipment like main battle tanks would not fit into the narrow-body C-130. A new transport aircraft under development, the C-17, would deliver the Army's large, heavy equipment directly into forward bases previously accessible only by the C-130.

The C-17 came under attack from Congress, in part because Lockheed did not produce it. All three of our cargo mainstays—the C-130, C-141, and C-5—had been built in Lockheed's plant at Marietta, Georgia. Putting work into that factory suited the purposes of Sam Nunn, the Georgia senator and chairman of the Senate Armed Services Committee. But Lockheed had lost out in the competition to build the new wide-body jet transport, the contract going instead to the old Douglas plant in Long Beach, California. The Lockheed lobby, including Nunn, was not happy about it. Over on the House side, Armed Services Committee Chairman Les Aspin was also on the offensive. He didn't have an airplane factory in his district, but he had lots of heartburn about the C-17 program, charging bad management by McDonnell Douglas and, worse, deception on the government side. I thought he might be right in some of his criticism but disagreed entirely with the contention that he and his committee had been misled by the testimony of Air Force officials, including senior uniformed officers.

Much of the trouble in the C-17 program sprang from trying to execute a fixed-price contract. This contracting approach, popular with the Reagan administration, sought to give industry big incentives to control cost. If spending went through the roof, the contractor would have to foot the bill. Alternatively, industry management would seek ways to reduce cost so it could make more profit inside the fixed price. At least this was the theory, and it may make sense for mass-producing lawn mowers, but for relatively short runs of high-tech equipment, it's a recipe for turning a company upside down. Defense contractors knew this but nevertheless bid (and underbid) for contracts because it was the only way to get work. So the C-17 was in a constant cost crunch, with McDonnell Douglas not strong enough financially to handle a serious cash bleed. The senior military officers who got into trouble with Aspin did so primarily because they tried to be creative in keeping the company afloat, it not being clear what public interest was served by letting it go under.[42]

Another problem with the C-17: it was what you might call semi-joint. The Army was a serious partner when it came to stating requirements but not when it came to providing money. Like the baby who keeps banging his cereal spoon on the high-chair tray, it was all appetite and no assets. Take the famous case of the paratrooper seat. The initial Army specification called for a fiberglass seat that would hold a soldier weight of 310 pounds. Over

---

42 Eventually, McDonnell Douglas and the Air Force agreed to tear up the contract and replace it with a "cost-plus" arrangement, with each side putting up money to "cure" the program. The more-permanent fix involved the company's merger into Boeing as part of much-needed, industry-wide consolidation.

the decade the aircraft was in development, the Army increased the weight in increments to 400 pounds. We opposed the change because it seemed unreasonable and would take time and cost money, none of which cut any ice with the Army. After a three-year fight, we gave up and did a redesign. The outcome was actually pretty good because we got larger, stronger seats made of a Kevlar composite that provided both better protection and more comfort. But it added weight to the airplane, took time, and cost money, just as we knew it would.

Managing an Earthquake

For creating C-17 program turbulence, however, neither the faulty contracting approach nor the Army could hold a candle to Congress. Puts and takes each year had us constantly reshuffling, starting and stopping, stretching and rephasing. Both our intuition and experience tell us that constant change can be even more damaging than highly debatable but enduring decisions. Congressional meddling made running the C-17 program like trying to manage an earthquake. More than anything else, the program needed to be left alone.

Even before being sworn in as chief, I made a point of going to the C-17 plant at Long Beach. The company had produced and flown several prototypes already and the first production article was nearing completion. But work was way behind schedule and over cost. Top management at Douglas seemed asleep, the factory directionless. It was a mess, confirming Les Aspin's conclusions, if not his rationale.

The C-17 was going to be a great transport if we could keep it alive, so I made a polite phone call to John McDonnell, then CEO at McDonnell Douglas. New management appeared at Long Beach. I also sent a charge of high voltage through the Air Force's acquisition wiring diagram, getting the attention of people involved in program oversight. Ever so slowly the C-17 program began to right itself.

Enter Aspin

Neither Nunn nor Aspin were happy, Nunn because of the constituent issue and Aspin because he thought we'd lied to him. There was nothing I could do to please Nunn. As for Aspin, he got the upper hand when he came to the Pentagon as President Clinton's new secretary of defense. In one of his first actions, he demanded a review of the C-17 program, which resulted in a "request" that I fire three senior officers and two civilian officials, all because of perceived malfeasance. Former congressional staffers who had followed Aspin across the Potomac made it plain the demand for scalps was not negotiable.

I thought hard about what to do. I didn't like the way we'd managed the program but was convinced any mistakes made were honest. Nonetheless, I was getting direction from a brand new civilian boss. Swallowing hard, I asked four of the five to take their punishment, which they did. Following tradition, two of the officers requested retirement by sending me short, hand-written notes, showing a lot of class.

I thought one of the civilians in question, Darleen Druyun, had done impressive work on a variety of acquisition programs. She was quirky and a little off center, but I liked her and thought I had a shot at saving her, not least because of the Clinton administration's high-profile advocacy for women. I went downstairs to see Aspin privately, telling him I was willing to follow orders with all five of the "guilty" parties, but recommending he make an exception for Druyun because of her potential to continue making a valuable contribution. He relented, and we were allowed to keep her. She subsequently rose to considerable prominence and power as a senior Air Force acquisition official.[43]

John Deutch

Having extracted his pound of flesh, Aspin turned the C-17 program over to his acquisition deputy, John Deutch, to be "fixed." I

---

43 For me, at least, Druyun subsequently did good work. Some years after I left, she was charged, convicted and sent to prison for arranging a high-paying job for herself at Boeing, while at the same time negotiating Air Force contracts favorable to that company.

found Deutch an odd duck, a man of large ambition at work in a building where custom required self-centered career pursuit to wear camouflage. He believed himself smarter than anybody else, when, in fact, he was only very clever. Deutch treated me and the other service chiefs with exaggerated deference, always calling us "sir," with no hint of condescension. This was a clue to the undermining weakness—wanting so obviously to be liked—that made him an easy target for every kind of flattery. When we prepared him properly, he did the right thing on Air Force programs, but we were always careful to show how our recommendations would allow him to make decisions motivated by good government, rather than any narrow interest we brought to the table.

Over the period of a few months, Deutch worked on the C-17 program with me and with Ron Fogleman, by then serving as commander of Air Mobility Command. We (mostly Fogleman) led Deutch through a series of briefings that built up his understanding of how and why the C-17 offered such a good solution to long-standing mobility problems and—voila!—suddenly the C-17 was back on track, an outstanding example of how intelligent oversight can mend even a very troubled program.

After Aspin left office, Bill Perry became SECDEF and Deutch moved up to be Perry's deputy. Of course, Deutch subsequently went to Langley to succeed Jim Woolsey as director of Central Intelligence.[44]

Delivering the C-17

In July 1993, I flew the first C-17 delivered to an operating base—Charleston AFB, South Carolina. General Binnie Peay, the Army's vice chief of staff, rode in the jump seat. The aircraft

---

44 Deutch left the CIA after 18 months, replaced by George Tenet. Following his departure, charges surfaced that he'd been (to put the best face on it) careless with classified materials. A more or less continuous brouhaha continued until Clinton preempted it on his last day of office by pardoning Deutch.

featured a side-stick controller rather than the traditional big airplane control wheel. I'd worried about this for some time, as Douglas had put the thing on the pilot's left console. The copilot's stick was on his right, so aircrews would spend years learning to fly right-handed, only to switch when they moved into the left seat to become pilot-in-command. This didn't make much sense to me beforehand, but after shooting a few touch-and-goes, I saw the jet was so easy to fly it wouldn't make much difference.

Among others, the state's two senators, Strom Thurmond and Ernest Hollings, were at Charleston to hear me call the C-17 "the new cornerstone of the nation's mobility fleet." Our experience with the aircraft ever since has confirmed this assessment.

Haiti and North Korea

In March 1993, North Korea announced it planned to withdraw from the Nuclear Nonproliferation Treaty and would refuse to allow continued inspection of its nuclear sites. We had direct, two-party talks in June and July. These negotiations deadlocked, and over the next few months we pursued a two-track approach, pushing for graduated international sanctions and at the same time planning a military response. The Joint Staff (during this time coming under the chairmanship of John Shalikashvili) and field commanders in the Pacific and Korea worked nights and weekends on military options. By the spring of 1994, North Korea was unloading spent fuel rods from its 5-megawatt reactor that could be reprocessed into weapon-grade fissile material. In June 1994 we announced reinforcement of our forces in the South, including the movement (by surface ship, so it would take a while) of Patriot missile defenses.

But also in June, Jimmy Carter rode to the rescue, visiting Pyongyang as a "private citizen" and getting agreement from Kim Il Sung on outline terms leading eventually to the so-called Agreed Framework, under which North Korea would abandon its graphite-moderated nuclear reactors for less threatening light-water reactors that we would provide. Carter deserved the Noble Peace Prize he won, partly as a result of this effort. Nevertheless, we all felt the air go out of the balloon we had pumped pretty hard to inflate.

At the same time we were working on the North Korea nuclear issue, the Haitian refugee problem heated to a boil. Jean-Bertrand Aristide had been elected president of Haiti in 1991 and deposed shortly thereafter in a military coup led by General Raoul Cédras. The Cédras regime was responsible for an alarming increase in the level of violence and a large-scale exodus of citizens to Florida. (The US Coast Guard rescued more than 41,000 Haitians in 1991 and 1992.) The United States and United Nations worked hard to restore legitimate civilian rule, and made some progress. However, in early October 1993, armed "civilians" turned back the USS Harlan County, carrying UN military personnel into Port-au-Prince. Thereafter, Southern Command and the Joint Staff started planning an invasion. We spent a lot of time on the effort and even kicked off the opening phases of the invasion in mid-September 1994. We got close to forcible entry, but another last-minute deal negotiated by Jimmy Carter, with Sam Nunn and Colin Powell assisting, led to an uneventful landing of US troops who were able to occupy the island and disarm junta supporters.

Should North Korea ever develop nuclear weapons it would impinge directly on the vital interests of four great powers: China, Russia, and Japan, because they are close neighbors, and the United States because of our history with and continued presence in South Korea. Moreover, nuclear arms in North Korea could quickly become a threat to US territory in Guam, or even Hawaii, Alaska, and the US West Coast, longer term. By contrast, though Haiti was nearby, a source of refugees, and a country we had occupied from 1915 to 1934, it could hardly be argued that a vital national interest required military intervention there.

I was on the sidelines for both these crises, little more than an interested observer at JCS deliberations. What struck me was we worked at least as hard on Haiti as we did on North Korea—if anything, maybe harder on Haiti. After all, there was no film footage of North Koreans bolting together nuclear bombs, but we kept seeing drowning Haitians every night on the evening news. Understandably, Washington reacts to graphics. But we pay a president to decide what's important, what the country should be working on hardest. No doubt Clinton was a fast learner, but at least early in his presidency he showed no real talent for setting national security priorities.

Airborne Laser

One morning a small group of officers came to me with a briefing the thrust of which was we might be able to package a high-power laser in a wide-body jet and defeat incoming ballistic missiles. Until quite recently, we hadn't shown we could deal with a significant problem: atmospheric disturbances that complicate the tracking and aiming problem. But now, some highly classified research work promised a solution. These officers wanted $50 million to do additional research and begin sketching out a program.

We didn't have $50 million to spare, but the idea intrigued me. As long ago as the mid-1960s, when the Vietnam War more or less forced us to adopt the Navy's F-4, there had been some loose talk about putting a laser, instead of a conventional gun, in our version of the aircraft, a concept quickly dismissed as impractical owing to weight, power, and cooling considerations. Now, three decades later, it might be possible to package such a system in a very large airplane.

My problem was, if the initial $50 million exploratory investment revealed no show stoppers, we'd need a lot more money to produce a flying prototype, at least an order of magnitude more. And then, if the prototype worked, we'd need to build a squadron—maybe 20 aircraft or so—with the planes costing a billion dollars or more, each. The problem would go away if, somewhere along the line, we found the concept unworkable, but could we stand good news?

I told them to go ahead. We'd find the $50 million.

Sheila Widnall

Beginning 13 July, I served a short hitch as secretary of the Air Force, the first uniformed officer to do so. The Clinton administration was slow in nominating and getting new service secretaries confirmed, so Mike Donley, a holdover from the Bush administration, had been kept on for a while as an interim. Donley was not a hit with Aspin, who finally decided to let him go, even if appointing me acting secretary undercut the principle of civilian control of the military—sort of.

I was now in a position to tell myself what to do but hadn't figured out how to leverage this blessing by the time we got Sheila Widnall, the first woman secretary of any service, and a first-rate one at that. I admired Secretary Widnall, who came to the Air Force from MIT, where she'd earned a doctorate, stayed on to teach aeronautics, and become one of the most prominent American women in science and engineering. Smart and surprisingly tough, she consistently made the right choices, for the right reasons, in issues brought to her for decision. She loved to fly, making me envy how often she found an opening to do this. From beginning to end, she was a respected friend, as well as boss.

Dinner with Hillary

On Tuesday evening, 10 August, the president and Mrs. Clinton hosted a White House dinner in honor of senior military commanders. Ellie was out of town, so I went unaccompanied. As luck would have it, I was seated next to the first lady. An excess of ego made me wonder whether this arrangement was purposeful, perhaps a semiofficial sniff check in connection with Colin Powell's succession. If it was, I was a multidimensional failure. Never gifted at small talk, the occasion brutally exposed my social shortcomings. I tried hard, and too obviously, but could find no common ground. Maybe opposites attract: Hillary seemed as distant as Bill was approachable. The silences lengthened; I considered escape tactics. Empathy was supposed to be her long suit. Maybe I could fain a limp. Then we could talk about how hard it is to remove all the shrapnel when you undergo expedient battlefield surgery. She fled me at speed following the conquest of dessert. I cannot remember a more uncomfortable evening.

Tuskegee Airmen

In August I spoke to the 22nd National Convention of the Tuskegee Airmen, in Sacramento, saying how proud the Air Force was of this group. I was told this was the first time a chief of staff had addressed their national convention. Afterward, Sam O'Dennis was delegated to offer me honorary membership. I told him instead I wanted to be a dues-paying, actual member. I became Tuskegee Airman number 3062.

UAVs

Unmanned aerial vehicles (UAVs) had been employed in various combat roles for a long time. The impetus to increase their use for spying was pushed hard after Gary Powers got his U-2 shot down by the Russians in 1960. Sometimes you'd rather not risk the embarrassment of human capture. Then, too, there are locations—space is one of these—where it's just too expensive to man-rate the vehicle.

The Israelis made good use of UAVs as faker targets in their dramatic 1982 victory over the Syrian Air Force in the Bekaa Valley. Horner did something similar in the opening minutes of Desert Storm, inducing ground-based defenses to spend their ammunition on drones, in the process exposing their own positions.

Inside the Pentagon, UAVs had lots of backing from civilian budget analysts whose soundest argument was that, going back to Richthofen, fighter pilots had shown themselves to be ambitious, glory-seeking egomaniacs, arrogant, and unpleasant to deal with. By contrast, drones didn't talk back. In points that were easier to counter, they also asserted UAVs were not less effective in combat and cheaper to buy. When the Clinton administration came in, the strength of the UAV lobby was greatly enhanced.

Even though I thought drones had, for the moment, limited combat value, I would have gladly spent more on them, if they were cheap enough to be regarded as disposable, throwaway items. In fact, we were already operating drones, and that's exactly the way we did treat them. Those that did not come back were written off without even a momentary pang of conscience, as the accidents involved no eye-catching human loss. But the OSD position was we should give drones a greatly expanded combat role and fund their procurement and operations with money taken from the manned aircraft accounts.

In considering an enhanced role for UAVs, I began with reservations about their effectiveness in a fast-moving combat environment. In my judgment—and maybe not forever, but certainly for the foreseeable future—drones of a size large enough to carry weaponry were sure to lose any contest with manned fighter aircraft. Therefore, we could use UAVs in an offensive combat role only if we commanded the air. In this respect, drones were just like any other piece of equipment on the modern battlefield; their use, indeed their continued existence, depended on air superiority. And achieving air superiority required manned aircraft, precisely what we were being asked to exchange for UAVs.

My thinking was reinforced by skepticism about projected cost savings. The human brain is, after all, a very advanced information processor. Moreover, it can be acquired at relatively low cost. (It is, to be sure, the product of unskilled labor.) In the early 1990s, there was not much data on cost, but drones designed for roles beyond basic low-altitude reconnaissance would surely turn out to be expensive.[45] I argued that, for that moment, the only place sophisticated drones were cost effective was in orbit, or for

---

45 A lot of time and money has since been spent trying to prove UAVs are more cost effective than manned aircraft. This may be correct, one of these days, but the track record so far has been disappointing with regard to both cost and effectiveness. The recent data are closely held, but as of the turn of this century, the Defense Department had started at least nine UAV programs that eventually were canceled. More than $1 billion was spent on the Army's Aquila program alone before it was terminated. I do not know the actual numbers, but it looks like Global Hawk, a high-altitude, long-endurance reconnaissance drone, may cost more than twice as much as an F-16 and have an accident rate two orders of magnitude worse.

planetary exploration, where the cost of supporting human beings was radically high.

Besides, if it made so much sense, why not unmanned combat systems at the Earth's surface? UAVs maneuver in three spatial dimensions, plus the dimension of time is more unforgiving. Technically, operating an unmanned tank or naval combatant ought to be an easier problem.

Here was yet another issue about which I judged we were in a losing battle, long term. But during my time the Air Force was able to hold the line pretty well.[46]

Israeli-Palestinian Agreement

On 13 September 1993, I was seated on the White House lawn for the signing ceremony of what was billed as the Israeli-Palestinian Agreement. Visibly ill at ease, Yitzhak Rabin got cornered into shaking hands with Yasser Arafat.

UK Visit

In October 1993, as part of a visit to the United Kingdom, Mike Graydon and I flew up to Leuchars, the RAF station located near Edinburgh. Mike had scheduled me to fly the interceptor version of the Tornado fighter, like the F-4, a two-seater. We went to the base the day before to spend some time in the simulator so I could get used to the cockpit setup and figure out how to start the jet. The next morning, Mike and I took off as a two-ship and did some defensive patrolling against other aircraft simulating hostile penetration of British airspace. Later that same day, we drove round to play the Old Course at Saint Andrews. My total score was in the stratosphere, but I managed to birdie both nine and eighteen. Mike also birdied nine, but I rolled a short putt in on top of his. Eighteen

---

46 For modern, Type A war, I'd argue that putting human beings close to the action is still best. But the armed drone could be one of the answers to effectiveness in Type B war, where we have otherwise been rather unsuccessful. If so, this may be a case where Special Operations Forces should command the deep battle, because of their special relationship with the intelligence community.

was just dumb luck, a curling, side-hill 40-footer I had no business making.

So I knew exactly what heaven is like: a fighter sortie in the morning, followed in the afternoon by a round at the birthplace of golf, with birdies when the bets are pressed.

The F-35

The F-16 had been procured, along with the F-15, as the low end of a high/low mix. At the time, we thought it wouldn't be a spectacular performer at any particular task, but would be OK for many, and cheap enough to let us fill out a projected 40-wing fighter force. Of course, the little jet fooled us by performing beautifully, doing everything we asked and more. But it had an 8,000-hour airframe life and would have to be retired beginning no later than about 2015, and maybe sooner, depending on how hard we used it. We had to start thinking about the F-16 replacement.

We followed a winding and tortured path to the Joint Strike Fighter (eventually, the F-35). I mention here only the highlights. First, we could have decided to upgrade the F-16, producing something like the Block 60 aircraft later built for the United Arab Emirates. This would be a highly capable airplane and much less expensive than starting from scratch with a new design, so lots of people inside the Air Force supported this approach, and, naturally, it had the backing of the manufacturer, Lockheed.

But there was no practical way the F-16 could be made truly stealthy. It was small, hard to see in a fight, and had a diminutive radar cross section, but we had not designed it from the wheels up for stealth, so there was a limit to what we could do regarding signature suppression. This fact made it an easy call for me. I thought we should never buy another nonstealthy combat aircraft, and had said so in public. We'd stopped buying the F-15E, a great jet and a solid performer in Desert Storm, for that reason (and because we had to free up dollars for other programs). There was a brief fight inside the Air Force but, by mid-1992, I was able to tell the House Armed Services Committee, "When I speak (of an F-16 successor aircraft) I mean an entirely new small fighter design." By this time we were calling the F-16 replacement program the Multi-Role Fighter (MRF). Early concept work predicted quite good performance and reasonable cost. We knew there was also a large foreign market, which would further mitigate costs.

Meanwhile, the Navy was trying to build a stealthy, medium-range ground attack aircraft to replace the A-6. Eventually designated the A-12, this was a flying wing design, a sort of miniature B-2. The Navy wanted side-by-side seating, a bad decision making stealth harder to achieve because of increased frontal cross section, and presenting interesting problems in carrying structural loads across the back of the airplane.

The A-12 never saw the light of day. Following the disclosure of severe cost and schedule overruns, the program was canceled in 1991. But the Navy quickly started another program aimed at more or less the same objectives. The CNO, Frank Kelso, asked that I bring the Air Force into this program, fashioned the A-X, to help spread the development cost. Experience warned me the cost benefits would be theoretical, but I agreed anyway because an Air Force version of the A-X could replace the F-111, and eventually the F-117 and F-15E. If anything could be salvaged from the earlier A-12 work, we might be able to squeeze in A-X procurement toward the end of the F-22 production run and just before we ramped up funding for our F-16 replacement, the Multi-Role Fighter.

I flew out to the McDonnell Douglas plant at St. Louis to take a look at leftovers from the canceled A-12 effort. What I saw made me feel good about Air Force programs, bad as they sometimes were, and pretty well convinced me the A-X was not going to make it, at least not before we'd need to spend our money on the MRF. We continued the formality of A-X support, but the Navy got crosswise with Congress trying to hurry the program and tied itself in knots with internal arguments about an air-to-air capability that might be added to the airplane so it could replace the F-14 as well as the A-6. In less than a year, the scheduled date to field the A-X slipped two years.

The Bottom-Up Review canceled the A-X and (sadly) our MRF, and pushed the Navy and us together into a program called Joint Advanced Strike Technology (JAST), which quickly became the Joint Strike Fighter (JSF), and eventually the F-35. The F-35 was meant to replace a variety of legacy aircraft, everything from our A-10 and F-16, to the Marine Corps' Harrier and F/A-18A/B, to just about every type of shooter on a carrier deck.

It was not difficult to see why the Navy needed such an aircraft. They had aircraft carriers and needed to populate the decks. They were late getting into the stealth business, with the result they'd been forced, at high cost, to develop a follow-on version of the F/A-18, the F/A-18E/F, which, owing to its observability, was obsolete at birth and would in any case only just about meet performance requirements laid down for the F/A-18A/B. The F-35 program gave the Navy a chance to get the F-18 experience behind them and enter the modern world of stealthy attack.

While the Navy's requirement was solid, the modifications needed to produce their version of the F-35 would make it a quite different aircraft. It would have to be beefed up for carrier deck operations. In a typical engineering spiral, it would therefore need to carry more fuel to get the required range. The wing would be bigger (eventually, 540 square feet versus 450), which meant it would be even heavier and have to be beefed up some more for carrier-deck operations. In the end, the Navy's F-35 would cost a lot more (at least a 30 percent premium) and many of the supposed economies of logistic commonality evaporated.

The Marine Corps said the F-35 had to have short-takeoff and vertical-landing performance, even though Marine STOVL fighters had no record of combat use—hadn't even deployed to a crisis area except in the company of other, non-STOVL air units. Since the F-35 program sought minimum life-cycle cost, a common engine was mandated for all versions. Putting a STOVL engine in the JSF penalized the Air Force and Navy because a cheaper, lower-risk engine optimized for high-speed flight and greater fuel economy would have been a much better match for Air Force and Navy requirements. Moreover, the larger Air Force buy subsidized the significant cost and risk inherent in the STOVL specification.

Marine Corps participation in the program should have raised the larger question of why they needed an aircraft capable of covering the full spectrum of missions, from grass-strip CAS to high-speed deep strike. (Indeed, we all ought to wonder why the United States needs three fast-jet air forces.) But no one in authority in the Department of Defense questioned the Marine requirement, an example of bureaucratic and political clout controlling acquisition decisions.

On a cost, schedule, and performance basis, I think it undeniable that the country would have come out ahead had the Air Force been allowed to pursue the Multi-Role Fighter. The compromises required to lash together the various requirements meant the Air Force would never get the aircraft it should have had. The F-35 will be stealthy and will turn out to be a good airplane. Just not surprisingly good, like the F-16.

In the end, multiservice procurement of major combat end items is not about improving performance. The saving grace of such programs is their potential to contain cost, though of course they don't do that either.

Going to Central Europe

Following the collapse of the Warsaw Pact, we had a grand opportunity to establish airman-to-airman relations in Central and Eastern Europe. I thought it important to exploit this opening and was, I believe, the first US service chief in the post-Cold War era to make official visits to Poland, Romania, the Czech Republic, Bulgaria, and the Slovak Republic. The air chiefs of these countries responded enthusiastically, part of the euphoria of being free at last to reach out to the West.

During my initial visit to the Polish Air Force, I arrived at Warsaw's airport in the late afternoon and was met by their air chief, Jerzy Gotowala. He took me straightaway to the Chopin Museum.

This is in the Ostrogski Palace, which sounds rather grand but is instead a modest structure. There, in a small, upstairs auditorium, the substantial Madam Maria Korecka appeared in formal dress, sat down at the piano and filled the evening with waltzes, mazurkas, etudes, a polonaise. Afterward, Gotowala gave her a well-deserved bouquet. Perhaps six of us attended this evening recital, an indelible memory.

In Slovakia, Stefan Gombik's aircrews were virtually grounded, there being little money available for flying training. He arranged for television coverage of my visit and asked that I criticize his government on the grounds that shorting his Air Force endangered flight safety. I managed to get through the interview without damaging US-Slovak relations, but Gombik was not happy with me.

Gombik also insisted that I fly the L-29 (the aptly nicknamed "Albatross"), a trainer aircraft Slovakia was interested in marketing to other air forces. I had scheduled only a very brief visit to Bratislava and in the trip planning, my staff had repeatedly said no to the flight because of time constraints. However, as I stepped from Speckled Trout onto Slovak soil, they walked me directly to a nearby L-29. I got strapped in, but had a hard time communicating with the instructor pilot in the rear seat. The interphone was one of those World War II contraptions with a throat mike you had to press up against your vocal chords, like John Wayne in *Flying Leathernecks*. I couldn't get it to work but it didn't matter, since the guy in back spoke no English. A crew chief got the airplane started and once the chocks were pulled I couldn't taxi straight. I kept looking for a nose wheel steering switch but it turned out the aircraft is taxied (like the T-33) with differential braking, which I should have guessed, but didn't. So, the IP taxied us to the runway and got us lined up. I took the aircraft, knowing I could steer it with rudder once we got the takeoff roll underway. I got airborne, did about 10 minutes of aerobatics, and landed. After touchdown, I raised my hands to signal to the IP that he had control of rollout and taxi back. After shutdown, I asked a translator to tell the crew chief that the exhaust gas temperature gage had failed in flight. It had simply gone to zero and since the engine was still running, I knew it was a false indication. However, this is an important indicator of engine condition, so I thought they should fix it before the next flight. After a brief conference in Slovakian, I was told that the IP had "taken command" of the EGT gage, which (incredibly) could indicate in only one cockpit at a time.

In the Czech Republic, I toured an air base the Russians had abandoned, formerly a key installation in the Warsaw Pact air order of battle. It was no real surprise to see the buildings gutted—windows broken, wiring pulled out, plumbing fixtures removed or shattered. But the acreage had been turned into an environmental catastrophe, thick with every kind of industrial pollution. It will be years before the Central European countries clean up the mess the Russians left.

The US ambassador in Prague hosted a small dinner for my party and a few high-ranking Czech military. Beforehand, I asked to make the after-dinner toast. The embassy staff consented, looking nervous, as though anticipating a rift in US-Czech relations. My toast was brief, but I worked in references to both Dvorak and Smetana. This maneuver was greeted with smiles all round. Even the ambassador seemed pleased, if a bit surprised.

Senior-Officer Promotion

I'd had to deal with a sensitive personnel issue even before I swore in as chief. For many years, the Air Force had used a two-track system to grade the performance of full colonels and generals of one- and two-star rank. Officers holding these grades continued to be evaluated in "open" forms available to them for review, but in addition the general officer next above them in the chain of command rated their performance in handwritten, "closed" forms. The ratee could not see closed forms; indeed, they were available only to very senior officers and promotion boards. That such a rating system even existed was protected information; I learned of it only when I got involved in writing closed forms. Naturally, promotion boards saw the closed form as a more candid assessment of potential. While not entirely ignoring open-form evaluations, they came close to doing so.

In addition to the closed form, four-star generals submitted to each promotion board a recommended promotion list that lined up candidates working for them in an order of merit. The president of a promotion board reviewed these lists, with the result that board recommendations usually did not stray far from the wishes of sitting four-stars.

After the promotion board had completed its work but before its members were released for return to normal duties, the board president briefed the chief and secretary, which opened the possibility, at least, that the board president could be sent back with instructions to do some tweaking of the list. As a consequence of these various procedures, Air Force four-stars, especially the chief, were in firm control of senior-officer promotion.

As I came to Washington to assume duties as chief of staff, I had no argument with the way this system worked. I was myself the product of it. Anyway, who better to choose future Air Force leadership than the people at the top, people who had given their lives to building the organization, who had themselves been tested and found to be the most competent? However, the Senate Armed Services Committee—especially its chairman, Sam Nunn, and his senior staff assistant, Arnold Punaro—had serious concerns about our practices, which they regarded as circumventing strict guidelines that barred "communicating" with promotion boards while they were in session. The long-standing prohibition on communication was meant to protect promotion boards from any attempt to influence their deliberations. One could argue that the processes used by the Air Force—including closed-form evaluation, four-star order-of-merit lists, and prebriefing results to the chief and secretary—violated the spirit, if not the letter of the law. Moreover, we'd never revealed that this was how we picked and promoted generals. Nunn felt we had been much less than candid with him and made the point forcefully in my confirmation hearings and in behind-the-scenes arm-twisting. I didn't try to defend the system, admitting our procedures were suspect and promising to review and change them. The secretary and I subsequently did so, reforming the senior-officer promotion system and bringing it in line with mandated policy. In a speech I made at about the same time, I said,

> No matter how bad the problem, no matter how difficult the circumstances, the Air Force as an institution does not, will not, and cannot accept anything less than absolute, rock-solid, uncompromising integrity.

Frankly, I was never comfortable talking about integrity, a quality, like patriotism, too often meant for display. Especially in our nation's capital, when someone gets lyrical about integrity, it's time to button up your wallet pocket. Often, integrity is a perishable, eroded by the give-and-take needed to get anything done. In time, my character too would come under attack, especially in connection with the Glosson Affair (see below), and my successor would be seen as needing to tackle the job of "restoring Air Force integrity."

But coming clean in this early encounter with Sam Nunn and Arnold Punaro paid dividends over the next four years. Nearing the end of my term, in an October 1994 headline, *Defense News* called Air Force credibility a "front burner" issue with the Senate Armed Services Committee. Even so, the accompanying article quoted Punaro as having "nothing but praise" for me:

> McPeak is straightforward, outspoken and blunt, sometimes to his detriment . . . When he comes over here and says something, we think it's accurate. My view is you can take what he says to the bank.

The Glosson Affair

Returning from my trip to Central European air forces, I walked into a gathering controversy involving one of my closest associates, Buster Glosson, and three other senior Air Force officers, two of whom, Lt. Gen. Mike Ryan and Maj. Gen. Dick Myers, would later achieve high station.[47] Ryan, Myers, and Lt. Gen. John Nowak, then serving on the Air Staff as DCS/Logistics, had been tagged for duty as members of the FY 94 Promotion Board considering brigadier generals for promotion to two-star. During my absence, these three officers reported to the vice chief, Mike Cairns, that Glosson had talked to each of them, declaring that he knew I wanted to block the promotion of a certain officer. Had such conversations occurred, they would have been highly irregular, exactly the sort of improper communication with promotion boards that I had pledged to end. Glosson denied the charges. He may have chatted with Ryan and the others, but he had in no way tried to influence their promotion board deliberations. It was not obvious how the stories of the two sides could be reconciled, so, just prior to my return, Cairns asked the inspector general to start an investigation.

Had I been present for duty when the argument started, it's just possible I could have straightened it out with minimum internal bleeding. But once a formal investigation was launched, there was no way to turn it off. In any case, I was myself involved. If the charges were true, Glosson had acted in my name, making a claim he represented my wishes. Everybody knew Glosson and I were close, so others could assume he might in fact be the vehicle for undertaking something I wanted done quietly.

Any assessment of lineups in this dispute would have to favor the Ryan/Myers side. Both men were highly regarded by everybody,

---

47 Ryan went on to run the air combat operations in Bosnia-Herzegovina that led directly to the Dayton Peace Accords. On promotion to four-star, he became commander of US Air Forces in Europe in 1996. In 1997, he became the Air Force's 16th chief of staff, following the footsteps of his father, General John D. Ryan, our seventh chief of staff. Myers served successively as commander, Fifth Air Force; commander, Pacific Air Forces; commander in chief, US Space Command and NORAD; vice chairman of the Joint Chiefs of Staff, and in 2001, became the 15th chairman of the JCS.

including me. I liked them, had played a role in their recent respective career successes, and would continue to help them following resolution of the Glosson Affair. They were absolutely straight, widely credited with rock-solid honesty. In a sense, they represented the best the Air Force had to offer, maybe not brilliant, but plenty smart, and absolutely reliable, highly effective, old school insiders.

By contrast, Glosson was extraordinarily bright, a gifted maverick, as much an outsider as it was possible to be and still make headway in a big bureaucracy. His perceived freelancing had gotten him in trouble with Larry Welch, a prototypical insider, and nearly ended his career. But I was different, something of a maverick myself and, as I got more authority, keen to spot others and provide protective cover. Glosson had done much to resuscitate his career with a superstar performance in Desert Storm, and Don Rice and I had completed the rehabilitation by giving him first the key job as the secretary's liaison with Congress, then promoting and putting him in the important three-star DCS/Operations position, after only a year's service as a two-star. But my link to Glosson went beyond sponsorship. Mavericks often make others uncomfortable and are not always easy to like. Not so with Glosson. Our relationship was built on affection as well as professional respect.

With the change in administration, Secretary Rice was no longer there to help Glosson. The new secretary, Sheila Widnall, was also high on Glosson, though perhaps not as supportive as Rice. She wanted to let the IG's investigation go wherever it went and deal with the findings, which was exactly the right approach, of course. In view of the personalities involved, she asked that the DOD IG get involved in what then became a dual investigation.

Meanwhile, downstairs in OSD, Glosson had lots of powerful support. The new SECDEF, Les Aspin, admired Glosson, as did some influential staffers Aspin had brought with him from Capitol Hill. Moreover, Glosson had strong allies in Congress, including

Senator Sam Nunn. If the investigation came down against Glosson, I'd have repair work to do on the Third Floor and across the Potomac.

I could see no way the Air Force would escape damage in this affair. We were either going to lose Glosson or the other three, neither outcome being good. Glosson hired a very able lawyer[48] and made a fight of it, attacking the motives of his accusers and also of the Air Force's investigating officer, Lt. Gen. Eugene Fischer, our inspector general. Glosson maintained Fischer had a grudge against him. But the investigation showed clearly that the claimed facts on each side were simply not compatible. Somebody was

---

48 Terrence O'Donnell, a savvy, well-connected partner at the Williams & Connolly law firm. If I ever got into bad trouble, I'd want Terry O'Donnell on the case. He was an Air Force Academy graduate and Air Force veteran. He'd served presidents Nixon and Ford in a variety of second-level White House staff positions and was Dick Cheney's general council in the Pentagon during the administration of George H. W. Bush. His father, Emmett "Rosie" O'Donnell, was one of the Air Force's most colorful general officers.

In the Glosson Affair, another lawyer, Charles Gittens, assisted O'Donnell. Gittens achieved additional prominence in 2002 when he was hired to defend Major Harry Schmidt of the Illinois Air National Guard, then facing charges in connection with a friendly fire incident in Afghanistan. Schmidt, a one-time instructor at the Navy's Top Gun school, released a bomb that killed four soldiers of Princess Patricia's Light Infantry, the first Canadian combat losses since the Korean War. Eight others were wounded. It turned out that Maj. Schmidt had taken amphetamines—our old friend the "go" pill—supposed to keep him alert on the long legs into and out of Afghanistan. I had effectively banned use of these drugs after Desert Storm, but in 1996, Lt. Gen. John Jumper, then the DCS/Ops and later the 17th Air Force chief of staff, reinstated their use, citing the length of air missions then being flown into the former Yugoslavia. Not surprisingly, Gittens publicly questioned the safety and common sense of making pilots take "uppers" before sending them into combat. Subsequently, Schmidt and his wingman escaped court-martial for involuntary manslaughter and dereliction of duty—the Air Force decided not to press charges—receiving instead administrative punishment that ended their careers as fighter pilots.

shading the truth, if not outright lying, and there was no way Glosson's version could stand up against the reinforced strength of the three other highly respected senior officers.

By mid-November, the IG reported his conclusion that Glosson was lying and that he had improperly communicated with promotion board members. The IG found no evidence of any involvement by me in the affair. Glosson and his lawyers countered with a long memorandum that quibbled about details in the testimony of his accusers and suggested that the three, and especially Mike Ryan, had embellished and twisted the facts as part of a campaign to damage Glosson's future prospects. The thesis was that Glosson and Ryan were natural rivals for top leadership roles and Ryan was acting to undercut the competition.

The "Glosson as victim" idea gathered momentum among his friends in the Office of the Secretary of Defense, where "a senior Defense Department official" observed to the *New York Times*:

> Unfortunately, we have an Inspector General report that has a number of flaws in it . . . These are very serious allegations, but there are a number of opinions expressed and the methodology is open to question.

There followed much internal discussion about what to do with the investigation findings. The threat to Glosson was that Secretary Widnall would take fairly harsh action, including perhaps a severe reprimand and forfeiture of pay, or even reduction in grade to major general, something she had authority to do. About the best Glosson could expect was to be allowed to retire in the highest grade he had held, lieutenant general.

In early December, 1993, I went to Les Aspin privately and got his support for what the secretary and I proposed to do. In view of Glosson's long and distinguished service, Secretary Widnall was willing to give him only a Letter of Admonishment, the softest form of nonjudicial punishment. Nonetheless, this rare public censure of a senior officer would put an end to his career prospects. He would be allowed to retire from the Air Force at three-star rank.

Aspin agreed, whereupon I called in Glosson, told him he would be admonished and to submit retirement papers after a cosmetic interval. That should have been the end of it.

Unhappily, when we submitted Glosson's name to the Senate for retirement in grade, Senator Charles Grassley of Iowa made an issue of it, asserting Glosson should be demoted because of the "dark cloud" over his name. This meant that Glosson had to again fire up the whole machinery of self-defense, with the Air Force getting further tarred in the process. It then emerged that the investigating officer, Air Force inspector general Eugene Fischer, was under something of a dark cloud of his own, having been accused of sexual harassment in the summer of 1993. In fact, the circumstances were ambiguous, but I had quietly asked Fischer to retire anyway, and he had agreed to do so but needed for personal reasons to postpone his exit until November. When the Glosson Affair kicked off in October, I had no real choice but to further delay Fischer's departure so he could finish the investigation.

Glosson had earlier raised the possibility of bad blood between him and Fischer to explain away the IG findings. This now became the news. The *Air Force Times* quoted a "Senate source" as saying, "There's at least some possibility that the (investigation) report is biased (against Glosson) or is playing into the competition that goes on among general officers." Trying to help his friend, John Deutch, by now moved up to deputy secretary of defense, wrote Grassley to say, "After repeated review of all the case materials, we do not support the conclusion—nor do I believe—that Lt. Gen. Glosson lied during the investigation."

Back in the Pentagon, Glosson's position—and mine, for that matter—was increasingly painful. Maybe this wasn't the O. J. Simpson trial, but the Air Force was having a family fight in public. As the affair dragged on, senior officers took sides, never helpful for an outfit that depends on unit cohesion. My overriding concern was to keep the Air Force flying and pick up some tailwind and, for that to happen, I needed among other things an

A new president meets with the Joint Chiefs in the "tank": CNO Frank Kelso, CSA Gordy Sullivan, CJCS Colin Powell, the president, Secretary Aspin, VCJCS David Jeremiah, me, CMC Carl Mundy.

Air House: Secretary Sheila Widnall and I at dinner.

Working session in the tank: Joining Powell and me at the table (from left): Chuck Horner, commander NORAD and Space Command; Bill Kime, Coast Guard commandant; Secretary Aspin, Undersecretary for Acquisition John Deutch.

Traveling with CMS Gary Pfingston, my senior enlisted adviser. His stripes are bolder, with three chevrons above the rockers, our redesign for the modern uniform.

Air Force headquarters staff, 1993. Seated, from left: John Jaquish, Mike Carns, me, Tom McInerney, Trevor Hammond. Standing: Carl O'Berry, Billy Boles, Rusty Sloan, Gene Fischer, Buster Glosson.

Air Force master photographer Ron Hall took many of the photos used in this memoir. But this one, in the chief's office, is by the noted portraitist William S. McIntosh. Hap Arnold's winged star, restored to use as an Air Force symbol, is woven into the rug.

Thunderbirds visit the chief.

I show Thunderbird lead Dan Darnell how to do a loop. He doesn't seem impressed.

effective DCS/Ops.[49] Glosson was preoccupied with his own problems and in any case anxious to be out the door and started on Phase Two of Life. At length, he came to me and said he was willing to accept retirement as a major general, in order to get the process closed, but he would continue to fight the matter from outside the Air Force.

Glosson left the Pentagon on 30 June 1994, a retired two-star. But that didn't end the affair. The *Air Force Times* did a cover story on 18 July 1994, with the headline, "Senate may probe Glosson's claims he was railroaded." In response, Secretary of Defense Bill Perry, who had replaced Aspin, ordered a new investigation to investigate the investigation. I was not shown the product of this new investigation, but later that summer the *Washington Times* quoted a "Senate source" familiar with the findings as saying it "cleared him (Glosson) of the charge of having lied."

On 8 October, the Senate, Nunn in the lead, voted 59-30 to restore to Glosson, in retirement, his third star.

I was genuinely saddened by this whole episode, losing a friend as well as a valued adviser. I had no role in the matter, except in trying to end it so as to limit damage to the Air Force. I did not ask Glosson's help in blocking any officer's promotion. My approach was to get the best officers promoted as quickly as I could, which had the effect of shuffling them to the top and worked much better than any deliberate effort to hold back the less able.

Incidentally, the three accusing officers, Ryan, Myers, and Nowak, were excused from participation in the FY 94 two-star promotion board and replaced by others. The officer whose advancement Glosson was charged with trying to head off was in fact selected for promotion by this board.

---

49 I had already nominated Lt. Gen. Joe Ralston, an old friend, a brilliant officer, future vice chairman of the JCS and NATO SACEUR, to replace Glosson, and was by this time concerned to get him in place as quickly as I could.

Defense Reform Movement

The defense reform movement had just about worn out its welcome by the time I became chief. Frankly, that was too bad, because I admired people like John Boyd and Chuck Spinney, who had ideas and pumped a lot of energy into the process.

The main argument I had with the defense reformers was they seemed to spend all their time on technology issues, arguing loudly (and often wrongly, in my view) in favor of what they saw as a simple, reliable, low-tech approach. (They sang the praises of the F-86 and positively loved the A-10!) Their formulation was "high-tech vs. rugged and simple," with rugged and simple being the only thing that works in combat. They cited the example of AIM-7 Sparrow, a radar-guided missile that achieved only .09 kills per shot against North Vietnamese interceptors. Admittedly, the missile was a loser, but training also played a big part. The top three US aces scored 14 of their 16 kills with the AIM-7. When Steve Richie, our first Vietnam ace, pulled the trigger, his probability of kill with the AIM-7 was .39.

Moreover, the AIM-7 being too complex for its time did not mean we should give up on the long-range air fight, stick with AIM-9 and a dogfighter like the early version of the F-16, and go for visual kills. Technology is yet another case where we need to pick the simplest approach that meets the requirement, and nothing simpler. Remember, the F-86 was actually the most sophisticated fighter of its day, a relatively expensive winner that achieved a healthy kill ratio against the less costly and far simpler MiG-15.

The defense reform movement should have paid more attention to how combat units are organized. Here's where we need simple, reliable, rugged structures, and have anything but.

Requirements vs. Specifications

In connection with equipping the Air Force, one of the most important reforms occurred in my first year, when Secretary Rice agreed the Air Staff should supervise operational requirements. The services could not purchase important equipment—a tank, a ship, an aircraft—without an established and validated "requirement" for the capability. A requirement statement described the main features needed in new equipment. We want a bayonet that's about so many inches long, ends in a point, is sharp on one side, is able to open a can of beans, and so forth. I thought writing these statements was important work and clearly a responsibility that should remain in military hands. A user needs to say what kind of bayonet he needs, not some civilian bureaucrat. Of course, civilians make many important decisions during system design, development and production, and I had no problem with that. In fact, it's a real advantage to have former industry leaders working in the Pentagon and active on the business side of large acquisition programs. But why would we ever want a civilian—any civilian—to describe the sort of equipment required for combat?

I drew a distinction between requirements and specifications. Users generate requirements, identifying a needed military capability. For instance, the operational user could say he needs a bomber that penetrates hostile defenses and survives. Such a requirement would not normally be written up as part of the contract let to industry, though it would be used as the basis for postproduction operational testing. By contrast, the acquisition community generates a specification, spelling out design details or performance levels. The specification could, for instance, call for our bomber to appear to be a certain size when illuminated from a given angle by radar of a particular frequency. A specification of this type, stated in discrete, measurable terms, does become part of a contract, and we subsequently measure spec compliance in development testing.

This is an important distinction, so I'll underscore it: In development test, we measure whether new hardware meets contract specifications. How big does our bomber appear when seen by radar? We want to know whether it meets the specification. In operational test, we ask an entirely different question: can we penetrate and survive? We want to know whether it satisfies the requirement.

Naturally, much thought goes into specifications, and we're serious about meeting them. Ultimately, however, we need equipment that matches requirements. In theory, at least, a new system may meet none of the contract specifications and still satisfy the requirement quite well. Or it could meet all the specs and have no military worth whatever.

The Goldwater-Nichols Act transferred oversight of important procurement programs to the service secretariats. Our secretariat had a deputy for acquisition (SAF/AQ), a political appointee, often a skilled and experienced industry executive. This personage had overall supervisory authority over contracting and other business aspects of system acquisition. Riding herd on specifications was a good job for him. That is not to say it's easy to translate a military requirement into a set of design specifications. It's quite hard, but there's no reason to think you have to be wearing a uniform while doing it. (Moreover, we always kept some of our brightest officers in SAF/AQ, charged with making sure requirements got translated properly into specifications.) SAF/AQ was also a good candidate to oversee development test, done mostly by the contractor to demonstrate spec compliance.

At the beginning of my term, headquarters responsibility for requirements was also located in SAF/AQ, an accidental consequence of the way the Air Staff was organized at the time of the Goldwater-Nichols Act. Secretary Rice allowed me to rescue the function and establish, under the deputy chief of staff for plans and operations, a director of requirements (AF/XOR), making the operations deputy the Air Force's advocate for requirements. I went further, ruling that a requirement became official only when signed off by my office. By the time I entered my final year, I'd reviewed and approved 31 operational requirement documents, and my deputy, Mike Carns, had signed off 48 more in my name. Another couple of hundred were in work. The point was simple: these were Air Force requirements. If you didn't have a requirement document held by XOR and signed off by the chief, you didn't have a requirement, which meant you had no way to get a program started or funded.

It must be clear why this was important. Establishing reliable, stable requirements is essential because any change moves the program's goal posts, with ruinous consequences for schedule and cost in system development. But because it takes so long to field new weapon systems, there's a certain amount of unavoidable instability in military requirements. The world is a dynamic place. Technology evolves. The threat changes. So I knew we could not avoid some instability—indeed, had to have some if we wished to produce, in the end, equipment that would be effective in combat. But I wanted to stabilize requirements as much as I could. The operator, the user—the customer—shouldn't be part of the instability problem. Thus, we made it hard to establish a requirement, and hard to change it, once established.

Then, confident about the requirement, we could take a more relaxed approach to specifications. Every time one of our development programs failed to meet any of thousands of specifications, we got clobbered in the press and around town. The critics claimed to have seen it many times before: either the specification was important, in which case the equipment failing it was useless, or it was not important, in which case we were gold-plating. Unhappily, we often overreacted, dumping money into spec compliance in a pointless effort to make sure we were never guilty as charged (hence, the C-5's famous "$600 toilet seat").

I wanted to change this picture. If I saw in *Aviation Week* that the B-2 was not quite as stealthy as we had hoped—at a certain aspect or in a certain radar frequency—I'd be interested and make inquiries. I'd want to know what we were doing about it. But strict spec compliance was not my game. Specifications can and should be changed, especially if they're cost drivers. Then again, if I learned a certain piece of military equipment under development wouldn't do its prospective job, couldn't meet the user's established requirement, that system was in serious trouble.

Operational Test

Of course, before we fielded a weapon system, user representatives needed to test it under realistic operating conditions to ensure it met the stated military requirement. The agency charged with doing this, the Air Force Operational Test and Evaluation Center, was already in existence and reporting to the chief of staff before the 1991 reorganization, so that part of the organization did not need fixing.

Acquisition Reform

On balance, the United States makes and fields the world's best military equipment. Nevertheless, the Pentagon is regularly buffeted by procurement scandal involving cost overrun, schedule slip, or operational deficiency in its programs. Repeated "reforms," including Goldwater-Nichols, which moved nearly all responsibility for weapon system acquisition away from service military staffs and into civilian secretariats, have not changed this unpleasant outcome. The reason: equipment procurement is a joint venture formed by the executive and legislative branches and can't be fixed unless both parties participate.

Important procurement programs have a long life. It now takes decades to move from the ambition of a concept, to the establishment of that moving target called a requirement, into research and design, on to development and test, forward into production and, at long last, to receipt of shiny new hardware at frontline units. In every year of this long process, responsible officers must go back to both the House and Senate and get the program authorized and appropriated, with permission coming from one set of committees and money from another. Every year, congressmen, senators, and their staffs fiddle with the program, resulting in more or less constant turmoil. With very few exceptions, for any large system, there is not one multiyear program, but multiple one-year programs, making efficient management more or less impossible. The only reason the arrangement produces equipment at any price and on any schedule is that lots of good people work their tails off.

The acquisition system could not be better designed to fail, and it regularly does just that. True reform is possible only if committee chairmen and senior members give up the power inherent in annual review. To say the least, this is unlikely. Nevertheless, we can anticipate many more tilts at the windmill, attempts to fix the system without tackling its underlying shortcoming.

Regarding further reform of the part that belongs exclusively to the executive branch, here are two rules I would follow: (1) At the front end of system acquisition, uniformed military officers (users) must write and certify equipment requirements. (2) Before equipment is issued to operating units, uniformed military officers (users) must do operational test and evaluation (trials) to verify that the equipment meets the requirement.

Fix whatever else you like.

Chapter 6

Bosnia

For the life of me, I could not visualize a cone intersecting a plane in space.

—Colin Powell, *My American Journey*

With the official demise of the Soviet Union in December 1991, we could claim, finally, to have won World War II. Now the problem was to win World War I. As the Cold War glaciers retreated, they exposed the detritus of earlier conflict, suspended during the superpower competition but now unfrozen. Nowhere was this truer than in the Balkans, where the synthetic compound that was Yugoslavia could no longer be held together.

As I arrived at the Pentagon in November 1990, the situation had been unstable for some time. In early summer 1991 both Slovenia and Croatia declared their independence. With 90 percent ethnic solidarity, Slovenia was able to break away with only a brief period of fighting. In Croatia, a Serbian minority of about 12 percent fought hard for a while, with outside help from Belgrade, but gradually lost or was evicted. Bosnia and Herzegovina opted for independence in December 1991. Here, where ethnicities were more evenly distributed, it was an ugly fight of all against all—though in general,

Muslim Bosnians aligned against Orthodox Serbs, with Catholic Slovenes shifting to provide a makeweight, as suited their purposes.[50] The conflict took place in Europe's backyard and should have been in its in-basket, but we had trained the Europeans to follow, always excepting the French, and they therefore waited for us to lead.

On the ground in Bosnia, it was a pretty one-sided affair, the Serbs much better organized and armed than the Muslims. The UN Security Council embargoed arms shipments to all sides, a shameless baby step that subsequently did nothing to slow the Serbs. In April 1992, Nationalist Serb snipers fired on peaceful demonstrators in Sarajevo, an act regarded as the beginning of civil war. At about the same time, the Yugoslav People's Army (JNA) formally discharged its Bosnian Serb soldiers, allowing them to keep their weapons. Very quickly, Serbian forces held something like 60 percent of the country (they had made up about 30 percent of Bosnia's population), including the high ground around Sarajevo, effectively laying siege to the city. In May a mortar shell launched into Sarajevo killed 16 people waiting in a bread line. On 30 May the Security Council imposed economic and other sanctions on "Yugoslavia," meaning Serbia.

---

50 The reader must excuse a vast oversimplification. In this geography there were many contestants. Indeed, the main groups were Bosnian Muslim and Bosnian Serb, but there were also Bosnian Croats, Croat Muslims, Chetniks, and Albanians, all of whom fielded partisans. The Yugoslav People's Army (JNA) and other non-Bosnians from Serbia and Croatia were deeply involved, and both sides enjoyed niche support from a number of other countries—Iranian Muslim fundamentalists, for example. Everybody involved had a different concept of "victory" tied to his own purposes: territorial, religious, personal adventure, private gain. The military capabilities and martial qualities of those present for duty were a crosscut through history: agrarian (ill armed, ill trained, ill organized, undisciplined); industrial (high quality, mass produced, firepower intensive); and modern (precision guided, high productivity, low collateral damage). Often, targeted forces were less vulnerable to traditional military power, and traditional power itself less useful in producing desired operational effects. This was postmodern war at its best—or worst.

UN Protection Force

By summer 1992, the United Nations was deeply involved in both peacekeeping and humanitarian relief. The UN Protection Force (UNPROFOR), initially established to oversee the cease-fire in Croatia, had its mandate extended into Bosnia. A Canadian battalion broke through Serb roadblocks on 2 July 1992, reopening Sarajevo's airport. After that, the UN High Commissioner for Refugees (UNHCR) coordinated a relief effort, the muscle provided by US, British, and French aircraft lifting supplies into the city.[51] By August, UNPROFOR, now installed in Bosnia, was reporting incidents of ethnic cleansing, the Serbian practice of driving off or killing Muslims to create ethnically pure real estate. Soon, the media displayed nasty images of death camps and other artifacts of mass murder and rape. In October 1992 the Security Council established a no-fly zone over Bosnia, and NATO aircraft (AEW, their version of the AWACS) began monitoring Bosnian airspace.

Lift and Strike

The outgoing Bush administration had limited US involvement to humanitarian assistance and support for the no-fly zone. We offered no troops to UNPROFOR even though, at an initial strength of about 14,000 in Bosnia, it was badly undermanned. The Serbs continued to encircle and bombard Bosnian towns and to obstruct delivery of relief supplies wherever they could. The final days of the Bush administration saw some discussion of an option called lift and strike, a proposal that would lift the UN embargo so Bosnians could be armed and strike Serbian military equipment and formations from the air. Colin Powell, among others, opposed this much more active involvement and, in any case, the

---

51 Operation Provide Promise lasted three and a half years. In all, the US Air Force eventually put 4,197 sorties into Sarajevo, where approaches and departures required some fancy flying to dodge Serbian ground fire. We flew an additional 2,200 sorties over besieged Bosnian cities, dropping food and supplies.

Europeans, with troops on the ground in UNPROFOR, were distinctly unenthusiastic.

Breaking with Powell

In JCS deliberations, I pushed the strike part of lift and strike as a low-risk approach with high potential to make a difference.[52] I did not take the line that we ought to intervene. There were high-minded reasons for doing so, but to intervene or not was a political question. I was suggesting only that we give the president a low-risk option for doing so. Powell, his authority ironically strengthened by airpower's success in Desert Storm, would hear none of it. As the chairman said in his memoir, *My American Journey*, he ran for cover whenever he heard talk of "nice, tidy, allegedly low-cost, incremental, may-work options that are floated around with great regularity all over this town." I was one of the people floating the option, and, as always when I took on Powell, I got nowhere.

Powell believed that when we involve ourselves somewhere militarily, we should do so on a massive scale—after all, this was the Powell Doctrine—and he defined massive as involving plenty of ground troops. Everybody (me included) thought that throwing a large number of US ground troops into Bosnia risked an uncertain outcome. Concluding the syllogism, not intervening was the only sensible option. I disagreed with the first premise, thinking intervention need not be massive, in the sense of requiring lots of ground troops, to be successful. Moreover, even if unsuccessful, air intervention could be done at low risk to ourselves and without making the situation worse for the Bosnians.

In Bosnia the pressing operational question was whether we might end the siege of Muslim towns by aerial attack of Serbian

---

52 Note that, as used here, "strike" means independent air attack: finding and damaging or destroying Serbian military assets far enough away from friendly forces or populations so we would not need detailed integration with UN troops on the ground. Strike is thus easier (and less risky) than close air support, which I regarded as pretty hard to do anywhere—and harder than that in the Bosnian context.

gun emplacements. Because we had little reason to worry about primitive Serbian air defenses, the heart of the matter was whether we could take out the guns. Powell worried that, once declared for action and with our reputation on the line, airpower would (yet again) fail, and we'd be obliged to go in on the ground to remove the guns, a pot-limit bet none of us wanted to make. This was the source of Powell's observation that he got "nervous when so-called experts suggest that all we need is a little surgical bombing."

It often struck me that nearly all the uniformed officers, including Powell, who during this period advanced theory concerning the difficulty and danger of attacking targets from the air, shared a characteristic: they had never participated in the aerial attack of any target. Supposedly, Powell himself kept in his office a photograph of well-camouflaged Serbian gun emplacements, showing it to visitors in order to ridicule the idea of airpower's usefulness. (If Powell had such a photograph, he did not share it with me, so I can't confirm this particular item of gossip.) The profession of arms is as specialized as any other. If you have a question about infantry tactics, ask an infantryman, preferably one with something more than sandbox experience in a one-*g* classroom. If you want to use airplanes to attack guns, ask me, or someone like me.

During my time in the JCS, the air intervention option was never seriously discussed, thanks in large part to Powell's opposition. When Bosnia was on the agenda, Powell, Vice Chairman Dave Jeremiah, and the other service chiefs fretted about "mission creep," stayed clear of "slippery slopes," agonized over "exit strategy." Everyone's speaking part seemed polished and practiced. When I could get a word in edgewise, I made clear my contrary view. But I had difficulty being heard, Powell's fingers on the volume knob. We took no votes—not unusual since the Joint Chiefs act mostly by consensus—so Powell could report, accurately, that the service chiefs supported his views.

The upshot was we stood still while Serbian thugs pushed NATO troops around. We watched while hundreds of thousands of lives were taken and maybe 2 million people displaced, all done in the most brutish way. Considering the killing that continued until 1995, when at last we mounted a miniature air campaign that forced the Serbs into peace talks, my observations may seem edged with bitterness or aimed at settling personal scores, so I hurry to make clear my feelings at the time about Colin Powell. Above all, Powell was a professional. He wasn't picking low-hanging fruit in some tidy policy grove. Instead, every day he took a hoe to the great weedy mess that is the real world. The "help" he got from "all over this town" came mostly from people who wanted to impose imaginary coherence on an international scene that was by nature disorderly, or who had an agenda or ideology (with me, was it the efficacy of airpower?), or who were amateurs, as when Madeleine Albright famously suggested she might "borrow" the Army, since Powell didn't want to use it. Powell had the brains to formulate a consistent worldview and the backbone and bureaucratic skill to push it against all comers. To this powerful combination of qualities he added considerable personal charm. (I liked him a lot, which did not make it any easier to disagree with him.) He was by some distance the most effective public servant I'd ever known.

And, on balance, I found much to admire in the substance of Powell's ideas. I didn't think, for instance, he ever more or less automatically looked for a way to avoid international commitment, a charge leveled against him. He knew as well as anybody that being a great power imposed special costs and responsibilities, all the more so in the wake of the Soviet collapse, when we no longer had a peer competitor, but stood alone at the summit of power. Nearly always, the argument between Powell and me came down to a different assessment of military risk. I was convinced that when our responsibility to lead took the form of required military action, airpower gave us advantages that Powell didn't believe in and wouldn't use. Thus, on some matters and depending on the situation, I couldn't support a view I regarded as too cautious.

Enter the Clinton Administration

During the 1992 presidential campaign, candidate Clinton was critical of Bush for not responding more assertively to the crisis in Bosnia. Clinton's stump speeches mentioned the "high cost of paralysis in the face of genocide," emphasizing that "history has shown that you can't allow the mass extermination of people and just sit by and watch it happen." He advocated lifting the UN arms embargo that "prevents Bosnians from defending themselves effectively" and proposed using American airpower to counter Serbian aggression, at the same time drawing a line against using US ground troops in any capacity. In other words, lift and strike—all of which made sense to me.

Once in office, however, Clinton seemed unable to figure out what to do or how to do it. In early February 1993, former US secretary of state Cyrus Vance and former UK foreign minister David Owen advanced a plan to divide Bosnia and grant about 40 percent of the territory to the Serbs. (By then, Serbian irregular forces, backed by the JNA, controlled about 70 percent of Bosnia.) Clinton decided this proposal rewarded Serbian aggression and instead of backing it, appointed a special American envoy, Reginald Bartholomew, to "build on the Vance-Owen negotiations in a way that can move toward a just, workable, and durable solution." This was a polite way of telling the parties we were taking over the negotiations. The problem is, when we take over something, we become responsible for it. If the initiative produced agreement, we would have the job of enforcing it. If it failed, we would have failed. And the Clinton team had not arrived at an answer to the central question of whether and how to impose a solution on Serbian authorities. The *Washington Post* quoted a "senior US official" on 9 February: "Do you or don't you use American military power, and for what purpose?" Indeed. Colin Powell had thought long and hard about this very good question, one presidential candidates might usefully mull over before occupying the Oval Office.

The Bartholomew initiative went nowhere.

Operation Deny Flight

Meanwhile, the United Nations, using reports from both the NATO AEW aircraft and ground observers, counted nearly 500 violations of the no-fly zone during the roughly six-month period from mid-October 1992 to mid-April 1993. During one of these, in March 1993, three Serbian aircraft bombed Bosnian villages east of Srebrenica. Early in April, NATO authorities offered to provide combat aircraft to enforce the no-fly zone, and the United Nations accepted the offer. As NATO's preeminent air force, we played a leading role in the enforcement action, which we called Operation Deny Flight. At the outset, it amounted to little more than burning holes in Bosnian airspace while the killing continued on the ground.

Debating an Air Campaign

By this point, Sarajevo had been under siege for a year. Srebrenica, recently designated a "safe area" by the United Nations, teetered on the brink of falling to the Serbs. Now with combat aircraft in the air over Bosnia, I once again argued we might, without calamitous consequences, become more active. This time, my views became public. *ABC Evening News* ran the following exchange on 28 April 1993:

> PETER JENNINGS: In Washington today, President Clinton is still struggling with whether the US should get militarily involved in Bosnia-Herzegovina. There are, he said, a lot of practical questions that must be answered. And today some of America's most senior generals have been telling Congress what they think the US military might accomplish on the Bosnian battlefield. Here's ABC's John McWethy.
>
> JOHN MCWETHY: The US Air Force used precision bombing with deadly results two years ago in Iraq. Today the Air Force chief of staff said they could do the same against Serb artillery in Bosnia.
>
> GENERAL MCPEAK: Give us time and we'll drive across the top of every one of those artillery positions and put it out of business.

MCWETHY: General McPeak could not promise such a campaign would force the Serbs to stop fighting, but he predicted it would definitely get their attention.

MCPEAK: We can make it very difficult for the people on the ground to—you know, we can work on their morale pretty good on this problem, because we can do this at virtually no risk to ourselves.

MCWETHY: McPeak says Serb antiaircraft missiles and guns are old and not very effective. But his optimism is not shared by another group of generals who do planning and operations for the Joint Chiefs. They said air strikes would have little or no effect on the Serbs unless they were accompanied by ground troops, something the president has ruled out.

MAJOR GENERAL MICHAEL RYAN (assistant to the chairman, Joint Chiefs of Staff): Airpower alone isn't going to do it, for a couple of reasons. Even if you are able to take out the majority of artillery, they still have mortars and small arms that you can't get at with airpower.

MCWETHY: But taking out the big guns would remove the primary advantage that the Serbs now have over the Muslims. Even so, the generals claim that would not stop the fighting or the atrocities. One senator was clearly frustrated by what he was hearing.

SENATOR STROM THURMOND: What's taking place there is worse than what Hitler did. Can we do nothing?

MAJOR GENERAL JOHN SHEEHAN (director of operations, Joint Chiefs of Staff): I cannot, in my mind, think of a military operation short of total intervention that will cause a cessation of the rape, the pillaging, and the murder you speak about.

MCWETHY: As opposition to air strikes appears to be mounting in Congress and at the Pentagon, President Clinton got two important new signals of support. The British said today that they would reluctantly go along with the bombing campaign. And Canada, which has had troops in Bosnia longer than anyone else, indicated that it would support President Clinton if he sought new authority in the United Nations for use of force.

John McWethy, ABC News, Washington.[53]

Clinton Adrift

In May, Sarajevo, Tuzla, Bihac, Zepa, and Gorazde joined Srebrenica as declared safe areas by the United Nations. The designation did little to protect the populations, swelling fast as refugees flooded in from the countryside. Meanwhile, President Clinton was reading Robert Kaplan's *Balkan Ghosts: A Journey through History*. Published in 1993, this is a well-written account of Kaplan's travels through the Balkans in the late 1980s and early 1990s. In a nutshell, the thesis: ethnic violence there is endemic and unstoppable, the people killing each other for centuries. And the implication: stay out of the fight.[54] I recall Powell's saying at a JCS meeting that he'd given the book to Clinton.

---

53 Maj. Gen. Mike Ryan, USAF, and Maj. Gen. Jack Sheehan, USMC, expressed their views at hearings to confirm their nominations (by Powell) for promotion and appointment to three-star Joint Staff positions, so one might expect them to support their new boss. Still, I was a little disillusioned by the testimony. In 1995 Ryan would himself run the brief air campaign that brought the Serbs to Dayton (and, of course, he was a future Air Force chief of staff). If he had genuine misgivings about the effectiveness of independent air attack, he certainly slew that dragon by his own hand. Jack Sheehan, too, should have known better, as he was one of the best thinkers in any color uniform.

54 Mr. Kaplan has since claimed he never intended that anyone draw this conclusion. In his foreword to the paperback edition of *Balkan Ghosts*, he writes,

> . . . a difficult ethnic history will not, by itself, necessarily cause the loss of hundreds of thousands of lives in conditions resembling the Holocaust. For that calamity, one needs additional factors: Western confusion and inaction which, in turn, create a power vacuum. Without these other elements, the horrors of the 1990s might not have occurred.

For whatever reason, Clinton seemed adrift, casting about for a political approach having the look and feel of real action, but without substance or accompanying risk. In Washington all talk of independent air attack stopped, though the United Nations did some work with NATO on the problem of how to provide close air support for UNPROFOR troops. For now, Clinton watched and waited, going only so far as to order humanitarian aid airlifted to the newly designated safe-area cities.

Sarajevo Visit

On 20 May 1993, I flew a C-141 into Aviano Air Base, Italy, delivering stores to our main base supporting the Bosnian airlift and no-fly zone. I was briefed on activities at Aviano, then, on the morning of 21 May, flew a C-130 with an all-Reserve crew from the 758th Airlift Squadron (Greater Pittsburgh) into Sarajevo. On the ground, I put on a steel hat and flak vest for (literally) a quick trot to the headquarters of the UNPROFOR in Bosnia, then under British command. We didn't park aircraft at Sarajevo, so my C-130 unloaded supplies without delay and took off. After meeting with senior UNPROFOR officers and stopping at the offices of the UN High Commissioner for Refugees, supervising the relief effort, I climbed into another C-130, this one from the 105th Airlift Squadron, Tennessee Air National Guard. We landed at Vicenza, Italy, where the Fifth Allied Tactical Air Force (5ATAF) had a combined air operations center (CAOC) running the NATO air effort. An old friend, Maj. Gen. "Bear" Chambers, was in charge there.

Gorazde Airdrop

From Vicenza I flew up to the large base at Rhein-Main, Germany, where we were staging C-130 night drops into besieged Bosnian cities. Yugoslav "inspectors" at Rhein-Main—a Bosnian, a Serb, and a Croat—watched what we loaded into the airplanes, making sure it was blankets and beans, not bullets and bombs. I flew out that evening in the lead aircraft of a three-ship formation of C-130s on a mission to drop MREs (meals ready to eat) into Gorazde, located along the Drina River in the mountains of eastern

Bosnia, quite near the Serbian border and on the main road from central Serbia to the Adriatic. By early 1993, Gorazde had been under siege for nearly a year, but its Muslim population had nevertheless doubled when Serbians "cleansed" the Drina valley east of the city.

The airdrop procedure was invented for the Bosnia exercise, an example of GI ingenuity. Large cardboard boxes, their edges cut to within six inches of the bottom, were heaped up with individual MREs and marshaled in the cargo compartment. Lengths of webbing held the boxes together in flight. Over the objective, the boxes were slid out the back of the aircraft, breaking up as they hit the airstream. MREs scattered and rained into the city, a particular benefit to children, the sick, or elderly, who might not be able to get outside of town to a proper drop zone. The drop altitude was fairly high, to keep us above the Serbian heavy-weapons envelope in this mountainous terrain, but the MRE containers, shaped like small tetrahedrons, tumbled in flight and had so much drag they did not attain great velocity during free fall. Supposedly, there was no danger to folks on the ground. Taking an MRE hit was said to be about like being struck by a softball. (Maybe so, but I'd stay indoors.) Reports we got back from many missions said we put a lot of food into refugee stomachs and not much into the hands of the opposition.

Back at Rhein-Main, I held a news conference, praising the C-130 crews. The drops were a "technically awesome feat, and we made it look easy." The debate in the United States over whether we should get involved in Bosnia was hard to fathom:

> Our Bosnian airlift has now passed the duration of the famous Berlin airlift, becoming the longest running humanitarian air effort ever . . . We've been engaged for 19 months, more or less painlessly, as such things are judged.

Christopher Mission

The muscular and praiseworthy lift and strike had been President Clinton's first option for Bosnia, shelved early as his new administration wrung its hands for months about intractable 1,000-year Balkan rivalries. At length, continued Serbian truculence produced enough embarrassment so that, in May 1993, Clinton dispatched Secretary of State Warren Christopher to Europe to line up allied support for a more forceful approach. The visit was prepared badly and managed worse. After all, the Brits and French actually had soldiers on the ground, in UNPROFOR—outmanned and outgunned, virtual hostages. Now along comes this new Clinton crowd, fresh from the backwoods of Little Rock, with no troops at the sharp end, but wanting to get snotty with the Serbs. No way. Christopher came back with his tail between his legs, US prestige tarnished.

Press Conference

About the same time, in mid-June 1993, I held a Pentagon press conference to deal with public aspects of the Norm Campbell Affair.[55] In the course of this event, someone asked me a question:

> Q: General, a couple of months ago, you were the only member of the Joint Chiefs speaking out about possible air strikes in Bosnia. Pardon me, you were the only one who seemed to feel they could be done, they were doable, there would not be unnecessary losses to US crews. You recently took a ride in a C-130 over Bosnia. Are your views the same that we get involved there? Can we still do air strikes safely and effectively?
>
> A: I was recently in Yugoslavia. I landed in Sarajevo and delivered flour there ... Later ... I made a night drop on Gorazde, one of the Eastern Muslim villages ...
>
> On the bombing, my comments are part of the public record, so I would urge people to go back and read what I said. I have never advocated bombing in Bosnia, or elsewhere for that matter. When asked what was practical, what could be done ... what the military risks were—would we lose aircrews, would there be collateral

---

55 See chapter 8.

damage—I've tried to provide an estimate based on my understanding of air operations . . . It's up to the president and his senior policy advisers to make decisions about when to do this. But my judgment is that, if called on to conduct more aggressive air operations, we can do it in Bosnia, or anywhere else the president decides to do it.

Close Air Support for the UN Protection Force

The continuing atrocities impelled the United Nations and NATO to contemplate stronger measures, including in particular close air support for UNPROFOR troops being treated badly by the Serbs. CAS is always tricky. Doing it safely (which is to say, without killing your own guys) and successfully (timeliness being an important aspect of success) depends on competence, which can develop only through training and experience. NATO air forces, except ours, had little CAS training and no experience. UN leadership and most of the UNPROFOR ground troops were entirely innocent of either quality.

The rules of engagement eventually decided on were fairly straightforward, though written so as to promote caution. We would limit all CAS to the degree, intensity, and duration needed to achieve specific objectives, with minimal collateral damage and no risk to friendly forces. We would conduct all CAS missions under the control of a forward air controller, with weapons released only when the aircrew had positively identified the target and after FAC clearance. Following a little classroom and practical training, the secretary-general informed the Security Council in mid-August 1993 that the United Nations "had the operational capability to use airpower in support of UNPROFOR."

The immediate technical issue was command arrangements: how aircraft in a NATO chain of command might support ground troops in a UN chain of command. UNPROFOR troops needing CAS would likely need it quickly or not at all. But to get it, they'd have to send requests to the UN-designated ground commander in Bosnia, who forwarded them to UNPROFOR's overall commander, responsible to the UN secretary-general. UNPROFOR's headquarters was at Zagreb, in Croatia. If everybody up the UN line signed off, UNPROFOR's staff would transmit necessary approvals back into Bosnia, to the air operations center at Sarajevo, which would forward them to the 5ATAF operations center in Vicenza, where NATO authority to task the aircraft resided.

This was not going to work.[56]

Chairman Shalikashvili

In October 1993, Colin Powell retired, and John Shalikashvili took over as chairman of the JCS. Shali had been Powell's assistant and then served as Supreme Allied Commander, Europe, giving him a rich understanding of what was going on in the former Yugoslavia. In the spring of 1991, he'd commanded Provide Comfort, the relief operation that returned hundreds of thousands of Kurdish refugees to northern Iraq. Thus, he had outstanding credentials for dealing with the Bosnia issue. Perhaps he lacked Powell's clout, but he was plenty smart, and he worked the boss's problem—the country's problem—never his own. He was conservative when it came to committing US combat forces to overseas intervention, but not dogmatic about it.

'Pinprick' Close Air Support

On 5 February 1994, Serbian shells lobbed into Sarajevo caused the so-called Marketplace Massacre, 60 people dead and more than 200 wounded. NATO followed by ordering the Serbs to withdraw

---

56 By contrast, command arrangements for Deny Flight, the enforcement of the no-fly zone, while complex, were workable. The commander of 5ATAF, who ran the operation from Vicenza, exercised tactical control of both AEW aircraft and fighters, tasking the latter into orbits where they were on call. AEW aircraft monitored the airspace, identified flights not authorized by the United Nations, and vectored the fighters to intercept, escort, turn away, or engage as needed. The effort was expensive and anything but leakproof, but at least we had enough flexibility to allow for timely action—witness the subsequent downing of several Serbian combat aircraft.

artillery at least 20 kilometers away from the city and authorizing air attack against Serbian gun positions when requested by UN authorities. In late February, US F-16s shot down four Krajina-based Serbian Galeb jet aircraft, caught in the act of bombing Bosnian targets. This was NATO's first hot combat in the 50-plus years since its founding.

A series of Keystone Kops air-support episodes occurred during the spring, summer, and fall of 1994. In March, for instance, UNPROFOR made its first request to NATO for CAS. Aircraft arrived at the scene, near Bihac, where French troops were under fire, but were turned back by a UN forward air control party on the ground. In April, UNPROFOR troops at Gorazde asked for help, a request that required and received approval by the special representative of the UN secretary-general. Two F-16s dropped bombs under the direction of a UN FAC. The same thing happened the next day, with two Marine Corps F/A-18 aircraft bombing and strafing targets. In August the Serbs seized a number of heavy weapons they had previously turned over for storage, despite warnings from UNPROFOR not to do it. At UNPROFOR's request, NATO launched aircraft and, despite barely workable weather, the pilots managed to locate something to attack—maybe a 76 mm antitank gun. The Serbs were impressed enough to return the heavy weapons they'd hijacked. In September two British Jaguars and a US A-10 hit a Serbian tank after it attacked and wounded a French soldier. But a practiced game of chicken, played skillfully by the Serbs, and the convoluted request-and-approval process adopted by NATO and the United Nations virtually assured the ineffectiveness of airpower. Indeed, we later called this, accurately, a period of "pinprick" bombing. Preparing to step down as chief, I found it dispiriting.

Getting to Dayton

After I left the Pentagon, former president Jimmy Carter brokered a truce between Bosnian Serbs and Muslims that held up reasonably well for four months. Then on 24 May 1995, when Serbian forces again ignored a UN order to remove weapons from the

Sarajevo area, NATO aircraft attacked a Serb ammunition depot. In retaliation, Serbs began shelling Muslim safe areas. An ineffectual flurry of NATO bombing led to the Serbs seizing 300 UN peacekeepers as hostages against further air attacks.

On 6 July 1995, Serbian forces attacked Srebrenica, now under the protection of 600 lightly armed Dutch troops. Bosnian fighters in the town asked for return of weapons they had surrendered to the peacekeepers. Request denied. The Dutch commander, Col. Thom Karremans, called for close air support. French General Bernard Janvier, in the UN chain of command, refused initially, then reversed himself after repeated pleas from the Dutch. In any case, Serbian attacks stopped before the planes arrived, and the air strike was postponed. On 9 July the Serbs attacked Dutch observation posts, taking about 30 soldiers hostage. Karremans told town leaders NATO would launch massive air attacks against the Serbs if they did not withdraw. In fact the Serbs did not pull back, but at 9:00 a.m. on 11 July Karremans got word he had submitted his request for CAS on the wrong form. At 10:30 a.m., a resubmitted request reached General Janvier, but NATO aircraft had to return to base in Italy for fuel after being airborne since 6:00 a.m. At 2:30 p.m., Dutch F-16s dropped two bombs on Serb positions. The Serbs responded with a threat to kill their Dutch hostages, causing the suspension of further bombing. Later that day, the Serbian commander, Ratko Mladic, entered Srebrenica, summoned Colonel Karremans, and delivered an ultimatum that the Muslims must hand in all weapons to guarantee their lives. On 12 July buses arrived to evacuate Muslims, but the Serbs kept males aged 12 to 77 for "questioning" about "suspected war crimes." On the 13th, the Dutch handed over about 5,000 Muslims whom they had sheltered at their base at Potocari. In return, the Serbs released 14 Dutch hostages. Following negotiations between the United Nations and the Serbs, the Dutch were at last permitted to exit Srebrenica, leaving behind their weapons, food, and medical supplies. Serbian forces subsequently killed perhaps as many as 7,000 unarmed Muslim men and boys, Europe's worst atrocity since World War II.

Finally, we'd had enough of the Serbs, and a proper NATO air campaign—Operation Deliberate Force—began in the early morning hours of 30 August 1995. It ended just three weeks later, on 20 September, when the Serbs agreed to negotiate.[57] If we subtract bad-weather days and bombing halts, only 10 days of actual air attack were needed before Serbia's Slobodan Milosevic cried "uncle." It took just 3,515 NATO air sorties, about a day's work in the 1991 Gulf War, to persuade the Serbs to negotiate in earnest. These sorties released only 1,026 munitions, 708 of them precision guided. In Vietnam, two-tenths of 1 percent of our bombs were of this type. In Desert Storm, despite the public perception of a "video war," less than 10 percent of the bombs were PGMs. In Deliberate Force, 70 percent of the bombs we dropped were "smart." Notwithstanding the frequently awful weather, NATO aircrews hit 97 percent of their targets and destroyed or seriously damaged 80 percent.[58] One French fighter, a Mirage 2000, was shot down near Pale (apparently by shoulder-fired SAM), the only aircraft lost in Deliberate Force.

---

57 Immediately, the opinion was put about that this success sprang not from the effectiveness of airpower, employed alone, but from the threat of follow-up ground combat. The rationale reminds us of Ptolemy's addition of hypothetical epicycles to calculated planetary orbits to show their conformity with an Earth-centered cosmology.

58 In another independent air war conducted in the skies over Kosovo in 1999, NATO claimed a 99.6 percent accuracy rate, which meant that only one side suffered. For 78 days, NATO aircraft pounded the Serbian army and its infrastructure precisely and accurately, hurting the army and devastating the infrastructure. Despite the weight of bombs dropped, Serbian civilian casualties were amazingly light, estimated at fewer than 1,500 dead. We lost one aircraft. To the surprise of some, Milosevic again capitulated, causing yet another uncomfortable scramble to find the alternative universe in which unsupported air attack never works.

The result was a victory for the West, but one that added no luster. As Warren Bass wrote in *Foreign Affairs*:

> In the end, the very policies that the administration balked at in May 1993—using military force and firm leadership of the Europeans—were the ones that stopped the war in the autumn of 1995. According to Warren Zimmermann, the last US ambassador to Yugoslavia, the cost of delay was more than 100,000 lives.

In November 2004, Bosnian Serb authorities admitted responsibility for the massacre at Srebrenica and apologized officially, after years of playing down the extent of the violence that occurred there in 1995.

※ ※ ※

The theme of this affair might be the near impotence of an immensely powerful West to end savagery in less-favored states. But we didn't try hard enough. No American blood was spilled in Bosnia, a substantial achievement. On the other hand, while we fiddled, the country became a ruins, full of pain and graveyards.

The choice for the United States is never likely to be between paying the price of intervention and opting for profitless but risk-free nonintervention. The choice will usually come down to the cost of intervention versus the cost of nonintervention, with neither option all that attractive. But if history tells us anything, it is that some ideas—Fascism, Stalinism, Maoism, Khmer Rougeism—demand a relentless opposition. Someone—usually the most powerful—must take the first steps to intercede. This is a political decision, and in this instance our political purposefulness and ability to lead were certainly suspect.

But even on the military side, we acted like meat inspectors: the president tossed a sausage in the door, we checked it for quality and cleanliness, found it didn't meet standards, and threw it back. Our military capacity was not in question, except inasmuch as capacity also includes the intangibles of judgment and courage.

Chapter 7

The War on Biology Part I: Women in Combat

There was a portion of the world's history which he regarded as the time of wars, but it, he thought, had been long gone over the horizon and had disappeared forever.
—Stephen Crane, *The Red Badge of Courage*

Eight thousand active duty women—one of them, my niece, SSgt Shannon McGinnis—deployed away from home station to support Desert Storm. But women have served in uniform—honorably, competently, bravely, albeit in relatively small numbers—in all of America's wars. Thus, when Congress established a separate Air Force in 1947, it included women, but capped their end strength at 2 percent. The ceiling created no difficulty at the time, as only 0.4 percent of the enlisted force and 1.4 percent of officers (mostly nurses) were women. Each of the services had a women's auxiliary—in our case, the Women in the Air Force (WAF)—separated administratively from males. Congress also limited promotion opportunity for women, authorizing no female generals. Each service could have only one female colonel of the line—for us, the

247

director of the WAF. And Congress explicitly barred women from combat positions in the Air Force, Marines, and Navy.[59]

The 2 percent end-strength ceiling was removed in 1967. By the early 1970s, nearly 4 percent of our officers were women, and the Air Force had promoted its first female general, Jeanne Holm.[60] The end of conscription and the movement to all-volunteer armed forces coincided with a series of reforms in the early to mid-1970s. The year 1972 saw the first women commissioned from college ROTC programs. In 1974 the Air Force stopped the policy of discharging women who became pregnant. The next year, we integrated basic training—the first service to do so. The WAF was disestablished in 1976, and women joined men in a gender-neutral administrative system. The same year, we opened pilot training to women. In 1980 the first women graduated from the Air Force Academy.

As traditional barriers fell, women responded by staying in the Air Force at increased rates. For example, of the 1975 accession-year group, 25 percent of the male and 23 percent of the female officers were still serving in 1994. The retention story was the same for enlisted women. Better "keep" rates, approaching those for men, reflected our success in improving opportunity for women.

By the time I came to Washington as chief, Air Force women were able, by and large, to work at any job and, given the opportunity, they did well in newly opened career fields. Nearing the end of my term, we had 300 female pilots and 100 or so navigators. Women were not just aircrew members, but experimental test pilots, even astronauts. Five hundred ten women held squadron- and group-level command positions. At that point, women led 12 percent of our aircraft- and missile-maintenance squadrons. The number of female lieutenant colonels on active duty increased

---

59 Though not covered by the 1948 Combat Exclusion Act, the Army maintained its own regulatory exclusion.
60 In 1973 Maj. Gen. Jeanne Holm became the first woman of any service to achieve two-star rank.

500 percent from 1967 to 1994 and, by that time, five women had become Air Force generals.

Some inside the Air Force were not enthusiastic about enhanced career prospects for women, but for the most part we willingly led the country (and the other services) in this regard. We wanted women to succeed, so a little reverse discrimination may have occurred, as seen, for example, in our promotion results. By the mid-1990s, we had selected women for brigadier general at a higher rate than men for a decade. At the 1994 Colonels' Board, women outperformed men by better than 15 percentage points. It wasn't that we rushed to "man" the affirmative-action barricades, or to do women a "favor." Quite the contrary, we saw that women were properly in the Air Force to stay and, given a chance, did high-quality work. We simply wanted to make sure they got the chance.

Fraternization

Traditionally, military service has been characterized by discipline and obedience in a rigid hierarchy of command. Any institution formed on such a framework requires strict barriers between those of greater and lesser rank to prevent development of an easy familiarity that might encourage one person to question the authority of another. Fraternization—too friendly a relationship between a senior and a junior—is what happens when these barriers are transgressed.

For the military, the most significant social divide is the one separating officers from enlisted personnel. The boundary is something of an anachronism—the fossil remnant of a time when officers were "gentlemen" and other ranks were not—and forces at work in society at large will conspire to further reduce its potency. Americans do not think of themselves as having an aristocracy that, according to the natural order, produces an officer corps conditioned by birth to prod a reluctant cannon fodder into the line of fire. The blurring of social stratification is especially notable in the Air Force, an all-volunteer, technology-driven meritocracy from its inception. For us, there was never much need for officers to intimidate a recalcitrant enlisted force. In any case, with notable exceptions, it was the officers who did the actual fighting—officers we expected to think for themselves, to understand the commander's intent, and to (constructively) disobey orders when necessary to get the job done. We therefore have made little use of social structures designed to facilitate mindless obedience.

Many Air Force officers (me among them) formed close relationships with enlisted personnel. I would have found it hard not to "fraternize" with my nearest blood relatives, a niece and nephew, who enlisted in the Air Force. It's no exaggeration to say that Sgt. C. D. James was a friend, as well as my Thunderbird crew chief. I was particularly close to the security men assigned to me in Washington—Charlie Hall, Paul Hilterbrick, and Mike Newsome. A condition of easy familiarity did exist between me and them—at least I thought so—without this leading to any breakdown of discipline. But, as always, some in the Air Force were more comfortable when operating within sharply defined social categories. They saw the issue in crude black and white, were alarmed to discover fraternization everywhere, and were not ready to let the issue go. Thus, from time to time, I was advised by experts to *take charge*, to clarify and codify how we should regulate the officer/enlisted relationship. I saw the issue in shades of grey and thought the less said the better.

Across Gender Lines

With the appearance of more women in the ranks, fraternization between the sexes naturally took on greater significance. Usually, the relationship was voluntary and willing. Increasingly, Air Force men and women, officer and enlisted, married one another, creating the most obvious case of easy familiarity. At one time, the military frowned on the practice of holding hands in uniform, even if the affectionate couple was married and both parties were on the same side of the officer/enlisted divide. Obviously, the Air Force should impose no fraternization barrier between husband and wife, but what if an officer is engaged to an enlisted person? What are the rules for service members who are merely dating? Should we have different rules for men and women in the same, as opposed to separate, chains of command? Between service members in the same unit, as opposed to on the same base? Between Air Force men and women and service members of the Army, Navy, or Marine Corps? The permutations were endless.

Thinking the best way to ensure lawlessness was to have too many laws, I set only one rule. The military's central nervous system is the chain of command running from the president through sequential subordinates to the lowest-ranking airman. This system must work properly to secure the safety of the republic. We therefore must keep it free of pollution by actual or perceived abuse of power. I made it clear to commanders at every level they were obliged to keep their hands off people who worked for them and extended the prohibition to all general officers, whether in command or not. My practice was to make sure commanders and general officers understood that any in-house liaison, no matter how congenial or loving, would constitute a punishable misuse of the power entrusted to them. I retired one very senior officer early and at reduced rank because he ran afoul of this simple rule.

Adultery

When cases of adultery came to my attention, I tried to look the other way, if possible. Here, the problem often was military lawyers, called judge advocates, or JAGs. A good JAG is the commander's best friend, finding ways to get the mission done while avoiding legal quicksand. Occasionally, however, I had to deal with a JAG who assigned himself the role of commander's guardian, the keeper of disciplinary crown jewels.[61]

The JAG always had a prima facie case that adultery demanded

---

61 Legal advice is a case—weather forecasting, another—where you *must* ask for expert opinion. However, American taxpayers have a right to expect that commanders—not lawyers or weather forecasters—will run the Air Force.

punishment since it was defined as an offense by the Uniform Code of Military Justice, the set of laws passed by Congress to regulate the armed forces. Thus, to ignore a case of adultery required a certain hardheadedness, especially when the JAG, holding the legal and moral high ground, wanted to prosecute. Nevertheless, with adultery, my experience showed the strict letter of the law was often in tension with reason and moderation. In my view, what consenting adults did in private was their business, assuming it did not involve a power relationship, as with a commander or general officer.

Many who would otherwise agree with this approach have castigated the military for seeming to regard adultery as a strictly male privilege, the indiscretions of female members being pursued with vigor. This simply was not so in the Air Force I led. I had neither the energy nor inclination to single out women for special treatment. Where the charges alleged *only* adultery, I do not recall pursuing a single case against either a male or female member. Unhappily, other kinds of actionable behavior—"unbecoming" public conduct, false swearing, disobedience, spousal abuse, and so forth—often complicated the case.

Sexual Harassment

As a growing number of women were grouped with men in high-pressure, frontline jobs, service leaders were bound to think about their role, if any, in regulating the sexual behavior of subordinates. One could argue that commanders have no legitimate role, any more than civilian employers have the right to manage the private lives of workers. I based my contrary view on the notion that the military profession is not just another job. We hold commanders responsible for the welfare and, above all, the operational effectiveness of their units, which no doubt can be undermined by inappropriate, sexually related behavior.

The services must provide a work environment that supports mission accomplishment. This means, among other things, one free of harassment of any sort. When men and women work together, there will likely be some sexual harassment of females by males. (A reverse case of female harassment of males never came to my attention.) Make no mistake, real crimes, like rape or assault, and real problems, like sexual harassment, are particularly loathsome in the military, given the special commitment service people make to one another.

When I took over as chief, the Air Force's sexual harassment caseload was low by comparison with earlier times and with the other services. In part this may have sprung from our policy of not tolerating this type of behavior. When harassment incidents came to the attention of commanders, our policy called for taking them seriously and dealing with them promptly. Nevertheless, while I was chief, the frequency of sexual-harassment complaints nearly tripled, from 0.7 (1991) to 1.7 (1993) complaints per 1,000 uniformed members. (On investigation, about 70 percent of such complaints turned out to be valid.) I'd like to think the rate increased because we made it clear women who complained would get a fair hearing and did not need to fear reprisal. So the uptick may have been a signal the system was working. In any case, the number of complaints started coming down in 1994, perhaps because our zero-tolerance attitude got through to more people.

The Tailhook Affair

Early in my tenure, the Navy's Tailhook affair brought the issue of sexual harassment to a boil. Naval aviators had a tradition of meeting once a year for a symposium on naval aviation named after the device that engages deck cables when coming aboard an aircraft carrier. More than 4,000 naval aviators attended the 35th Annual Tailhook Symposium, held in Las Vegas in September 1991. Naturally, it was the perfect excuse for a party. Though the event was described as tamer than other recent gatherings, subsequent investigation identified 90 victims of indecent assault. One evening, during a particularly raucous party, Navy Lt. Paula Coughlin and 26 other Navy women were attacked by at least 70 male Navy and Marine Corps officers. When Lieutenant

Coughlin complained, the Navy's inspector general looked into the matter and issued a report showing many senior officers had attended Tailhook and had been aware of indecent acts and assaults. However, the report skipped over Secretary of the Navy Lawrence Garrett's presence at the scene, an omission amplifying public criticism and the demand for independent review. Finally, the DOD inspector general got involved, issued a devastating report and referred back to the Navy a list of 140 individuals for possible courts-martial or other disciplinary action. The report identified 32 active duty flag officers who had attended Tailhook, including the current CNO, my friend Admiral Frank Kelso, and a future CNO, Rear Adm. Jay Johnson.

There was a widespread feeling that Tailhook had happened not because of the egregious actions of a few drunken aviators, or even a broader reluctance of military leaders to insist on fair treatment for servicewomen, but because disrespect for servicewomen was implicit in the assignment policy barring them from combat duties. So Tailhook turned out to be a watershed event in that it gave rise to public demands for the military to show its commitment to equality in a very specific way: opening combat duties to women.

The Combat Exclusion

Notwithstanding the remarkable progress made by women in the Air Force and the other services, as we entered the decade of the '90s, women still could not hold military positions officially designated as combat jobs. When the demand now arose to repeal this "combat exclusion," I was an early, high visibility opponent of doing so. Before completing my first year in office, I told *Armed Forces Journal International*:

> . . . my attitude is one of ambivalence. On the one hand, I believe the services ought to reflect the best aspects of our society: where if you've got the capabilities, nobody should stop you from doing something because of your race, religion, sex, age, or anything else. We have a lot of highly capable women in the Air Force, and I would like them to have unlimited opportunity.

But, personally, I have a problem with it. For me, combat is a grim activity. I'm not talking about the risk, because women are already at risk in their noncombat jobs. Some were killed in Desert Storm. But combat, for me, is not about dying. It's about killing. There's no qualification needed for dying. It's killing that has to be learned. And I'm reluctant to ask women to kill people when I'm available to do it myself. It's hard enough to ask men to go do it, as I recently found.

. . . We're probably going to open up all jobs to women, and I will not be real comfortable with that. But that's probably the way it's going to come out.

In opposing repeal of the combat exclusion, I had many covert allies but almost no public support. Without exception, senior Navy aviators I knew shared my views, but the backlash from Tailhook effectively muzzled them. The senior leadership of the Army and Marine Corps felt it essential to keep women out of ground maneuver units—infantry, armor, and artillery. Though unenthusiastic about women in combat aviation, they were willing to give this up to protect the ground combat arms. By default, I became the spokesman for a view that, after Tailhook, was pretty obviously going to be a loser.

Ensuing Debate

As a general rule, countries have not deliberately sent their women into combat.[62] America was now about to alter this policy. Moreover, such a change might be both required and desirable. But we did not learn this in the debate that followed. An informed discussion of the proposition might start with the question "What are

---

62 John Keegan, the eminent military historian, was quoted in the *New York Times Book Review*:

> Women . . . rarely fight among themselves and they never, in any military sense, fight men. If warfare is as old as history and as universal as mankind, we must enter the supremely important limitation that it is an entirely masculine activity.

armed forces for?" If they exist to fight and win the country's wars, it seemed to me that those seeking fundamental change in the gender composition of combat units carried a special burden of proof. Perhaps soldiers fight better in combat units containing a mixture of sexes, though I heard no one make this assertion. In fact, we categorically failed to address the implications of such a change for the combat effectiveness of military formations. Instead, advocates for women (I considered myself one, though maybe not of the doctrinaire variety) shifted the burden of proof, arguing there should be no ceiling on career opportunity and that women could never reach the top of the military profession unless they got a crack at the fighting—a fair point. Accordingly, it was up to people like me, who sought to exclude women from active combat, to prove that enrolling them would somehow reduce the effectiveness of the combat force.

The Individual and the Team

In considering how to make that case, there were at hand many convincing but unusable arguments. For example, while I believed that, typically, men sustain the rigors of combat better than women, certainly many women are as steadfast as some men. Again, in my view, men are more likely than women to possess the physical skills needed to pilot combat aircraft, but surely at least a few women have flying ability to match anyone's. I never used generalizations about masculine or feminine capacity because it would be silly to argue we could find no woman who possessed in full measure the attributes needed for success in any kind of combat task.

However, it is a misjudgment to imagine that individual performance is what matters in combat. Combat is not a contest between persons, like poker or boxing. It's not "singles." Combat is a team event, with success or failure depending on group cooperation and morale. This is true even of fighter pilots, those aces presented as champions of single combat. Airmen fly into battle together, in formation. The fight can and sometimes does degenerate into a melee, with every man for himself, but when it does, things have gotten out of hand. We want to fight as a team. So the gender-related behavior that concerns us here is not about personal capacity but about the social dynamics of relationships and groups. The issue is not whether one woman, or some women, or even women in general possess the requisite individual skills for combat, but whether and how including women in the fight affects the performance of the team.

Unit Cohesion

Unit cohesion is a multidimensional term without a precise, pedigreed meaning in the English language. It captures a value not directly observable or measurable—easy to recognize but hard to describe. I think of it as a strong sense of community, a sense of trust, a shared willingness to intervene. Establishing such a feeling in combat units is of crucial importance because the relationship between the individual and the group determines a person's willingness to fight, even to die, for the group.

It's a lot easier to get unit cohesion if you start with kindred material. That's why many of the world's armed forces have recruited healthy young men in a rather narrow age band, and even from a specific community or region. The Ottoman Empire took boys from Christian families in the Balkans and turned them into the much-feared Janissaries. The British have had their Welsh Guards, for instance, or Highland regiments, or Gurkhas. The superior combat performance of such groups is a well-documented phenomenon, examples so plentiful as to need no further elaboration. We even see something of the sort in the civilian world, where group solidarity seems to spring up spontaneously among individuals with common social experience based on religion, race, ethnic group, age, or gender.

The Limits of Training

Today's military cannot bank on the ready-made cohesion flowing from either selective recruiting or free association. To put it mildly, America's armed forces are drawn from a diverse population. (For us, cohesion may be the wrong term, technically. Perhaps better would be "adhesion," in its sense of bonding dissimilar materials.)

On joining the Air Force, young men—and, increasingly, young women—from every part of the country, of every racial, religious, or ethnic background, some speaking English only haltingly, meet one another for the first time at an air base in Texas, and we undertake to make them part of a disciplined, cohesive team. This is not the same problem as that facing, say, the air force of Portugal, a country whose political boundaries have not changed in centuries, whose population is completely uniform in religion, and whose territory is exactly congruent with its language.

Under the circumstances, how can we produce cohesive units? We do our best by making much of what is good about the service and the country. Most Americans have a commitment to universal values such as liberty and equality—good subjects to start with in the process of indoctrinating basic trainees. We even try to turn the absence of a unifying culture into an asset. After all, we are a great country in large part because all sorts of people live here, assimilate, and prosper. But since we lack an underlying common culture, these concepts provide only a modest foundation for unit cohesion. So, this isn't work to be done just once in the controlled environment of basic training. Taking disparate human material and forging it into units that are at the same time cohesive and tolerant of considerable diversity is a continuing leadership job for field commanders.

Combat versus Support

Though important in every kind of military formation, cohesion is a make-or-break factor only in combat units. Not all Air Force units are combat outfits, not even a majority. And even in air combat units, most people play a supporting role. The cohesiveness of support units or of supporting individuals in combat units is important but much less likely to be determining in battle. It's the cohesion of the combat aircrew force, the warriors, that's important, and their training is quite different. Already, before flying training starts, the attrition is heavy. Aviators are officers, so the requirement to complete a college degree sifts out many. Sharp eyesight, good reflexes, and a high standard of physical fitness are specified. Batteries of special psychological and physical tests separate those thought to have low potential for success. Preflight screening identifies the most certain victims of airsickness and those who become easily disoriented in space and time. At each stage of primary and basic flying training, more aspirants wash out. Then, on graduation and the award of wings, only a fraction of the new pilots are taken into combat crew training. Most are siphoned off into transport, tanker, or other support aviation. At the combat crew training stage, still more attrition occurs. Surviving and getting, finally, to a combat squadron produces the feeling of having joined a carefully culled elite.

That's when the real competition starts. In a fighter squadron, you prove yourself every day. At the gunnery range, there's a bet on every practice bomb and every bullet hole in the strafing panel. If it's air-to-air work, gun-camera film is painstakingly analyzed to satisfy tracking and kill claims. Debriefings are merciless, any imperfection quickly exposed. Pilots vie for designation as a "select crew," or squadron "top gun," for selection to attend Fighter Weapons School, or for membership on the team that enters Gunsmoke and William Tell competitions. Sport, even off-duty play, is taken seriously. Rivalries as fierce as any schoolyard's establish a pecking order that might in other settings disrupt and divide, but somehow works to unify when turned to the benefit of the team. Deployments take aircrews away from home and enforce togetherness in a bachelor setting. Finally, the job-rating process, assignment system, voluntary return to civilian life, and accidents chip away at the crew force relentlessly, removing the less skilled, less dedicated, or less lucky, while repeatedly convincing those who remain of their special status. If you start with good people and if they're properly led, at the end of such a process, you get unit cohesion —a combat team ready to fight anybody.

How would this change with women in the mix? Well, when we collaborate, it seems clear we call on primitive patterns of behavior, evolved over millions of years of living and working in groups. Granted there are interactions between nature and nurture, but genetic heritage must be a guiding, if not controlling force in determining many aspects of group conduct. (Indeed, the scholarly evidence accumulates to show that much animal—including human—behavior obeys deeply embedded biological rules.) For instance, some say men possess special psychological resources for bonding with one another, derived from the primitive need to hunt cooperatively. On its face, this proposition would seem convincing, but its implications are so definitive for the issue at hand that perhaps we should not trust it to settle the argument. We would do better to rely on a more modest observation that must be so commonplace as to be nearly universal: how people behave with members of their own sex differs considerably from how they behave when members of the opposite sex are present.

Sexual nuance invades every aspect of adult human relationships. We seem to have no choice other than to send and receive signals as we unconsciously assess the biological and cultural cues that establish sexual identity during even the most ordinary human interactions. Because of this more or less fixed natural ingredient, our common sense tells us that a combat unit mixing men and women will inevitably be characterized by a different set of relationships than will an all-male version. Sexuality unavoidably colors these relationships. The change will not likely enhance unit cohesiveness. On the contrary, unit cohesion has so far been built on male bonding, which must be put at risk when men compete for the attention of women.

I never assumed biology was the whole story. We can regulate conduct by effective training. But the issue for me was the degree to which we can or should rely on training programs to entirely transform instinctive human behavior. In answering this question, we should not ignore the obvious: our best institutions, like liberal democracy or market economics, work because—unlike socialism, radical feminism, or other utopian schemes—they do not operate at cross-purposes with human nature. Military leaders who encourage male bonding reinforce a powerful natural instinct, the tendency of men to band together for competitive purposes and to seek domination in status hierarchies. By contrast, those who try to get healthy men and women in their early 20s to ignore each other's sexuality attempt something quite unnatural. Any military regimen or training mandate designed to eliminate or even markedly attenuate human sexuality is so unrealistic as to be laughable.[63]

Congressional Testimony

On balance, the foregoing argument that assigning women to combat units would change them and that the change would very likely reduce their reliability and effectiveness seemed to me unassailable. But I could see no way to condense this view into a few phrases or a catchy slogan that might sway an inside-the-Beltway audience. "Identity" politics had produced a generation of officeholders especially sensitive to pressure from interest groups. I therefore judged that I was not going to win; that is, I could not stop the movement to declare women eligible for Air Force combat jobs.

The situation became clear in July 1992, when, in the wake of the Tailhook scandal, the House Armed Services Committee called

---

63 In 2002, in response to gender-related problems at the Air Force Academy, the secretary of the Air Force, the Honorable James Roche, ordered removal of a poetic fragment "BRING ME MEN" from a stone arch, framed by a background of mountains as viewed from the cadet parade ground.

We used to ridicule the Soviet practice of including a "political commissar" in the outfit, a fellow who enjoyed status on a par with the unit commander but whose concern was political correctness instead of combat effectiveness. Of course, civilian service secretaries are commissars of a sort, but, unlike Roche, most of them have not taken their role as political nanny seriously. Beginning to end, Roche was a disaster for the Air Force, so this little drama only adds to a bill of attainder too long and detailed for treatment here.

the service chiefs to testify on sexual harassment. Congresswoman Patricia Schroeder, a snappy, well-practiced foil on women's issues, summed up the case, remarking that the witness table seemed reserved for men only—that even officer aides accompanying the chiefs were entirely male:

> There aren't even any women in the second row! I mean, where do women go? I mean, what do they do and how do we deal with those attitudes? There just doesn't seem to be the respect even among the top leaders that women are contributing anything.

Sure enough, the chiefs (me included) ducked for cover, each of us searching for and pointing out female staff scattered in the audience. On the issue of women in combat, this exchange was typical of what passed for debate—strident and uninformed, each side denouncing motives rather than examining convictions.

Although I was realistic enough to understand I was on the losing side, I tried a number of approaches. At the July 1992 House hearing cited above, I testified:

> I believe the combat exclusion law is discrimination against women. And, second, that it works to their disadvantage in a career context. I still think it is not a good idea for me to order women into combat. Combat is about killing people. I'm afraid that even though logic tells us women can do that as well as men, I have a very traditional attitude about wives and mothers and daughters being ordered to kill people.

This was not the oft-heard contention that women cannot kill because their instinct is to give life, to nurture, though that is certainly true of many women. The point was we'd always have males in the chain of command who (like me) would not relish the prospect of causing women to join any sort of murderous fight, never mind a fight with the other side's men. The argument had internal validity, but I intended to frame it in a way that would compel male advocates for women in combat to confess they were willing to stand aside while women did the fighting, a proposition I hoped would make them uncomfortable. It didn't work. Unblinkingly, men like Senator Ted Kennedy stepped up: "The time has come to repeal the archaic and arbitrary statutes that exclude women." I had underestimated the capacity to tolerate embarrassment.

Testifying before the Senate Armed Services Committee, I tried another tack. Asked by Senator William Cohen of Maine whether I would always assign a male pilot to a combat position, even if a female was better qualified, I answered, "It does not make much sense, but that is the way I feel." My point was it's logical that the better pilot, male or female, should be used, but it is *only* logical. In dealing with human relationships, it doesn't pay to be fanatically logical. This is especially true when it comes to matters involving sexuality. Combat itself is too crazily stupid, glorious, hideous—human—for us to believe that logic can tell us everything we need to know about it.

DACOWITS

A variation on this theme occurred in April 1993, just as the issue was coming to a head. In an appearance before the largely female Defense Advisory Committee on Women in the Services (DACOWITS), I said I thought it a mistake to open bomber and fighter cockpit assignments to women. According to news accounts, one of the conferees, Navy Lt. Kara Hultgren, then flying EA-6B electronic jammer aircraft out of Naval Air Station Key West, "jumped to her feet" and "peppered" me with pointed questions. I was quoted as replying, "I'm dealing with a human-relations problem, and not all human-relations problems yield to logic. I can't offer a syllogism showing how I arrived at my view."

Newsmen later sought out Lieutenant Hultgren, who reportedly said,

> He admitted that his whole premise is illogical. It's nonsense to say that unit cohesion would suffer. I can say

confidently that almost every man in my squadron would say, "I would fly with women in combat," without hesitation.⁶⁴

Divided Air Force

Portraying my opponents as relying only on cold, objective logic when the case called for an understanding of human feeling and emotion didn't work either. Nothing was going to work. Even inside the Air Force, I ran into considerable opposition. The *Air Force Times* regularly panned my position. Some senior officers, like General Bob Herres, former vice chairman of the Joint Chiefs, found the equal-career-opportunity argument compelling. A former chief I respected, Larry Welch, thought I was tilting at windmills and advised me privately to give my energy to matters I could influence favorably for the Air Force. "Besides," Welch told me, "there's a slight chance you may be wrong," a remark I soon borrowed. Both these men had fine combat records but, like many who opposed me on this issue, they were not hard-core warrior types, having risen instead on the strength of intellectual and bureaucratic skills.

Aspin's Announcement

Shortly after coming to the Pentagon as our new secretary of defense, Les Aspin ordered a change in assignment policy, allowing women to be combat aviators but continuing to exclude them from the ground combat arms. On 28 April 1993, Secretary Aspin announced the new policy at a Pentagon press conference, staged with all the service chiefs standing behind him. On Cable News Network, Jamie McIntyre described the scene:

> MCINTYRE: The plan got a four-star salute, even from the Air Force chief of staff, who made no secret of his personal opposition.

---

64 Lieutenant Hultgren subsequently became the first female naval combat pilot. She was killed in October 1994, trying to land her F-14 aboard the USS *Abraham Lincoln*. Her male backseater ejected and survived.

GENERAL MCPEAK: The secretary made a decision, so I'm comfortable with it. And there's always a small chance that I was wrong (laughter).

In the *Washington Times*, Wesley Pruden was not kind:

> General McPeak, who once said he would take a female pilot assigned to his squadron as his own wingman because he would have the decency not to doom (another) pilot under his command, is eager this week to be the majorette for the band assigned to wreck his Air Force.

A more charitable view would be that I'd taken full advantage of the opportunity to state my views and had been overruled. As I said during the Aspin press conference,

> We had a discussion period in which my views were asked, and I gave an honest opinion. If I hadn't, I think the secretary should have fired me. Now the secretary has made a decision, and it is my job to implement that decision as well as I can. And if I don't do that, he should fire me for that.

Obeying Orders

It was a bad mistake, in my view, to mix women into the combat crew force. On the other hand, of 16,500 pilots we had at the time, only 295—less than 2 percent—were women, nearly all of them serving in support aviation. It seemed unlikely we would have more than a few female combat aircrews anytime soon. Moreover, the country faced no immediate threat. Nevertheless, this issue brought me as close to early departure from office as any I faced in four years as chief. The excuse for staying was the usual lame one: my leaving would not have affected the outcome.

Because I stayed, I was obliged to do my best to ensure the success of the new policy. Anticipating Aspin's decision, I'd already asked Billy Boles, the deputy chief of staff for personnel, to identify some female pilots who seemed to have high potential to make good in combat units. Based on his recommendations, I picked six and brought three of them—2nd Lt. Jeannie Flynn, Capt. Sharon

Preszler, and Capt. Martha McSally—to Washington. I asked for a second session with the Pentagon press corps following Secretary Aspin's announcement and introduced these three to the public.

By virtue of her immediate reassignment to combat crew training in the F-15E, Jeannie Flynn became our first female combat pilot, making an attractive poster girl for the change. Her credentials were typical of this handpicked group. She had a bachelor's degree in aerospace engineering from the University of Texas, as well as a master's in aeronautics and astronautics from Stanford, and she had recently graduated first in her flying training class of 31 men and two women. She'd wanted a fighter assignment, in fact, had picked one from the offerings at the end of pilot training. But because of the gender restriction, we'd packed her off to C-141 training, which she had just begun. I terminated her transport training and sent her to Seymour Johnson, the F-15E base in North Carolina.

Both Captains Preszler and McSally were well out of training and in operational units. Preszler had a degree in computer science and mathematics from the University of California–Davis. She'd gone first to navigator school, becoming an instructor navigator before being selected for pilot training. She was flying the C-21, a small jet transport. An Air Force Academy graduate with a master's degree from Harvard, McSally was an instructor pilot flying T-38s at a Texas flying training base.[65] Such women as these ought to have the best shot at making the grade in combat squadrons.

Going beyond this initial move, I directed a series of actions

---

65 McSally later caused a stir when she publicly blasted the Air Force for cooperating with Saudi Arabia in enforcing dress rules requiring her to wear long sleeves when off base in that country. In his book, *It Doesn't Take a Hero*, Norm Schwarzkopf makes the best observation about such an attitude: "The law of the land here happens to be Saudi law. So just like we require them to obey our laws in the United States, they have every right to require us to obey their laws here."

aimed at sustaining a flow of high-quality female pilots into the combat force:

First, we immediately established gender-neutral pilot training. That is, we reviewed our training programs to remove any aspect of organizational gender bias.

Second, we instituted a gender-neutral assignment system, to include combat aircraft.

Third, we screened all female pilots trained since 1991 (when I had ordered a return to the merit assignment system) and afforded them the same opportunity to select fighters and bombers their male counterparts had enjoyed at the time of graduation. I intended that this directive, a kind of affirmative action, would correct the "mistakes" of the past—within reasonable limits.

Finally, we screened all female flying instructors to identify the top performers in Training Command and targeted this group for assignment to fighters and bombers, using the same assignment policies we employed for male instructor pilots.

The Exceptions

The decision to give access to combat cockpits opened more opportunity to women in the Air Force and the other services. Nevertheless, some jobs remained closed. Of most significance, we would continue to exclude women from service in the infantry, armor, and artillery units of the Army, Marine Corps, and Special Operations Force. It certainly made sense to me to retain the all-male policy for ground combat units. But, interestingly, it was not the unit cohesion argument that prevailed in this instance. Army and Marine Corps leadership argued that ground combat makes demands no woman can meet. While I agreed it was silly, even dangerous, to expect a cross section of female soldiers to perform the same physical tasks as male counterparts, this was much different from claiming there was no woman in America with upper body strength to match our weakest infantryman. The success of the Army/Marine Corps argument and the failure of my own was yet more evidence that, when formulating high policy, it's not enough simply to be right.

The continued ground-combat exclusion had the effect of perpetuating some restrictions on the assignment of Air Force women. These related to skills that might put them in situations involving direct ground combat. For instance, about 500 active duty jobs in the Air Force's "combat control" career field stayed closed to women. Combat controllers parachute into drop zones and demolish obstacles, set up navigation aids, take weather observations, and otherwise prepare for the arrival of Army airborne units. Another 500 or so aircrew positions in the helicopter force supporting Special Operations Command remained closed to women. The logic seemed a bit tortured in these cases, but the Army and Marine Corps had successfully separated "direct ground combat" from other forms of fighting, so it became necessary to honor this somewhat artificial boundary where our people worked in tandem with ground maneuver units.

An interesting, unintended side effect of the new rules: opening aviation assignments made a few female officers eligible for combat duties. Perpetuating restrictions in ground combat meant that, by and large, the exclusion of enlisted females would continue. I often wondered whether feminist advocacy groups even noticed that the vast majority of women in uniform—the enlisted force—did not rally to their cause. In a way, combat flying became a sort of indulgence enjoyed by women of privilege, but the pressure groups pushing the politics of identity scarcely objected. They seemed content to fashion a world in which only an elite upper crust of military women remained free to choose what to do and what to be.

A few other restrictions remained in effect, but by 1994 the Air Force had opened more than 99 percent of its jobs to women.

✈ ✈ ✈

When I was growing up, the rites of the playground demanded stoicism, made boys ashamed of expressing weakness or vulnerability. Fighting, though, was fairly stylized. Participants could remove eyeglasses. Onlookers stopped particularly one-sided fights. And boys did not fight girls. I do not believe suspending such rules would have made the playground—or the battleground, for that matter—a better place.

As I listened in Washington to the "spokespersons" for women, it was clear they, too, had no wish for girls to be beaten up by boys. Instead, the most radical feminists seemed to feel that boys should not fight boys either—that boys should change. They were revolted by male attitudes toward violence, power, and status, as well as by the male tendency to band together for competitive purposes, all of which they saw as wholly the product of a patriarchal culture, crying out for change. Their real agenda? To feminize the warrior elites, these little boys who never outgrew the playground; to rechannel, if not eliminate, male preoccupations with hierarchy and domination; to soften the traditional masculine virtues of toughness, aggression, and willingness to use force when necessary; to use the political power of women to produce kinder, gentler armed forces.

The matter of gender was pretty close to the center of my understanding of the warrior's place in society. What does it say about *us* if we let women do the fighting, if we let *our* women fight *their* men? This was the issue for me, and in the long sweep of history, that may be the wrong issue. It may be true that less sexist societies are less warlike and, for a society, this is a good thing. I would, myself, prefer Athens to Sparta. But I was convinced that armed forces are the exceptional case, that we might not want them to mirror society, that we ought to be very careful about making them less warlike.

When peace breaks out, soldiers are such an easy target. They're already separated, a special human community with its own traditions, language, art, values. It has to be that way. Stripped of its distinctive content and intangible rewards, the military life is simply another government job, characterized by family separation, red tape, forcible relocation, bad pay, and equipment supplied by the lowest bidder. This is good enough for careerists, for timeservers who see the military as a five-day workweek, with the opportunity for early retirement. But to prepare warriors for a life of hardship, the military must remain a kind of adventure, apart from the civilian world and full of strange customs. To be a fighter pilot, or a paratrooper, a submariner or a Seal, is to join a self-contained, resolutely idealistic society, largely unnoticed and surprisingly uncorrupted by the world at large. I did not see how including women in this community would enhance prospects of success in battle. Indeed, I believed doing so, in the end, would weaken the warrior culture—which is OK, I suppose, unless we ever again have a real fight on our hands.

For the record, war has not so far been the occasional interruption of a normality called peace.

Chapter 8

The War on Biology Part II: Gays in the Military

We few, we happy few, we band of brothers . . .
—Shakespeare, *Henry V*

During the 1992 presidential campaign, Governor Bill Clinton promised to end the practice of excluding declared homosexuals from military service. He later softened the proposal somewhat with assurances that we would continue to forbid open homosexual conduct, just as we prohibited outrageous heterosexual activity, and here the linkage to the Navy's Tailhook scandal was obvious. Subsequently, the matter did not get much attention in campaign debates but, following Clinton's election, there was a lot of public speculation and press comment, not to mention a certain amount of head scratching inside the Pentagon.

It is probably true, as gay advocates assert, that homosexuals have served in our armed forces since the country's beginnings. The argument for allowing them to do so openly is animated by our most humane and progressive instincts, the highest ideals of Western liberalism. Here, I use the term liberal in its classic sense: a set of attitudes grounded in the belief that a proper goal of government is to protect individual autonomy against coercion from whatever source—state, church, or society. As a citizen, I favor this brand of liberalism. Over the years, much damage has been done by fashionable restriction of minority expression. When in doubt, we should prefer public policies that err on the side of personal freedom.

It is elementary civics, though, that some issues transcend the individual. The neighborhood, too, has rights, perhaps the clearest case occurring when a country prepares its citizens for war. Here, the overriding concern must be the success and safety of our young people drawn together in combat formations. My view—shared in this instance by the other service chiefs—was that allowing open homosexuality in ranks would adversely affect unit cohesiveness and therefore compromise combat efficiency.

Finessing the Cohesion Issue

By and large, spokesmen for gay rights ignored the cohesion issue, beginning their case with the seemingly businesslike argument that what's important is an individual's own performance. Military standards should address precisely that: performance. The policy of prohibiting open homosexuality was based not on deficient individual performance, but on a definition of the individual self, an odd exception to the American idea that people should be judged by their actions rather than their makeup. As even conservative icon William F. Buckley observed, "A gay sergeant who obeys military regulations shouldn't endanger the republic, or even his platoon."

The point was brought home forcefully when several homosexuals with spotless military records came out of the closet. SSgt. Thomas Paniccia, an 11-year Air Force veteran with high job ratings, declared his homosexuality on national television. Another who became well known was Margarethe Cammermeyer, a colonel in the Army National Guard, a wife and mother, a nurse decorated for service in Vietnam (Glenn Close played the role in the HBO production). President Clinton and others made much of her case.

Here, they asserted, was direct evidence it was flat wrong to claim, as the Defense Department did, that homosexuality was "incompatible" with military service.

Gay-advocacy groups went further. They estimated one in 10 Americans was homosexual and the composition of the military was likely no different, which implied there were perhaps as many as 200,000 gays in uniform. But the services discharged only about 1,500 a year for homosexuality. In effect, many thousands of gay soldiers, sailors, airmen, and Marines must live in a state of peaceful coexistence with heterosexual troops.

There was more to this line of argument than wishful thinking, or a postdiscovery sense of commonality: the oft-observed tendency of, say, unemployed workers to overestimate the jobless rate. This was propaganda. For example, in his book *Conduct Unbecoming: Gays and Lesbians in the U.S. Military*, published in the spring of 1993, Randy Shilts claimed:

> ". . . at least one gay man has served in the astronaut program . . . The Navy and Marine Corps had at least one gay person at four-star rank since 1981, and at least one gay man has served on the Joint Chiefs of Staff in that time."[66]

Some also argued that sexual identity was not a "preference" but an innate and immutable characteristic, akin to race. It was therefore not "abnormal," but simply not the sexual complexion of the majority. If true, the bar on openly gay service was analogous to the racial-exclusion policies of 50 years earlier.

The new president and others clearly did see "gays in the military" as a rights issue, asserting parallels with the civil rights movement and posing as vigorous opponents of discrimination. By ending the prohibition on openly gay service, Clinton supposed he would follow in the footsteps of President Truman, whose famous 1948 executive order was seen as having ended racial segregation in the armed forces.

---

66 Mr. Shilts died in 1994, age 42, of AIDS.

Even when the matter of unit cohesiveness was acknowledged as important and was understood to involve more than the question of individual performance or civil rights, gay advocates claimed that Tailhook and other harassment incidents showed the problem was not sexual orientation but sexual misconduct. The remedy was responsible leadership, to enforce existing standards of behavior for all service members, gay and straight, male and female. The argument seemed to be, "Sure, open homosexuals will be harassed and excluded, but Tailhook shows that's happening already to women. What's needed is better training, better discipline, better leadership, and that will solve the 'inclusion,' or cohesion problem."

Finally, training costs were cited as a concern. The Government Accounting Office, Congress's auditing arm, produced an estimate that the services spent nearly $500 million during the decade of the '80s to train replacements for discharged homosexuals. Many, including the president, cited this figure during the subsequent debate.

Training Cost

I had no idea where the GAO came up with this $500 million figure. For the record, during the decade of the '80s, the Air Force put more than 800,000 people through various basic and advanced training programs. Like each of the services, we maintained a training base to handle this continuous workload. For the whole decade, the operating cost of the Air Force training base was about $30 billion. Over that same period, it made no measurable difference that we incidentally separated something like 3,000 people—about one-third of 1 percent of the number trained—on account of homosexuality. As one might guess, most such separations occurred in the first few weeks of basic training, before the more expensive technical training began. Many of the separations would have occurred in any case, since they were the result of "conduct" and not simple "declaration." In any event, we could not have materially reduced the size or cost of the training base by keeping all 3,000 of the separated gays. This also held true for the other services. So training cost was not an entirely phony issue, but to talk about $500 million amounted to a gross, and perhaps deliberate, distortion.

Closeted versus Open Homosexuality

Nor did the argument that closeted homosexuals had served honorably and well cut much ice with me. Over the years, I'd known a handful of airmen of homosexual orientation. Those who were discreet served without difficulty. I was convinced the figure was nothing like the 10 percent claimed by gay proponents, or even 5 percent, but certainly it was not zero percent. So the point that undeclared homosexuals have a record of honorable service is correct, and no one should deny it. As long as neither they nor we acknowledge it and their behavior is circumspect, we have a tendency to live and let live. Colonel Cammermeyer was not an obstacle to unit excellence before she declared her homosexuality, proving only that closeted homosexuality was not the issue.

What the Cammermeyer case and others like it showed was we ought to distrust simplistic solutions to complex social problems. When it came to closeted homosexuality, people in uniform were quite capable of adopting a sophisticated middle position. It was the Clinton initiative that forced a choice. We had to be either for or against open homosexuality in our ranks. It was this insistence that we recognize and accommodate open homosexuality that I judged would corrode unit cohesion.

Civil Rights

Much of the pro-gay argumentation tacitly assumed there is a "right" to serve in the armed forces. This bothered me because I regard a citizen's rights as a basic protection against the law, a shield warding off the sometimes-menacing power of the majority. We ought to worry when every supposedly desirable social goal is cast as a "right," when rights proliferate and are as a consequence cheapened.

Whereas the nation has often required able-bodied men to serve, no citizen can claim a constitutional right to enter the armed forces.

The view that such a right exists rests on the notion that serving in the armed forces is a job, like any other in our society, and therefore the antidiscrimination laws relating to civilian employment should apply with equal force to the services.[67] It may seem hopelessly idealistic, but my view was that serving the nation in uniform amounted to a calling, different in many ways from other "jobs." (One of the ways is your employer can order and enforce action that puts your life at risk.) Uniformed service to the country should be regarded a civic privilege, not a civil right.

And I wondered why the many other well-established forms of discrimination weren't burning political issues. People could not serve in uniform if they were too old or too young, too fat or too thin, too tall or too short, handicapped, not sufficiently well educated, and so forth. So why did discrimination against gay people rise to the status of a civil rights issue, but the practice of barring from service, say, men shorter than four feet, eight inches did not?

In brief, the services excluded from entry, without challenge, many categories of people. On balance it seemed to me there could be no valid assertion of a universal "right" to serve in the armed forces, and therefore exclusion from service was not a legitimate civil rights issue.

Truman's Executive Order

There also was some misunderstanding about Truman's executive order of 1948. No doubt it was a landmark in the long struggle to achieve full rights for African Americans. However, it was a necessary but not sufficient inducement for the armed forces to do the right thing. The divergent experience of the services illustrates the point.

---

67 The Air Force employed about a quarter of a million civilians during my time as chief. These civilians had "jobs" and were treated quite differently from active duty military. Sexual orientation was an issue only for those civilians who concurrently served in uniform, like National Guard "weekend warriors."

The Air Force had prepared itself for racial integration. General Carl Spaatz, our first chief of staff, went on record as favoring the elimination of segregation even before issuance of the executive order, though not because of any idealism. For Spaatz and many other senior airmen, the issue was efficiency. Segregation was wasteful because it made poor use of manpower. It seemed clear the Air Force would include at least some and more likely a growing number of black officers and enlisted men. Organized into all-black units, they were underemployed and largely ineffective. During and after World War II, the Tuskegee Airmen aroused much sympathy, but even their combat performance had been uneven. (Perhaps their most important accomplishment was to prove conclusively that black airmen were both brave and competent, destroying the myth of intrinsic inferiority.) Therefore, the most important senior uniformed officers—including Spaatz and his successor, Hoyt Vandenberg, as well as such notables as Curtis LeMay—believed that integrated units would make the most efficient use of black manpower. The Air Force's first secretary, Stuart Symington, also gave racial integration a strong push.

As a consequence, the integration of blacks in the Air Force is one of the great success stories of the civil rights movement. Truman's executive order established a mechanism to insure Defense Department compliance, the Committee on Equality of Treatment and Opportunity, popularly named, after its chairman, the Fahy Committee. When the Fahy Committee was briefed on our plans to integrate, it elected to stand aside and let the Air Force conduct its own program. Within six months, we created 1,300 integrated units. Negro service units disappeared; three years after the new policy was introduced, there were none.

On the other hand, the Army and Navy were models of passive resistance. The Air Force had nearly completed integration before the Army started. Technically, Truman's order made no reference to ending segregation, speaking only of equality of opportunity and treatment. The Army therefore argued it was in full compliance.

Its subsequent racial integration was forced on it because of combat losses in all-white units during the first months of the Korean Conflict. The Navy continued its policy of tokenism into the 1960s, with a black steward corps still waiting tables 10 years after the executive order.

Thus, it is a misunderstanding to think that Truman passed his hand over the Pentagon and brought racial justice to the armed forces. Only after the leaders of each service committed their institutions did we make real progress. Even so, all the services had to put an additional, massive effort into revamping equal-opportunity policies following the racial tensions that surfaced in the Army during the Vietnam War. Active, continuing, and committed leadership was the key to achieving racial integration without disabling loss of unit cohesion.

That being the case, my main problem with allowing open homosexuality in our ranks was I couldn't figure out a way to provide leadership for it. While I believed that all people are created equal, I did not believe such equality extended to all ideas or all cultures. And since I didn't know how to promote the assimilation of this particular form of diversity, I could see no way to prevent it from undermining unit cohesion.

Air Force Attitudes

In the last analysis, however, mine was a subjective assessment. I could cite no empirical evidence to support the claim. Accordingly, in the interval between Clinton's election and his inaugural, I asked for a survey of Air Force attitudes. We chose 800 respondents from a demographic cross section. (The otherwise random selection did include 100 serving unit commanders.) I got the results in December 1992. To summarize its highlights, on the central issue of whether open homosexuality should be permitted, Air Force people were opposed by a substantial margin. The result was fairly consistent up and down the ranks, though women were twice as supportive of the proposed change as men. Even so, women mostly opposed the idea. Overwhelmingly, Air Force people believed the proposal would negatively affect unit cohesion, which, if true, would impair combat performance. Moreover, flying officers and operational commanders, the backbone of our combat capability, were by far the most negative in their attitude toward open homosexuality.[68]

This survey of Air Force attitudes, and my part in ordering it, came in for some criticism. Following Clinton's inaugural, OSD staffers ordered us to keep the findings under wraps. Accordingly, we denied at least three Freedom of Information requests on the grounds we'd collected the data for internal use only. However, as is usually the case in Washington, the survey results found their way into the public domain. The survey was then denounced on account of cost, claimed to be $20,000. (No basis existed for this or any other price tag. We did the survey by telephone, the cheapest approach.)

Memo for the President-Elect

On 14 December 1992, the *Air Force Times* informed its readers in bold headlines: "McPeak Talks of Resigning over Gay Issue." The *Times* claimed that all the chiefs opposed the president but quoted "several sources" as saying that I was "the most vocal of the hard-liners," threatening to fall on my sword. In his autobiography, Colin Powell refers to me as "the most truculent" of the chiefs, which I take as a good-faith observation on his part. As a matter of fact, in confidential JCS discussions, I had strongly opposed accepting openly gay service, but it was pretty hard to get into an argument with the other chiefs on this subject. The publicity casting me in the role of die-hard opponent may have been part of the inevitable jockeying for position during Powell's last months of active

---

68 Charles Moskos, the Northwestern University professor considered a leading authority on military sociology, did some polling for the Army a couple of months later, the results tracking nicely with ours.

service. The president would soon select a new chairman and perhaps someone wanted to show daylight between me and the president on this matter.[69]

My actual position was summed up in a memo I wrote at about the same time the *Air Force Times* story appeared. During the interval between election and inaugural, a transition team showed up in the Pentagon and began putting together recommendations for the new administration on policy and personnel appointments. Team members asked me (and presumably the other chiefs) to draw up an "eyes only" memorandum for the new president, stating my views on important defense issues. They emphasized this memo should be a personal product, not staff work, and assured me the president-elect would read it. In the end, I wrote a brief paper—two-and-a-half pages, double spaced—that said, in part:

> Gays. This ought not to be—but is—the number one topic of conversation whenever I meet with officers and airmen. Accordingly, I put it first. It's not a showstopper, but the services need wiggle room. I suggest a phased approach. In the first phase:
>
> (a) Rescind the ban. Start by removing the DOD policy that prohibits uniformed service by homosexuals. This policy is a little silly anyway since we have always had gays in the military. It is declared or announced homosexuality that gives us the problem, and the services could simply stop asking the question. Gays would no longer be forced either to lie or be barred from service. In brief, near-term, we don't ask—and they don't announce. This would be characterized by many as asking gays to stay in the closet for a while longer. Nevertheless, taking this step allows for at least a technical claim that the ban on gay

---

69 In its 1 February 1993 cover story, *Newsweek* magazine claimed the Joint Chiefs had threatened resignation en masse, but omitted my name when designating the chiefs most hostile to the new administration's goals.

service has been rescinded. We could start "not asking the question" immediately.

(b) Deal with conduct. The Air Force does this already. About half of our involuntary discharges for homosexuality involve conduct rather than "declaration." But the total number of homosexual discharges is very small: only 115 in fiscal year '92—about 15 times fewer than we separated for being overweight. The number is small because we don't peek through bedroom windows. Rather, homosexual misconduct (like egregious heterosexual behavior) is dealt with when it is brought forcefully to our attention. So, all services can stop any aspect of a "witch hunt." This step, too, could be taken immediately.

In the next phase:

(c) Study the impact of allowing service by declared homosexuals. Open—as opposed to closeted—homosexuality involves some rather difficult administrative problems for the services. Thoughtful examination of these problems, either through the normal staffing process or by an outside group of graybeards, would shed needed light and provide more time for the services to adjust.

This phased approach is one I could support publicly—and perhaps the other service chiefs could, as well—as one helping to defuse the issue while at the same time making good on your pledge to promote change.

Agenda Setting

I implied in this memo that homosexuality in the armed forces should not be high on the list of national security concerns. It was not, perhaps, the sort of issue a new president should put at the top of his agenda. What was the evidence for this? Well, in the decade of the '80s, the number of uniformed personnel in the active Air Force averaged about 550,000. To sustain this strength, we brought in and let go about 65,000 people a year. Three-quarters of the people we let go separated voluntarily—either retired from active duty or finished their term of service and returned to civilian life. About a quarter of our separations were involuntary, most of them because of poor performance—people who either would not or could not meet our disciplinary or work standards. On a percentage basis, we separated much smaller numbers because of such factors as drug or alcohol abuse, poor physical condition, or homosexuality. Only 1 to 2 percent of our *involuntary* separations were for homosexuality. The figures remained remarkably stable, never more than 2 percent or less than about 1 percent.

In 1992, when gays in the military surfaced as a national issue, I kept close track of our numbers. That year we were in a drawdown, so we separated 81,500 people, but only about 10,000 of them involuntarily. Of these, 115 separations were for homosexuality, as I noted in my memo to the president-elect. In 1992, in other words, homosexuality was a factor in about one-eighth of 1 percent of our total separations and in only about 1 percent of involuntary separations. We involuntarily separated four times as many people for drug or alcohol abuse and 15 times as many for being overweight. Moreover, as I also pointed out in the memo, about half the 115 homosexual separations involved behavior of a kind that would continue to be actionable, even under the president's proposals.

We all expect the president to set the national agenda, to identify and bring to center stage important questions we need to answer collectively. Indeed, agenda setting lies at the heart of a president's real power. Naturally, for those with some personal involvement or for gay-rights advocates, the way the services deal with homosexuality was a high-priority matter. But based on Air Force experience at least, one had to wonder whether there were not other national security concerns of considerably greater importance.

Conduct, Orientation, Status

Within a few days of his inaugural, President Clinton called the Joint Chiefs to the White House for a meeting on this topic. I thought a good bit about what I would say when my turn came. I did not know whether the president had read my memo, which he might anyway have regarded as an insult rather than wise counsel, so I prepared to go over some of the material again.

In organizing my thoughts for the meeting, I found it useful to differentiate among three concepts: conduct, orientation, and status.

Conduct, of course, was easiest to understand since it is behavior, what a person does. It's external; if present at the scene, we notice conduct, witness it. Conduct was also the aspect easiest to agree on. All parties agreed we should consider homosexual conduct proscribed behavior, leading to dismissal from the service.

It was the other two concepts, orientation and status, that were a little slippery. It seemed to me one could best think of orientation as the direction along which a person wished to move, at the end of which was the objective person one wished to become. In this sense, orientation was entirely an internal condition. On the other hand, status was much more than simply an internal matter. It involved the relationship between the individual and society. The community granted status, often in law or some credentialing process.

I felt it was a mistake to confuse these concepts. People may have a pilot orientation—be inclined to become pilots, maybe even behave like pilots—but they do not achieve the status of pilot until they get wings or a license from the FAA. Perhaps a better contemporary example: two people may wish to marry, may even conduct themselves as though they were married, but it is with the marriage certificate that the community accords the status of married couple. Thus, there is a rite of passage from orientation to status. Some sort of official recognition is granted. When we go to a doctor, we may not be much interested in medical orientation, but we do like to see on the office wall the documents that confer status.

For years, Defense Department regulations had contained the unambiguous assertion that homosexuality was incompatible with military service. The standard entry form used to in-process prospective members required the applicant to answer the question, "Are you a homosexual?" The form itself defined the term as "sexual desire or behavior directed at a person of one's own sex." So this was an all-purpose question because it asked about both orientation and conduct, and answering it established status. In other words, checking the "yes" block and handing the form to the recruiter—a government official—constituted a rite of passage. (By the way, persons with a homosexual orientation or a record of homosexual conduct, for that matter, could check the "no" block, could lie about it. Many did, thus avoiding homosexual status and thereafter serving honorably and well.)

In brief, orientation is what someone wanted to be and status is what the community certifies he or she is—and it's a mistake not to differentiate between these ideas. But the public case made by members of the new Clinton administration relied heavily on fudging the distinction. Indeed, as events unfolded, their press statements used these two terms as though they were interchangeable.

White House Meeting

I had these thoughts in mind when the president summoned us to the Roosevelt Room on Monday evening, 25 January, during the new administration's first days. The vice president, Al Gore, was at the president's side, the two of them flanked by their senior national security advisers, Tony Lake, Sandy Berger, and Leon Fuerth. George Stephanopoulos took a chair on the wall behind the president. On our side of the table, Colin Powell, Vice Chairman Dave Jeremiah, and the four service chiefs lined up with the new secretary of defense, Les Aspin. The chiefs spoke in turn, the others making clear their opposition to lifting the ban on homosexual service. I spoke last.

I explained why I thought it important to distinguish among the notions of orientation, status, and conduct, and wondered whether we might use this approach to find a way out of the difficulty. All sides agreed we should not permit outrageous conduct of any kind, either homo- or heterosexual, so conduct was not an issue. Since orientation itself did not pose a problem, the services might agree to stop asking the question of entry candidates. Were we to do so, the president could claim he'd ended discrimination because he would have caused us to withdraw the procedure requiring homosexuals to lie if they wished to enter the military. Moreover, the services could agree to stop intrusive investigations aimed at rooting out closeted homosexuals. We didn't do much of this sort of morals police work anyway, if for no other reason than our investigative agencies had more important business. But in return, we needed flexibility on the question of status. We could not sign up to permitting open homosexuality in our units, which would have a devastating impact on unit cohesion. In effect, I proposed a "don't ask, don't tell" approach—exactly where we eventually ended up, after the president had formed much scar tissue.

Clinton and his aides heard us out, listening carefully to what we had to say. At meeting's end, the president came around to our side of the table, shaking hands and patting each of us on the back. He used my first name, saying, "Tony, you should have been a lawyer!" Of course, I was flattered, stammering something to the effect that I'd try to regard this as a compliment. Then and later, I found President Clinton to be a man of considerable charm. I went away from this first meeting—and I think the other service chiefs did too—thinking, "Here is a good ol' boy from Arkansas who understands our problem."

Immediate Aftermath

I got some nice publicity out of the meeting. *US News and World Report* quoted the president as telling aides afterward, "Boy . . . McPeak really had it." (It was one of those insider leaks I always objected to because nobody ever seemed to print mine.) But the chiefs collectively came in for much criticism in the wake of this Monday evening meeting. Most of the news coverage started with the assumption senior military leaders had no business negotiating with the commander in chief.[70] Our job was to take orders. Anything less amounted to a replay of the Truman-MacArthur episode.

I agreed completely that, in the end, the president is the boss. However, it's a bad misreading of the situation to assert the

---

70 See, for example, the 26 January 1993 *New York Times* editorial, "Who's in Charge of the Military?"

president shouldn't ask the chiefs for their honest opinion on any matter affecting the armed forces. It's also a mistake to expect them to fall in line automatically behind any particular administration's political platform. The chiefs serve whatever administration is in office but, unlike the service secretaries, they are not part of any administration. This no doubt frustrates some presidents, but is a source of strength for the country. Citizens have a right to expect the chiefs to give the president their best advice, untainted by politics.

Be that as it may, any good feelings generated by the meeting at the White House did not last. The president held a remarkable news conference on 29 January. In response to query, the president asserted he hadn't made "military gay rights week" the new administration's first order of business. "The Joint Chiefs asked for a meeting about a number of issues, [of] which this was only one," he said. (I have no memory either of asking for the meeting or of discussing anything else.) Regarding gays in the military, he said, in part,

> . . . the issue is whether men and women, who can and have served with real distinction, should be excluded from military service solely on the basis of their status . . .
>
> I have asked the Secretary of Defense to submit by July 15th a draft executive order . . . which would end the present policy of the exclusion from military service solely on the basis of sexual orientation.

There it was, the conflation of status and orientation to depict them as more or less the same thing. At best, this indicated the general untrustworthiness of language; at worst, it showed that in this argument words had become weapons, not carriers of thought or meaningful discourse.

At this same press conference, the president fielded another question about a district-court ruling handed down the day before, holding the military ban on homosexuals unconstitutional. He responded to the effect that, if the administration and the services did not cooperate quickly, "there is a not insignificant chance" that the courts would rescind the ban "without the opportunity to deal with this whole range of practical issues" that he was trying to help us solve. In short, if we didn't behave, the courts would get us. As a matter of fact, though the Pentagon had lost a number of cases in the lower courts, these were regularly reversed on appeal, judges being properly reluctant to undertake the administration of the armed forces.

Toward the end of his news conference, the president said,

> I want to make it very clear that this is a very narrow issue. It is whether a person, in the absence of any other disqualifying conduct, can simply say that he or she is homosexual and stay in the service.

Ordinarily, we can assume people are what they say they are. But in the ensuing national debate about gays in the military, the Clinton administration tried to turn this due-course assumption on its head. If we continued to prohibit homosexual behavior, as all sides agreed we would, then what were we to assume about any person who claimed to be homosexual? In the end game, some suggested the Pentagon set up a procedure to allow declared homosexuals to prove they had not engaged in characteristic behavior. This was nonsense worthy of Alice's looking glass, and we all recognized it as such.[71]

Presidential Memorandum

Within a few days of our White House meeting, the president issued a memorandum having the rather grand title, *Ending Discrimination on the Basis of Sexual Orientation in the Armed Forces*. This memo gave Secretary Aspin six months to draft an executive order for the president's signature and required a study showing how we could carry out the change in a way that was "practical, realistic, and consistent with the high standards

---

71 As Frank Kameny, a leader in the "Gay Liberation" movement, said, "I haven't worked for 30 years to give gays the right to be celibate."

of combat effectiveness and unit cohesion." Naturally, the memo pleased no one. Gay advocates were let down because the president had seemed to promise immediate action, not a six-month study. Antigay activists noted the mandated study would not address the merits of the idea but how to dress it up as *not* a bad idea. For our part, the services entered a sort of Bermuda Triangle.

First, there were, as always, a few "status" cases already in the pipeline. What were we to do with these? The services naturally took the view that we should continue to play by the rules until they were changed, which would now certainly be no sooner than six months. Powerful outside voices supported this approach, including some people in the president's own party who pointed out that Article 1 of the Constitution gave exclusively to Congress the power to "make rules for the regulation of land and naval forces." Some members of Congress made it clear they would hold the services accountable for any failure to execute faithfully the rules and regulations they had put in place. On the other hand, respondents in ongoing status cases now claimed they had declared themselves only because they'd believed the president when he promised immediate change, so the administration could not allow business as usual without seeming to betray the very people it had sought to help.

Enter Sam Nunn

By early February, Secretary Aspin issued administrative guidance that reflected a kind of goofy compromise worked out between the president and a senator who had by then become increasingly active on the issue—Sam Nunn, chairman of the Senate Armed Services Committee. In brief, we were told to stop asking the question (which was OK). No change would occur in the treatment of uncontested conduct or status cases (also OK). As for status cases in which the individual was contesting separation, we were to process the case through all the phases, including normal discharge action. These cases would then be taken outside Defense to the Justice Department and referred to the attorney general, who could "suspend" the discharge until the president acted on the SECDEF's forthcoming study. Persons whose discharge was suspended in this way would nevertheless be separated from active duty and placed in a "standby reserve." They would have an option to return to active duty, on request, if the policy eventually changed. Finally, commanding officers were given the authority to reassign personnel during the course of separation proceedings.

It was pretty hard to see how this sort of "suspended" discharge was much better than the actual kind. We were to physically separate people and return them to their home of record. Their ID cards were to be taken away. Their access to military facilities would be restricted, like any other civilian. None of us quite understood what this "standby reserve" was, but to be sure you did not get paid or receive medical treatment and other benefits. In addition, the authority of commanders seemed to have been strengthened by the grant of arbitrary reassignment power, which the Air Force, at least, had not requested.

As it turned out, we never had to face these lawyerly complexities. Congress quickly took the action away from the president, a development we will turn to in a moment, and no contested status case got all the way through to a conclusion. Two Air Force cases started, but we handled them methodically and they were still unresolved when events took down the whole rickety procedure.

Studying the Problem

Meanwhile, we began the study that was to outline steps we could take to insure declared homosexuals could serve in the military without damaging unit cohesion. This was going to take some imagination, but we plunged in, determined to give it our best shot. The longer we looked at the problem, the harder it got.

For example, Secretary Aspin's preliminary guidance had directed us to stop asking the question, to blank it out on entry forms. Now we wondered whether we shouldn't continue to ask it. If homosexuality did not bar people from service, why not determine the standing of those willing to declare it? Perhaps we should code declared homosexuals in our personnel data systems and follow whether they received fair treatment in recruitment, training, and promotion. This kind of tracking had proved essential in advancing opportunities for blacks and women. It was exactly the sort of information we always needed in response to congressional and public inquiry. We might also use such information to mandate more frequent HIV testing, to assist in assigning dormitory rooms, to prevent sending people to serve in countries that considered homosexuality a crime, or to make sure gays had representation on promotion boards. This approach might seem to constitute unwarranted prying into the private lives of servicemen and women, but was better regarded as added proof that military service is not just another job.

We thought about whether we should exclude declared homosexuals from certain career fields, such as the chaplaincy or especially health-care delivery. What would we do for our people at remote locations where, say, the only doctor or dentist available in one-deep positions was a declared homosexual?

We asked ourselves what to do about the impact on the frontline blood supply. Most countries, including the United States, disqualified gay men from donating blood. Here, the policy protected the public interest in a safe emergency blood supply. So far as I knew, gays had not yet argued that treating them differently in this regard violated their civil rights, given the absence of any constitutionally protected right to donate blood.

These concerns may seem a bit overwrought, even hysterical, but I've only scratched the surface. We also considered the question of whether we should allow gay and lesbian groups to organize on our bases and sponsor social events. Some worried about how to protect Boy Scout troops, hosted on many of our installations. Others supposed homosexuals would volunteer in disproportionate numbers for assignment at certain locations, creating gay enclaves. And so forth. Frankly, this kind of speculation ran directly counter to and subverted the increasing tolerance that had emerged in this country, in part because of a mostly admirable campaign against irrational hatred, led by gays themselves. There are many ways to be masculine in our society. But the fact, welcomed by many of us, that homosexuals were moving much more freely in almost all walks of civilian life did little to erase the rationale for exclusion from the military, which rested on basic differences between the two lifestyles.

In the end, we never came up with a plan to change the rules that we thought would not affect unit cohesion.

Backlash

Inside the professional military, the president's proposal encountered intense resistance. Everywhere I went, Air Force people showed open contempt for Clinton. It didn't help that he had less interest, experience, understanding, or credibility in military affairs than any president since the 1920s. The well-known contortions he went through to avoid service in Vietnam did nothing to strengthen his hand.

In March the president tried out some of his celebrated charm on the crew of the aircraft carrier *Theodore Roosevelt*. He was greeted by a chorus of catcalls. I thought the erosion of respect for the office of the commander in chief had gone far enough, so on 24 March transmitted a "personal for" message to all commanders down to squadron level, which said, in part,

> Perhaps it is time to remind ourselves about core values, including the principle of a chain of command that runs from the president right down to our newest airman. We simply must not permit today's debates about . . . social issues to divide us from the society we serve or to undercut the strength and integrity of the chain of command.

In reporting this message, the *Washington Post* noted I had a personal interest in courting the president's favor: "Many Pentagon officials believe he aspires to Powell's job and has even been campaigning for it. Air Force officials, not surprisingly, deny the memo should be read as a job application." The *Wall Street Journal* took a similar tack, noting without elaboration that I was "one of two current chiefs seen as having a shot" at the chairmanship.

The Campbell Affair

In late May, an old friend and fellow fighter pilot, Maj. Gen. Harold "Norm" Campbell, in extemporaneous after-dinner remarks at Soesterberg Air Base in the Netherlands, referred to the president as a "skirt-chasing, dope-smoking draft dodger," or words to that effect. We did an investigation and offered Campbell nonjudicial punishment, which he accepted. (The alternative would have been a court-martial, which I was prepared to pursue.) Campbell was reprimanded, fined about $7,000, and permitted to submit his retirement paperwork.[72] I couldn't help musing that we had, here, a case strikingly similar to the central issue concerning gay service. Although the organization can stand quiet doubts about the president's fitness to serve as commander in chief, we cannot tolerate open expression of such feelings.

Schroeder to Powell

Congresswoman Patricia Schroeder, enhancing her record as Pentagon gadfly, wrote to General Powell in April asking him to explain the difference between the ban on gays and the previous restrictions concerning service by blacks. Lumping blacks with homosexuals certainly could be viewed as an affront to most African Americans and Powell plainly thought the letter insulting. His reply pointed out that "skin color is a benign, nonbehavioral characteristic," while sexual orientation was "perhaps the most profound of human behavioral characteristics." Comparison of the two was a convenient but invalid argument.

Powell's answer was splendid, but I would have gone further. The different races have been around for the past 100,000 years or so, a blink of the eye in evolutionary time. Since the races can

---

72 By tradition, general officers request retirement in a handwritten note to the chief. Campbell's note was one of the most eloquent and moving I ever received.

and do interbreed, the boundary line between them is quite fuzzy. The same is certainly not true of the sexes. In fact, the proper analogy between homosexuals and heterosexuals is that between men and women. Sexual orientation is, after all, sexual orientation. The issue had to do with mixing sexes, not races.

Congress Steps In

Meanwhile, civilian opposition to the president gained momentum. It is a clear misreading of the law and the Constitution to believe the president's powers as commander in chief are absolute. The Armed Services Committees routinely produce Authorization Acts in which they insert language to stop or endlessly complicate any administration proposal not of their liking. This means that a president opting for sweeping change in the armed forces must have at least the tacit and preferably the enthusiastic support of Congress. But now a bill was introduced requiring the implementation of Clinton's proposed change by law rather than by executive order. Another bill would prohibit extending to homosexual partners the benefits provided to military spouses. John Warner, ranking minority member of the Senate Armed Services Committee, put forward legislation that would have established a right to separate for service members who had religious, moral, or personal objections to the change, opening the prospect of a mass exodus of our best people, with large consequences for readiness and real, as contrasted with GAO estimated, impact on training costs. Both houses held hearings during which respected authorities testified against the proposed change. It became more and more obvious that the president would not have enough support if his proposal came to a vote.

Nevertheless, inside the Pentagon at least, the administration held the line. The study the services had been directed to do got nowhere, so the Rand Corporation was hired to do a parallel study. The sum of $1.3 million was paid to researchers who issued a report that, sure enough, found open homosexuality in the armed forces was not necessarily a bad thing. A quick reading of this study was enough to show it had no chance of improving sociology's standing as a science. But it was already obvious this counter study and other administration pressures brought to bear on the services violated the First Rule of Holes; to wit: when you're in one, stop digging.

Finally, on 11 May, Senators Nunn and Warner went to Norfolk, Virginia, and took a ride in an attack submarine. That evening's network news showed the senators in conversation with sailors, some in their bunks, in what could only be described as close quarters. These pictures had an enormous impact on the video-conscious White House staff. After this date, the administration was a lot easier to work with. Indeed, within a few days, the president signaled his willingness to compromise: a front-page headline in the *Washington Post* proclaimed, "Clinton Shifts on Ending Gay Ban."

Don't Ask, Don't Tell

By mid-July, the president, the Joint Chiefs in tow, appeared before a military audience at the National Defense University and announced what he called an "honorable compromise." The door would open for homosexuals to serve, but only if they did not acknowledge their homosexuality. Alleged "witch hunts"—investigations launched with less than credible evidence—would stop. The compromise contained wording the chiefs had insisted on: any homosexual declaration was, by definition, a type of homosexual conduct and therefore a dismissible offense.

We had arrived, finally, at "don't ask, don't tell."

❂ ❂ ❂

Years later, in an interview in *Rolling Stone*, President Clinton offered his version of events:

> I think it backfired partly because the people that were against it were clever enough to force it. I tried to slow it down, but the first week I was president, Senator Dole—who, I think, saw it as an opportunity—decided to push a vote in the Senate disapproving of the change in the

policy. I tried to put it off for six months, and the Joint Chiefs came down and raised hell about it.

I wanted to do it the way Harry Truman integrated the military. He issued an executive order and gave the military leaders a couple of years to figure out how best to do it. But a lot of the gay groups wanted it done right away and had no earthly idea what kind of reaction would come. They were shocked by the amount of congressional opposition.

A lot of people thought I compromised with the military. That's not what happened . . . I could not sustain my policy in either house.

And it was only then that I worked out with Colin Powell this dumbass "don't ask, don't tell" thing. I went to the Army War College [sic] and explained what the policy was going to be, based on the agreement we'd reached together. Then they wrote that into law, and then we had several years of problems, where it was not being implemented in any way consistent with the speech I gave at the War College—of which General Powell had agreed with every word.

When we begin explaining things, we have to employ language, and language itself takes a little explaining. Here, Clinton adopts a style in which words, already imperfect avatars of meaning, are commandeered for public use, coerced into shedding their private and personal definitions. Language is, after all, a form of common property, and all of us ought to object to this form of hijacking.

❦ ❦ ❦

Armies have to care about what succeeds in war. Sometimes they win or lose because of material factors. They should therefore concern themselves with questions such as which side has the greater numbers, the best equipment, or the more generous supply support. But armies are sure to lose if they pay no attention to the *ideas* that succeed in battle. Over the years, we have learned that unit cohesion is one such idea.

By design, combat forces must continue to work under the

most terrible conditions. We know, or ought to, that warriors are inspired by comradeship, by the knowledge that they survive only through relying on one another. Bonding, loyalty, and teamwork are the traits that combat units must cultivate to prevail. To undermine cohesion is to endanger everyone. Hence, every service makes much of customs and practices designed to create conditions of solidarity that by nature clash with individual freedom of expression and other civic values. It is understandable that some civilians see these ingredients of the military lifestyle as a sort of absurd, tough-guy game played by overgrown boys.

But we know from hard experience that men fight well not for God, or even for country, but for the guy next to them in ranks.

Chapter 9

Somalia

So there were effectively two separate forces pinned down now, and their commanders were not talking to each other.
—Mark Bowden, *Black Hawk Down*

Somalia became an independent country in 1960, when former colonial powers Italy and Britain relinquished control. It occupied an area in the Horn of Africa slightly smaller than Texas, of some strategic and almost no economic value. A place of dust storms and drought, there are no natural harbors or navigable rivers, the forest has been stripped away, the land overgrazed, the soil eroded, the water polluted. By the early 1990s, more than 8 million people were trying to eke out a living, generating less than $5 billion a year in product, placing them among the world's poorest citizens. The equator runs through the country a few miles south of the capital, Mogadishu, which is situated in barren coastal lowland that's either too hot, or hotter than that.

During the Cold War, Somalia's location along the southern approaches to the Red Sea and Suez Canal produced a desultory competition between us and the Russians. Each side pumped in a little aid money. In 1969 a military coup led by General Mohamed

Siad Barre established a socialist-Islamic state aligned, at first, with the Soviet Union. In 1977–78, Somalia fought and lost a short war with Ethiopia over control of the disputed Ogaden region, in the process forfeiting Soviet and picking up US sponsorship. Clan and tribal disputes fueled continuous and escalating internal conflict that climaxed in January 1991, when Siad Barre was ousted and rebels seized Mogadishu. Ali Mahdi Muhammad took control of the north part of town and proclaimed himself president, while General Muhammad Farah Aydid did the same thing on the south side. The contest for control between Ali Mahdi, Aydid, and various other factions meant continued lawlessness and economic disruption. Perhaps as many as 300,000 people died of starvation in the year following Siad Barre's ouster.

In March 1992, the warlords agreed to a cease-fire and the UN Security Council deployed unarmed military monitors, organized as the UN Operation in Somalia (UNOSOM). A humanitarian effort called Operation Provide Relief started up under UNOSOM auspices. The Air Force sent 10 C-130s and about 400 people to stage airlift support out of Mombasa, Kenya, into Mogadishu and other Somali towns.

UNOSOM had an authorized strength of only 50, with Brig. Gen. Imtiaz Shaheen of Pakistan designated the chief military observer. Later, Pakistan agreed to provide a 500-man security unit, but even this was much too small a presence to stabilize the situation in Mogadishu. Subsequently, Somalis looted relief flights on landing, hijacked food convoys, assaulted aid workers. The United Nations appealed to its membership for more serious help and, with only days left in his administration, President Bush offered US leadership for an international force aimed at increased security for relief operations.[73] On 9 December 1992 US Marines splashed ashore

---

73 At about this same time, of course, Chairman Powell and others were resisting military involvement in Bosnia. The offer to help in Somalia quieted criticism of our passivity and was seen as low risk, since we (mistakenly) believed a "humanitarian" effort would incur no casualties.

into the klieg lights of a well-documented amphibious "assault," the start of Operation Restore Hope. UNITAF, the short name for the US-led Unified Task Force, included about 38,000 soldiers (21,000 US) from 23 countries. In a matter of weeks, food was being delivered to all areas of southern and central Somalia, and factional fighting decreased somewhat.

By the following March, the United Nations had decided on an expanded, "nation-building" role for UNOSOM. UNOSOM II took over UNITAF's enforcement role, with a mandate to disarm Somalis and restore law and order. For the first time in history the United Nations intervened where it had not been invited.

Thirty countries offered troops to UNOSOM II, which had an initial strength of 28,000. UNITAF handed off command on 4 May 1993. The secretary-general appointed retired US Admiral Jonathan Howe as his special representative and Lt. Gen. Çevik Bir of Turkey as force commander. Bir's deputy, the US Army's Maj. Gen. Thomas Montgomery, wore a UN blue beret as part of the peacemaking force and a separate hat as commander, US Forces Somalia. In the US military chain of command, Montgomery reported to the commander of Central Command, Marine Corps General Joseph Hoar, who had succeeded Norm Schwarzkopf in charge of US military operations in the Middle East and the Horn of Africa. (Headquarters CENTCOM remained at MacDill AFB, in Florida.)

President Clinton supported the expansion of the UN mandate but simultaneously ordered a reduction of American troops, so that by June, only 1,200 or so US combat troops remained in-country, mostly in the form of a battalion-sized quick response force (QRF) from the 10th Mountain Division. This QRF was held outside UNOSOM II as an independent US command reporting to General Montgomery. (Even so, Montgomery had only tactical control of the QRF, meaning he could use it in an emergency. Operational control resided with Hoar, who retained approval authority for any planned QRF operation.)

Under the terms of an agreement signed by all parties, the Somalis had promised to disarm and store weapons at sites that could be inspected by UNOSOM II troops. On 5 June 1993 a badly mishandled inspection at one of the storage sites belonging to the Aydid faction sparked a series of running gunfights that killed 25 Pakistani soldiers and wounded another 54, with 10 reported missing. The UN Security Council issued a call for the arrest of those responsible, without naming Aydid, but within a few days, US and UN troops were attacking targets in Mogadishu known to be associated with him. The United Nations was now at war with Aydid.

In mid-June, Admiral Howe ordered Aydid's arrest and offered a $25,000 reward. For the next three months, Aydid lived a charmed life. Even when a US air raid flattened his house, he escaped unharmed. But the action forced Aydid underground, and Howe asked Washington to send Special Forces to help capture him. In August, Secretary of Defense Les Aspin directed deployment of a joint special operations task force called Task Force Ranger (TF Ranger).

A composite unit with a strength of about 450, the task force consisted mostly of 130 hard-core operators from Squadron C of 1st Special Forces Detachment-Delta (Delta Force); Bravo Company, 3rd Battalion of the 75th Ranger Regiment; and a package of 16 helicopters from the 160th Special Operations Aviation Regiment ("Night Stalkers"), which included MH-60 Black Hawks and MH-6 Little Birds. Partly due to constraints laid on by CENTCOM, TF Ranger deployed without Air Force AC-130 gunships, the usual platform for providing industrial-strength close air support to special operations forces. The Army's Maj. Gen. William Garrison, commander of Delta Force, led TF Ranger. Almost immediately, Garrison started conducting raids into Mogadishu, with good success at first.

The Quick Reaction Force would have to backstop TF Ranger if it got in trouble, and the 10th Mountain Division troops making up the QRF were very fine light infantry, fully living up to their great heritage. By the time TF Ranger arrived, they had months of experience in-country and had already taken losses during operations into Mogadishu and elsewhere in Somalia. But the new guys in town, the rangers, were an elite outfit, arguably the best infantry on the planet, especially when fighting at night—their specialty. Naturally, some friendly tension arose between these two outfits. There was also tension—not altogether friendly—inside TF Ranger itself. In particular, special operations troops are an elite of the elite, and that's true in capital letters for Delta Force, the Army's handpicked counterterrorism unit, torturously trained for a narrow range of important, very risky jobs, like hostage rescue. An insider subsequently described Delta Force special operators in TF Ranger as "very aloof . . . [They] don't want to work with other people." The Somalis had their clan infighting. We had ours.

Tension within and between military organizations is not necessarily bad. In fact, a talented commander can use it creatively. But at the end of the day, combat is a team sport. Inside the team, someone with authority over all the players has to regulate the competition and keep it in bounds. To say the least, command arrangements in Mogadishu were not suited to this purpose. Like the QRF, TF Ranger was not part of UNOSOM II, but, unlike the QRF, neither was it part of US Forces Somalia. Garrison did not work for Montgomery but reported directly to their mutual boss, General Hoar. In *Black Hawk Down*, Mark Bowden says that Montgomery had "never been particularly happy about the presence of Garrison's Task Force Ranger, which had flown in and begun its own secret missions independent of the force structure already in place."[74] And Garrison, a special operator of long standing, apparently continued to talk regularly to his normal, in-garrison

---

74 Montgomery has since stated he and Garrison were on good terms, talked to each other every day, shared intelligence. OK, but that's not the same thing as having one guy in charge at the point of contact.

boss—Army General Wayne Downing, commander of US Special Operations Command.⁷⁵ Thus, in these difficult and dangerous circumstances, we had two US general officers—and aside from them a Pakistani UN commander—in charge of different aspects of military operations in and around Mogadishu. There was not one belly button to push, no one person clearly responsible for success or failure. This was one of the oldest mistakes in the book and not one we could rely on Secretary Aspin to understand or fix.

By contrast, it was pretty clear that Aydid was in charge on his side. He divided his part of Mogadishu into 18 sectors, each with an on-scene tactical commander who reported to him. He was better organized than we were, and he hadn't gone to National War College.

In early September 1993, Montgomery sent Hoar a call for heavier forces, including tanks and armored fighting vehicles, to protect US logistics convoys and installations. Hoar scaled back the request by more than 75 percent and forwarded it to SECDEF through the Joint Chiefs of Staff. Colin Powell took the request to Aspin, but the secretary elected not to approve it, believing that heavier forces were not essential to carrying out the mission.⁷⁶

On 3 October 1993 TF Ranger launched an operation into south Mogadishu aimed at capturing a number of Aydid's key aides. During the operation, Somali militiamen shot down two US helicopters. In the hardest ground fighting since Desert Storm, 18 US

---

75 Downing has been quoted as saying, "I kept telling (Garrison) . . . to be patient, be careful, eventually you will get a shot at Aydid . . . I told him that (1) he needed to be careful in populated areas, and (2) in certain circumstances do not go near the Bakara market . . . We did not have good intelligence on that part of the city." Wayne Downing was a superb officer and this was good advice, but it's the sort of thing you hope would come from the joint commander—in this case, Joe Hoar.

76 Aspin later said he did not want to augment US forces in Somalia while we were trying to reduce our presence there. But he also conceded, "Had I known at the time what I knew after the events of [October 3–4], I would have made a very different decision."

soldiers were killed, 75 wounded, and one helicopter pilot captured. The bodies of US soldiers were subjected to public acts of outrage, the scenes broadcast by television around the world. Following these events, we reinforced the QRF with tanks and armored fighting vehicles and brought TF Ranger home. At the same time, President Clinton announced his intention to withdraw all US troops from Somalia by 31 March 1994.

❂ ❂ ❂

In mid-January 1994, I decided to take a quick look at our airlift support into Somalia. I had a standing invitation from my counterpart in Kenya, so I flew there via Ascension Island, giving me a chance to visit one of the sites doing down-range support for space shots out of the Cape.

In Nairobi and outside it at Laikipia Air Base, Maj. Gen. Duncan Wachira showed me what there was to see of Kenya's air force. But the highlight of the visit was an hour-long, one-on-one session with President Daniel arap Moi in the garden of his official residence. I did some heavy-duty listening in what was a monologue, rather than a conversation. Moi's regime was notorious for corruption, economic buffoonery, autocratic rule, election stealing, and massive human rights violations, but he lectured me at length on the many benefits to a democratic Kenya of his continued leadership.

I had no idea why I was singled out for this punishment, except that long ago, in 1982, only four years into his presidency, a Kenyan Air Force enlisted man, Hezekiah Ochuka, had led a failed coup attempt. He managed to take over the radio station and rule the country for about six hours, after which the rebellion was crushed. Moi detained all 2,000 air force personnel, hanged Ochuka, and disbanded the air force. It was later reconstituted as a new unit called the 82 Air Force and put under strict army control. (Wachira's headquarters was at Moi Air Base, located on the old Nairobi Airport, not to be confused with Moi International Airport, in Mombasa.) Anyway, maybe Moi was getting even with me for being an airman.

I flew from Nairobi down to Mombasa, where I jumped in a C-130 for the hop to Mogadishu. Once on the ground, I met with Maj. Gen. Montgomery and got briefed on his setup.

The military calls the document illustrating command relationships a "wiring diagram," terminology that has leaked into private-sector use. In the age of postmodern warfare, all professionals know the solid, straight lines and square corners of military wiring diagrams are a deception. Nowadays, we should regard these drawings as works of impressionism, at best. But in Mogadishu the printout of command relationships was more akin to the sketches of M. C. Escher, though to be fair the eye can at least follow the action as Escher transforms fish to fowl or devises stairs that cannot possibly join floor to floor. Here at the scene of the action, the viewer was welcome to see in the wiring diagram whatever he wished.

Back from Somalia, I sought out Colin Powell, reporting that even now, after it was too late, we should do something about the ugliness of our command arrangements in Mogadishu. Powell said, "Tony, you're a genius at organization, but let me work this problem."

The reference to my passion for making Air Force organizational structures simpler and stronger was meant to flatter, and did. But beyond the feel-good part, I was once again impressed by a man not very interested in the way things ought to be. Powell always worked with what he was given and always got something done. He was the best kind of bureaucrat—a pragmatist whose regular contact with hard-charging ax grinders made him a cautious, thoughtful, fact-driven compromiser.

That said, if organizing our work in Somalia was his problem, he didn't solve it.

In March 1994, the last US ground troops left Somalia. Just over two years later, General Muhammad Farah Aydid died of gunshot wounds taken in a firefight with militias seeking to wrest from him control of south Mogadishu. His third son, Hussein, succeeded him as president of a self-proclaimed republic. Hussein Aydid had migrated to the United States at the age of 14 and lived in Los Angeles for 16 years, becoming a naturalized citizen and joining the Marine Corps Reserve. He'd come ashore as part of the UNITAF operation but had been transferred back stateside when the manhunt for his father started. He subsequently demobilized, returned to Somalia and married. Faction elders chose him to replace his father.

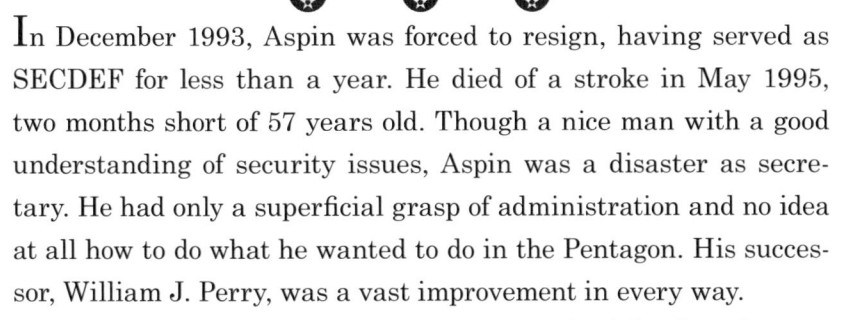

❂ ❂ ❂

In December 1993, Aspin was forced to resign, having served as SECDEF for less than a year. He died of a stroke in May 1995, two months short of 57 years old. Though a nice man with a good understanding of security issues, Aspin was a disaster as secretary. He had only a superficial grasp of administration and no idea at all how to do what he wanted to do in the Pentagon. His successor, William J. Perry, was a vast improvement in every way.

Still, the failure in Mogadishu was not Aspin's, though some shifted blame to him because of his refusal to send in armor. We, military professionals who were supposed to know better, were the ones who allowed our forces to be organized so badly. The failure was ours.

Chapter 10

Roles and Missions

Given the costs associated with unnecessary duplication, DoD must make every effort to ensure that appropriate jurisdictional boundaries are established. It is not clear that the rigorous analysis required to establish these boundaries has been conducted at any time since enactment of the National Security Act of 1947.
—Defense Organization: The Need for Change
(Locher Report), 16 October 1985

With the establishment of more unified defense structures following World War II, it was assumed the country would be both better protected and better off—could buy more security for fewer dollars—because the services would specialize, divide the work, and rely on one another. This notion lies at the heart of the concept known as jointness. But true jointness has been hard to achieve because the legacy services have opposed every attempt to reduce their autonomy.

By comparison with officers of other services, airmen have been more comfortable with jointness. We came out of the Army and from the beginning relied on it to capture and protect air bases and on the Navy to clear sea-lanes and deliver the tonnage of fuel and munitions needed to sustain our operations. We had no interest in creating our own army or navy to accomplish these tasks, not least because trying to do everything is a recipe for operational mediocrity. In general, airmen aimed for excellence in relation to air combat, rather than seeking lowest-common-denominator self-sufficiency.

Resistance to jointness on the part of the legacy services sprang not from any inherent evil, but from experience and honestly held differences about how combat power should be organized. From aviation's beginnings, each possessed its own air combat arm. Why should they now give up ownership of make-or-break capabilities and become dependent on someone else to provide them? If he grasps nothing else, an experienced commander knows about "friction," the uncertainty, the "fog" of war. That he will protect the capacity to act alone may be taken as a cultural imperative. So jointness, which in the end requires specialization and dependence on others, has been hard for some of our ablest officers to swallow.

A century ago, the thirst for self-sufficiency did not result in costly overlap or duplication of effort. The very apparatus of war had to be specialized for employment on either land or water. (The Marines, seagoing men-at-arms, had not yet staked a claim to sustained combat in the interior.) Thus, each service operated in its own sphere, with the beach a sharp demarcation line, and only occasional action—like shore bombardment, coastal defense, or raids ashore—at the seam.

The invention of the airplane changed things. This new contrivance showed no respect for coastlines. In addition, while at first armies and navies used aircraft only in ancillary tasks—observation, artillery spotting, scouting—it quickly became obvious that combat aviation would not be limited to a supporting role. Even when designed specifically to restrict employment, the technical capabilities of aircraft allowed for overflow into unexpected and increasingly important uses, an evolution airmen exploited with zest. Thus, the newfangled technology was in itself disruptive.

But the establishment of an independent Air Force made adaptation much harder for the other services because the upstart institution presented itself together with a claim to the technology. Soon thereafter, combat aviation systems became the center of contention about budgets and force levels, ownership of these systems turning into a fight for institutional prestige. This double spillover—from a supporting to a leading role and from gadget to budget—heightened emotion at the same time the constraints of physical geography were removed as a reliable referee of capability overlap. The result has been a jurisdictional dispute now lasting 60 years or more, an argument about which union will get the work. Much is at stake for the services here, since genuine roles-and-missions reform would make for winners and losers. But, so far at least, institutional strength has held off a day of reckoning.

Four Air Forces

By the 1990s, Sam Nunn, then chairman of the Senate Armed Services Committee, could lament that America had "the only military in the world with four air forces." He meant the Army, Navy, and Marine Corps all fielded costly combat aviation arms that overlapped in equipment and capability and competed for roles with the Air Force—an observation so obvious one wonders why someone in the Pentagon hadn't noticed. If it is true that the services ought to concentrate on core competencies, then the evident, systemic duplication already exerted a cost by diluting and dissipating the defense effort. But worse, it undermined combat effectiveness. We've learned the hard way that when supposedly friendly fighting forces enter the air arena with hostile attitudes about cooperation and central control, optimizing an air campaign, or even deconflicting it, is very nearly impossible. Nevertheless, the competition is precisely in this aerial arena, and each service feels it has to stay in the game, has to continue pushing chips into the pot.

The result has been extravagance of two sorts. Whereas in the past, we've often not had enough airpower, the pursuit of market share has led the services to buy too much, funding it at the expense of other forms of needed military capability. It's hard to fault the services, since air superiority is the key enabler making all the other impedimenta of modern war usable—indeed, survivable. Still, our military capabilities should be balanced and, for now, are not.

The other objectionable extra expense has been in the large establishments set up to equip and support aviation units. Aside from space systems, the hardware for aviation is the most expensive bought by the Pentagon and needs intensive management. Any new airplane must be officially required, programmed, funded, designed, developed, produced, tested before issue, maintained while in use, and finally disposed of by storage, sale, or destruction at the end of useful life. Each service has its own far-flung infrastructure—crowds of people, libraries of regulations, huge facilities—to superintend these processes, and it is all "tail" in the tooth-to-tail equation.

We need some of this filigree—over time, the system wouldn't work without it—but carbon-copy duplication for each service? Only a very rich government could afford to organize defenses in this way. Countries born in the age of aviation, confronted with real security problems, and challenged by genuine resource constraints—Israel, or the People's Republic of China come to mind—have been smarter about producing integrated defenses. In Israel, everything that flies or shoots at airplanes belongs to the air force, but they call it the Israeli Defense Forces/Air Force and the implied fusion is a fact as well as an abstraction. In much the same way, the air force of the People's Republic of China is known as the People's Liberation Army Air Force (PLAAF). Some other young countries have defense organizations that mirror US or Soviet sponsors, but most of them are present or former satellites with little need for cleverness. In the late 1940s—at the same time the US Air Force was established and the legacy services were working hard to "dis"integrate airpower—both Israel and China knew there was serious work at hand and, starting with a more or less clean sheet of paper, decided to weave integrated air capabilities into unified defenses.

The Canadian experience is interesting. Though its security problems do not rise to the level of those facing Israel or China, Canada is sincere about defense and has only small resources to put against the problem. In 1964 a sole chief of defense staff replaced the individual service chiefs and in 1968 the services were consolidated. At present, Canada's Forces comprise four commands—Maritime, Land, Air, and Support. Air Command owns and operates everything that flies, including helicopters and maritime patrol aircraft, with Land Command and Maritime Command having operational control (tasking) of aircraft operating in support of their activities. The government justified unification of Canada's armed forces as a cost-reduction measure and put it through against fierce service opposition. It has worked well, and unification is now a dead issue in Canada.

The evolution of the Russian Air Force offers another striking recent example of how countries pressed for resources organize with greater care. In the good old days, the Soviets had an air force with offensive and transport capabilities; another one, Voyska PVO (Air Defense Troops), that operated interceptor aircraft and surface-to-air missiles; and still another one that belonged to the army. (This was the model for Warsaw Pact and other copycat structures, including Iraq's, and would be held up to scorn, except our own scheme resembles it too much.) Having fallen on hard times, the Russians reorganized. In 1998 PVO merged into a unified Russian Federation Air Force. Helicopter units transferred from the army to the RFAF in late 2002. (It remains to be seen whether the army will accept this arrangement.) Again, these moves were forced because of cost, so the more important benefit of improved combat performance was involuntary.

Army

In passing, we should note that, at times, the largest of our four air forces has been the Army's. During the Vietnam War, for instance, they operated more aircraft (counting helicopters) than the other three services combined. But it is our approach to air defense that raises the roles-and-missions issue, *par excellence*. Air defense operations occur in a unified medium and need to be centrally controlled to advance the prospects of effective combat action. There are many reasons for this, the most obvious being that surface-to-air missile (SAM) and fighter-interceptor envelopes overlap and create a real danger of fratricide.

If we look at "best of breed" air defenses around the world, the United States stands alone in placing SAMs and interceptor aircraft in different institutions. In Britain, France, Germany, Italy, Japan, China, and Israel, it is the air force that owns and operates SAMs. The old-style Soviet system separated the air force from the Air Defense Force (PVO), but at least PVO had responsibility for both piloted interceptors and SAMs. Our Marine Corps Air Wing incorporates ground-based air defenses, such as Hawk missile squadrons. At sea, our Navy thoroughly integrates fleet air defense. What the Navy calls the Anti-Air Warfare Commander controls all parts of the system—interceptors, SAMs, guns—and everybody in the system wears a Navy uniform. The Navy does this because there is no other organizing scheme that, in stressful conditions, can be trusted to defend against air attack and at the same time bring carrier-based aircraft back aboard ship. The ground forces of many countries retain short-range, man-portable or otherwise highly mobile systems for last-ditch self-defense, but no country that knows what it's doing "dis-integrates" medium- and high-altitude air defenses as the United States does by splitting the business, giving interceptor aircraft to the Air Force and SAMs to the Army.[77]

As a result of this "dis-integration," the air defense system in a theater of operations has to be jerry-rigged. The standard way to do this is for the joint commander to designate an Area Air Defense Commander (AADC), by tradition the senior airman, who is supposed to have operational control of all elements of the system, including the Army's medium- and long-range SAMs.

Operational control is a weak reed on which to lean in a supercharged combat environment. (There is no substitute for *command*.) But it has so far been of little consequence because to date the Air Force has fought the air battle deep inside unfriendly territory—over the Yalu, over Hanoi, over Baghdad. Not a single hostile fighter aircraft has appeared above our ground troops in more than half a century. In such circumstances, Army SAMs can stay "guns tight" that is, be ordered to hold fire unless coming under direct attack. Hence, we have no reason to think "dis-integrated" air defenses are effective. Ours have not been put to the test.[78]

Responsibility for theater-wide air and missile defense should be

---

77 I'm not certain why we ever allowed this mistake in the first place, but it must have had something to do with the Army's Air Defense Artillery branch not wanting, in 1947, to follow pilots into a new Air Force that pilots were sure to dominate. The time to overrule parochial interests of this sort is before the country is again attacked—this time by, say, cruise missiles, or armed drones. We need and should have highly integrated national air defenses.

78 No US Army surface-to-air missile has ever been fired in anger at an enemy aircraft, an astonishing fact that should have had some impact on our thinking. During the Second Iraq War, Army Patriot missiles did mistakenly shoot down a couple of friendly aircraft—one US Navy, one RAF—hard to believe because the Iraqi Air Force never showed signs of life during the entire engagement. This inexplicable mistake lifted the fig leaf of operational control of Army air defenses.

consolidated in the Air Force, the sensible approach that ought to have been followed in 1947. I do not mean we should take away from the Army the short-range SAMs that protect troops on the move. Our ground forces have not had to defend themselves from enemy air attack in decades, but clearly organic firepower should be available if they ever have to do so. The same logic does not apply to medium- and high-altitude air defense, which are mostly for protecting rear areas and fixed installations. For theater-wide air defense, the need for integrated detection, tracking, identification, and engagement strongly argues for single service responsibility. SAM systems like Patriot should be moved to the Air Force, which should also assume responsibility for national air and missile defense.

The other overarching roles-and-missions issue with the Army is close air support (CAS). The Army does some of its own close air support but, owing to the speed, range, and weight-lifting shortcomings of helicopter gunships, relies on the Air Force for big league CAS. To serve this requirement, the Air Force procured and operates the A-10, an aircraft with capabilities so limited it is suitable only for close air support. The Air Force has also set up and operates organizational structures that mirror the Army's: forward air control teams at battalion level, and operations centers at division and corps levels. This elaborate and costly structure is required because the Army must reach across departmental lines for critical support it needs on a routine basis.

Of course, the Marine Corps is organized differently. Every Marine division has an associated air wing that trains, works with, and gets to know its ground counterpart. I've never heard a Marine complain about the air support their system provides.

Trading off CAS

In the summer of 1993, I tried to make a modest start on the problem of putting more fully integrated service capabilities into an integrated defense structure. I went privately to Army Chief of

Staff Gordon Sullivan and proposed he take over the close air support role. We would transfer A-10 squadrons to the Army in the context of a grand bargain in which the Air Force assumed responsibility for theater air and missile defense. I argued this scheme would make for much better integration of combat roles by giving clear authority and responsibility in delineated battle space to each service. Among other benefits, it should reduce fratricide, a problem in Desert Storm (and since).

Sullivan balked at the idea, wanting first of all, I suppose, not to give up air and missile defense. But with regard to transferring close air support, he had three objections. First, he claimed it would be an entirely new role for the Army, that they did not do CAS. In this, he resolutely refused to abandon his service's doctrinal position: the Army *defined* what helicopters do as *not* close air support. Well, what attack helicopters do walks like CAS and talks like CAS; I've done a bit of CAS myself, and it sure looks like CAS to me. In any case, it was unworthy of Sullivan to fall back on Army groupthink as a device for turning away rational argument in a matter as serious as how to improve battlefield performance.

His second argument was to poor-mouth, saying Air Force A-10 squadrons were too expensive for the Army. This too was posturing. I'd offered to transfer the aircraft and associated funding in return for Patriot and Hawk battalions, with their associated funding. In any case, the A-10 was cheap by comparison with the Army's advanced helicopters. The Comanche attack helicopter, then in development, was projected to cost a good bit more than an F-16, and we'd purchased about four A-10s for the price of an F-16.[79]

Finally, Sullivan objected that taking on the CAS role and fixed-wing A-10 aircraft would tie the Army to air bases. Of course, the

---

79 The RAH-66 Comanche program was canceled in 2004, before mass production began but after a reported $7 billion had been spent on development.

Army already operated fixed-wing aircraft in a theater of operations for both intelligence collection and administrative airlift. In any case, the argument made sense only if you believed the Army could run away from air bases and operate in isolation from the support flowing to it through the theater logistic infrastructure. Based on recent combat history, it was possible to claim the exact opposite—that, far from being independent of air bases, one of the Army's pivotal jobs was to capture and protect them.

Nothing came of my proposal.

Navy

The Navy fields a first-rate air force that is useful in any event, but would be especially so if the United States were ever denied access to air bases on land. We need and should have some of this sort of capability, though it is almost never the case that there are no alternatives. Thus, in a roles-and-missions context, the dispute between the Air Force and Navy is not about whether we need aircraft carriers, but how many we need, with cost considerations often left out or played down because of bureaucratic and political factors. Other ways of stating the issue: what fraction of the country's fighter aviation must be configured, at high expense, for the possibility that we cannot acquire bases ashore? How much insurance should we buy to protect against blocked access to land basing?

Let's do a *gedankenexperiment:* suppose the Navy operated large-deck aircraft carriers for the benefit of the Air Force, as it does amphibious carriers for the Marine Corps. That is, what if the aircraft and squadrons flying off supercarriers belonged to the Air Force, instead of the Navy?[80] The prediction: the Air Force would be very enthusiastic about aircraft carriers and the Navy would allocate a much higher percentage of its budget to smaller surface

---

80 It's certain the Navy's institutional strength would prevent this from happening, and I think that's a good thing.

combatants and submarines. In my view, both outcomes would serve the national interest.

By the way, countries thinking about conflict with us couldn't care less whether carrier-based air squadrons were Navy or Air Force. As for deterring "Type A" war—the best and highest reason to procure massive, industrial machinery like aircraft carriers—opposing intelligence estimates would not change because the squadrons were under new management.

Marine Corps

At Marine Corps behest, Title 10 of the US Code "requires" the Marine Corps to maintain three active air wings. But it is the Marines who decide the strength and composition of these organizations. The Marine Air Wing incorporates all fixed-wing aircraft and helicopters, surface-to-air missile defenses, and the technical apparatus—radars, control centers, forward observers, etc.—providing command and control for both offensive and defensive air operations. This is exactly how you would describe operational excellence in organizing air capabilities.

As for size, at this writing, each of the three active Marine wings possesses about 400 "shooter" aircraft—by which I mean fighters and attack helicopters—an inventory equivalent to five or six standard Air Force fighter wings. In addition, a Marine Air Wing will likely have several squadrons of transport helicopters, two squadrons of reconnaissance and electronic warfare aircraft, and a squadron of aerial refueling tankers. Our Navy's army has its own air force.

The Marines task-organize combat forces of various sizes, always according to the same model. Pro forma, the largest unit is a Marine Expeditionary Force, the MEF commander being a three-star general. Reporting to him are a two-star in charge of a Marine Division and a two-star in charge of the Marine Air Wing, which together form the vaunted air-ground team. Thus, there is a single seam between ground and air, and the MEF Commander has unambiguous authority to police the boundary. The Marines

Air Force headquarters staff, 1994. From left, seated: Billy Boles, Tom Moorman, me, Jim Fain, Dick Hawley. Standing: John Nowak, Joe Ralston, Erv Rokke, Mark Anderson.

At RAF Leuchars, I fly the RAF's Tornado interceptor, thanks to Air Chief Marshal Mike Graydon.

New Chairman John Shalikashvili has dinner at Air House with the military high command of the United States, and their husbands.

With Secretary Widnall at the National Geographic Society, to accept the Thomas White Space Trophy.

At my retirement from active service, the four-star generals of the Air Force. Next to me, Ron Yates, Mike Loh, Ron Fogleman, Chuck Boyd, Butch Viccellio, Skip Rutherford, Tom Moorman, Jim Jamerson, Joe Ashy, John Lorber. The painting quotes Isaiah 6:8: "Whom shall I send, and who will go for us? Then said I, Here am I. Send me."

Official Pentagon portrait.

are justifiably proud of how well this air-ground team works. We have every reason to believe that joint employment in a theater of operations ought to be organized in precisely the same way.

Thus, while masquerading as a single service, the Marine Corps is more like a joint force, with a comprehensive range of both land and air capabilities. But there is more to the Marine Corps story. The Navy sails a dozen or so "big deck" aircraft carriers in the roughly 100,000-tons displacement class. In addition, they operate another dozen or so "jump jet" carriers in the 40,000-ton class on behalf of the Marines. Each of these ships is larger than any aircraft carrier built during World War II and about the same size as France's *Charles de Gaulle*.[81] Our Navy's army's air force has its own navy.

The Marines are well organized for operations they undertake alone. It's when they mix with the forces of the other services that the trouble starts. They've tried to solve this problem by claiming some chunk of territory for their own. In NATO during the Cold War, they exercised and planned to operate in Norway. In the Korean War, they operated along the East Coast; in Vietnam, in I Corps. In Desert Storm, they spearheaded the drive into Kuwait City, at a remove from the Army's VII and XVII Corps, who were involved in the flanking maneuver. In each of these cases, the Marines looked for isolation that might have been possible in a smaller, lower-intensity conflict. But these were large operations, many Marines were deployed, and in every case they needed support from the other services, creating the complex relationships they sought to avoid. As things now stand, the problem is chronic; the Marines are very unlikely to be issued a war of their own.

The integration and organizational excellence seen in the configuration of Marine Corps combat units suggests an elegant solution

---

81 As this is written, only Russia's *Kuznetsov* (55,000 tons) and China's *Liaoning* (67,500 tons) are larger than the Wasp-class aircraft carriers operated for the Marine Corps.

to the problem of jointness. Why not simply do away with the Army, Navy, and Air Force and put everybody in a Marine Corps uniform?

Special Operations Force (SOF)

Along with the Marines, the Special Operations Force illustrates how stand-alone joint forces incorporating land, sea, and air assets should be organized. The SOF includes the Army's Special Forces and Rangers, the Navy's Seal Teams, and the special operations commands of the Air Force and Marine Corps. All of these organizations are committed to the joint Special Operations Command (SOCOM).

Regarding SOF, the services have only themselves to blame for its creation. For years we systematically neglected the need for highly trained specialists to conduct deep raids, hostage rescues, and the like. The Army's attitude was particularly ambivalent. The fact that the hush-hush, counterterror Delta Force belonged to them was offset by the distaste many senior officers felt for anything that smacked of an elite. The Army saw itself as a reflection of America, a cross section rather than a privileged cream of the crop, an attitude giving the Marine Corps, the "un-Army," a recruiting edge with young men who want to be different, out of the ordinary. But the antipathy was seen also in the other services. As late as 1987, the Air Force had never promoted to general any officer who might be considered a career special operator. Accordingly, special forces capabilities languished, creating an opening politicians exploited. President Kennedy started the interference, making a darling of the Green Berets, whom he regarded as the foil for an incurably orthodox conventional military.

If we could begin again, the services might be merged into a single armed force, with everyone wearing the same uniform. Inside that unified structure, force capabilities would be organized against the range of possible military tasks. A special unit would be formed to conduct high-profile, risky, but small-scale operations, like antiterrorism or hostage rescue. This unit would incorporate the seagoing and air support elements needed to accomplish its mission. Everyone involved would live, train, and practice the trade together. For the moment, this "clean sheet of paper" approach seems out of reach.

An alternative approach would have been to direct the Army to build such an organization, in-house. Delta Force was and is the ground-based foundation of such an enterprise. There would have been strong resistance, but sea and air capabilities could have been stood up inside the Army, wearing Army uniforms and living and working together, to produce an integrated capability. However, lacking Seals and major-league air support, Delta Force had to reach across departmental boundaries for essential capabilities, a fatal flaw that produced, for instance, the failure at Desert One of the 1980 Operation Eagle Claw, mounted by the Carter administration to rescue American hostages held in Iran. It was the collapse of Eagle Claw more than anything else that led to the creation of the joint Special Operations Command.

By definition, missions like hostage rescue ought to be relatively small, stealthy, and precise. (That's what makes them "special.") In today's SOF, the officer commanding such an operation has clear authority over the land, sea, and air elements involved, and regulates all the seams. The setup is first-rate, sharing many of the virtues of Marine Corps organization. (Often such operations will fall apart anyway, owing to inherent risk or difficulty in execution, but failure should not be traceable to faulty organization, as was the case for the doomed Eagle Claw.)

The SOF has also been very good at the role of foreign internal defense, in which they help build up the armed forces in a cooperating country. It's a "go there and stay there" mission, a full-time assignment, and of course language and cultural skills are important. Moreover, the SOF has been effective in the deep battle, conducting raids, attacking concealed targets or safe havens, sometimes taking out target system operators and leaving the equipment intact.

Note that the operational roles envisioned here—antiterrorism, hostage rescue, foreign internal defense, participation as an auxiliary in the deep battle—are relatively small scale, commonly involving teams of a handful of men, certainly no more than a few hundred at most. But with the inclusion of the Army's Rangers, the SOF is now rather large—as this is written, more than 60,000 soldiers, sailors, airmen, and Marines—a bigger combat force than can contemporaneously be fielded by, for example, Great Britain. Moreover, expansion of the SOF has siphoned off military skills required in the routine operations of the regular service components. For example, in Desert Storm, the Navy was tasked to conduct intercept operations as part of the blockade of Iraq. The Navy component commander used Seal teams to conduct numerous boarding and takedown missions in both the Red Sea and the Persian Gulf, removing them from the Special Operations component, where they could not be kept fully employed.

As for the Rangers, what's "special" about them is that they are highly trained and motivated light infantry, experts in direct action missions behind enemy lines, airfield seizures, ambushes, and interdiction raids. These shock troops may be the best night-fighting force in the world. Unlike the Green Berets, who must speak foreign languages and train and advise other countries' military forces, Rangers are strictly fighters. If they are not to be part of the Army component in a theater of operations, we ought to ask ourselves what it is we want the Army for.

It bears repeating that the organization of the SOF, like that of the Marine Corps, contains much merit if, and only if, they operate alone. The big problem comes when the SOF must act in concert with regular service components in joint operations, in which case they represent another army and another air force, even to some degree another navy, creating additional seams with conventional forces. In Type A conflict, what should happen is that much, if not most of the SOF, is broken up and elements of it returned to and put under the command of regular service component commanders. (This is what should have happened with the AC-130s in Desert

Storm.) But if that's how we're going to fight, shouldn't we organize this way beforehand?

Well, perhaps the SOF is so well organized as a joint force that we want it to command more-or-less conventional military operations up to a certain size, wherever they occur. (If this is so, the SOF has a direct competitor in the Marine Corps, also a joint force in readiness, which is the reason the Marines were so reluctant for so long to commit any part of the Corps to the SOF—in fact, had to be ordered to do so in 2005.) The Special Operations component of a joint command might take on any operational mission, helped as needed by the regular service components in-theater. Or the CONUS-based Special Operations Command might deploy forces and take charge of conventional operations in a theater, again supported by the regular service components. (Either of these alternatives makes the in-place joint theater commander a redundant reporting layer, a sort of fifth wheel.) For theater-wide operations, the SOF will likely always be too small, unless we do away with the regular service components and put everybody in the SOF. (This is not a bad idea, but for an even better one, see above, Marine Corps.)

The operational difficulty of integrating the SOF has been conjoined with a congressional grant of budgeting authority to Special Operations Command. SOCOM now has its own major force program (a special budget tracking category) and direct congressional authorization and appropriation lines. Therefore SOCOM (and its service components) needs the full panoply of staff support to manage requirements and monitor programming, budgeting, and equipment acquisition, just as if it were an entirely separate service. As a result, SOF headquarters end strength now certainly exceeds the manpower requirements of any reasonably sized raid or hostage rescue operation.

As this is written, the Special Operations Force makes the claim that it is trained and equipped to respond "across the spectrum of security threats around the globe." And that, of course, is precisely the problem. It needs to be reshaped so that it responds to "special" threats—counterterrorism, hostage rescue, foreign internal defense, and participation in the deep battle being the premier roles here envisaged—that are beyond the scope of the regular armed forces. For the United States, the SOF now constitutes a third competing, differently organized, army. Like the Marine Corps, it would be better if it were smaller.

Air Force

So, we have three armies. Why not a fourth, to match our purported number of air forces? Well, it's not something US airmen hanker after, but it's not unusual for air forces to have their own army. The Brits have the RAF Regiment, charged with defense of their bases. One squadron of the RAF Regiment has a parachute capability, which reminds us that in World War II, it was the Luftwaffe that incorporated Germany's parachute infantry. Herman Goring, head of the Luftwaffe, formed the first parachute regiments starting in 1935. In May 1941, the Luftwaffe captured the island of Crete in history's first example of a large-scale airborne invasion. Kurt Student, a Luftwaffe general and World War I fighter ace, was chief of parachute troops in World War II and active in supervising the Crete operation. Though successful, the Germans took heavy casualties, and Hitler lost confidence in airborne operations. Nonetheless, Luftwaffe parachute troops played a key role in the daring 1943 rescue of Mussolini.

The US Air Force has resisted getting into the army business, concentrating (until rather recently) on its core competence, combat in the Earth's atmosphere. By precedent and tradition, our lightly armed Air Police have looked after security only "inside the fence," with either the Army or the host nation responsible from the base perimeter out into the surrounding countryside. However, in the aftermath of the 1996 Khobar Towers bombing that killed 19 airmen at Dhahran, Saudi Arabia, and the report of a task force (chaired by retired Army General Wayne Downing) that laid much blame for this incident at the feet of the Air Force, even though the bomb had been planted and was set off in a parking lot *outside* the base perimeter fence, the Air Force has been prodded into expanding its concept for base security and is on the way to creating its own small army for ground combat operations around air bases. Of course, doing so vastly increases the complexity of service component relationships in the rear battle.

Note that the Air Force is not building close-in air defenses for air bases, but rather defense against ground attack that extends outside and well beyond the perimeter fence—for the moment, not a core competence of the US Air Force. In general, close air defense of air bases has been ignored.

With the spectacular exception of Japan's attacks in the opening days of World War II, we don't have a lot of experience with our bases coming under aerial attack. In Vietnam we were subject to occasional shelling or acts of sabotage, but we took the survivability of our air bases for granted. On the other hand, every study done by the Air Force showed the effectiveness of close air defense of bases, this notwithstanding the fact that our own security force was lightly armed and incapable of close air defense.

The Army hasn't shown much enthusiasm for tactical, close air defense of static positions, like air bases. They (rightly) believe in maneuver and want their equipment to contribute to the combined arms fight against opposing ground forces. For many years, the Army did man SHORAD, or short-range air defense systems, at air bases in Germany, but did so with equipment that was highly mobile and could be taken away when the Army moved. I was never happy with this arrangement. The situation was even worse in places like Turkey, South Korea, or the United Kingdom, where we resorted to a variety of expedients, including buying the equipment and paying the manpower costs to have outfits like the RAF Regiment do the job.

As chief, I tried to correct this situation by moving money around in our budget submissions to procure short-range air defense missiles, which we would then have issued to our security forces. The dollars I put at risk were simply raked off the table by OSD analysts, meaning we had to forfeit money we could have used on other Air Force needs, an excellent example of how to punish initiative. We were in the position of not being able to interest the Army in close air defense of our bases and also of not being allowed to do it ourselves.

Chairman's Role in Roles and Missions

The Chairman of the Joint Chiefs of Staff is the only senior uniformed officer in a position to address systemic roles-and-missions issues, like those outlined above, with nominal objectivity. Thus, among its other provisions, the Goldwater-Nichols Act required the chairman to review and report on service roles and missions every three years. The first such review, done by Admiral Crowe, had no observable content. The second, by General Powell, was also an air ball, though (typical of Powell) it recommended some tinkering at the margins.

It's hard to blame these two smart, hard-working chairmen. After all, part of the chairman's ability to respond to real world events involves the enthusiastic cooperation of the services, not easy to get if he insists on lighting up roles-and-missions debates. Moreover, there is no off-the-shelf, proven formula for settling the issues. The fight over roles and missions embodies elements of symbolism, bargaining, and persuasion for which there is no answer in common sense or logical abstraction. On these issues, the secretary of defense, or even the president, must lead.

Clinton

On 13 August 1992, as part of the run-up to the general election, then governor Clinton gave a speech before the Los Angeles World Affairs Council. Clinton did not often address security issues, this speech being perhaps his most important pronouncement on the subject during his campaign. There is much to admire in the text:

> ... the (Bush) administration talks of strategic change but basically, simply shrinks the existing Cold War force structure ... Leadership demands more than a "Cold War Minus" ... The administration's "base force" plan leaves us with a military that ... is burdened with redundancy ... I agree with Senator Nunn that it is time to take a fresh look at the basic organization of our armed forces. We have four separate air forces—one each for the Marines, Army, Navy, and Air Force ... While respecting each service's unique capabilities, we can reduce redundancies, save billions of dollars, and get better teamwork ... As president, I will order the Pentagon ... to hammer out a new understanding about consolidating and coordinating military roles and missions in the 1990s and beyond ... My administration will make security and savings compatible.

This statement makes it clear that someone in the Clinton camp, perhaps even the candidate himself, understood important defense issues. But, as was so often the case, Clinton was long on ideas and short on implementation. His immediate postelection priority was gays in the military. This was followed by the Bottom-Up Review, which gave us Cold War Minus, Minus.

Commission on Roles and Missions (CORM)

By the 1990s, despite an entirely changed international security environment, a 10-year revolution in military affairs, Powell's Base Force proposals, and the Bottom-Up Review, the services had not changed nearly enough to catch up with post-Cold War realities. Reflecting their dissatisfaction with the lack of progress, Congress authorized a Commission on Roles and Missions of the Armed Forces to perform yet another high-level review.

DOD's failure to come to grips with capability overlap and duplication had been studied regularly and often by capable, well-intentioned civilian and military authorities, mostly without making much of a dent. But this new Commission on Roles and Missions (CORM) had marching orders that were specific: (1) review the current allocation of roles, missions, and functions among the armed forces, (2) evaluate and report on alternative allocations, and (3) make recommendations for change.

This broad congressional mandate should have been the best opportunity yet to examine basic ideas about organizing armed defenses. Accordingly, my counterparts in the other services started an immediate search for ways to make sure nothing came of it. In looking over the commissioners, it seemed to me my brother service chiefs had nothing to worry about. CORM Chairman John P. White of Harvard University (later, deputy secretary of defense) and the others were reasonable people—experienced, levelheaded—who could be counted on to agree the system was basically sound and needed only fine-tuning.

I knew the CORM would ask me to appear before it, and I had to decide how to testify. In some ways, this would be a painful choice. Hard experience has led the service chiefs to avoid discussing the more combustible roles-and-missions issues. In the late 1940s, several senior Navy officers retired following a nasty fight with the Air Force about who should do strategic bombing. No one came out of that episode looking good. Over the years, the Army learned not to pick fights with the Marine Corps. Thus, whenever the roles-and-missions question comes up, the service chiefs huddle carefully, like porcupines in winter.

Entering the mid-1990s, the constraints on free discussion were, if anything, even tighter. The Goldwater-Nichols legislation created a demand for political correctness, the window dressing prized more highly than the goods. In this setting, any Air Force advocacy for change would be dismissed as old-fashioned interservice bickering, out of step with the times, an affront to jointness itself. Whatever jointness might mean in the context of a roles-and-missions debate, it wouldn't pay to be against it.

On the other hand, the principal roles-and-mission issue was how to organize combat aviation, with only the Air Force in a position to rationalize and reduce its cost. In this respect, as always, the very existence of the Air Force constituted a latent threat to the institutional interests of the other services. But the threat would become real only if I spoke up. Naturally, the other services hoped I wouldn't rock the boat. But my view—indeed, my conviction—was the Air Force should consolidate its position in the air combat arena, the military operations segment it had been created to serve. I did not see how I could finesse the issue, let alone why I should want to. I therefore decided to commit truth. The objective was important enough to undergo the certain denunciation bound to follow my abandoning the script.

The commission had been tasked—specifically, in writing—to *evaluate alternatives* and *recommend changes* to the present allocation of roles and missions. (In the end, it did neither.) In thinking through the alternatives and recommended changes I might suggest, I discarded immediately the notion that we should abolish the services altogether and put everybody in the same uniform, a utopian ideal, clearly out of reach. Next, I thought it unlikely I could convince the CORM we should put all air capabilities in one service and fold that organization into a more tightly unified defense establishment. The operational virtue of truly integrated air operations would seem obvious, but this was precisely the question the services were dug in on, and the commissioners would likely think my views less objective than those of the other chiefs. Although I should not concede the argument, I probably couldn't win it on the basis of personal testimony. It therefore came down to devising a scheme for establishing acceptable limits to service autonomy in air operations—which I judged would not work either. But if I could get some ideas on record with this CORM, perhaps a future roles-and-missions study would circle back and take account of them.[82]

---

82 The commission's acronym reminds us that, in botany, a *corm* is a bulblike underground stem that stores food. Some plants, like the crocus, use corms to survive winter or other adverse conditions.

Defining 'Roles,' 'Missions,' 'Functions'

"Roles and missions" is a term of art for how military work should be divided among the services and, at least as far as combat aviation goes, isn't. It will be obvious from what appears above that I came to the roles-and-missions debate with certain convictions, but one idea that may not be so obvious is I thought we could have no fruitful discussion unless we agreed on what the terms meant. What is a "mission"? A "role"? I knew of no settled definitions; indeed, some of the parties seemed to prefer a little ambiguity, sought refuge in jargon meant to obscure rather than clarify.

In my opinion, a *mission* is a purpose, a requirement to do something. It therefore must include an active verb: repel boarders, take the hill, liberate Kuwait.

On the other hand, both roles and functions are processes. A role is an *operational* process, activity relating directly to mission accomplishment. Roles are (or should be) performed by people wearing uniforms and are characterized by their decentralized nature and immediate impact. That is, they take place wherever they must on a battlefield or in a theater of operations, and their result—bad or good—usually is an obvious and quick physical change in the situation. By contrast, a function is a *support* process. Logistics, communications, and transportation are all functions, and all are types of support. They are very important in that they enable the accomplishment of combat roles efficiently over time, but there will likely be some delay before we feel the repercussions of any failure.

One can think about these terms by imagining the theatrical production as a metaphor for combat. (I like this because it evokes a "theater" of operations.) Let's say we decide to produce *A Midsummer Night's Dream*. That's the *mission*. We'll hire actors to play parts, or *roles*. We'll also need support—lighting, set design, costumes, ticket sales. Call these *functions*.

Looking at the problem this way helps us understand it is the producer who stages the play and therefore he's the guy with the mission. As we now organize for combat, the joint commander is the producer.

This is a point so important I'll risk repeating it: the *mission* belongs to the joint commander. In principle, there is no competition for the mission.[83] The services provide formations to perform combat *roles*, developing these units out of the familiar "organize, train, and equip" *functions* of Title 10, US Code. Thus, the competition, and the controversy, is about roles and functions.

We know what the roles are in *A Midsummer Night's Dream*, but what are they in war? To my way of thinking (and here I refer to modern, industrial, or Type A war) the classic ground roles are infantry, artillery, and armor; for air, we might list air superiority, deep attack, and close air support; at sea, surface warfare, fleet air defense, amphibious attack, and submarine warfare.

The offering is by no means complete, but some conclusions are obvious. Roles are not simply important. It wouldn't make any sense to stage a play and leave out a speaking part. Someone *must* perform each role. A measure of how well we are prepared to perform roles is called *readiness*, the word itself an indication of the weight we give this matter.[84]

Functions are also important but have less urgency. We can stage our play, at least for a while, without ushers. In much the

---

83 At least, there should be none among the service chiefs, or between them and joint commanders. Unhappily, in the real world there can be competition between joint commands (see chapter 9, Somalia). If it happens, it's our fault. Combat is a two-sided game, the outcome uncertain not least because the opponent is an independent variable. But how we organize for combat is one of the few things under our sole control. Thus, if on our side more than one person can claim responsibility for the mission, we've no one to blame but ourselves.

84 We can understand why warriors compete for roles, and we should not want it otherwise. To have a role is to be somebody, to be where the action is. As De Gaulle said, "Glory only sleeps with those who have always dreamed of her," which is true, and sounds better in French.

same way, we need accountants and lawyers, maintenance depots and commissaries, and these jobs need to be done well. But functions are mostly not tooth, but tail, and the proper metric is not readiness, but *sustainability*.

However—and it's an important point—we should be mindful that *function* is a catchall category including an assortment of markedly different activities, creating lots of opportunity for classification error, even by professionals. A pilot performs combat roles in a front-line squadron. When assigned to a schoolhouse to train other pilots, he may fly the same type of aircraft and do much the same sort of thing as before. But combat crew training is a function. In much the same way, a military policeman stands guard at a stateside installation, performing the function of base security. In a time of active operations, he may deploy forward into the role of rear area security. In this way, some peacetime functions provide the essential rotation base for operational roles.

Pilots and policemen are examples—there are many more—of players who jump back and forth between roles and what we might call "retail" functions. With few exceptions, all service departments perform all retail functions for themselves. All have uniformed doctors, communicators, computer experts, engineers, police, historians, recreation specialists, chaplains, and so forth, the full range of support activities needed to keep modern communities working and headquarters staffs filled.

These retail functions have become a target for civilianization and contracting out.[85] We should be careful about this. First, many activities thought to be functions have turned out to be core operational processes in the postmodern, "Type B" wars we've so far seen in the twenty-first century. Engineers, police, civil affairs, medical support, and the like, constitute roles in Type B war, and

---

85 As this is written, civilian contract guards control access to many US military installations. This makes no sense for many reasons, not least our need for a substantial military police rotation base.

accordingly should be kept under service component command to ensure proper battlefield integration.

Besides, even in peacetime there is little to gain and much to lose by centralizing, civilianizing, or out-sourcing retail functions. It's hard to see how creating, say, a unified Defense Department Chaplain Service saves much money. The total number of chaplains required would remain virtually the same. But the commander at an airfield or fort or naval station should get retail functional support from people in the same uniform he wears because this helps create teams that have high motivation and a mission focus difficult to achieve otherwise. Clearly, any marginal savings is not worth the risk in terms of unit cohesion and morale.

These same arguments do not apply to what we might call wholesale functions, large business-type activities like aircraft maintenance depots, POL purchase, bulk storage of common use items, or long-haul communications. Wholesale functions occur well away from the battlefield, are already manned mostly by civilians, and are surprisingly expensive. We should have been able to save money and enhance service by outsourcing wholesale functions to the civilian sector and getting some competition going. Instead, many have been concentrated in growing, proliferating defense agencies.

Centralizing wholesale functions and *keeping them in-house* has not worked well. Outfits like, say, the Defense Commissary Agency or the Defense Finance and Accounting Service, were consolidated at the behest of Defense Department (and against strong service opposition) with a view to improving customer support and driving down cost. I know of no convincing evidence that either thing has happened. Indeed, the centralization of these wholesale functions and their removal from service jurisdiction has created conditions reminiscent of Soviet agriculture. Spinning them out to the commercial sector would have been a good idea, but there is no longer much chance of this happening, since the collectivized functions, even more concentrated and civilianized than before, have congressional representation. However, one way or another, these wholesale business activities provide few thrills and the services are well rid of them.

In any case, the roles-and-missions debate is concerned only secondarily with either retail or wholesale functions, which we might more properly consider in a tooth-to-tail debate. Whether we need two experimental test pilot schools is a matter of some consequence, but it's primarily a management issue. We should not let low-hanging fruit like this divert our attention from first-order roles-and-missions issues.

Saving Money on Roles and Missions

Being given a *role* is what authorizes a service to organize, train, and equip units to perform that role. Thus, having a role links first to force structure, size, and training (and therefore the service culture), and then to equipment requirements (and therefore hardware acquisition).

Again, this is an important point, so I will repeat it. When a service is told to provide combat forces to perform a role it is able to stake a legitimate claim on the country's resources. It follows that when more than one service is charged with the same role, a competition is sure to occur, and the claim on resources is bound to be immoderate, even outrageous. Thus, the key to excellent, affordable national defense is to be judicious in assigning roles.

Most combat roles are difficult to define so as to exclude at least some capability overlap. We should accept that, even welcome it. Were we to produce a play, we'd want an understudy or two available in case one of the stars gets sick. But we certainly would not hire more than one highly paid performer to play each role. It's not just the matter of expense (though that's a pretty good reason) but prima donnas have to be looked after, want their own dressing rooms, get in each other's way, and it's exactly the same in combat. So, always, the question is, how much role overlap and duplication is enough? Or, maybe better said, how much can we stand?

Without question, the joint commander should be self-sufficient regarding the availability of airpower. He has the mission. He's the one who requires generalized self-sufficiency. He should have all the airpower and ground power and maritime power he needs, plus a little. The right roles-and-missions question is, how much self-sufficiency can we afford to buy for the service components that work for the joint commander? We can afford some, we should have some, but we should remember that the push for component self-sufficiency is very expensive, especially when the commodity being purchased is airpower.

If we are to keep the services in more or less their present form, we can solve the expense problem and improve operational performance only by establishing role limits in the context of a theater of operations, and then aligning service functional responsibilities (organize, train, and equip) with component war-fighting roles. Accordingly, we should begin by thinking about how to organize for combat.

Organizing for Type A War

The joint commander has a mission in a theater of operations. The theater consists of terrain to some specified depth, together with adjacent air and waters. As some of the geography is in unfriendly hands, there is an area, or some areas, in which we have troops configured for or engaged in ground combat. We'll call this area the "close battle." There is some extent of more-or-less friendly terrain through which we supply troops engaged in the close battle. We'll call this the "rear battle." Beyond the close battle and extending into hostile territory to the depth of the theater is an area we'll call the "deep battle." Finally, above all the terrain to the edge of space is a region we'll call the "high battle."[86]

Combat roles are tied to battles. For instance, all infantry combat is, by definition, part of the close battle, wherever under way, in whatever part of the theater. Theater air defense is, by definition,

---

86 There is, of course, a space battle, above the high battle. I argue elsewhere that a new, independent service, a US Space Force, should have component responsibility for it.

always and ever part of the high battle. Air interdiction is done only in the deep battle.

The joint commander specifies a land commander responsible for the close and rear battles. Likely, he's from the Army, but could be a Marine, if that service provides the preponderance of troop strength. In any event, it's the joint commander's call. The joint commander also identifies an air commander responsible for the deep and high battles. Again, this officer probably comes from the Air Force but could be a naval aviator or even a qualified officer from one of the other components.

In assigned battle space, the respective land and air commanders are responsible for integrating combat operations. All roles in the close and rear battles, including close air support and what we might call close air defense, come under the regulation of the land commander. Accordingly, the land commander controls some airspace—however much is needed to integrate CAS and close air defense with the other roles of the ground battle. We can think of the close battle as a combined arms operation, including associated air support, with streamlined command arrangements.

The joint commander has responsibility for integrating all battles. He draws the lines—what we call battlefield control measures, or "seams"—that demark the battle space of each. Only he can do this, as only he has unambiguous authority over forces operating on each side of the seams.

For instance, the joint commander establishes the boundary between the close and deep battles, a line with some of the features of today's fire support coordination line (FSCL). The joint commander sets the altitude limit of the land commander's owned airspace, a battlefield control measure called a floor. In fact, it's a floor for the high battle—more a ceiling for the close battle—and a likely choice is the maximum effective altitude of man-portable surface-to-air missiles. In this low-altitude airspace, friendly aircraft—many of them helicopters, but also fixed-wing CAS aircraft—operate under command of the land commander.

The deep battle has no floor or ceiling because the high battle extends from any flying altitude down to the surface. (Airmen will be forgiven for thinking the deep battle is part of the high battle.) Thus, all roles performed in the high and deep battles, including theater air defense, interdiction and deep attack, are the responsibility of air commander, and under his command, no matter which service provides the combat resource.[87]

In my testimony to the commission, I intended to argue that an organizing framework calling for close, rear, high, and deep battles, with associated responsibilities and control measures, was right, operationally. Because of its simplicity, such a scheme would stand up better under the pressure of combat. It could be tailored for independent naval or amphibious engagement, special operations action, or where ground forces operate in a variety of spots simultaneously, in a distributed style, rather than along a single, contiguous front line. It would be suitable for sequential air, naval, and land campaigns, or for parallel, near-simultaneous operations in all dimensions. We should adopt something like it, not because we have less money to spend on defense, or because our forces have different jobs to do in the post-Cold War era (though, again, these are excellent reasons), but because it offers a straightforward and reliable way to organize armed forces to perform all Type A military tasks, scaled to any size.

Getting from Effectiveness to Savings

This simpler, more reliable organizing scheme would also be a big opportunity to cut defense costs, but only if we take the next step: aligning each service's "organize, train, and equip" functional responsibilities with the roles its component could expect to play in joint operations. We would permit only the Army and Marine Corps

---

87 Service components seeking to preserve autonomy will prefer some other relationship: cooperation, coordination, operational control, tactical control. But when the task is hard, the military bond that makes sense is *command*, not any of the pale substitutes.

to organize, train, and equip for combat roles in the close and rear battles, meaning these services, exclusively, could state requirements for, program, develop, purchase, and maintain equipment used in these battles, including fixed-wing aircraft for close air support and short-range missiles for close air defense. By the same token, these services would lose the authority to acquire forces or equipment for the high battle (like the Army's Patriot) or deep battle (like the Army's Joint Tactical Missile System or the Marine Corps' fast jets). We would charge the Air Force and Navy, and only them, with developing and programming high and deep battle systems, like theater air defense, interdiction, and deep attack.

It doesn't often happen that a service loses a role. (One of the few examples was the Army's loss of the land-based intercontinental ballistic missile role to the Air Force.) So we should underscore that when a service relinquishes responsibility for a certain role it must give up the full cascade effect that a fundamental change in organization portends. The losing service must be totally driven from that role. A certain ruthlessness is required here, a quick kill much preferred to lingering death. But that is the way to achieve savings, along with enhanced combat effectiveness.

Argument against Roles-and-Missions Reform

It has been argued that service roles should not be narrowly circumscribed because doing so reduces the joint commander's flexibility. According to this propaganda line, each of the service components provides a variety of tools. The joint commander needs and will use all the tools he can get from the toolbox.

In the abstract, we should wholeheartedly agree, the question being, whose toolbox needs all the tools? The idea that each of the several service components should have its own toolbox full of Swiss Army knives is a formula for jack-of-all-trades mediocrity. What the joint commander needs in *his* toolbox are world-class core competencies in the rear, close, deep, and high battles and, within economic limits, some duplication in order to hedge against single strand failure.

The argument is often dressed up as a pitch for "balanced forces," capable of meeting threats "across the spectrum of conflict." Specialization, according to this view, creates a set of forces optimized against only narrow slices of the threat. But, again, it's the joint commander who must have access to "balanced" forces. It is lavish beyond even our means to suppose that every service component should be "balanced" against all possible threats.

What about Type B War?

Postmodern, Type B war brings with it a new set of techniques and military problems we haven't solved—not yet. I suppose we will make incremental progress, eventually understanding what combat roles are needed and assigning them to services, along with appropriate battlefield control measures. The point is, when we have figured it out, we should be judicious in assigning Type B combat roles, knowing the services pick up the associated organize, train, and equip functions. Assuming we're after effective, affordable Type B capabilities, we need to avoid redundancy in assigning roles.

In any case, we'll continue to build Type A forces for some time, maybe indefinitely. This is because there is always the possibility we will be challenged by a modern, industrialized state, an existential rather than marginal threat. Our continuing to be prepared for Type A war will likely prevent it from happening, just as our readiness for nuclear war has so far deterred that threat. And anyway, for the moment, the money (and the potential savings) is in Type A systems. For example, as this is written, the Defense Department is procuring the F-35, a single-seat fighter, meant to replace the Air Force F-16, the Navy F/A-18 and the Marine Corps Harrier. In the scheme proposed here, the Marine Corps would have joined the Army in stating the need for a close air support aircraft. Freed from the design-stressing (and largely imaginary) Marine Corps requirement for vertical/short takeoff and land (V/STOL) performance, the Air Force and the Navy would have bought a less expensive, higher performance, stealthy fighter that would have been a popular international sales candidate.

Commander in Chief's Trophy

I headed for the White House again in the spring of 1994 to receive the Commander in Chief's Trophy. Each year the president recognizes the service academy football team that wins in tri-cornered competition, graduating team members invited to the ceremony. Of course, I'd watched the Falcons play West Point and Annapolis in rotation during annual four-star gatherings we held at the Air Force Academy. Our players, underweight by college varsity standards, bulked up during the season and had to lose much of this heft to meet Air Force standards at commissioning. In the Rose Garden, I hardly recognized these slender cadets, grown lean since I'd seen them play.

I picked up the Commander in Chief silverware four times in a row, a record I'm unjustifiably proud of, as the credit goes entirely to Coach Fisher DeBerry and the program he established over many years at Colorado Springs.[88] Early in my tenure as chief I designed a set of cufflinks for recently retired four-star generals, presented on the first occasion of their attendance at special briefings we held annually, called Senior Statesman meetings. These cufflinks were meant only for retired four-stars, but I made an exception, giving a pair to Coach DeBerry.

Nixon Funeral

President Nixon's funeral was held in Yorba Linda, California, in late April 1994. All the service chiefs attended. TV cameras videotaping the crowd returned often to scan our front-row seats. The congressional delegation occupied the next few rows behind us, scrums of representatives and senators chewing the political fat. One of the senators, Bob Packwood of Oregon, sat just behind me,

---

88 I thought at the time this record was unbeatable, as the chief's term is only four years, and very hard even to match, the vagaries of college football being what they are. But in the 14 seasons from 1989 to 2002, we won the Commander in Chief's Trophy 13 times, losing only in 1996 (to Army). Accordingly, Mike Ryan, who succeeded Ron Fogleman as chief, tied my four-win record almost immediately.

apart from the rest. Packwood was a member of some consequence, chairman of the powerful, tax-writing Finance Committee, but I knew him only slightly. He was not on Armed Services, not someone closely involved in defense issues. He was taking water just then, revelations circulating about unsavory conduct with young women in his Washington office. None of his colleagues seemed to want film footage with him in the picture, so they had been careful to leave empty chairs on either side of him. He looked forlorn, out-of-place. I turned to remind him we were both Oregonians, eliciting an enthusiastic, puppyish response.

Expanding the CONJEFAMER Idea

I hosted the 1994 CONJEFAMER meeting, a gathering of the hemisphere's senior airmen. I asked Dr. Bill Parry, then secretary of defense, to address the group. In briefing him before his appearance, I mentioned these meetings had been going on for 25 years or so and had been very useful. Among other benefits, if trouble popped up anywhere in the hemisphere, I could pick up the phone and talk to the other air chief on a first-name basis. When, in 1992, a Peruvian fighter aircraft accidentally fired on one of our C-130s, killing one of the crew, my relationship with Chino Velarde helped defuse an otherwise tense situation. Secretary Perry thought we were onto something. He subsequently invited Western Hemisphere defense ministers to a conference set up along the same lines as CONJEFAMER.

I tried with some success to expand the scope of CONJEFAMER. Canada's Air Force had held back for a long time, accepting only "observer" status, but finally did join in after my appeal to Canadian counterpart and friend, Dave Huddleston. The Mexican Air Force was never allowed to join because Mexico's Army controlled their budget and was unwilling to underwrite the very small cost involved. I wanted to invite the Cuban Air Force but was blocked from doing so by OSD's International Security apparatus, which laid the blame on the State Department. I have no way of knowing whether State actually objected, but it makes sense they would, as they have never been keen to have amateur "help" in handling the country's foreign affairs.

I took the hemisphere's air chiefs to dinner at the Smithsonian's National Air and Space Museum. I'd hosted dinner there before, on one particularly memorable evening to honor Anne Morrow Lindbergh. Claire Booth Luce attended and made remarks. On another occasion, Senator Barry Goldwater was guest of honor. Dinner is served on the mezzanine floor. Here, one can dine by candlelight in the presence of the Wright flyer, the *Spirit of St. Louis*, Glenn's *Friendship 7*, and many other fabulous artifacts of aviation. Airmen will find no other dining room quite so impressive.

Flying the MiG-29

In May 1994, during a visit to Germany, Pim Kuebart arranged for me to fly the MiG-29 at Preschen, one of the former East German air bases he'd inherited as a consequence of reunification. Kuebart had settled Fighter Wing 73 there, equipped with two dozen MiG-29s, NATO code-named Fulcrum.[89] Kuebart was having management fits as a result of acquiring the regiments of the former East German Air Force. It was particularly hard for him to find ranking officers from the East ("Ossis") who met Western leadership standards. In the end, he turned loose almost all the East German officers above the grade of major.

I flew the two-seat version of the MiG-29, accompanied by the squadron commander, a lieutenant colonel from the West (Wessi) who had been trained in the United States. I expected what I found, a sturdy aircraft with lots of power, impressive maneuverability, and very little attention given to human factors in cockpit design. It was virtually impossible to see anything at six o'clock, or even over the side, since the canopy rails were very high. The impression was one of sitting in a bathtub, reinforced by a control stick uncomfortably long, seeming to rise chin high. The gages were metric and

---

89 More recently, Fighter Wing 73 "Steinhoff," in honor of the legendary fighter ace and Luftwaffe four-star general.

in Cyrillic script, which was not so bothersome, but the attitude indicator worked backwards. Western instruments gyro stabilize an artificial horizon and display aircraft attitude with respect to it. This duplicates visual flight, with the earth's profile providing a stable reference on which the pilot orients the aircraft. For some reason, Russian aero engineers decided to stabilize the miniature aircraft and make the horizon move to depict relative attitude. This may not sound like much of a problem, but I found it disorienting during an instrument approach at the end of the sortie. My Luftwaffe instructor pilot understood, saying his Wessi pilots had eventually gotten used to it.

D-day Anniversary

On Saturday, 4 June 1994, I was at Cambridge American Cemetery with Secretary Widnall for a D-day 50th anniversary memorial service. The cemetery holds 3,812 American war dead and also a 500-foot-long Wall of the Missing, inscribed with the names of 5,125 more, including Army Air Corps bandleader Glenn Miller. John Major, the prime minister, and President Clinton were featured speakers. Walter Cronkite did introductions. The weather was appropriately miserable, maybe a 500-foot ceiling and a mile visibility. The program called for a "vintage fly-by," and a B-17 and P-51 did manage to get under the stuff for a really low pass, the Mustang's Merlin engine producing that beautiful, deep-throated moan.

Later, Air Chief Marshal Mike Graydon and I traveled to Portsmouth for a dinner held at the Guildhall, which had been bombed out in January 1941. The head table accommodated 13 people, including 10 royals, Viscount Montgomery of Alamein, His Excellency Mr. Lech Walesa, and the Baroness Thatcher. The queen wore a diamond tiara that coruscated shafts of light around the hall as she swung her head from the Honorable William J. Clinton, on her left, to His Excellency Monsieur François Mitterrand, on the other side. Mike and I were seated at banquet table Q, in a good position to watch the queen's hair dance with fire. Across the table, in a civilian black-tie outfit, sat my old buddy from Tuy Hoa,

Col. Bruce W. Carr, USAF (Ret.), an unexpected pleasure added to a splendid evening.

Next morning I flew Speckled Trout to France as D-day celebrations moved to Normandy's Invasion beaches. I landed at Cherbourg, and an Army Blackhawk helicopter took our party to a farm field near the fabled Sainte-Mère-Église, where about forty 70-year old veterans of the 82nd and 101st Airborne Divisions were going to relive some of the fun of World War II. When this was first proposed, I would not authorize use of Air Force C-130s, so these guys simply hired a transport aircraft and made a couple of practice jumps, breaking various body parts. As the exercise gained momentum (and publicity), I relented on the theory that at least we would do it right. Still, I kept my fingers crossed. In the event, we flew them right across the drop zone at precisely the right time, and they all came out and floated to ground without misadventure.

The same could not be said of Mrs. Pamela Harriman, our ambassador to France, who sat with me to watch the proceedings. She had worn diamond earrings of considerable caratage, one of which somehow came loose. We spent much time inspecting deep grass around and under the reviewing stand, without success.

President Clinton showed up late (as usual) for his speech at Omaha Beach, and it was getting dark before we climbed in the Blackhawk for the short hop back to Cherbourg. Weather was lowering, and the airport, sitting on something of a plateau, gradually socked in. The chopper crew made several runs at it, using the asphalt method of navigation. Finally, they scared me enough I got on a headset and told them to put it down next to the road. We scrambled out; I waved down a passing car and got to use my survival French. We squeezed in with a Norman family and drove to the airport, where I caused our driver some dismay by whisking the party through security and onto the flight line. But then I ducked on board Speckled Trout, collected the last of our gift inventory and handed it to a surprised but happy ally.

Mike Boorda

I managed to build a bad relationship with Mike Boorda, distressing since I'd been on warm terms with Frank Kelso, his predecessor as chief of naval operations. Boorda was the first Jewish officer ever to head the Navy. Even more remarkable, he had not graduated from the Naval Academy, or even from a college ROTC program. He'd served in ranks for years before being picked to go to Officer Candidate School. He had plenty of operational experience, but was known primarily as a personnel specialist. For a guy like this to become CNO, he had to be unusually able. So, there were at the outset many reasons to be favorably disposed toward Boorda. I should have liked him, and almost immediately didn't.

Twice, Boorda was effective in prying loose large sums of money from the Air Force. In the most egregious case, the services were required to set aside dollars every year for correction of environmental remediation at installations being shut down in the base closure process, creating something like a trust fund for this purpose. The Navy shorted their fund so they could spend more on other priorities. We funded our obligation fully—dumb on my part—but were rather deliberate in working our way through the closure process, with the result that a large amount of unobligated Air Force money built up in our account. I wasn't concerned because the funding profile would self-adjust in the out-years. But the Navy's less rigorous approach to the base closure process got them through the wickets quicker and they were smarter working angles on the remediation problem, so they ended up with the capacity to obligate more money than they had accumulated. The Navy argued this was an opportunity. They should be allowed to tap the unused funds set aside by the Air Force, whose slowness to spend it, of course, proved we didn't know what we were doing. I cried foul. This was Air Force money, taken out of squadrons and airplanes. At OSD insistence, we'd faced up to the requirement and funded it fully. The funds were multiyear, not about to expire. They would be available as the Air Force got each base closure package wrapped up—the point being, do it right, not necessarily fast. The Navy simply hadn't taken enough of a hit in its own budget to cover its base closure costs and was now trying to hand us the tab.

In private, I braced Boorda and he denied any knowledge of the Navy effort to pick our pocket. Service chiefs have a lot to do, but I reckoned not so much he could be blissfully unaware of a budgeting issue involving hundreds of millions of dollars, as this one did. So, he lied. Worse, because of the Navy's bureaucratic strength, he got the money.

Boorda and I had another argument when I tried to reduce funding for KC-135 aerial tanker modifications that would allow for multistation, "probe-and-drogue" refueling. Increasingly, the Navy relied on the Air Force for air refueling support, but they still did air refueling by having the receiver aircraft insert a probe into a basket, called a drogue, hooked to the end of a hose trailing behind the tanker. Air Force fighters had for years used the same technique, but bombers and transports used a different style, called boom refueling, in which an operator on board the tanker inserts a fuel pipe into a receptacle on the receiver aircraft. To give us more flexibility with the tanker fleet (and to reduce weight and complexity in fighter aircraft designs) we finally standardized on boom refueling and gradually switched all our aircraft, including fighters, over to this style. The KC-135 could be configured for either probe-and-drogue or boom refueling, but not both, so we were required to juggle the schedule or reconfigure tankers, depending on whether they were to refuel Air Force or Navy aircraft.

Maintaining a probe-and-drogue capability complicated our tanker operations, but we were very willing to do it. However, the Navy also wanted to be able to refuel from more than one station on the tanker. To be precise, they wanted us to buy underwing pods that would enclose and reel out drogues, enabling us to refuel three aircraft at a time from a KC-135. We agreed to do this and programmed money to buy the pods and modify the tankers.

However, reductions to the Air Force budget put all our programs under heavy pressure. We canceled or cut back deeply many high-priority Air Force initiatives. As a way to distribute the pain, I proposed cutting the probe-and-drogue pod program in half, meaning all our KC-135s would continue to support Navy air refueling, but only half of them would be able to refuel three Navy fighters at once.

The Navy objected to cutting back this program and tabled it as an issue for consideration by the Defense Resources Board (DRB), a high-level committee chaired by the deputy SECDEF and including other senior OSD officials, the chairman of the JCS, the service secretaries, and chiefs. When the DRB took up the matter, Boorda jumped in immediately and began to lecture on air refueling. The Navy had to have probe-and-drogue; it was better, easier to do, safer—so on and so forth—all of this reading from notes.

I was hard for me to sit through this. Boorda's occupational strength was in personnel administration; he'd been the Navy's flesh peddler. Not only was he not a pilot, he wasn't even what I thought of as a hard-core operator. I doubted he had any up-close and personal experience with aerial fuel transfer. On the other hand, probably nobody in the Air Force, let alone the Navy, had more hookups than me. My experience went back to the prop-driven KB-50 and included single-point and multipoint, and probe-and-drogue as well as boom refueling. I'd forgotten more about air refueling than Boorda would ever know, and all present understood this, so Boorda's harangue was met with an embarrassed silence he seemed not to notice.[90]

Boorda finished his presentation, and the group turned to me.

---

90 Matter of fact, I sort of agreed with some of the points Boorda made. I always liked probe-and-drogue because it gave the receiver aircraft a feeling of increased control, fighter pilots being the original control freaks. On the other hand, boom refueling was as easy (or easier), as safe (or safer), and removed hardware from the fighter, making it lighter—always a good thing.

The real issue here was "jointness," and I knew I was going to lose. It didn't make any difference that we would continue to support the Navy, and do so even better than before. We had to over-service the Navy requirement and further short Air Force priorities as an indication of sincerity about jointness. I said we would restore the probe-and-drogue pod program to full funding. Let's go on to the next issue. But I never forgot Boorda's Lessons on Air Refueling.

Mike Boorda didn't understand the pivotal difference between values—culturally driven and temporal—and virtue—spiritual and eternal. The matter of values is about the bargain we make with others—our family, our service, our country. Loyalty is a value, patriotism, a value. By contrast, we have to make the virtue deal with ourselves. Honesty is a virtue.

The world would certainly be an easier place if values always aligned with virtue, but unhappily these two are often in tension, as when honesty requires you to do or say things that may be disloyal to the group. As you rise in an organization, the conflict case, the tug-of-war between values and virtue, becomes more and more common. What we call integrity, a unified sense of oneself, involves the willingness to choose virtue over values when a choice is unavoidable. This was the choice Mike Boorda couldn't make. He loved the Navy, thought he owed it everything. The Navy was his value system. And he put service above self, selflessness being one of the great values.

It turned out Boorda loved the Navy more than life. Some months after I retired, he committed suicide. The press was about to reveal that for years he had improperly attached devices to decorations he wore, identifying these awards had been earned under combat conditions. Over at least some of his long period of service, Navy boards considering Boorda for promotion would have seen official photographs sporting the questionable garlands, so it could be argued he'd provided inaccurate, self-serving information, and a cloud would arise over the advancement that had positioned him to become CNO.

The post-suicide civilian commentary missed the point entirely, stressing how sad it was that Boorda killed himself over an item so inconsequential as a couple of award devices. I'm not a big fan of decorations, but there's nothing ambiguous about the rules for earning them. And one thing all professionals of every service can do is read decorations at a glance. Inside the Navy, Boorda had made an issue of character, going around giving speeches on integrity (always a cautionary signal). Now his own integrity was about to be examined in the most painful, public way. Based on what I'd seen, it would not withstand scrutiny. In the end, Mike Boorda shot himself in the chest rather than see his Navy tarnished by any mistake he'd made.

In *The Last Battle*, C. S. Lewis has the dying centaur, Roonwit, send a message to King Tirian: ". . . remember that all worlds draw to an end and that noble death is a treasure which no one is too poor to buy." Lewis had served in the trenches of World War I and would have seen a little dying, but I have no doubt that hard-core military professionals will discern the sentimental foolishness in the centaur's view. Even so, in death, Mike Boorda achieved a sort of nobility. He found more courage than I could have in the circumstances. And courage is a virtue.

China Visit

I was invited to China in September to visit my counterpart, Cao Shuanqming, Commander of the People's Liberation Army Air Force (PLAAF). He was the replacement for Wong Hai, the long-serving air chief who had fallen from grace, having sided with the "liberals" on how to handle the 1989 Tiananmen Square protests. I first met Wong when I'd accompanied Charlie Gabriel on a visit to China. A fighter ace from the Korean War, Wong took Gabriel and me to the PLAAF museum to see his MiG-15, decorated with 13 small US flags. Wong had been shot down three times, once at a place and on a date that corresponded with one of Charlie Gabriel's two kills. The men were convinced that Gabriel had in fact shot down Wong.

When Wong came to the United States to return Gabriel's visit, I was detailed as escort officer, spending enough time with him to kid him about kill claims. (I told him we hadn't lost 13 aircraft total, let alone to one guy.)

When the conservative hard-liners won out, Wong lost face, and eventually his job, after which he was put under house arrest. I tried to communicate with him through his son, Steve Wong, who had moved to the United States and was working for McDonnell-Douglas. In fact, I arraigned to meet Steve Wong when I visited the C-17 factory at Long Beach, one of the first places I went after being named chief. I brought along a leather flying jacket I wanted the younger Wong to send to his father. He later wrote me to say Wong Hai was delighted with the jacket and asked me to accept in return a nice Chinese painting.[91]

Wong was still alive in September 1994 when we arrived in Beijing for the official visit. I asked the Chinese to let me see him. No dice. Not even our ambassador, J. Stapleton Roy, could get them to bend on the issue. But it was a good trip, one I think helped Sino-US relations. I met with their minister of defense, Chi Haotoan. The government press release had him referring to me as "an old friend," this being my third official trip to mainland China.

Out in the countryside, the commander at one of the PLAAF's fighter bases took me through his supply warehouse, a surprisingly small structure, about the size of a Quonset hut. The shelves were nearly bare, but at intervals the odd spare part was stocked—a wheel here, generator there. It didn't seem like much to me. I'd had seven immense warehouses at Upper Heyford when I was running the 20th Wing, and they were always full to overflowing, though

---

91 The main rule officers are obliged to observe regarding gifts like this is they must be of nominal value. Otherwise the government carts them off to a warehouse, after which I don't know what happens. But I managed to keep the painting from Wong Hai.

often not with the stuff I needed. This Chinese commander seemed proud of his skimpy inventory. I pressed the interpreter for an explanation and probably missed something in translation, but what I think the Chinese commander said was he received supplies once a year, in January, and it was a great achievement still to have any spare parts at all, this late in the year.

OSD's Cast of Characters

In my time, a deputy and five undersecretaries assisted the secretary of defense. Dick Cheney's deputy was Don Atwood, a nice man who left no fingerprints whatever on any of the Pentagon's formidable problems. When Les Aspin took over as President Clinton's first SECDEF, his deputy was Bill Perry. Perry had previous Pentagon experience as the assistant for acquisition and had funded much of the early signature reduction technology leading up to the F-117. He consequently had a good claim to being the Father of Stealth, or at least one of the fathers. Like Atwood, Perry was a gentleman, easy to like and work with, but he was in addition a real contributor, not just on the technology issues he understood so well, but also on international security policy, where his judgment was superb. The best part: Perry was entirely selfless, focused on externals—the problem, impediments to be removed, timing. When Aspin self-destructed, Perry moved up to secretary, an immense improvement. The only count against Perry was his failure to address the roles-and-missions issue. Even here, I credited him with judging he had enough to do without fighting windmills that could fight back.

Perry's replacement as deputy was John Deutch, Perry's equal in intelligence, though not in judgment. Unlike Perry, Deutch couldn't separate himself from a problem, though often he found a solution anyway.

Of SECDEF's senior assistants, the undersecretary for policy was arguably the most important, regarded as number three in protocol pecking order. Paul Wolfowitz was Cheney's USD/P. I'd known Wolfowitz slightly when he served in Indonesia as ambassador. He was very smart, a little scary in his ability to grasp and manipulate concepts. At the table, he didn't always argue issues well because his vocal chords couldn't keep up with his brain. He recognized this and slowed down presentations, paying out thoughts carefully, but the almost physical effort was never hidden from view, taking away from his persuasiveness. He, too, was courteous and considerate, a man who paid attention to the small niceties of rank and position important in a military context, without seeming self-conscious or in any way condescending in doing so.

The very capable Jim Lilley occupied the rung just below Wolfowitz as assistant secretary for International Security Affairs (ASD/ISA). Listening to Jim Lilley was never a waste of time.

Walt Slocombe, who as far as I could see gave new meaning to the term "passivity," succeeded Wolfowitz in the Clinton administration. Things happened *to* Slocombe. He certainly left behind no traces in the Pentagon's halls. But his assistant was the formidable Chas Freeman, perhaps the ablest of the civilian leaders I worked with. Freeman was a sort of Socrates. Quiet, thoughtful, he penetrated beyond the province of smart into that foreign country called wisdom. Near the end of my tenure, Joe Nye, another superstar, replaced Freeman.

On balance, OSD's civilian lineup was pretty impressive, especially Perry, Lilley, and Freeman.

Briefing the Tank

In preparing for my appearance in front of the Commission on Roles and Missions, I thought I'd better run proposed testimony by the other chiefs as a matter of professional courtesy. I asked John Shalikashvili to allow me to give my CORM pitch in the tank, the secure, second-floor conference room where the chiefs met two or three times a week. He agreed. On the day, I didn't get very far into the briefing before Gordy Sullivan exploded, ending his outburst with a tight-lipped warning that I should not doubt his courage.

As was often the case with Sullivan, I had no idea what to think of this utterance. Of course, I didn't question his bravery. But there sure was an issue about his willingness to engage in a contest of ideas. His taking the matter as a personal affront effectively ended my effort to prebrief the chairman and other chiefs.

Sullivan had a reputation for brains, maybe seen inside the Army as well earned. Viewed from outside, his most important observable trait was a gift for opaque expression. For me, he was a brown dwarf, faint at the start and dimming with time, but just possibly a tiny contributor to the dark matter that seems to outweigh the luminous mass of the universe, and therefore not to be dismissed entirely.

Having gotten only a glimpse of my proposed CORM testimony, Sullivan and Boorda tried to get a restraining order, but they couldn't convince Shali, certainly one of the most open-minded and progressive chairmen in history, to shut me up.

CORM Testimony

My appearance before the commission came in September 1994, only weeks ahead of scheduled retirement. I was the first service chief to appear, the others wanting to key their testimony off mine. I outlined my ideas in a presentation lasting a full two hours. The central theme was we needed to more clearly define the combat roles for which services organize, equip, and train forces and that a stylized battlefield of the kind I describe elsewhere in these pages could be the basis for such a definition.

The CORM Report

The commission reported its findings, *Directions for Defense*, in May 1995. It was clear that my views had made no impression. The commission offered a number of careful recommendations, mostly regarding what I describe here as support functions. Perhaps the report's most lasting contribution was to recommend doing yet another study. It sidestepped the very roles-and-missions issues Congress had asked it to address. Over and over, the report asserted that the question needed to change from "who does what" to "who needs what." This captured the high ground, of course. It's hard to disagree about the superior standing of, say, the joint commander's war-fighting needs, as compared with a service's institutional self-interest. However, although a joint commander might be indifferent regarding the source of a military capability—he may be little concerned about whether close air support is provided by the Army, Navy, Air Force, or Marines, or whether the troops being supported are soldiers, Marines, or special operators—these are matters of institutional life and death for the services, who, back in Washington, are responsible for spending the money.

Had I been in Dr. White's place, awaiting appointment as deputy secretary of defense, perhaps I might have wondered about sponsoring recommendations that would alienate most of the military establishment. Still, I suppose if Congress had wanted the commission to hold itself above the roles-and-missions fight, it would have given it another name.

In a fitting curtain line, Dr. White sent a note to me in retirement (addressed to Gen. Anthony A. McPeak) thanking me for giving the roles-and-missions issue "energy it needed at a critical time."

❂ ❂ ❂

Those who wish to avoid honest debate about roles and missions sometimes start by asserting the Air Force thinks itself the most important service, that we claim the way to victory lies always and only through the air. The pioneer airpower advocates were certainly guilty as charged, but this hobbyhorse has now been rocked long and hard enough. The issue is not whether any one service can do the job by itself. It can't. It's about how to defend the country better, and at lower cost.

Chapter 11

Followed by More

Flying men, guarding the nation's border,
We'll be there, followed by more . . .
                    —"Air Force Song"

The breakup of the Soviet Union presented a radically different situation, a world transformed from the one in which we found ourselves for two generations. The fear that a hostile power would dominate the Eurasian landmass—at the same time a long-established peril and a contemporary anxiety—disappeared and was not at once replaced. On the other hand, the Soviet withdrawal unlocked new and poorly understood menaces that had been fixed in ice during the period of the Cold War.

We neither foresaw nor planned for these developments, though there had been a lively and long-running debate about the sort of power relationship that might emerge in a post-Cold War world. The most common and best-argued case envisioned a multipolar arrangement. Assuming we won, the United States would have enhanced status as a great power, but whatever endured of the Soviet Union would occupy a place of importance; China would gain increased standing; some sort of European entity might emerge; Japan, or India, even Brazil could play a role. In the event, this didn't happen, at least not immediately. In the first phase of the post-Cold War period, we settled into a unipolar condition, the United States standing alone at the apex of world power.

The new international environment had its impact on domestic politics. First came many attempts to further limit American involvement overseas, especially military engagement. The bitter residue of Vietnam still influenced thinking, and the interventions in Beirut, Grenada, Panama, Somalia, the Balkans, and Haiti, as well as our failure to remove Saddam Hussein at the end of the first Gulf War, provided much ammunition for those pressing the case against American commitment abroad, except when we were pushed to the wall.

There is always room for honest debate about specific interventions, but I regard as nonsense the more extreme versions of this argument. Of course we should be conservative about military intervention. There are many instruments available for use by a great power—economic, political, diplomatic, financial, cultural—and all should be employed before resorting to force. But when gentle argument or soft coercion fails and military action is the only effective option, the opposition case takes the form of truisms: it's risky (as if the security environment was otherwise risk-free); we shouldn't be "the world's policeman" (whatever that means); we should intervene only when it is in our (otherwise undefined) national interest.

Of course, in prospect, our actions should be proportionate and suit national purposes. And up to the end of the second Clinton administration, no recent intervention failed this test. We did not go to Haiti to make it the 51st state or fly over Kosovo so we might put our president's face on Serbian postage stamps. These and other late twentieth-century military interventions took place when things seemed out of control and had the potential for explosive escalation, and where stabilizing the situation would work to our advantage. This suits my notion of action in the national interest.

Furthermore, I believe we ought to be concerned about the free movement of people, ideas, and commerce, meaning we should help preserve collective security in a disjointed world. Often, simply helping will not be enough. In dangerous situations, others will hold back unless and until we act. Leadership is thus part of the price of being a great power. There are other costs—economic and, not least, human—and we have no realistic alternative to shouldering them. Our future success will be measured not in the number of engagements we avoid, but in how well we execute after we commit.

The Soviet demise had another, less obvious, impact. The old threat-strategy-force planning model no longer worked. In both the Base Force exercise and the Bottom-Up Review we found the essence of this approach—sizing forces to prevail in imagined but believable scenarios—increasingly difficult to sustain. In the absence of graphic, easily understood threats, we needed to invent a new calculus to structure and size the force and articulate its intended uses to a skeptical public—a problem unsolved at this writing. Until the new analytical tools become available, we'll have to settle for witness testimony—subjective, first-order approximations from people we hope know what they're talking about. What follows is my contribution.

If we start first with size, we reached the high-water mark of recent active duty end strength—nearly 2.2 million people—in 1987. By the end of the twentieth century, we had drawn down to 1.4 million. We cannot reasonably expect the scale of likely military operations to exceed what we did in Korea, Vietnam, or Desert Storm, and in each case, we deployed about half a million men. If we double this for safety and to provide a rotation base, the size of our active force could be about a million. Judging by history, even a million men permanently under arms would constitute a dangerously large force, but such size seems in keeping with the requirement to provide global leadership in the post-Cold War era.

Regarding structure, we should configure the active military to carry the full load in anticipated conflict short of general war. This means that certain support functions, like military police, civil affairs, psychological and information warfare, should be reclassified as combat roles and moved from the reserves back into the active force. We should backfill the reserves with "heavy" equipment like tanks and tube artillery, large chunks of which no longer need to be kept at highest readiness. Shifting capabilities in this way would lighten active forces and make them more deployable, avoid the necessity of recalling reserves for every small engagement, and disburse heavy equipment in conditions that allow for throttled-back, lower-cost use.

When needed, we should in any case integrate reserves in smaller units. The Air Force has had good success in keeping squadron-sized reserve formations at high readiness, available for immediate recall and attachment to regular line wings. To maintain quality at a higher echelon—say the brigade or division level for ground forces—is a much more complex undertaking for anyone, active or reserve. It's not a part-time job. Better to build reserve companies or battalions for emergency integration with active duty Army brigades. We'll pay a political price for this approach because it will be obvious that reserve structure above battalion level is administrative in nature and has only a peacetime role. That said, this is probably the best way for reserves to make a meaningful, early contribution in circumstances involving a genuine national emergency.

But the post-Cold War upheaval in potential threats, military requirements, and combat missions begs for much greater change, touching not only the size and structure, but also the character of our forces. We should move, and move quickly, from concepts of linear, industrial-age war to nonlinear, information-age operations, featuring vastly increased tempo, rapid movement, and great depth.

What characteristics should the new-style forces have? We know the location, direction, and timing of threats will be difficult to predict. This reality, along with reduced forward basing and a citizenry increasingly casualty averse, argues that speed, range, and precise lethality are far more important than size. We must redesign our forces for rapid, long-range movement to any point of contact, and for immediate effectiveness upon arrival. No more Desert Storms—painful, heavy-footed buildups to some anticlimactic combat phase. We should measure our timelines for availability anywhere in the world in hours, and our readiness for combat in minutes after arrival. This is a very large part of the actuality and perception of our continued global engagement, even where we are not physically in place.

Thus, we need a different kind of force, smaller and changed in its nature. However—and this is an important caveat—having won the Cold War, we will seek relief from the defense burden. We are unlikely to finance the equipage and sustainability needs of even a smaller force unless we act vigorously to reduce the duplication of military capabilities among the services and amputate much of the logistic support tail that our combat forces drag behind them. Assuming we find the courage to face the roles-and-missions and tooth-to-tail issues, we can create conditions allowing for prudent reduction in the size of our forces and transfer a substantial amount of money to investment accounts, providing the wherewithal to modernize our forces for the post-Cold War world.

It's said the calendar's appointment of years does not track well with history's turning points. Accordingly, we may think of the nineteenth century as elongated, stretching from the French Revolution to World War I. The twentieth century having thus been delayed a decade or two, we might also regard it as closing ahead of its allotted time, starting in 1989 with the fall of the Berlin Wall, followed in short order by the rapid disintegration of the Soviet Union. If this view is correct, I can stake a claim to being the first Air Force chief of the "real" twenty-first century.

I did what I could to prepare the Air Force for a new millennium.

Organization, training, equipage, I ignored nothing I thought of consequence, trying to build and shape structures better suited to fight the country's air wars. I led my service as I had learned to fly, not by extraordinary talent, but by effort and concentration. And, just as one cannot master the internal work of flying (or even entirely explain it), there is a ceiling on what can be achieved through raw application. Beyond a certain point, something more, some natural gift is required. Thus, as with flying, I never quite succeeded—or quite failed either.

Logbook

Crew Position	Total
Pilot	4,112
Instructor Pilot	809
Copilot/other	1,372
Total Rated Hours	6,293
Combat Hours	646
Total Sorties	3,279
Combat Sorties	285

Mission Ready/Capable:

Aircraft	Total Hours
F-100C/D/F	2,466
F-104C/D/G/TF	674
F-4E	196
F-111A/E	154
F-16A/B	187
F-15A/B/C/D	174

Current and/or Left Seat Qualified:

Aircraft	Total Hours
T-33	123
T-39	232
C-20 (Gulfstream)	519
C-21 (Learjet)	154
C-135	1,365

Other Aircraft Flown:

A-1	B-1B	B-52G	C-12	C-17	C-117		C-130
C-137	C-141	E-8	Embrar 312	Hawk 50	IAO 63		KC-10
L-20	L-29	MiG-29	Mirage 2000	Mystere 20	O-2		OV-10
P-9	P-51	S-211	T-1	T-28	T-29		T-34
	T-37	T-38	Tornado	U-6	UH-1		

The times were in figures, the dull specifics which were supposed to record the passage of intervals in our lives, and serve as official recognition that a certain amount of experience and consequent wisdom had dribbled into our aerial selves. The numerals, in summation, represented much more than this. For they said that our marrows had been both frozen and melted, our quotients of courage drained and replenished, and our ability to act in fear, proven . . . Altogether, the numerals stated that we knew how to remove ourselves and others out of our natural element, in all seasons, and in all circumstances and conditions, and return the lot safely to earth.
 —Ernest K. Gann, *Fate Is the Hunter*

Appendix: Battlefield Control Measures

Key West Agreement: The National Security Act of 1947 unified the old War and Navy Departments, creating a Department of Defense. It also established an independent Department of the Air Force. There followed a scramble in which the Army and Navy sought to retain roles and missions that should logically have been given to the new service, highlighted by a noisy dispute between the Air Force and the Navy over responsibility for "strategic" warfare. In early 1948, the first secretary of defense, James Forrestal, fed up with the bickering, did what any modern CEO would do: he convened an off-site conference. This one took place at Key West, Florida. Some great military figures were there—Omar Bradley, Tooey Spaatz, Louis Denfield. They agreed to a set of compromises that muted Pentagon infighting temporarily by papering over underlying issues. Even so, Forrestal's first annual report, published toward the end of 1948, admitted, "I would be less than candid ... if I did not underline the fact that there are still great areas in which the viewpoints of the services have not come together." He put the most divisive issue simply: "What is to be the use, and who is to be the user of airpower?"

In the abstract, the problem faced at Key West should not have been difficult: the Army works on land, the Navy at sea, the Air Force in the air, a situation that ought to have determined the allocation of primary roles-and-missions responsibility and would have produced natural jurisdictional boundaries at the earth's surface and along oceanic coastlines. But a new world of air capabilities was being imposed on powerful, entrenched bureaucracies. Each service recognized the crucial role airpower would play in modern battle and naturally wanted its own ability both to mount aerial attack and to defend against it. The question should never have been whether, collectively, we needed such capabilities, but rather how much of these capabilities each service must have of its own. The outcome at Key West was to cut and paste airpower to suit institutional interests.

The Key West Agreement therefore created our "four air forces," allocating roles and missions to the services pretty much as we still do today. About the only formal change since Key West has been to tack on roles when some new technology, like satellite reconnaissance or electronic warfare, could not be ignored. In such cases, almost without exception, the solution has been to give the same new responsibilities to each service. Thus, for example, every department has the same tasking in space and, as a consequence, every department has a space command. (Think of it—three space commands! Even so, it should have been a surprise that the first American to orbit Earth was a Marine, stretching the limits of the Marine air-ground team concept.)

It is an important point and bears repeating: the allocation of roles and missions is essentially the same today as it was in 1947, despite vast changes in our world position, despite a half century of very rapid technical advance, despite the Goldwater-Nichols legislation and other important impulses toward jointness and, perhaps most important, despite the tremendous growth in the nature, size, and cost of our defense establishment.

I suppose you could argue that by some improbable stroke of luck, the Key West Agreement hit on exactly the right formula for parceling out responsibilities and that's why it has not been revisited in a fundamental way. Judged strictly by results, I do not believe our performance in battle since World War II has validated the half-century-old design. Of course there has been some splendid work done, but insiders know the record is spotty enough to support a comprehensive rethinking of roles-and-missions issues. So, the much more likely case is that no miracle occurred at Key West, that the solution cooked up there was never adequate from the beginning, and that we have operated for more than half a century with a patchwork compromise, a committee design that, to the extent it has worked at all, proves only that good people can achieve middling results with any system, if they have enough money and lives to spend.

Title 10, US Code: The Key West Agreement was the basis for the law applicable to the Department of Defense and to each of the services, Title 10 of the United States Code. As amended through the early 1990s, Title 10 identifies "functions" that must be performed by the military departments. For instance, listed among the "Primary Functions of the Air Force" is "to organize, train, equip, and provide forces for the conduct of prompt and sustained combat operations in the air."

But Title 10 goes further to specify the *composition* of each of the services:

> In general, the Army, within the Department of the Army, includes land combat and Service forces and such aviation and water transport as may be organic therein . . .
>
> The Navy, within the Department of the Navy, includes, in general, naval combat and Service forces and such aviation as may be organic therein . . .
>
> The Marine Corps, within the Department of the Navy, shall be so organized as to include not less than three combat divisions and three air wings, and such other land combat, aviation, and other Services as may be organic therein . . .

Clearly, the phrase "such aviation as may be organic therein" is a binding that will wrap any kind of graft. But, in the case of the Navy, Title 10 goes further:

> All naval aviation shall be integrated with the naval Service as part thereof within the Department of the Navy. Naval aviation consists of combat and Service and training

forces, and includes land-based aviation, air transport essential for naval operations, all air weapons and techniques involved in the operations and activities of the Navy, and the entire remainder of the aeronautical organization of the Navy, together with the personnel therefore.

And, finally:

In general, the Air Force includes aviation forces both combat and Service not otherwise assigned.

As can be seen, Title 10 sets the "four air forces" in concrete. A quick reading of its provisions speaks volumes about the pushing and shoving that occupies the services, both inside the Pentagon, in their relations with one another, and outside, in their relations with Congress and the public. The Air Force has not done well in this tug-of-war. Surely the organizers of an independent Air Force did not envision an outfit consisting of aviation forces "not otherwise assigned." What the country needed (and still needs) was for airpower capabilities to be unified in an integrated national defense.

Core Competence: Fundamental knowledge or expertise in a specific role or function. The term entered the vernacular in recent years as a way of guiding businesses in a competitive marketplace to concentrate on what they're good at. But the economics of specialization rest on the well-tested theory of comparative advantage, according to which parties that trade with each other maximize wealth creation by doing *only* what they do best, even if one side does *everything* better than the other.

When challenged to name anything discovered by the social sciences that was both true and nontrivial, Paul Samuelson cited the theory of comparative advantage:

That it is logically true need not be argued before a mathematician; that it is not trivial is attested by the thousands of important and intelligent men who have never been able to grasp the doctrine for themselves or believe it after it was explained to them.

Seams: Once people combine their efforts and specialize for greater productivity, seams at the boundary of different sorts of activity are unavoidable. Work may be divided by shift (time), by geography (distance), by type (function), or in other ways. Every work boundary represents a tradeoff, a decision about which organizational characteristics to reinforce and which problems to live with. Thus, no organization, even the most elementary, will be able to optimize itself for all seam issues.

Consider the relatively simple case of a basketball team. Our side has only five players on the floor at any time, but there are guards, forwards, and a center. Even these categories do not fully describe the degree of specialization (e.g., "point" guard; "power" forward). Our players may all be seven feet tall, but somebody has to play guard because the good teams will kill us if all our guys stand around under the basket. (As an analogue to some of our recent combat experience, we probably could get away with it against weak-enough opposition.) So, our team specializes, and specialization creates complex relationships ("seams") among the players. It is the coach's job to produce an integrated effort, obviously including the important and difficult matter of regulating constantly changing player relationships (seam management).

Complex organizations, like armed forces, find it very hard to get the seams right. Nonetheless good organizational design, including careful boundary placement, greatly increases the odds that the constituent parts will be capable of self-regulation and high performance. There are no easy answers but, once a decision to divide the work has been made, here are a couple of reliable rules for seam management:

Rule One: Decrease seams to the lowest practical number. Fewer is better. Unnecessary seams cause no end of trouble, the District of Columbia's dozen or so overlapping police jurisdictions being a domestic example having a certain slapstick quality.

The Russians illustrated the point convincingly in Chechnya. There, despite overwhelming numbers, a big technical edge and superior firepower, the Russians had their hands full trying to control a few thousand Chechen rebels. Why? At the time, 12 Russian ministries or agencies fielded armed ground units. These included the army, navy, and air force, of course, but also such diverse groups as the Interior Ministry, federal border guards, and Civil Security Agency. (In 1995, their federal railway troops alone had a strength of 10,000 men.) The fighting in Chechnya was not the consolidated responsibility of the regular army, but shared with paratroops (which belonged to the air force), marines, Interior Ministry troops and militia units. Reverses on the ground often resulted from a lack of coordination among the various kinds of troops involved. On 3 April 2000, in reporting the deaths of 43 Russian soldiers killed in an ambush, the New York Times noted that, "the Kremlin has sent a hodgepodge of military units under command arrangements that seem to invite disaster." Here is a tale of too many seams, creating complexity of geometric, not linear, proportions, and paid for in lives. (For an example closer to home, see chapter 9, Somalia.)

We all understand intuitively the virtue of a "seamless" organization. But how do we organize for seamlessness? A commonsense approach is to subordinate needed resources within the organization that uses them on a regular basis. Otherwise, the mission cannot be completed without constantly reaching across departmental seams for essential support. For instance, if each of the services is to continue having its own air force—that is, if we are never to rationalize the organizational structure of our armed services—then close air support should be owned and operated by the Army.

Rule Two: Where there must be seams, make them strong. An organization may go rotten at the core but it frays at the edges. A knowing enemy will find and attack the seams; they should be designed to take stress. Strong seams can be created only by someone with full authority over the organizational entities operating on each side of the specified boundary. As an example of how to ignore this simple rule, consider the fire support coordination line (FSCL), a battlefield control measure established by a ground force commander having control over activities on only one side of the line.

Battlefield Control Measures: In military parlance, seams are regulated by battlefield control measures, lines drawn on a map describing responsibilities of cooperating commanders in the dimensions of space and time—assembly areas, departure points, assault positions, objectives, phase points, etc. In what follows, I set out operational-level battlefield control measures for a stylized Type A war.

Type A War: Modern, industrial war, featuring mechanized forces, a type of conflict roughly coterminous with the twentieth century. It's the sort of war we came to know something about and got fairly good at.

Desert Storm was a Type A war, perhaps the last we'll fight for a while. This is because the side possessing air superiority prevails in Type A war. Thus, while one can visualize a future Type A war—say between India and Pakistan—our overwhelming air superiority makes it unlikely others will challenge us in modern, industrial combat anytime soon, a situation much to be desired.

This is not to say we can stop paying attention. Airpower is in many ways an American birthright, starting with the Wright brothers and running through Lindbergh and Doolittle to Yeager and beyond. Nevertheless, in World War I we had to fly French airplanes, and our condition at the start of the World War II wasn't much better. If we want Type A war to go away, we'd better stay ready for it.

Close Battle: A battlefield control measure marking off the area in which opposing ground forces are in contact. In Type A war, the close battle extends from friendly forward positions out to the limit of conventional artillery fires—no farther than, say, about 50 kilometers—where the deep battle begins. The close battle includes airspace up to the maximum range of man-portable surface-to-air missiles, perhaps 3,000 meters altitude.

Rear Battle: A battlefield control measure incorporating territory in more-or-less friendly hands extending from the area of active close combat to the rear, including theater air base and other support infrastructure. Like the close battle, the rear battle includes airspace up to some altitude, allowing for fixed-wing, helicopter, and light UAV operations under the operational control of the ground forces commander.

Deep Battle: A battlefield control measure describing the area forward from the further edge of the close battle to the limits of the theater. Because of the aircraft's speed and range, the deep battle is the natural realm of land- and sea-based air forces, though the Special Operations Force assigned to a theater can lend a hand. In fact, airpower and special operations are likely to be the only combat elements routinely at work the deep battle. Therefore, integration of airpower and special operations is critical to the success of both efforts.

High Battle: A battlefield control measure marking off airspace in a theater of operations under control of an air component commander. This would include all airspace from any flying altitude down to the surface in the deep battle, and above 3,000 meters or so in the close and rear battles.

Space Battle: When we get serious about war in space, we'll need another battlefield control measure, the space battle, fought above the others, with a seam at the edge of the atmosphere. Combat roles in the space battle will include satellite warfare, long-range ballistic missile attack, and anti-ballistic missile defense. Functions will include overhead reconnaissance of all types, communications, weather, and navigation support. The space battle should be placed under the command of the space component of the joint command in a theater of operations.

Reducing Overlap: Our forces fight jointly on a mission basis but are programmed and budgeted, by and large, on a service basis. And since Title 10 is promiscuous in assigning roles and functions, each service can and does establish requirements, set up programs, and budget for systems that compete for combat roles in every corner of the battlefield. *Some* overlap and duplication is a good idea. The commander needs flexibility, a Plan B when things go pear-shaped. But the post-Cold War challenge to both restructure and downsize puts a premium on making effective use of the defense dollar. That should translate (but has not, to date) into wringing out the *excessive* duplication and overlap that was virtually guaranteed by the Key West Agreement and institutionalized in Title 10. What must be done is to find a way to restrict service autonomy and impose a focus on core competencies. The twin dividends: (1) a sharp increase in combat efficiency and, (2) vastly reduced cost.

The key is to recognize that battlefield control measures can be established for Type A war such that combat roles are delineated and assigned to specific services. We should start by giving the Army unambiguous responsibility to "organize, train, and equip" for combat roles in the close and rear battle. Thus, the Army would establish procedures, develop tactics, set performance standards, select and train personnel, exercise units, write equipment requirements, acquire hardware, and so forth, for the set of combat roles in the close and rear battle, including close defense of air bases. The Marines should be assigned secondary responsibility with respect to these roles, and the Navy and Air Force prevented from doing any of these things.

In the same way, the Air Force should have primary responsibility for combat roles in the high and deep battles, with the Navy having collateral responsibility.

(Of course, there is a maritime battle and an amphibious battle, not addressed here, for which the Navy and Marine Corps should have primary responsibility to "organize, train, and equip," with collateral responsibilities assigned to the Army and Air Force.)

So far in the twenty-first century, fighting Type A war has not been the military problem of interest. Nevertheless, we will (and should) continue to prepare for it, in the same way that we stay ready for nuclear war, even though to date we have not had to fight one. If we ever again must fight a Type A war, the organizing scheme proposed here would produce the benefit of improved combat performance. If we do not, the enduring value of setting limits on service autonomy in their Title 10 "organize, train, and equip" functions comes from saving a lot of money.

Type B War: Postmodern war. At the moment, and perhaps only temporarily, we've moved away from centralized, Type A engagements toward a period of more disorderly conflict. The pendulum will probably swing back but, for now, geographically defined states have lost control of large-scale violence.

Type B war has a long history and is at the same time an innovation for which we haven't yet figured out an antidote. In fact, almost certainly there is no military cure, warlike remedies not being a good fit for problems that are primarily economic, political, or cultural. Long term, what will matter in a Type B security environment is governance—say, the safety of civilians in a large city, or keeping the electricity on, or providing clean water. Military forces can come to the rescue, can temporarily impose order, can continue to assist over time, but the central problems needing a solution are civilian, not military, and need to be dealt with by indigenous civil authority.

A Type B war may feature a brief opening phase in which traditional combat roles—air superiority, infantry, artillery, deep attack, etc.—are important. But this will likely be followed by an extended period during which these activities, while perhaps not disappearing entirely, will be overshadowed by roles like peacekeeping, civil affairs, reconstruction, or antiterrorism. None of these roles is new. The Army performed many of them on the frontier in the years following our Civil War and both the Army and Marine Corps picked up a lot of experience in the Philippines, Central America, and the Caribbean in the early twentieth century. In addition, repeated use of US forces in constabulary and other missions short of major war has been a regular feature of the post-Cold War landscape.

With so much practice we should be good and getting better at

Type B combat roles, and it's a nice question why excellence is taking so long to become a core competency. I think there are a number of reasons. First, at the outset, at least, we weren't serious about what was not regarded by professionals as "real" war. (Tellingly, for a time we used a particularly unfortunate term: "Operations Other Than War.") Accordingly, the various combat roles important in Type B war were for a long time seen as leading nowhere, not career enhancing.

Second, we assumed that engagements of this kind were outside the scope of our enduring security interests. Where we got dragged in, we looked immediately for an "end state," or exit strategy, seeking to avoid that longer, maybe more difficult phase in which we would act as an adjunct to civil authority. But there are few parts of the globe where America has nothing at stake. When might America's interest in a stable Europe, or a peaceful Middle East, or a secure East Asia end? What is our exit strategy from the affairs of the Western Hemisphere, or even Africa?

So, in a big and to some degree continuing miscalculation, we have not focused sufficiently on organizing, training, and equipping to perform peacemaking, peacekeeping, and similar duties that have become part of our customary workload, assuming that readiness to perform these roles is subsumed as a lesser included case in Type A capabilities. But the modes of conflict are so unlike that our overwhelming superiority in Type A war has not been enough to win, or perhaps even to understand what winning is, in Type B war.

For instance, our experience in Somalia showed that the sole remaining superpower was ill equipped mentally or physically for the challenge posed by a failed state with no infrastructure, national authority, or targetable military forces. Events elsewhere, in Bosnia, Rwanda, East Timor, Sierra Leone, Kenya, and Tanzania, revealed a real scarcity of applicable and deployable military assets.

Can our forces be reshaped for success in Type B war? No doubt.

But it will not be easily done. Success will come down to whether our services are "learning" organizations that can adjust to new and rapidly changing conditions. The services, the Army, especially, but also the Navy and Air Force, are large, slow-moving bureaucracies, and may not be up to the task. So far the Marine Corps and Special Operations Force have shown the most promise. But we'd better get going. What used to be called irregular war is nowadays irregular only to us.

By the way, successful suicide bombing requires both stealth and precision, the hallmarks of modern war. This shows that while the equipment used by the other side in Type B war may be low-tech, the ideas are not. And it is this battle of ideas that we must win.

Asymmetrical War: Two sides fight each other using entirely different modes of warfare. For the United States, it has come down recently to fighting Type A war against opponents who fight Type B war.

In asymmetrical war, time is the most important strategic variable, with victory going to the side that hangs on longest. This is not good news for us because, typically, the Type B enemy has nowhere to go and nothing else to do; hanging on is his core competence. By contrast, while our citizens now seem sophisticated enough to put their children at risk in pursuit of limited objectives, they will tolerate such a commitment over time only behind sensible political leadership, perhaps a contradiction of terms. In recent experience, we have been unable to achieve stated purposes within time constraints established by falling public support and as a consequence have simply left the field and tried to describe our exit as something other than defeat.

It is anyway not clear that "victory" is itself an uncomplicated thing in the case of asymmetrical warfare. Goals, too, can be asymmetrical, creating the theoretical possibility that both sides can win, if their purposes are limited. Here, I'll deviate from good practice and assert that we will *never* win against Type B opposition if we insist on establishing Clausewitzian goals, like total destruction or unconditional surrender. Such an approach requires more time and more force than we seem willing to commit and is anyway likely to deliver results that are nothing special, or even counterproductive.

Thus, the key to "winning" in asymmetrical war is to limit our objectives, while at the same time trying to persuade the opponent to limit his—that is to say, to change his behavior. Victory will in any case be elusive. Perhaps the only way to prevail in asymmetrical warfare is to make it symmetrical. That means joining the enemy in Type B war, and being good at it.

Index

Page locators in *italics* indicate photographs.

1st Air Commando Wing, 99, 100
1st Bombardment Wing, 73
1st Fighter Group, 99
1st Fighter Wing, 74
1st Space Wing, 99–100
1st Special Forces Detachment-Delta (Delta Force), 300–301
1st Tactical Fighter Wing, 99
2nd Bomb Wing, 74
4th Fighter Group, Army Air Forces, 71
4th Fighter Wing, 100
5th Bomb Wing, 100
7th Bomb Wing, 101
8th Fighter Wing, 153
18th Wing, 100
20th Wing, 97
21st Space Wing, 100
23rd Fighter Group, Army Air Forces, 71–72
31st Fighter Wing, 98
49th Fighter Group and Wing, 74, 98
75th Ranger Regiment, 300
89th Wing, 97
90th Missile Wing, 100
"100-Hour War," Desert Storm ground operations, 27–29
100-Wing Air Force, 76–78, 90
160th Special Operations Aviation Regiment ("Night Stalkers"), 300
366th Wing, 102
509th Bomb Wing, 96–97
555th Fighter Squadron, 98

A

A-10 aircraft, 314–15
A-6 aircraft, 205
A-12 aircraft, 205
A-X aircraft, 205
AC-130 gunships, 23–24, 32, 300, 324–25
acquisition system reform, 224, 226–27
adultery, and women in the Air Force, 251–52
advanced medium-range air-to-air missile (AMRAAM), 18
African Americans: racial integration of the military, 276–78; Tuskegee Airmen, 26, 201, 277

AIM-7 Sparrow missile, 222
Air Combat Command (ACC) establishment, 82, 83, 87, 94, 101, 114–17
air division, 75–76
Air Education and Training Command (AETC), 83, 101, 113, 116–17, 146
Air Force: Army's view of Air Force role, 36–38; attitudes toward gays in the military, 278–79, 291; headquarters staff in 1991, *127*; headquarters staff in 1993, *219*; headquarters staff in 1994, *317*; and Title 10, US Code, 370. *See also* chief of staff duties and activities; equipment; reorganization; roles and missions; training
Air Force Academy, 83, 113, 17, 146–48, 150, 48, 261, 342
Air Force Audit Agency, 75
Air Force Band, 93–94
Air Force Combat Units of World War II, 99
Air Force Communications Command, 74–75
Air Force Logistics Command, 82
Air Force Materiel Command, 83, 117, 180–81
Air Force One, 97
Air Force Operational Test and Evaluation Center, 226
Air Force Reserve, 63
Air Force String Quartet, 93–94, *131*
Air Force Systems Command (AFSC), 82, 180
"Air House" residence, *125*, *129*, *130*, 159–61, *217*
Air Mobility Command (AMC), 114–16, 157–58, 196
Air National Guard, 63, 99
Air Staff reorganization, 84–85
Air Training Command (ATC), 83, 116–17
Air University (AU), 83
Air Weather Service (AWS), 65–66, 74–75
Airborne Laser Program, 59, 199
Airborne Warning and Control System (AWACS) aircraft, 13

381

aircraft carriers, 185–88
aircraft maintenance echelons, 69–71
airpower advocacy and impending
  Gulf War, 5–6
airpower capability, Desert Storm, 8–11
Al Dhafra, F-15 sortie, 13–14
Al Firdos bunker, 25–26
Al-Hijarah Scud missiles, 19
Al-Husayn Scud missiles, 19
Al Khafji, Battle of Al Khafji, 22–24, 39
Al Kharj airfield, 13
Albright, Madeleine, 233
Allen, Barbara, *130*
Allen, Lew, *130*
Alon, Joe, 118
Anderson, Jack, 118–20
Anderson, Mark, *317*
Andrews Field, 141, 159, 181
Arafat, Yasser, 203
Area Air Defense Commander
  (AADC), 312
Arens, Moshe, 118
Aristide, Jean-Bertrand, 198
Armitage, Richard, 105
arms reductions, START I and II
  accords, 105–6, 174
Army: Army helicopters in Desert
  Storm, 48; Army Special Forces
  and Rangers, 322, 324; and C-17
  specifications, 193–94; combat
  restrictions for women, 267–68;
  view of Air Force role, 36–38
Army Air Forces groups, 71–72
Army Signal Corps, 160
Arnold, Hap, 73, 90, 98, 164, 169
Ashy, Joe, *319*
Aspin, Les: Bottom-Up Review, 184;
  and Buster Glosson, 213, 215–16;
  and C-17 aircraft program, 192–93,
  194–96; combat exclusion repeal for
  women in the Air Force, 264–65;
  defense budget dynamics, 189; and
  gays in the military, 284, 287–88;
  meeting with JCS, *217*, *218*; Major
  Regional Contingency (MRC) force
  level requirements, 185–86; and
  "Option C" force reduction proposal,
  181–83; Somalia, 300, 302, 305
Assistant Director of Operations
  (ADO), 73
asymmetrical war, 378–79
Athanasios, Stathas, 103
Atwood, Don, 137, 151, 353
Aydid, Hussein, 305

Aydid, Muhammad Farah, 298, 300,
  302, 304–5

B

B-1 aircraft, 144
B-2 aircraft, 123, 176–77, 178
B-17 aircraft, 123
B-52 aircraft, 21
Baker, Jim, 11
Balkan Ghosts (Kaplan), 237
Barak, Ehud, 118
Barksdale Field, 74
Bartholomew, Reginald, 234
Base Force concept, 90–93
battle damage assessment (BDA), 51
Battle of Al Khafji, 22–24, 39
Battle of Majuba, 54
battlefield control measures, 28–29, 373
Ben-Nun, Avihu, 118
Berger, Sandy, 284
biological weapons and Desert Storm, 20
Bir, Çevik, 299
Black Eagles (play), 26
Black Hawk Down (Bowden), 301
"Black Hole" planning cell, Joint Task
  Force Middle East, 7–8
Boles, Billy, 113, 163, *219*, 265, *317*
Bolling Field, 159, 160
Bong, Richard I., 74
Boomer, Walt, 15
Boorda, Mike, 347–51, 355
Bosnia: and Clinton administration,
  234, 237–38, 239–40; and
  Colin Powell, 230–33; costs of
  nonintervention in, 246; Gorazde
  airdrop, 238–39; ground vs. air
  operations, 231–33, 235–37, 240–
  41; and John Shalikashvili, 242;
  Sarajevo visit, 238, 240; Operation
  Deliberate Force, 245–46; Operation
  Deny Flight, 235, 242; Operation
  Provide Promise, 230; and Reginald
  Bartholomew, 234; seizure of UN
  peacekeepers, 243–44; Srebrenica
  massacre, 244–45, 246; UN
  Protection Force (UNPROFOR),
  230–31, 238, 240, 241–43; and
  Warren Christopher, 240; Yugoslavia
  breakup, 228–29
Bottom-Up Review (BUR), 184–85, 189,
  190, 206, 329
Boyd, Chuck, *319*
Boyd, John, 222
Bradley, Omar, 367

Brereton, Lewis, 79
Brett, Rock, 97
British soldiers and scarlet uniforms, 53–54
Brokaw, Tom, 142
Brown Papers, 112–13
Brown, Skip, *130*
Buckley, William F., 272
budgets, defense budget dynamics and budget cuts, 175–77, 188–90
Burhan, Halis, 103
Bush, Barbara, 14, *132*, 175
Bush, George H. W.: Bosnia, 230–31, 234; Camp David farewell meeting, 174–75; Commander in Chief's Trophy awarded to Air Force, *127*, 342; Desert Storm preparations, 9, 11–12, 14, 17–18, *34*; Desert Storm victory, 61; and McPeak flying F-15 aircraft, 144; Somalia, 298; START I accords, 105; START II accord, 174; White House dinner and Ford's Theater production, 26
Butler, Lee, 88–89

C

C-5 aircraft, 192
C-17 aircraft, 192–97
C-130 aircraft, 115–16, 192, 238–39, 304
C-135 aircraft, 143
C-141 aircraft, 192, 238
Cammermeyer, Margarethe, 272–73, 275
Camp David meetings: Bush I farewell, 174–75; Desert Storm preparations, 11–12
Campbell, Harold "Norm," 292
Canadian armed forces, 310
Canadian military chiefs meeting, 140–41
Caniff, Milton, 100
Carlisle Barracks, 142
Carns, Mike, 94–95, 113, 212, *219*, 224
Carr, Bruce W., 346
carrier fleet, 185–88
Carter, Jimmy, 197, 198, 243
Cédras, Raoul, 198
Central Command Air Forces (CENTAF): airpower capability, 8–11; Desert Storm planning, 6–7, 79
Central Command (CENTCOM) Desert Storm planning, 6–7, 8
Central Europe visit, 207–9

centralized command and military effectiveness, 45–50
Certain Victory, 36, 37
Chain, Jack, 88
chain of command, 67–68
Chambers, "Bear," 238
Chanute AFB, 136
Charleston AFB, 196
Chechnya, 110, 371–72
"Checkmate" planning cell, 7–8
chemical weapons and Desert Storm, 20
Cheney, Dick: B-2 aircraft, 177; Base Force concept, 92; Desert Storm ground operations, 27; Desert Storm preparations, 11, 14; Strategic Command, 88; and McPeak flying F-15 aircraft, 142–43, 144; at McPeak's swearing in as chief of staff, *42*; meeting with the Rev. Billy Graham, *166*; and Terrence O'Donnell, 214
Chi Haotoan, 352
chief of staff duties and activities: appointment as fourteenth chief of staff, 1–2, 5–6, *41*, *42*; presenting Air Medals to Grumman JSTARS staff, 140; breakfast with Strom Thurmond, 145; Bush I farewell meeting at Camp David, 174–75; Canadian military chiefs meeting, 140–41; chief's office, *219*; China visit, 351–53; Clinton inaugural, 175; Commander in Chief's Trophy, *127*, 342; Conference of Jefes of American Air Forces (CONJEFAMER), 103–5, 343–44; Council on Foreign Relations dinner, 190–91; D-day 50th Anniversary, 345–46; dinner with Hillary Clinton, 200; Glosson Affair, 211–16, 221; Grey Eagle award, 161–62, *167*; Haitian refugee crisis, 198–99; Israel trip, 118; Israeli-Palestinian Agreement, 203; McPeak's; Mary McGrory meeting, 140; new uniform, *165*; Nixon funeral, 342–43; Piotr Deynekin meetings, 107–10, *128*, *129*, 144, *167*, *168*; Quarters Seven "Air House" residence, *125*, *129*, *130*, 159–61, *217*; Russia visit, 106–10, *128*, *129*; Secretary Sheila Widnall, 199–200, *217*; senior-officer promotions and Glosson Affair, 209–16, 221; single-seat aircraft flying, 141–44, 158, *168*;

chief of staff duties and activities: *(continued)*
    state dinners, 95, *166*, 200; State of the Union address, 89; Thunderbirds visit, *220*; Trent Lott meeting, 159; Tuskegee Airmen meeting, 201; UK visit, 203–4
China visit, 351–53
Chinese People's Liberation Army Air Force (PLAAF), 309, 351–52
Chopin Museum, 207–8
Christopher, Warren, 174, 240
civil rights and gays in the military, 275–76, 292–93
civilian deaths, Al Firdos bunker, 25–26
Clark Field closure, 105
Clinton, Bill: Base Force concept, 92; Bosnia, 234, 237–38, 239–40; and "Cold War Minus" and military redundancy, 92, 181–82, 328–29; D-day 50th anniversary, 345, 346; defense budget cuts, 190; Haitian refugee crisis, 198–99; inaugural gala, 175; Major Regional Contingency (MRC) force level requirements, 184–85; meeting with JCS, *217*; selection of Les Aspin as secretary of defense, 184, 195; Somalia, 299, 303; stance on gays in the military, 271, 272–73, 275, 278–79, 282–88, 293–95
Clinton, Hillary, 200
close air support (CAS), 37, 48, 52, 241–43, 313–15, 338
close battle, 373
closeted vs. open homosexuality, 275, 278–79, 280–81
coalition partners, Desert Storm airpower capability, 9–10
Cochran, Phil, 100
Cohen, William, 263
"Cold War Minus," 92, 181–82, 328–29
Colley, George, 54
command relationships "wiring diagram," 304
Commander in Chief's Trophy, *127*, 342
Commission on Roles and Missions (CORM), 329–31, 354–56
conduct, gays in the military, 283, 284–85, 287
Conduct Unbecoming (Shilts), 273
Conference of Jefes of American Air Forces (CONJEFAMER), 103–5, 343–44

core competence, 370
CORONA gatherings, 162, *166*
costs: acquisition system reform, 226–27; C-17 aircraft, 192–95; carrier fleet, 187–88; combat roles and service effectiveness, 336–37, 339–40; defense budget dynamics and budget cuts, 175–77, 188–90; F-22 aircraft, 179–80; of nonintervention in Bosnia, 246; operational requirements vs. specifications, 225–26; training, 136–37; training costs and gays in the military, 274–75; unmanned aerial vehicles (UAVs), 201–3. *See also* force reductions
Coughlin, Paula, 253–54
Council on Foreign Relations dinner, 190–91
Couric, Katie, 142
Croatia, 228–29
Cronkite, Walter, 345
Czech Republic visit, 209

D

D-day 50th anniversary, 345–46
Darnell, Don, *220*
Dayton Peace Accords, 212, 237
de Chastelain, John, 140–41
DeBerry, Fisher, 342
decentralization and Quality Air Force (QAF), 139
"decisive" military victories, 36–40
"decisiveness syndrome," logistic support for Desert Storm, 58–59
deep battle, 374
Defense Advisory Committee on Women in the Services (DACOWITS), 263–64
defense budget dynamics and budget cuts, 175–77, 188–90
Defense Planning Guidance (DPG) and force structure planning, 191–92
defense reform movement, 222
Delta Force, 300–301, 322, 323
Deming, W. E., 138
Denfield, Louis, 367
Department of the Interior, JCS meetings at Interior Department, 139–40, *217*, *218*
Deptula, Dave, 8
deputy commander for operations (DO), group reorganization, 72–73

deputy commander for resources (RM), group reorganization, 72–73
deputy group commanders, group reorganization, 72–73
"Desert Drizzle," 183–84
Desert Island Discs radio program, 93
Desert Shield, 7, 9, 187
Desert Storm: AC-130 gunship loss, 23–24; air campaign, 18–26; air campaign planning, 7–8, 10–11; Air Force role in "decisive" victory, 36–40; airpower advocacy and impending Gulf War, 5–6; Al Firdos bunker, 25–26; battle damage assessment (BDA), 51; Camp David meeting, 11–12; Chuck Horner and Central Command Air Forces (CENTAF), 6–7; end of operations, 29–31; fratricide, 35, 46, 51–52; ground operations, 26–29; Iraqi Air Force capability, 9–10; Iraqi Scud missile attacks, 19–22; joint command, 5–6, 14–17, 40, *43*, *44*, 45–50; JSTARS aircraft and the Battle of Al Khafji, 22–24, 39; logistic support for, 58–59; lopsided victory, 34–36, 38–39; and military intelligence, 50–51; and military readiness, 60–61; and missile defenses, 59–60; and oil-well fires, 22; precision and "smart" bombs, 54–56; press briefings and assessment of operations, 31–33, *44*; readiness assessment Gulf trip, 12–14, *43*; start of operations, 17–19; stealth and tactical surprise, 52–54; "tank plinking," 24–25; US Air Force capability, 8–9, 10–11; White House meetings, 14, *43*. *See also* Powell, Colin; Schwarzkopf, Norman
Deutch, John, 195–96, 216, *218*, 353
Deynekin, Nina, 109, *129*
Deynekin, Pyotr Stepanovich, 107–10, *128*, *129*, 144, *167*, *168*
Dhahran barracks attack, 21
Dole, Bob, 294
Donley, Mike, 200
"don't ask, don't tell," 280–81, 285, 294, 295
Doolittle, Jimmy, 79, 169
Downing, Wayne, 302, 326
drones, unmanned aerial vehicles (UAVs), 201–3
Druyun, Darleen, 195

Dudayev, Dzhokhar, 110
Dugan, Grace, *42*, *130*
Dugan, Mike, 5, 6, *42*, *130*

E
Eaker, Ira, 79, 90
Eakle, Denny, 163
Eberhart, Ed, 97
Eighth Air Force, 79, 192
Eisenhower, Dwight D., 15
end-strength ceiling, women in the Air Force, 247–48
enlisted professional military education (PME), 135–36
enlisted rank and insignia, 137–38
enlisted retention rates, 138
enlisted technical training, 124, 133–35
equipment: acquisition system reform, 226–27; Airborne Laser Program, 59, 199; B-2 aircraft, 123, 176–77; Bottom-Up Review (BUR), 206; C-17 aircraft, 192–97; defense budget dynamics and budget cuts, 175–77, 188–90; defense reform movement, 222; F-22 aircraft, 177–80; F-35 aircraft, 204–7; Joint Direct Attack Munition (JDAM), 55, 173–74; JSTARS aircraft, 22–24, 57, 140; Les Aspin and C-17 aircraft program, 192–93, 194–96; operational test of weapon systems, 226; operational requirements vs. specifications, 222–26; Ron Yates and Air Force Materiel Command, 180–81; unmanned aerial vehicles (UAVs), 201–3
Estefan, Gloria, 95

F
F-4 aircraft, 199
F-15 aircraft: Desert Storm, 19, 20; Desert Storm training exercises, 13–14; McPeak's flying of, 141–44, 158, *168*; replacement with F-22 aircraft, 177
F-16 aircraft, 13–14, 177–78, 204–5, 341
F-18 aircraft, 206
F-22 aircraft, 177–80
F-35 aircraft, 204–7, 341
F-111 aircraft, 24
F-117 aircraft, 53, 54, 74, 178
Fahy Committee, 277
Fain, Jim, *317*
Field Manual 100-5, Operations, 39
Fifteenth Air Force, 79

Fifth Air Force, 79
Fifth Allied Tactical Air Force, 238, 242
fire support coordination line (FSCL), 28–29, 339, 372–73
First Air Force, 99
Fischer, Eugene, 214, 216, *219*
fixed-price contracts, 193
flight-line maintenance, 69–71, 72
flight logbook, 363
flying-hour program, 155–56
flying training, 145–49
Flynn, Jeannie, 265–66
Fogleman, Ron, 157–58, 169, 196, *319*, 342
force reductions: Base Force concept, 92; Bottom-Up Review (BUR), 184–85, 189, 190, 206; and "Option C" force reduction proposal, 181–83; size of Air Force, 122
Ford's Theater, 26
foreign military sales (FMS) supervision, 85
Forrestal, James, 367
Fort Ross, 144
Fourteenth Air Force, 98
Francis, Fred, 141–42
Franks, Frederick, 28–29, 31
fraternization, 249–51
fratricide, 35, 46, 51–52, 214, 311, 314
Freeman, Chas, 354
friendly fire, 35, 51–52
Fuerth, Leon, 284

G

Gabriel, Charlie, 97, *130*, 351–52
Gabriel, Dottie, *130*
Garrett, Lawrence, 254
Garrison, William, 300, 301–2
gays in the military: Air Force attitudes toward, 278–79, 291; civil rights arguments, 275–76, 292–93; Clinton's stance on, 271, 272–73, 275, 278–79, 282–88, 293–95; closeted vs. open homosexuality, 275, 278–79, 280–81; Congressional stance on, 293–95; and "don't ask, don't tell," 280–81, 285, 294, 295; JCS discussions regarding, 279–80; and prioritization of national security concerns, 281–82; and Sam Nunn, 288–89; training costs argument, 274–75; Truman's executive order and racial integration, 276–78; and unit cohesion, 271–74, 278–79, 289–91, 295–96
Gittens, Charles, 214
Glosson, Buster, 7, 158–59, 184, 211–16, *219*, 221
"go pills," pilot use of amphetamines, 13, 86–87, 214
Golda (family dog), *125*, *129*
Goldwater, Barry, 344
Goldwater-Nichols reforms, 82, 85, 160, 180, 224, 226, 328, 330
Gombik, Stefan, 208
Goodpaster, Andy, 161
Gorazde airdrop, 238–39
Gorbachev, Mikhail, 26, 105, 106, 108
Gore, Al, 284
Gotowala, Jerzy, 207–8
Graham, the Rev. Billy, *166*
Grassley, Charles, 216
Gray, Al, 6, *44*, 92
Gray, Boyden, 175
Graydon, Mike, 203, 345
Grey Eagle award, 161–62, *167*
ground operations, Desert Storm, 26–29
ground vs. air operations, Bosnia, 231–33, 235–37, 240–41
guided air-to-ground munitions ("smart" bombs), 54–56, 173–74, 245
Gulf War. *See* Desert Storm
gunships, Spirit 03 (AC-130 gunship) loss, 23–24, 32

H

Haiti, 40
Haitian refugee crisis, 198–99
"half wars," Major Regional Contingency (MRC) force level requirements, 91–92, 184–88
Hall, Charlie, 250
Hammond, Trevor, *219*
Harkins, Paul, 15
Harriman, Pamela, 346
Hawley, Dick, *317*
Hays, Ron, 94
headquarters reorganization, 84–86
heraldic dinners, 162, *166*
heraldry and heritage preservation, 68, 78–79, 95–99, 101–2, 111
Hermitage Museum, 110
Herres, Bob, 264
Herzegovina, 228
Hickam Field, 118–19
Hickey, Tom, *127*

high battle, 374
Hilterbrick, Paul, 250
Hoar, Joseph, 299, 301, 302
Hod, Moti, 118
Hollings, Ernest, 197
Holloman Field, 74, 98
Holm, Jeanne, 248
homosexuality. *See* gays in the military
Hope, Bob, *126*
horizontal organizational design, Air Force reorganization, 66–67
Horner, Chuck: Battle of Al Khafji, 23–24; Desert Storm air campaign, 26, 46, 47–49, 80, 201; Desert Storm preparations, 6–7, 8–9, 10–11, 12; and Iraqi ground war, 29; nominated as Schwarzkopf's deputy, 16; heraldic dinner, *166*; "tank plinking," 24
Hosmer, Brad, *127*
Howe, Jonathan, 299, 300
Huddleston, Dave, 343
Hultgren, Kara, 263–64
human values promotion, Air Force reorganization, 68
Hurlburt Field, 99
Hussein, Saddam, 18, 20, 26–27, 30, 34, 95, 358

I
ICBM wings, 98
ICBMs and Air Combat Command (ACC) establishment, 114–16
identify friend or foe (IFF) problem, 51–52
insignia, enlisted rank and insignia, 137–38, 164, 169
Instant Thunder, 8
integrity, senior-officer promotions and Glosson Affair, 211–16, 221
intelligence, military, 50–51
Intermediate-Range Nuclear Forces (INF), 174
Iran, 19
Iraqi Air Force capability, Desert Storm, 9–10, 18–19
Iraqi Scud missile attacks, Desert Storm, 19–22
An Irish Airman Foresees His Death (poem), 140
Israel: Desert Storm, 19, 20, 21; Israeli Defense Forces/Air Force, 309; Israeli-Palestinian Agreement, 203; Six-Day War, 35

Israel trip, 118
Italian Air Force, 13–14
Ivry, David, 118

J
Jackson, Stonewall, 56
Jamerson, Jim, *319*
James, C. D., 250
Janvier, Bernard, 244
Jaquish, John, *127, 219*
Jennings, Peter, 235
Jeremiah, David, 30, *43, 44, 217,* 232, 284
Johnson, H. T., 157–58
Johnson, Jay, 254
Joint Advanced Strike Technology (JAST), 206
joint chiefs: JCS discussions regarding gays in the military, 279–80; JCS meeting at Interior Department, 139–40; meeting with Clinton regarding gays in the military, 281–86
joint command: Desert Storm, 14–17, 40, 45; and military effectiveness, 45–50; Special Operations Command (SOCOM), 322
Joint Direct Attack Munition (JDAM), 55, 173–74
joint force air component commander (JFACC), 49
Joint Primary Aircraft Training System (JPATS), 148–49
Joint Strike Fighter (JSF), 206
Joint Surveillance Target Attack Radar System (JSTARS) aircraft, 22–24, 57, 140
Joint Task Force Middle East, 7
Jones, Dave, *130*
Jones, Lois, *130*
Jordan, Vernon, 174
judge advocates (JAGs), 251–52
Jumper, John, 214

K
Kadena Field, 100
Kaplan, Robert, 237
Karremans, Thom, 244
KC-135 aircraft, 13, 141, 348–49
Keegan, John, 255
Keesler Technical Training Center, 97
Kelk, Jon, 18
Kelso, Frank, 6, *43, 44,* 149, 161, 205, *217,* 254, 347

Kennedy, John F., 322
Kennedy, Ted, 263
Kenney, George, 79
Kenya visit, 303–4
Key West Agreement, 367–69
Khamis Mushait air base, 13
Killey, Phil, 99
Kim Il Sung, 197
Kime, Bill, *218*
Kirov Ballet, 110
Kirtland Field, 116
Korean War: Chinese Army intervention, 56; and joint command, 15, 47; and racial integration of the Army, 278
Korecka, Maria, 208
Kuebart, Pim, 344
Kunsan Air Base, 153–54
Kurdish refugees, 242
Kuwait City, 27–28
Kuwaiti theater of operations (KTO), Desert Storm, 21–22

L

L-29 aircraft, 208–9
Lackland AFB, 124, 133
Lahm, Frank, 161
Lake, Tony, 284
Langley Field, 74, 99, 179, 187
Lanir, Avi, 118
Lapidot, Amos, 118
laser-guided bombs (LGBs), 55
leadership: Air Force reorganization, 71, 76–77, 80; chief of staff role, 1–2; enlisted professional military education (PME), 135–36; and joint command, 5–6; and unit cohesion, 258
LeMay, Curtis, 79, 277
lift and strike option, Bosnia, 230–31
Lilley, Jim, 354
Lincoln, Abraham, 26, 33, 78
Lindbergh, Anne Morrow, 344
logistic support for Desert Storm, 58–59
logistics group, reorganization, 72
Loh, Mike, 94, *127*, 178, *319*
Lorber, John, *319*
Lott, Trent, 159
Lowry AFB, 136
Luce, Claire Booth, 344
Luck, Gary, 29
Ludwig, Bob, *127*
Luftwaffe, and parachute infantry, 326

Luke Field, 116
Luke, Frank, 99
Lynch, Jim, 119

M

MacArthur, Douglas, 15, 56
MacDill AFB, 6
McDade, Joe, 183
McDonald, Chuck, 82, 86
McDonnell Douglas, 192–93, 194, 205
McDonnell, John, 194
McGinn, Cathy, 163
McGinnis, Kevin, 12–13
McGinnis, Norma, 12
McGinnis, Shannon, 12–13, 247
McGrory, Mary, 140
McInerney, Tom, *219*
McIntyre, Jamie, 264–65
McNamara, Robert, 189
McPeak, Ellie, *42*, 95, 109, *125*, *129*, *130*, *131*, *132*, 144, 161, 175
McSally, Martha, 266
McWethy, John 235–37
maintenance, aircraft maintenance echelons, 69–71
major air commands (MAJCOMs), 81–84
Major, John, 345
Major Regional Contingency (MRC) force level requirements, 91–92, 184–88
Marine Corps: air wings, 313, 316, 321–22; combat restrictions for women, 267–68; Desert Storm sortie allocation, 48; F-35 aircraft, 206–7; in Somalia, 298–99
"mass," as a principle of war, 56–58
Matthei, Fernando, 104
Maximoff, Field Marshall, 108–9, and "failsafe" control of Soviet nuclear systems, 108–109
May, Charlie, *127*
meals ready to eat (MREs) and Gorazde airdrop, 238–39
MiG-29 aircraft, 344–45
Military Airlift Command (MAC), 46–47, 81, 101, 114–16, 150
military effectiveness and joint command, 45–50
military intelligence, 50–51
Military Personnel Center, 153
military readiness, 60–61
Miller, Monte, *127*

Millie (Bush family dog), 14
Milosevic, Slobodan, 245
Minot Field, 100
missile defenses, 59–60, 178–79
mission-focused reorganization, 64–66
Mitterrand, François, 345
Mladic, Ratko, 244
Mogasdishu, Task Force Ranger and US operations in Mogadishu, 300–305
Moi, Daniel arap, 303
Moiseyev, Mikhail, 110
Montgomery, Thomas, 299, 301, 302, 304
Moore, Royal N., Jr., 48
Moorman, Tom, 113, *317*, *319*
Morale, Welfare and Recreation (MWR) office, 111
Moscow State Circus, 110
Moskos, Charles, 279
Mother Teresa, *131*
Mount Pinatubo eruption and closure of Clark Field, 105
Muhammad, Ali Mahdi, 298
Mulroney, Brian, 174
Multi-Role Fighter (MRF) aircraft, 205–7
Mundy, Carl, 190, 191, *217*
Murtha, Jack, 170
mutual assured destruction (MAD), 59
My American Journey (Powell), 228, 231
Myers, Dick, 212–13, 221

N

naming conventions, Air Force reorganization, 100–101
NATO Air Chiefs, 103
NATO aircraft in Bosnia, 230, 235, 238, 241–43, 244–45
Navy: air force, 315–16, 321; Desert Storm fleet defenses, 47–48; and Mike Boorda, 347–51; submarines, 57–58
NCO Academy, 124, 135–36
NCO clubs, 111–12
Nellis AFB, 144, *168*
Nelson, Mike, *127*
Newsome, Mike, 250
Next Generation Trainer (NGT) aircraft, 148–49
Nineteenth Air Force, 98
Ninth Air Force, 6–7, 79, 80
Nixon, Richard, 91, 140, 214, 342
no-fly zones, 95, 230, 235, 238, 242

North Korea, 197–99
Nowak, John, 212, 221, *317*
Nuclear Nonproliferation Treaty, 197
numbered air forces (NAFs), 78–80
Nunn, Sam, 17, 179–80, 192, 194–95, 198, 210–11, 214, 221, 294, 308
Nye, Joe, 354

O

O'Berry, Carl, *219*
Ochuka, Hezekiah, 303
O'Dennis, Sam, 201
O'Donnell, Emmett "Rosie," 214
O'Donnell, Terrence, *42*, 214
Office of the Secretary of Defense (OSD): and Air Force flying-hour program, 156; and Air Force training costs, 136–37; and Buster Glosson, 215–16; Defense Planning Guidance (DPG), 191–92; deputies and undersecretaries, 353–54; executive staff, 92; pilot production rate reductions, 151; and unmanned aerial vehicles (UAVs), 201–2
Olds, Robin, 97
on-the-job training, enlisted technical training, 133–35
Operation Deliberate Force, 245–46
Operation Deny Flight, 235, 242
Operation Desert Storm. *See* Desert Storm
Operation Eagle Claw, 323
Operation Just Cause, 40
Operation Northern Watch, 95
Operation Provide Promise, 230
Operation Provide Relief, 298
Operation Restore Hope, 299
Operation Southern Watch, 95
operational testing of weapon systems, 226
operational requirements: equipment requirements vs. specifications, 222–26; headquarters reorganization, 84–85
operations group, reorganization, 72
orientation, gays in the military, 283–85, 286–88, 289–90
overlap reduction, 374–76
Owen, David, 234

P

P-9 aircraft, 149
PACAF headquarters renovation, 118–20

Pacific Air Forces (PACAF), 81, 103, 116
Packwood, Bob, 342–43
Panama, 40
Paniccia, Thomas, 272
Parry, Bill, 343
Patriot air defense missile, 20–21
Pave Tack infrared sensors, 24
peacetime presence, Major Regional Contingency (MRC) force level requirements, 185–88
Pearl Harbor, 52, 327
Peay, Binnie, 196
People's Liberation Army Air Force (PLAAF), 309
Perry, Bill, 196, 221, 305, 353
personnel and payroll cuts, Air Force reorganization, 122–23
personnel classifications, 123–24
Peterson Field, 99–100
Pfingston, Gary, 163, *218*
physical fitness program, 87
pilot assignment after flight training, 149–50
pilot flying-hour program, 155–56
pilot production rate reductions, 150–51
pilot retention, 151–53, 154–55
Planning, Programming and Budgeting System (PPBS), 189
Poland visit, 207–8
post-Cold War world: Base Force concept, 90–93; Central Europe visit, 207–9; defense budget dynamics and budget cuts, 175–77, 188–90; F-22 aircraft, 180; force drawdowns, 76; Major Regional Contingency (MRC) force level requirements, 188; and missile defenses, 59; roles and missions in, 357–62
Powell, Alma, *132*
Powell, Colin: and airpower's importance during Desert Storm, 32–33; appointment of Mike Carns as vice chief of staff, 94; Base Force concept, 90–92; Bosnia, 230–33; civilian deaths in Al Firdos bunker, 25–26; Desert Storm ground operations, 27, 27–28; Desert Storm joint command, 5–6, 16–17, *43*, *44*; Desert Storm preparations, 11; Desert Storm victory, 35; dinner with the McPeaks, *132*; end of Desert Storm operations, 29–31; and gays in the military, 279, 284, 292, 295;

Haitian refugee crisis, 198; JCS Chairman roles and missions review, 328; joint Strategic Command, 88; leadership style, 12, 17, 45; and McPeak flying F-15 aircraft, 142–43, 144; Major Regional Contingency (MRC) force level requirements, 184–85; and Mikhail Moiseyev, 110; Powell Doctrine, 231; Somalia, 302, 304; START I accords, 106
Powers, Gary, 201
precision, and "smart" bombs, 54–56
presence, peacetime presence and Major Regional Contingency (MRC) force level requirements, 185–88
Preszler, Sharon, 265–66
Prince Sultan Air Base, 13
professional military education (PME), 135–36
promotions: senior-officer promotions and Glosson Affair, 209–16, 221; women in the Air Force, 249
Punaro, Arnold, 210, 211
Pushkin Museum, 110

Q

Quality Air Force (QAF), 139
Quarters Seven "Air House" residence, *125*, *129*, *130*, 159–61, *217*
quick response force (QRF) in Somalia, 299, 300–301, 303

R

Rabin, Yitzhak, 203
radar, stealth and tactical surprise, 52–53
RAF Regiment, 326, 327
Ralston, Joe, 221, *317*
RAND Corporation, 80, 293
Randolph Field, 153
Ranger (Bush family dog), 14
rank, enlisted rank and insignia, 137–38, 164, 169
readiness, military readiness, 60–61
rear battle, 373–74
regulations, 156–57
reorganization: 1990s budget declines, 63–64; Air Combat Command (ACC) establishment, 82, 83, 87, 94, 101, 114–17; Air Education and Training Command (AETC), 83, 101, 113, 116–17; Brown Papers, 112–13; chain of command strengthening,

67–68; Don Rice, 80–84, 85, 86, 88, 115–16, 120, *126*, *127*; flight-line aircraft maintenance, 69–71; group reorganization, 71–73; headquarters reorganization, 84–86; heraldry and heritage preservation, 68, 78–79, 95–99, 101–2, 111; horizontal organizational design, 66–67; human values promotion, 68; internal consensus, 112; joint Strategic Command, 87–89; Lee Butler, 88–89; major air commands (MAJCOMs), 81–84; Mike Carns, 94–95; mission-focused reorganization, 64–66; mistakes and lessons learned, 113–17; naming conventions, 100–101; numbered air forces (NAFs), 78–80; personnel and payroll cuts, 122–23; reasons for, 120–21; squadrons, 68–71; wings, 73–78, 99–100

Republican Guard (Iraqi army), 21, 28–29, 34

requirements vs. equipment specifications, 222–26

retention: enlisted retention rates, 138; pilot retention, 151–53, 154–55; volunteer assignment system, 153–55; women in the Air Force, 248–49

Rice, Don: and Buster Glosson, 213; equipage of Air Force, 173–74; F-22 aircraft, 178–79; and Joint Direct Attack Munition (JDAM), 55; operational requirements vs. specifications, 222–23, 224; photographs of, *126*, *127*; reorganization efforts, 35, 80–84, 85, 86, 88, 115–16, 120; and Total Quality Management (TQM), 139

Richie, Steve, 222
Rickenbacker, Eddie, 99
Ritchie, Steve, 98
Roche, James, 261
Rogers, Buck, 15
Rokke, Erv, *317*

roles and missions: air defense and the Army, 311-13; Air Force ground forces, 326–28; Clinton on roles and missions reform, 328–29; close air support (CAS) and the Army, 313–15; Commission on Roles and Missions (CORM), 329–31, 354–56; costs and service effectiveness, 336–37, 339–40; definitions of roles, missions, and functions, 332–36; four air forces, 308–11; JCS Chairman's role, 328; Marine Corps air wings, 313, 316, 321–22; Navy air force, 315–16, 321; "seams," 372–73; Special Operations Force (SOF), 322–26; and Type A wars, 337–39; and Type B wars, 341

Roy, J. Stapleton, 352
Royal Hellenic Air Force, 103
Russ, Bob, 94
Russia visit, 106–10, *128*, *129*
Russian Federation Air Force, 107–10, *128*, 310–11
Rutherford, Skip, *127*, *319*
Ryan, John D., 212
Ryan, Mike, 97, 212–13, 215, 221, 236, 237, 342

S

Salvatierra, Manual, 104–5
Sarajevo, 229, 237, 238, 242–43
Saudi Arabia, 19, 20
Schmidt, Harry, 214
Schroeder, Patricia, 262, 292
Schwarzkopf, Norman: Desert Storm air campaign, 22, 26; Desert Storm ground operations, 21, 23, 28–29; Desert Storm preparations, 8, 10, 12; and joint command, 14–17, 28, 40, 45, 47, 50; headquarters at MacDill AFB, 6; memoir, 266

Scott, Winfield, 78
Scowcroft, Brent, 11, 12, 14
Scud missile attacks, Desert Storm, 19–22
Second Air Force, 98
Secretariat, headquarters reorganization, 84–85
Selfridge, Tom, 161
Senate Armed Services Committee, 179, 192, 210, 288, 293, 308
senior-officer promotions and Glosson Affair, 209–16, 221
Serbia: and Yugoslavia breakup, 228–29. *See also* Bosnia
service obligation, Air Force pilots, 152
service roles: overlap reduction, 374–76; reform proposals, 337–41; and "seams," 372–73; Title 10, US Code, 369–70
Seventh Air Force, 79

sexual harassment and women in the Air Force, 252–54, 261–63
Shaffer, Sue, 143
Shaheen, Imtiaz, 298
Shalala, Donna, 175
Shalikashvili, John, 197, 242, *318*, 354, 355
Shaposhnikov, Yevgeny, 106, 107
Shaw AFB, South Carolina, 7
Sheehan, John, 236, 237
Sheppard AFB, 133
Siad Barre, Mohamed, 297–98
single-seat aircraft flying, 141–44, 158
Six-Day War, 35, 52
Skelton, Ike, 101
skip-echelon staffing, group reorganization, 72–73
Sloan, Rusty, *219*
Slocombe, Walt, 354
Slovakia visit, 208–9
Slovenia, 228–29
"smart" bombs, 54–56, 173–74, 245
Smith, Leo, *127*
Somalia: history, 297–98; Task Force Ranger and US operations in Mogadishu, 300–305; UN Operation in Somalia (UNOSOM), 298–300; Unified Task Force (UNITAF), 299
Soviet Union and post-Cold War world, 357–62
Spaatz, Carl "Tooey," 169, 277, 367
space battle, 374
Space Command, 114
Special Operations Command (SOCOM), 322, 325
Special Operations Force (SOF): AC-130 gunship loss during Desert Storm, 23–24, 32; ATC training, 116; combat restrictions for women, 267–68; and joint command, 48, 49; military "mass" versus small precise forces, 57
Speer, Albert, 192
Spinney, Chuck, 222
Spirit 03 (AC-130 gunship) loss, 23–24, 32
Srebrenica massacre, 244–45, 246
SS-1 Scud missiles, 19
START I accords, 105–6
START II accords, 174
state dinners, 95, 200
State of the Union address, 89

status, and gays in the military, 283–85, 286, 288
stealth and tactical surprise: ethical considerations, 56; and military "mass," 56–58; sensors and target location, 52–54
Stein, Paul, 113
Stephanopoulos, George, 284
Strait, George, 175
Strategic Air Command (SAC), 46, 81–82, 87–89, 114–16
Strategic Command, 87–89
Student, Kurt, 326
submarines, 57–58
Sullivan, Gordy, 39, 161, 190–91, *217*, 314, 354–55
Sununu, John H., 141
support group, reorganization, 72
surface-to-air missiles (SAMs), 18, 311–13
surprise, stealth and tactical surprise, 52–54
Suvorov, Alexander, 61

T

T-3 "Firefly" aircraft, 146–48
T-6 aircraft, 149
T-37 "Tweety Bird" aircraft, 148–49
T-41 aircraft, 146–47
T-46 aircraft, 148
Tactical Air Command (TAC), 81–82, 83, 94, 99, 101, 112, 114, 178, 179
tactical airpower (TACAIR), 182–83
Tactical Fighter Wing Equivalent (TFWE) metric, 89–90, 93
Tailhook scandal, 253–54, 271, 274
"tank plinking," Desert Storm, 24–25
target location: battle damage assessment (BDA), 51; sensors and target location, 50–51
Task Force Ranger and US operations in Mogadishu, 300–305
Tastan, Siyami, 103
technical training reforms, 135
Tedder, Arthur, 15
Tenet, George, 196
Thatcher, Margaret, 345
theater missile defense (TMD), 60
Thomas White Space Trophy, *318*
Thunderbirds visit, *220*
Thurmond, Strom, 145, 197, 236
Title 10, US Code, 369–70

Tomahawk missiles, 55
Tornado interceptor aircraft, 203, *317*
Total Quality Management (TQM), 138–39
training: Air Training Command (ATC), 83, 116–17; costs, 136–37; enlisted professional military education, 135–36; enlisted technical training, 124, 133–35; fighter assignments, 149–50; flying training, 145–49; personnel classifications, 123–24; pilot flying-hour program, 155–56; pilot production rate reductions, 150–51; pilot retention, 151–53, 154–55; technical training reforms, 135
transporter-erector-launchers (TELs), 20
Truman, Harry, 273, 295
Turkish Air Force, 103
Tuskegee Airmen, 26, 201, 277
Twelfth Air Force, 79, 145
Twentieth Air Force, 79, 98
Twining, Nate, 79
Tyndall Field, 99, 116
Type A wars, 40, 203, 316, 324–25, 333, 337–39, 373, 375–76, 378
Type B wars, 50, 203, 334–35, 341, 376–79

U

UH-1 helicopters, 160
UK visit, 203–4
UN High Commissioner for Refugees (UNHCR), 230
UN Operation in Somalia (UNOSOM), 298–300
UN Protection Force (UNPROFOR), 230–31, 238, 240, 241–43
uniform, redesigned, 162–64, *165*, 169–71, *218*
unit cohesion: and gays in the military, 271–74, 278–79, 289–91, 295–96; women in the Air Force, 257–61, 263–64, 267
United Arab Emirates (UAE), 9, 12–13
United Nations (UN): Haitian refugee crisis, 198; no-fly zones, 95, 230, 235, 238, 242; sanctions on Serbia, 229, 234; UN Resolution 678, 17–18
unmanned aerial vehicles (UAVs), 201–3
US Coast Guard, 198
USAFE, 81, 116

V

Vance, Cyrus, 234
Vandenberg, Hoyt, 79, 277
Velarde, Chino, 343
Viccellio, Butch, 16, 117, *127*, *319*
Vietnam War: F-4 aircraft, 199; and joint command, 15–16, 47; and racial tensions in the Army, 278; stealth and tactical surprise, 52–53
Voltaire, 56
volunteer assignment system, 153–54
Vuono, Carl, 6, *44*

W

Wachira, Duncan, 303
Walesa, Lech, 345
Waller, Cal, 17, 31
Warden, John, 7–8
warfare: classical theories of, 40, 45; and "decisive" military victories, 36–40
Warner, John, 293, 294
Warsaw Pact, 89, 106
weapon systems, operational test, 226
Welch, Eunice, *130*
Welch, Larry, 63, *130*, 160, 179, 213, 264
White, John P., 330, 356
White, Tommy, 103, 159
Whiteman Field, 97
Widnall, Sheila, 199–200, 213, 215, *217*, *318*, 345
Williams, Pete, 144
wing commanders, 76–78
wing reorganization, 73–78, 99–100
Wolfowitz, Paul, 92, 353–54
women in the Air Force: adultery, 251–52; combat exclusion repeal, 254–57, 264–68; combat vs. support roles and unit cohesion, 258–61; Defense Advisory Committee on Women in the Services (DACOWITS), 263–64; end-strength ceiling, 247–48; enhanced career prospects, 248–49; fraternization, 249–51; sexual harassment, 252–54, 261–63; Tailhook scandal, 253–54; unit cohesion, 257–61, 263–64, 267
Wong Hai, 351–52
Wong, Steve, 352
Woolsey, Jim, 196
World War I, 36, 37, 56

World War II: 1st Air Commando Wing, 100; Army Air Force losses, 96; Army Air Force groups, 71–72; Luftwaffe, 326; Pearl Harbor, 52, 327
Wright brothers, 160–61
Wright-Patterson Field, 181

Y

Yates, Ron, 82, 86, *166*, 180–81, *319*
Yazov, Dmitri, 107
Yeats, W. B., 140
Yeltsin, Boris, 106, 174
Yeosock, John, 15
Yugoslav People's Army (JNA), 229, 234
Yugoslavia breakup, 228–29

Z

Zimmermann, Warren, 246